PUBLIC MANAGEMENT IN TRANSITION
The orchestration of potentiality

Niels Åkerstrøm Andersen
and
Justine Grønbæk Pors

First published in Great Britain in 2016 by

Policy Press	North America office:
University of Bristol	Policy Press
1-9 Old Park Hill	c/o The University of Chicago Press
Bristol BS2 8BB	1427 East 60th Street
UK	Chicago, IL 60637, USA
t: +44 (0)117 954 5940	t: +1 773 702 7700
pp-info@bristol.ac.uk	f: +1 773 702 9756
www.policypress.co.uk	sales@press.uchicago.edu
	www.press.uchicago.edu

© Policy Press 2016

British Library Cataloguing in Publication Data
A catalogue record for this book is available from the British Library.

Library of Congress Cataloging-in-Publication Data
A catalog record for this book has been requested.

ISBN 978 1 44732 866 7 paperback
ISBN 978 1 44732 868-1 ePub
ISBN 978 1 44732 869 8 Mobi

The right of Niels Åkerstrøm Andersen and Justine Grønbæk Pors to be identified as authors of this work has been asserted by them in accordance with the Copyright, Designs and Patents Act 1988.

All rights reserved: no part of this publication may be reproduced, stored in a retrieval system, or transmitted in any form or by any means, electronic, mechanical, photocopying, recording, or otherwise without the prior permission of Policy Press.

The statements and opinions contained within this publication are solely those of the authors and not of the University of Bristol or Policy Press. The University of Bristol and Policy Press disclaim responsibility for any injury to persons or property resulting from any material published in this publication.

Every effort has been made to trace copyright holders and to obtain their permission for the use of copyright material. The publisher apologises for any errors or omissions in the above list and would be grateful if notified of any corrections that should be incorporated in future reprints or editions of this book.

Policy Press works to counter discrimination on grounds of gender, race, disability, age and sexuality.

Cover design by Hayes Design
Front cover: image kindly supplied by www.alamy.com

Contents

List of figures and tables — iv
Preface — vi
Foreword by Bob Jessop — ix

Introduction — 1

one	Keeping the future open	11
two	The impossibility of governing society	33
three	From bureaucracy to potentialisation	57
four	Welfare organisations as infinite potential	89
five	Searching for possibilities between disciplines and codes	103
six	From contract to partnership	131
seven	The playful employee	149
eight	Citizens as a resource	183
nine	The potentiality state	213

Conclusion: toward a premiseless management philosophy — 241

References — 255
Index — 271

List of figures and tables

Figures

I.1	Thematic figure of the outline of the book	9
1.1	Decision as form	15
1.2	Figures of temporality in the public sector of the 1960s and 1970s	17
1.3	Figures of temporality beginning in the 1980s in the public sector	19
1.4	Looking beyond the horizon	21
2.1	Changes in the differentiation of society	35
2.2	Function systems and their media and codes	37
3.1	Hierarchical self-description	62
3.2	Self-descriptions of planning	64
3.3	Sector administration	65
3.4	Supervision administration as self-description	70
3.5	Potentialisation as a fourth-order decision	76
3.6	Potentiality administration	80
4.1	The growing independence of welfare institutions	90
5.1	Formal institution	109
5.2	Homophonic welfare institutions	110
5.3	Heterophonic welfare organisation	118
5.4	A model for health in a social context	121
5.5	Patients at the centre	123
5.6	The core task at the centre	125
5.7	Communication-seeking organisation	128
6.1	Two forms of contractual hybrids	134
6.2	The contract that wanted to be community	146
7.1	The shaping of the medium of pedagogy by the figure of self-enrolment	156
7.2	The love code formed by self-enrolment	161
7.3	The medium of play shaped by self-enrolment	169
8.1	Hyper-responsibility as form	208

Tables

1.1	Public administration temporal figures over time	22
2.1	Society's function systems	41
2.2	Reflexivity of the function systems	48
3.1	Forms of administration	58
3.2	Summary of developments in public administration	82
4.1	Institutional forms	99

List of figures and tables

5.1	Toward the heterophonic and communication-seeking organisation	106
5.2	The relationship between communicative code and possible organisational self-description	119
6.1	Typology of contractualisation	132
6.2	Forms of contract	136
6.3	Contractual coupling of law, economy and organisation	137
6.4	Shifts in dimensions on the first and second order	143
6.5	Partnership observed by different function systems	145
6.6	Polycontextual partnership	147
7.1	Forms of membership	150
7.2	Love communication	160
7.3	Form, function and effects of self-enrolment	176
8.1	Forms of citizenry	183
8.2	Forms of citizen governance	191
8.3	First- and second-order audience roles	195
8.4	The articulation of responsibility over time	205
9.1	The law as structural coupling	216
9.2	Developments in the legal system	221
9.3	The form of state in transition	228
C.1	Developing forms	245

Preface

This book is about public organisations and welfare institutions, and the transformation of their conditions of management. Over time, rather tricky managerial conditions have been created by the growing complexity of management, and the reaction to this growing complexity. This has led to many paradoxical questions facing managers and welfare professionals, such as, 'How to manage by saying "Do as I tell you to. Be autonomous!"', 'How to make changes for an unknown future', 'How to encourage institutions to "think out of the box" and constantly reinvent themselves', 'How to manage an institution that has to connect many functions and professional perspectives while remaining fully flexible', 'How to get citizens to recognise themselves as active, responsible, fellow citizens?, and 'How to create employees who are creating themselves in the image of the organisation'.

In this book, we trace and discuss the making of these conditions for managing public organisations and welfare institutions. In particular, we pay attention to the growing tension between a desire to govern and a desire to produce change and new possibilities.

The book's subtitle – 'The orchestration of potentiality' – marks a tension that we perceive as fundamental to contemporary welfare management. On the one hand, welfare management is about governance, or more precisely, about the effort to create connections and consistency among the various and diverse activities of the welfare state. On the other hand, there is an immense focus on adaptability, change and innovation. We are told that without radical change, the very existence of our welfare society will be threatened.

This story affects not only the way we organise welfare, but also our core definitions of what welfare is. It has become imperative for our welfare functions to be in a continual state of reconceptualisation. Thus, a new responsibility of public managers is to seek out new conceptions of education, care, health and so on, beyond what we are able to imagine in the present. For lack of better words, we refer to this as 'potentialisation', that is, the creation of possibilities for renewal beyond our present conceptions. Governance therefore indicates the desire for consistency with respect to financial policies, quality and cross-departmental coordination. And potentialisation marks a seemingly opposite desire to open up, transgress what is perceived as traditional and given, and to 'think outside of the box'. Welfare management has to manoeuvre in this contradictory terrain.

This book has been written to bridge the areas of public administration, state theory, organisation theory and social theory. What bridges these perspectives is a historical diagnostic of the present. The concept of 'public management' has always suffered from its exclusion of questions of state and society. Public management has been perceived of as practical, neutral, technocratic and apolitical. So a central aim of this book is to reintroduce the political and societal to the field of management.

Preface

This book is a textbook for public policy, public management and leadership, public administration and management of welfare institutions such as schools, healthcare institutions, hospitals and so on. It is written primarily for postgraduate students and also for executive students such as those studying for a Master's of Public Administration (MPA). We write for the reflective manager who already knows quite a bit about management and who has experienced a need for a language with a slightly different angle on their management insights. The book is therefore written for welfare managers and students seeking insight into the insight they already possess.

We try to cover many policy fields, presenting cases from healthcare, education, social care, foreign aid, radicalisation, personal policy and so on. These cases reflect many levels of the public sector such as national ministries, local municipalities, single organisations as well as interactions between employees and citizens.

We would like to emphasise that we have not written a textbook that can be taught in isolation. Although the book has a wide scope in the sense that it seeks to combine many different facets (society, organisation and the individual), and although it contains examples from a variety of sectors and investigates the historical evolution of conditions of management, it remains vetted to a particular systems theoretical and contemporary diagnostic perspective as a means to achieve this broadness of scope – we have chosen a broad empirical perspective over a broad theoretical survey.

We are both from Copenhagen Business School in Denmark, and have been teaching public management for many years. We often give presentations for experienced managers at all levels, from chief executive civil servants in ministries, to managers in local municipalities to managers of public schools, daycare institutions, health institutions, social work administrations and so on. Our research also covers this span. Although our empirical examples come from Danish welfare society, the transformations of the conditions of management we describe are similar to major trends in other European countries. However, rather than downplaying the specificities that characterise the Danish cases, we have tried to turn these into a pedagogical advantage. On the one hand, 'the Danish case' represents an extreme case in European public welfare. But on the other, very little is actually invented in Denmark – Danish policy-makers often get their inspiration for new steering technologies from other European countries, and in particular, the UK. As we see it, however, Denmark is an interesting case because new ideas are often quite radically implemented in Denmark. Ten years ago, concepts such as 'relational coordination' and 'interprofessionality' emerged in international discussions. Such concepts are now being implemented in Denmark in almost all policy sectors, and from the top to the bottom of public sector hierarchies. This means that the effects have become very visible.

We hope that our Danish bias can play a productive role in the book, making the transformational trends very clear and visible, and thereby providing our readers with the possibility of critically assessing public management and perhaps appreciating just how strange and surprising recent developments in the public sector actually are. That is at least what we experience when we present our findings to international audiences.

We trace four historical 'layers' of public administration in this book: formal bureaucracy (from 1860), sector administration (from 1950), supervision administration (from 1980) and potentiality administration (from 2000). How these 'layers', their accumulations and various ways of intersecting unfold at particular sites obviously vary, not only from country to country, but from local government to local government, from policy sector to policy sector, and from welfare organisation to welfare organisation. We invite the reader to continuously consider how the suggested 'diagnoses of the present' relate to her particular organisational setting. Thus, we hope that, rather than as a singular and universal description of public management, the book will be read as a set of possibilities for observing and interpreting the specific entanglements of logics and dynamics that the reader encounters in her organisation.

Niels Åkerstrøm Andersen and Justine Grønbæk Pors
Copenhagen Business School
August 2015

Foreword

This is a sparklingly brilliant, positively irritating and doubly challenging book. It is *brilliant* because it provides a wonderful, clearly written introduction to 'welfare management' that sets sparks flying in many directions and can be used by critically engaged welfare practitioners as well as students and scholars of changing forms of government and governance. It is positively *irritating* in the sense of being provocative, inspiring and inducive to critical reflection and self-reflection. It is also *challenging* in a double manner. On the one hand, it draws on concepts, theories and perspectives that are more familiar in German-speaking and Scandinavian circles than in the Anglophone intellectual community outside some kinds of organisational studies. Relevant approaches include Niklas Luhmann's theory of modern, functionally differentiated societies, self-organising systems and the nature of organisational decisions; George Spencer Brown's laws of form and logic of distinctions; and wide-ranging ideas about paradox, reflexivity, the intellectual and practical benefits of adopting different perspectives and the implications of polycontextuality alongside many other thought-provoking concepts. So English language readers will welcome this book as an insightful introduction to these challenging ideas, especially as Niels Åkerstrøm Andersen and Justine Grønbæk Pors take care to present their theoretical approach step-by-step and provide practical examples to illustrate and support it. On the other hand, these examples provide challenging material that invites comparison with the problems that practitioners may confront in their daily lives or moments of reflection. This reflects the authors' extensive experience with self-reflexive managers in welfare management to develop their arguments. But their book is also relevant and challenging for those with broader macro-theoretical interests.

The authors' re-designation of the familiar field of public management as welfare management is indicative of the shift of terrain that they aim to promote and their attempt to 'queer' this all too often taken-for-granted analytical domain. The main theme is that the nature of public management has changed, at least in Denmark, and that this is reflected in growing concern with the management of self-management and with preparing for a future that cannot be predicted. There are obvious parallels in changing forms of governance elsewhere, although these have not been pursued with such consistency outside a Scandinavian context, in part because of the dominance of neoliberal ideologies about the superiority of market forces, the need for austerity, and so on. In all cases, however, the challenge is to develop welfare managers who are oriented to future potentials and potentialisation in a present world where there are no obvious decision-premises for planning. These arguments are developed theoretically, linked to an account of different stages in public administration and the shifting time horizons with which they are associated, and illustrated from different policy fields. The argument is developed systematically and coherently but never in a simple, linear way – which would be inconsistent with the complexity of the challenges in new forms of government and governance. Throughout the authors identify paradoxes, dilemmas, strategic choices, and the strategies adopted to deparadoxify paradoxes, finesse dilemmas and postpone choices or deny that they are choices. For a self-reflexive manager this will be full of provocation and a stimulus, as intended, to self-reflection.

As indicated above, this is a practical as well as theoretical work, intended for practising managers curious about, and interested in, the paradoxes, dilemmas, and strategic challenges of their work. Its chapters explore many policy fields and issues based on careful observation and case studies, so that any practitioner will find relevant material and provocative comparisons. It is also theoretically grounded (but wears its theory light – it is not afraid to spell out demanding theoretical issues but it always aims to bring out their practical implications too – and introduces them gradually rather than in one big bang approach). As an inveterate theorist, I learnt much from this theoretically as well as empirically on every page; I am sure that more evidence-based scholars and practitioners will learn much from the book too.

I am not aware of any rival to this book in the English language. This is partly because of its solid grounding in the Danish appropriation of the often abstruse German sociologist, Niklas Luhmann, and partly because of its grounding in the very different nature of Danish society and Danish political culture. But these are also strengths of the book because there is growing interest in the Scandinavian model given the increasing disenchantment with statism and neoliberalism. Thus I am confident that this book will transform its chosen field of intervention – but in a 'slow-burn' rather than 'brief splash' manner. This reflects the difficulties in challenging neoliberalism, even in the face of its failures – which are also an indicator of the need for this book.

Bob Jessop
Lancaster University
January 2016

Introduction

Since the beginning of the 1980s, there has been an explosion in the number of public sector management programmes, books, concepts, critiques, academics, seminars and consultants. Management is viewed as the solution to a broad range of problems in society: poor education, increasing healthcare costs and excessive bureaucracy in the welfare state. It seems that all that is required is more and improved management.

Management has become a career path for many in the public sector. It has become an expansive market for consultants, a place where academics can think up general answers to a broad range of specific problems. It is a zone where different concepts clash, concepts that separately promise to provide the most advanced solution, or at least one that is slightly better than the last one – Lean, systemic management, narrative management, network management, coaching, activity budgeting, co-creation, radical innovation, and many more. It is a field where people can profile themselves through applying a particular management approach: "Our municipality uses Lean…", "Our preschool works with trust management…".

This book is not an attempt to present yet another management concept, although we are not trying to suggest that new management concepts are pointless. Even though some management concepts may seem a bit too clever, we believe that quite a few of them are well-founded, well-written and serve a good purpose. They often contain important insights and practical implementation strategies. And there is a need for them. The objective of our book, however, is different. We ask: if management is the answer, what is the question? What do the many strands of new management literature provide answers to? Why are we are so concerned with management in the welfare state?

What we explore in this book is the 'machine' that drives the whole management field in the public sector, and that continues to compel us to seek out new ways of management. We are not simply looking for solutions to problems; we are also looking for the machine that produces the problems and that connects them to the solutions. We ask: what is the problem that particular problem–solution combinations in welfare management function as a solution to for?

What we are looking for, therefore, is a bit more abstract and lasting than many of the concrete management proposals currently on display in the vast management literature. We do not see 'abstract' and 'concrete' as actual opposites. Many management terms that we often consider to be concrete, are, in fact, rather non-specific and metaphorical. They naturalise and assume what they signify rather than specifying and defining it. Because these terms function as metaphors rather than concepts, they provide no resistance and trick us into believing that we know what we are talking about. We confuse lack of resistance and naturalised truths with concreteness. The question of how management, innovation and collaboration function in specific social operations requires abstract conceptual work in order to capture the forms that are repeated within and characterise existing practices. We look for the abstract forms that are repeated in the specific processes that guide the formation of expectations.

What machine drives the acceleration of expectations directed at management, and how does this have an impact on the possibilities for carrying out management practices?

This has already been mentioned in the Preface. Welfare management today is located in a site of tension between, on the one hand, governance expectations about consistency across fragmented sectors and, on the other, potentiality expectations about the continual transgression of existing horizons of expectations, actions and thoughts. This particular constellation has a rather remarkable history. It is the story of the radical transformation of the machine that produces management expectations. We trace this transformation as a shift from a machine that produces management expectations in the form of unambiguous, clear and factual premises to one that increasingly dissolves the idea of expectations as premises.

This shift explains why we have become so focused on management. As the premises for welfare practice become transient, transitory and ambiguous, the need for management increases. Moreover, there is an inherently tragic dimension to this shift. Management today does not simply establish clear premises for an organisation and its operations. It has become a machine for premise dissolution, requiring organisations and their employees to continually question their structures, habits, competences, naturalised assumptions and ways of thinking. Coaching managers provide no answers for their employees, only questions. Managers of strategic networks in municipal administrations do not explicitly propose and mandate strategies for their organisations, but invite them to participate in a strategic dialogue and to organise innovation games, which establish and undermine premises for strategic self-management processes in the different welfare organisations.

Today, the biggest challenge for welfare managers is the expectation that their leadership rests on the premise that all management premises are questioned. Thus, the basic premise for welfare management is the dissolution of premises! Welfare organisations are expected to continually incorporate reflections on whether a given action, procedure or even perception of welfare service quality could be construed differently. Welfare managers are expected to strategically experiment with their organisation's identity, performance and roles. And they are expected to be able to construct the organisation in many different ways depending on the specific challenge or situation. This book shows how today's welfare managers are required to deal with the fact that elements that were previously taken for granted as management objects no longer appear self-evident.

We show how today's managers are expected not only to ensure quality case management, but also to facilitate the mapping of the different potential perspectives from which a case can be viewed. Managers are expected to bring perspectivism into their employees' ways of viewing a given case in order to explore the potential solutions that different definitions of the case may give rise to. *This represents a shift from management based on factuality as given to factuality as contingent.*

We also show how managers are expected to create multidisciplinary organisations as a way of strategically seeking out the possibilities of approaching a case from the different perspectives of different disciplines. Managers are expected to ask: what do different professional forms of knowledge offer in terms of seeing a case from a different perspective? While a doctor offers diagnostics and treatments, perhaps more appropriate solutions can be achieved by seeing a problem as pedagogical in nature – a question of teaching patients to improve their overall health. *This represents a shift from professional knowledge as given to professional knowledge as contingent.*

At the same time, we notice a change in the relationship between the organisation and employee. Managers are expected to create conditions for individual employees' ability to take responsibility for their role in an organisation, which is in a continuous process of becoming something other than what it is. Employees are expected to develop their competences and personalities so that they can provide the organisation with its future needs. This means that the premises for what it means to be a member of an organisation are no longer given or fixed. *This represents a shift from membership as given to transient conditions for self-membership.*

Finally, welfare managers can no longer take for granted the framework within which their activities take place. They are presented with an excess of possibilities for how to possibly describe a given action or activity. *This represents a shift from a given whole to contingent, multiple wholes.*

Diagnosing the present: three motifs

Our aim is to provide a diagnosis of contemporary welfare management. Diagnoses of the present mean descriptions of the production of and changes to conditions for welfare management, so rather than assuming that management exists as some definite entity, independent of the specific development characteristics in the public sector, we explore the different forms that management takes, as described with a point of departure in the case of Denmark. We ask questions about the inner tensions produced by developments in society and in contemporary management ideals, which welfare managers have to contend with. Given specific management forms, what are the inner dynamic and productive contradictions that management is compelled to unfold? All social and communicative forms contain irresolvable tensions or even paradoxes, which have to be continually managed. Even with the emergence of a particular ideal or a specific management technology meant as a solution to a specific problem, the underlying tensions or paradoxes remain as a constant tension. In fact, new ideals and technologies may bring new tensions and problems, which welfare managers are required to seek out solutions to without the possibility of arriving at a lasting solution.

We approach contemporary management ideals, discourses and practices from a critical and analytical perspective. However, our aim is not to provide a normative critique in the sense of a comparison of our observations of reality with an existing ideal, and the conclusion that reality leaves a lot to be desired. Normative critique always results in disappointment with respect to the conditions of society and in the devaluation of certain people, organisations or parties, whose actions are deemed insufficient or wrong. Diagnoses of the present, by contrast, draws on a far more humble concept of criticism, which does not position itself outside society in order to judge it, but which also does not uncritically pursue the latest management concept or ideology. Rather, we ask how particular forms of management yield particular results and create particular risks. Faced with a problem or a new management ideal, we seldom ask which new problems and questions emerge with this type of thinking and these ideals (Andersen, 2003c).

The aim of this book is not to provide an unambiguous diagnosis of our welfare society. The objective is not to sum up the developments of recent years with terms such as 'the competition state', 'the network society', or 'the knowledge society'. Instead, we point to tensions within welfare management. As already mentioned, we look for the 'expectation machine', and trace it primarily in relation to three separate motifs. The first is the *relation between management and self-management*. The second is the *relation between differentiation and unity*. And the third is the *relation between simultaneity and temporal integration*. Throughout the book, we trace and unfold these three motifs.

Managing self-management

We begin with the assumption that effective management is about managing in a way so that it does not restrict the potential for self-management, but instead nurtures and cultivates potential. Management and self-management are not opposites but mutually condition each other. Or, in other words, independence is a condition of management because what makes sub-systems manageable is precisely their ability to self-manage. In short, management means the creation of premises for self-management. This creates a rather paradoxical constellation because management (precisely in order to manage effectively) must be capable of supporting the independence of the objects of its management. Today, the welfare state relies heavily on the individual institution's capacity for independent management. In fact, in recent years management reforms have focused on strategies for strengthening the capacity for self-management and strategic force in disparate areas of the welfare state.

Accordingly, we do not analyse developments in the public sector as a question of how the state has historically tightened or loosened its grip of individual institutions. We do not see the conditions of welfare management as a question of oscillating movements of decentralisation and recentralisation. Our argument is not simply that democracy, initiative and quality always develop from the ground up and is restricted by too much control from the top. Instead, our thesis is that the principle of management of self-management is pervasive in the public sector and creates specific premises for welfare management across its various forms. This logic appears throughout the welfare state and shapes relations between state and municipality, between municipalities, between management and employees, and between welfare professionals and citizens. This logic is repeated again and again, although it assumes different forms at different times and in relation to different questions. Historically, and at all levels of the welfare state, we observe increasingly sophisticated ways of integrating management and self-management. And it is precisely such points of integration that we trace and describe here. Thus, our first motif is the fact that the conditions for managing welfare primarily result from the different ways in which management and self-management become intertwined.

Differentiation and unity

Another prominent issue that shapes today's welfare state is the relation between differentiation and unity. Here, too, welfare management finds itself within a paradoxical tension between on the one hand, the demand for increasing differentiation in the form of increased professional specialisation and, on the other, demands for consistency, coordination and unity.

Society continues to develop in the direction of increasing levels of differentiation. The economic, legal and healthcare systems are becoming increasingly proficient at managing economic, legal and healthcare-related issues respectively, with limited regard to the functioning of other systems. However, at the same time, welfare functions require the coordination of a great number of institutions and different professional knowledge. Not only public, but also non-profit and private actors, each with their particular perspective and mode of operation, have to work together. There is at once increased differentiation and increased interdependence. We are interested in the way that efforts to formulate new forms of consistency across and integration between otherwise differentiated systems result not only in new forms of unity, but also in general tension between unity and differentiation that plays itself out in new and interesting ways. In other words, a new level of complexity is created, which welfare leaders have to contend with. Thus, our second motif suggests that the conditions for welfare management are shaped by the different ways in which the relation between differentiation and unity become intertwined.

Simultaneity and temporal integration

As society's differentiation makes it increasingly more difficult to factually coordinate and integrate many different interests, the integration effort becomes temporalised, that is, it becomes defined as a question of time and temporal organisation. There is a drive to change integration from being a practical challenge to a temporal challenge by deferring factual decisions into the future.

However, this requires the simultaneous organisation of society's temporality, which then becomes caught in various contradictions and paradoxes. We argue that there are two fundamental forms of temporality: operational and perceptual time.

Operational time is temporality linked to the operation of systems. Systems operate in time and exist only qua their operations. This means that systems only exist in the present. They are present neither in their past nor in their future. Everything happens simultaneously. All systems – social, biological or conscious – exist only in the present. This means that the operations of one system are unable to reach the operations of another, resulting in a state of uncontrollable simultaneity.

But there is also another temporality: *perceptual time*. This is time as experience. It is the time that is created by the individual system through its distinctions between the past, present and future. Systems can only operate in the present, but they are capable of distinguishing between the past and future, between something they have done and something they will do. However, these distinctions between the past and future always take place in the present. Time does not flow from the past into the present and toward the future. In the shift from the operations of one system to another, the entire distinction past–present–future also shifts. Thus, time is always time for an observing system. Perceptual time is linked to the individual system, which distinguishes between the past, present and future. Each system defines its own time.

So, not only does everything happen simultaneously, each system also has its own perception of time, which is linked to its respective 'systems logic'. We are all familiar with the way in which the political system's sense of time is linked to election terms and the way that this does not always coincide harmoniously with long-term political priorities. Likewise, anyone who has ever visited an Accident & Emergency knows that time is perceived differently in different situations. A patient is left to wait for long periods of time while the nurses are running around, busy at work. The healthcare system draws a distinction between urgent and non-urgent patients, which results in relative lower priority given to prevention and aftercare in favour of treatment. Or in the political system, ecological balances are rarely perceived as urgent, and by the time they are seen as urgent, it is often much too late to do anything. Every organisation is faced with the challenge that the time of the task, the time of the decision and the time of the strategy are entirely different. Thus, in a temporal dimension, the question of differentiation and unity translates into a question of temporal integration. How is it even possible to coordinate mutually dependent operations in the welfare society when everything takes place simultaneously and when each system creates its own perceptual temporality? Our third motif emerges from the question of how to organise and bind time when everything happens simultaneously and when all systems have different temporal structures. We explore how perceptual time is created historically in different systems, and the conditions this establishes for simultaneity and temporal organisation.

Introduction

Outline of the book

The book consists of nine chapters and a conclusion. Each chapter looks at the same thing: changes in the 'expectation machine'. How does the basic expectation machine shift so that the ability for expectations to serve as factual premises are challenged? How does this machine gradually transform into a machine for the production of expectations about future expectations, whose premises cannot be fixed in similar ways? What varies between chapters is the system reference. Our point of observation is shifted in the different chapters in order to investigate the question from the perspective of society, organisation and interaction respectively. Moreover, there is variation in our focus on central systems elements so that certain chapters emphasise the temporal dimension and others focus more heavily on the factual dimension. This allows us to describe the multiplicity of effects caused by shifts in the expectation machine, including a relatively simple description of the complexity of welfare management.

Chapter One addresses the history of perceptual time in the public sector. We believe that a particular shift in the perception of time in the early 1980s represents a central and irreversible dislocation in the development of public administration, which continues to produce a chain of effects. The fundamental issue here is the emergence of a new ideal about ongoing adaptability – not adaptation to any one thing, but simply adaptation to adaptability. The chapter functions as a cornerstone for the other chapters that follow.

In Chapter Two, society serves as the point of observation. We ask how society can be managed, and describe today's society as differentiated into a great number of function systems, each with their own particular logic. It is a centre-less society.

In Chapter Three, we use public administration as a whole as the point of observation. We look at the development of public administration over the past 150 years from a formal bureaucracy via sector and supervision administration to potentiality administration. We show how the inner complexity of public administration increases, how public administration finds increasingly more complex answers to such complexity, and how this further increases the inner complexity and makes management more difficult. The effect is a rather paradoxical management regime, which manages through messages such as 'Do as we say – act independently'.

In Chapter Four, we take the individual welfare institution as the point of observation. We describe the same development as Chapter Three, but with the individual institution as a system reference. How do expectations form in relation to the individual welfare organisation? When is the organisation met with expectations about management? Which management conditions apply when the institution is simultaneously expected to show independence and to observe the hierarchy? Paradoxically, welfare institutions have grown more independent at the same time as they are more heavily managed than ever before.

In Chapter Five, the point of observation remains the individual welfare organisation, but the focus here is on the development of the relation between the organisation and society's function systems. We show how the relation between the welfare institutions and society loses its self-evident character. There are no longer any given premises for the societal function that individual welfare institutions connect to. The complexity of the increasing differentiation in society encroaches on the individual institution, and manifests itself in the fact that the individual institution assumes responsibility for deciding on a growing number of issues, including economic, political, legal, educational and social issues. The question is whether the multiplicity of logics is managed more effectively at the level of individual welfare institutions than at the level of society. It is becoming increasingly more difficult for organisations to establish factual premises for their decisions.

In Chapter Six, our point of observation makes a small shift to the relation among welfare institutions. Increasing differentiation and independence also increases mutual dependence among welfare institutions, both within specific policy sectors and among them. At the same time, there is an increased demand for flexibility. We ask how welfare institutions create mutual expectations when the premise is constantly changing expectations.

In Chapter Seven, we zoom in on the relation between the employee and organisation, and describe how the ideals of adaptability and 'thinking outside the box' affect the management of public sector employees. A central question is how an organisation can create conditions for ensuring that individual employees take responsibility for self-enrolment in the organisation when it can no longer define clear and stable premises. Employees are made responsible for inventing themselves as a surplus of possibilities for the organisation.

In Chapter Eight, we focus on shifts in the expectations that the government directs at its citizens. Today, the state places much greater expectations on its citizens about their active participation in ensuring their own and others' quality of life. The most private becomes political.

In Chapter Nine, we begin to zoom back out. Here, the political system (and in part, the legal system) serves as the point of observation. We see the state as the political system's description of its own unity. We describe a shift in the political system from viewing the state as the given contextual premise for its actions to placing actions and operations at the centre, which transforms the state into a repertoire of alternative forms (for example, constitutional state, welfare state, network state and competition state) that can be chosen among.

Finally, in the Conclusion, we sum up these developments and reflect on which kind of management philosophy would match today's welfare management where it has become increasingly more difficult to establish factual premises for decisions.

The structure of the book is illustrated in Figure I.1 opposite. The chapters are structured so that they each describe the development that has shaped the conditions for management in a particular area. We ask how different development characteristics challenge welfare management in specific ways. We then go on to discuss how this affects welfare managers. Thus, we allow our analyses to produce descriptions of specific management paradoxes. Our hope is that our readers –

Figure I.1: Thematic figure of the outline of the book

whether they work as the manager of an institution or as a CEO, whether they are responsible for executive strategies and funds, or whether their job is to manage the daily operations at a preschool – can use the specific paradoxes to challenge their understanding of their specific management conditions.

Finally, our analyses also result in a set of questions. The thought is to provide managers with ways to reflect their own management practice and the possibilities for action presented within these pages. To facilitate the reading of the book, we have included three kinds of boxes throughout:

- *Example boxes.* Example boxes are square. They provide empirical illustrations of our diagnoses. The examples are not designed to justify or prove our diagnoses, but to facilitate reflection. They allow readers to consider the specific manifestations of our diagnoses in specific welfare organisations.
- *Concept boxes.* Concept boxes are grey. They are used to define concepts that are central to our line of thinking. These are concepts such as decision, leadership, interaction, system and organisation.
- *Reflection boxes.* Reflection boxes are round. In these, we formulate questions that individual welfare managers may ask themselves and use to increase their understanding of how our diagnoses create particular challenges for their management practice.

ONE

Keeping the future open

What does it mean to govern the public sector without knowing the possibilities and challenges of the future? How can we invest in a future that is basically unknown and uncertain? How can specific strategies for an organisation be planned, and simultaneously, how can its ability to adapt quickly to developments that cannot be predicted be strengthened? How can we educate public managers when we do not know which qualifications for management will be needed in the future?

These are the questions that drive today's demand for improved public management. They are the result of an ideal about constant adaptation, which began to influence the public sector in the 1980s. The ideal does not preach adaptation to a specific scenario, but rather adaptation to adaptation. This creates a radically transformed concept of time in organisations, which has subsequently spread like wildfire, causing fundamental changes to our ways of organising and managing in the public sector.

The problem today is not simply the difficulty in public administration of planning solutions to problems when the future turns out differently than what was expected. The challenge is more radically the fact that reality as it exists in the present is perceived as an obstacle for the ability to imagine the future, let alone formulate strategies in relation to it. The big question that many managers face today is how to formulate strategies for the future that do not lock public organisations into specific future scenarios, since this might reduce the organisation's flexibility and hence its capacity for rapid adaptation when the future turns out differently than expected. Today, the predominant trend appears to be a desire to adapt to a radically open future, which remains open at all times. The goal is to create organisations capable of adapting to something we have not yet predicted will happen.

The changes to the understanding of time in public organisations have fundamental implications for conditions of managing public organisations, what constitutes a decision, and for the relation between organisation and society, between organisation and employee, and between organisation and citizen. The conditions for any kind of management are precisely established through conceptions of what kind of future the organisation should direct itself toward. Therefore, we begin this book by tracing changes in the temporality of the public sector. In this chapter, we show how the effort to expect the unexpected turns welfare management into the management of organisations that want to make decisions but that at the same time are unwilling to let go of alternatives – organisations that seek to actualise possibilities without renouncing other potential possibilities. The chapters that follow pursue and push this question further via specific points of observation such as administration, welfare organisation, or the relation between organisation and employee.

> **Example 1.1: Investing in an unknown future**
>
> There is a sense in the public sector today that a manager's ability to imagine the future through calculation, scenarios and market projections speaks less to the future and more to present ideas about the future. Organisations become trapped in a double ambition of being both extremely involved in predicting the future while remaining conscious that the more specific their expectations of the future, the higher the risk of reducing the organisation's adaptability (Andersen and Pors, 2014, Pors and Andersen 2014).
>
> This creates a complex issue with regard to educational policies because, on the one hand, an educated workforce is considered society's most important resource, while on the other, there is no way to anticipate which qualifications and competences will be required in and by the future. This presents a challenge to the planning of future education. We expect the education system to be managed in a way so it remains independent of existing notions of necessary competences and avoids simply educating for a labour market shaped by existing and therefore limited technological possibilities (Pors, 2011a). The question is how to plan without tying the sector to particular scenarios, which would reduce its flexibility and hence adaptability.
>
> Similar complexity can be found in business policies where, on the one hand, massive investments in the present, particularly in technology, are seen as a potential future competitive advantage, while on the other, policy-makers are reluctant to tie those investments to particular industries. The challenge is to both invest in and hence commit to a particular future horizon while ensuring that this commitment does not have a negative affect on the organisation's ability to adapt to alternate futures.

Organisations and time

All organisations establish conditions of possibility through their descriptions of the past, present and future. The same applies in public administration, where a specific present is constructed through descriptions of a specific past from which one is departing and a specific future toward which one is moving. However, time does not denote a linear development from the past via the present to the future. Time does not flow through the systems like a river from the past via the present toward the future. Rather, in each operation, organisations establish their present as a tension between the past and the future. The future is defined as everything that cannot be changed and the future as a horizon of not yet realised possibilities. The past, therefore, is the past of the present in the same way that the future is the future of the present, which is why each operation re-configures time in a new way. Thus, it is not time that moves through the present. What changes from operation to operation is the entire distinction past-present-future (Luhmann, 1982a). Organisational present is continually produced through the indication of a particular past and a particular future. The present is precisely the tension between the way we perceive the past and the future at any given time (Koselleck, 1985; Andersen, 2011b). Management is often a question of portraying the present as a 'now', where specific decisions have to be made based on descriptions of a particular past that we are trying to escape and a particular future that we are moving toward. It is a question of creating the moment of decision, which cannot be postponed for even a moment. We know this from phrases such as 'The moment is now', 'The time is ripe', or by contrast, 'The time is not yet ripe for this decision'.

However, a particular past did not simply happen and a particular future does not simply arrive. The past and future are always relative to the present. From the perspective of a specific present, we can understand and describe the past and present in particular ways. The past, present and future, therefore, are never anything in and of themselves but come into being as organisations relate them to each other. Past-present-future is always time for an observer (Luhmann, 1982a, p 307).

This perception of time shifts the analytical interest away from the question of *what* time is to the question of *how* time is constructed. We explore time not as an independent phenomenon, but as projections – as references to the past and future – that systems use to organise their operations in the present. We are interested in exploring the way systems produce time as a way to structure their operations and make them more complex (Esposito, 2011, pp 20-1). To achieve a more precise understanding of the way time is managed in organisations, we need to enter the organisation's control room, its most fundamental mode of operation: the decision.

Decisions as the containment of future uncertainty

Organisations have developed a broad range of methods for handling their inability to know the future. Typically, future uncertainty is managed via decisions. Decisions absorb uncertainty about the future by making decisions about it here and now. The planning and decision of what will happen at certain times in the future is basically a method for turning the future into something that can be decided about in the present. Annual plans represent one method for managing the future. A child and youth policy department writes up a plan for the coming year, planning different events in January, March or September. In March, there is a strategy day for all daycare facilities, in August a management development project for all managers in training, and in October there are contract review meetings between the heads of schools and the director of education. Decisions work by introducing the future into the present and constructing it as something in relation to which decisions can be made. We might call this a kind of presentification of the future through which uncertainty about the future can be contained. The future no longer appears undefined. We can expect the first week of March to be about the final preparations for strategy day.

In this way, organisations seek to stabilise time by defining fixed images of the future as premises for present decisions (Frankel and Thygesen, 2012). The future is made present through decisions and planning, and hence decisions can be made about it. This creates the *future of the present*.

This does not mean that decisions unambiguously determine or control the future. Instead, expectations are established in the present about what will happen in the future. It might be decided at a meeting that making coffee and emptying the dishwasher is a collective responsibility, but it will not be known whether this *was* a decision until there is the smell of freshly brewed coffee and the sound of crockery being put away. Thus, decisions establish social expectations about future decisions. They accomplish this by constituting a distinction between fixed and open contingency (Luhmann, 1993a). Before a decision is made, there is a multiplicity of possibilities, but a decision chooses one (or several) of these. Accordingly, a decision splits the world into a 'before' and 'after'. The 'before' of the decision is defined as a time where many different outcomes to a particular situation could still be imagined, where much could still be changed (Luhmann, 2000b). Decisions create an image of 'before' as the site of *open contingency* with respect to the particular expectations that will shape the future. Following a decision, this contingency and openness with respect to the outcome appear in fixated form, that is, as the fact that the decision could have been made differently. We could have done one thing but did something else. Decision as form looks like this (Andersen, 2003a) (see Figure 1.1).

Figure 1.1 is not quite as reductive as it may appear. A decision is precisely the unity of the difference between fixated and open contingency. Both sides of the difference are necessary in order to have a decision (a decision is precisely the result of a choice, not a calculation or logical deduction) (von Foerster, 1989, 1992; Derrida, 1992a). Included in the act of decision, therefore, is that which was not decided – that which was rejected as a choice (see also Knudsen, 2006, 2012a). Thus, it is not simply that decisions fixate or reduce contingency. Contingency is given a new form through the awareness that the decision could have been made differently. Social contingency is simultaneously stabilised and opened up through the operation of decision because the stabilised expectations are always seen along with a horizon of other potential expectations. This is the paradox of decision: the reduction of contingency produces contingency (Stäheli, 1998, p 59; Luhmann, 2002b, p 123; Philippopoulos-Mihalopoulos, 2009, p 131).

Our thesis is that this fundamental way of defining the relation between the present and the future is turned on its head in today's organisations. Our argument is that the uncertainty of the future is no longer perceived simply as a risk that needs to be contained, but also as a resource. Thus, organisations

Figure 1.1: Decision as form

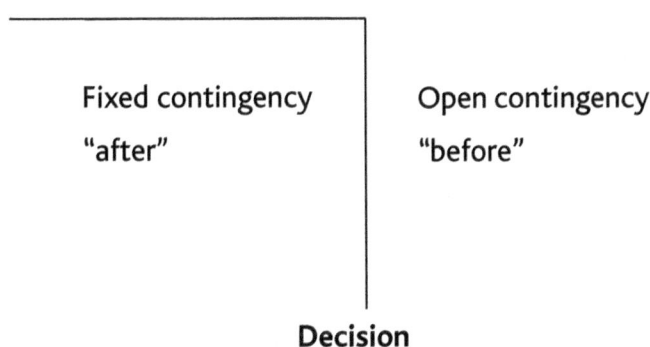

structure their operations not only by presentifying the future but also by futurising the present (Andersen and Pors, 2012). However, in order to pursue this logic we need to present the different perceptions of time that have historically characterised the public sector. We focus on this history as the development of definitions of the past-present-future relation. We are not using our exploration of such *figures of temporality* to claim that time itself *has* changed. We are not arguing that there is a shift from stability toward change or from minimal to increased changes. Such a diagnosis would be both incorrect and imprecise. But we do claim to be able to trace a development in the ways in which welfare organisations perceive and relate to time. And this development has a series of radical implications for welfare management.

Changing figures of temporality

We trace four different perceptions of time that occur at different points in the history of the public sector. These coincide with the four phases we return to in the following chapters. For now, we focus exclusively on the concept of *time*. In the chapters that follow we address other aspects of the developments within public administration, welfare organisations and the relations between organisation and employees and between state and citizen.

In the formal bureaucracy, developed from the late 1900s and onwards, we find a temporality figure according to which administrative decisions were made based on previous decisions. As we discuss elsewhere in the book, formal bureaucracy oriented itself toward the case itself. Administrative decisions referenced previous decisions, which made for a relatively predictable form of case management. In this scenario, the future remains but an externality, which an administrative decision is unable to account for or relate to. Hence the future was not a decisive factor, neither in the self-description of the bureaucracy nor as a reference for decisions. A decision established a past of previous cases relevant to a particular case, and the future was externalised as those things about which decisions could not be made. Thus, formal bureaucracy operated with a *present's past*.

The 1960s and 1970s was the time of planning. Developments in the public sector were about planned changes via reform and adaptation. Increased complexity within formal bureaucracy resulted in a need to restore unity and a sense of direction by means of central planning. Thus, planning was invented as a form of superstructure designed to supplement case management within the bureaucracy. Planning did not orient itself directly toward the individual case but focused on broader issues whose definition and prioritisation established premises for subsequent case management. Planning can be described as second-order administrative decisions, decisions about premises for subsequent administrative decisions (Luhmann, 1971).

The focus on planning meant that the future was described as calculable. Public councils and commissions identified specific developments in the world, and prescribed reforms designed to ensure that administrative units and policies adapted to the new conditions. The public sector was guided by the belief that the world was moving in one particular direction and that its job was to adapt to this movement. It was generally believed that historical analyses would deliver prescriptions based on which decisions could be made. Thus, change was always defined as change in relation to stability. Stability was perceived as the precondition for gaining knowledge, analysing development and identifying elements in need of reform. Stability was valuable as the condition for change.

Thus, from the 1960s on, the public sector increasingly recognised that the world was changing, although the relationship between time and case was articulated with priority placed on the factual rather than the temporal dimension. Factual analyses of history and social environment were seen as the conditions for change. The present was a question of analysing the past as a means to determine the future and conduct the appropriate planning in the present. Planning thus entailed *the future of the present*.

This logic of change can be summed up like this (see Figure 1.2). Around 1980, we see the emergence of a radically new figure of temporality in public institutions. The ideal is no longer about adapting to a particular scenario but about *adapting to adaptability*. The world and developments in it are no longer described in fixed terms – 'This is how things are developing'. The world is described in indefinite terms with phrases such as 'The world is growing increasingly complex', 'Changes are here to stay' and 'The world is a turbulent place'. How does an organisation relate to an environment that is described in such terms? The organisation is no longer adapting to anything in particular. It is supposed to adapt to the unknown. Therefore, the ideal is to adapt to adaptability. It is a question of the ability to continually be something else. Change management during this period is about maintaining the ability to change direction. Change no longer takes place on the basis of stability since the only stability is constant change and turbulence (Andersen and Born,

Figure 1.2: Figures of temporality in the public sector of the 1960s and 1970s

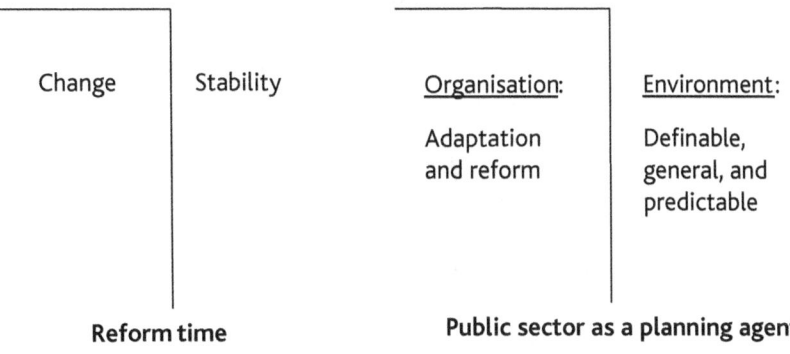

> **Concept 1.1: Time**
>
> Time cannot be known directly: the past is always gone, the future has not yet arrived, and the present dissolves before we can grasp it. And yet, time is a central aspect of our way of organising.
>
> The present is defined as the unity of the difference between past and future, or, in other words, between an experiential space and an expectational space. The experiential space is a *present past*, that is, experiences that have taken place. And the expectational horizon is a *present future*, which directs itself toward the not yet experienced (Koselleck, 1985; Luhmann, 2000a, pp 99-130). Each 'now' has its own past and its own future.
>
> Organisations create a *present future* as a way to manage, in the present, decisions about the future even though it is unknown. In other words, organisations seek to predict and plan the future, and establish norms that organise time and define stabilised ideas about the future as the premise for decisions in the present.

2000; Andersen, 2008b, 2013b; du Gay and Vikkelsø, 2012, p 122, 2013). The conception of what change is shifts from a movement toward something specific – a movement based on stability and leading to another stable condition once the movement is brought to an end – to change as a constant pulse. It is not change with a specific and final aim. It is not change in relation to something else. It is change or non-change. It is change aiming for more change. This has been given many different names by different critics. Clarke and Newman, for example, speak of 'the tyranny of transformation' and about 'the discourse of turbulence [...] where the only continuity is change itself' (Clarke and Newman, 1997, pp 39, 45).

Thus, beginning in the 1980s, the public sector adopted the ideal about adapting to adaptability. Organisations were expected to develop a set of tools to ensure continual changes to their modes of organisation, employment and relations. The key concept was strategy. Organisations were expected to continually ask themselves where they wanted to be in the future – to orient themselves toward future incarnations of themselves and their environment. The past was increasingly considered irrelevant. Past experiences were no longer to be trusted. Instead, the present was about guessing the future, providing future scenarios and replacing them with new future scenarios. Thus, the present becomes the present of the future. Where planning was about presentifying the future, making the future a present premise of decision-making, and thus absorbing uncertainty, strategy is a futurisation of the present, opening a contingent horizon of different possibilities.

We sum up the ideal about adapting to adaptability like this (see Figure 1.3) Since the 1980s, this perception of time has spread throughout the public sector in increasingly more radical and accelerated forms. In recent years, the public sector has begun to consider how traditional perceptions of the future – for example, strategy building and references to different images of the future such as the information society, the experience society or the knowledge society – contain the risk of tying public administration to specific future scenarios, which might not hold true. These images of the future might never have been perceived as actual or necessary truths. However, even perceived as contingent or interchangeable, they have functioned as references for decisions and for strategy building – and still function as such. But today, all such overarching narratives are being called into question. There is growing awareness of the fact that the future towards which we strategise will have transformed into something entirely different long before our strategic efforts have been implemented.

The public sector may glance at the private sector where previous behemoths such as Nokia shrink to almost nothing in a very short time and new giants emerge out of nowhere. Business gurus tell us that strength and size no longer give the same competitive edge as elasticity, flexibility and willingness to take risks. An article in the *Financial Times* (Pfeifer, 2013) concludes: 'Executives have to determine what is an appropriate strategy in a world of uncertainty.' The question is how to manage organisations in the present without running the risk of tying them to that present's limited ability to anticipate the future.

What is happening is an acceleration of the speed with which conceptions of the future replace one another. There is a sense that efforts to predict the future say more about the present than about the future. It is a bit like watching a sci-fi film from the 1970s. What springs to mind in the film's images of the future is not so much the future itself as the way these images reflect the present from which they derive. Reality might have turned out even more radical than what the filmmakers were able to imagine at the time of the film's making. Accordingly, what is already emerging, what can already be described and put into words, is considered to be the future of the present rather than something reflective of the 'real' future. The question is how to formulate strategies for the future based on the premise of having to expect the unexpected. The

Figure 1.3: Figures of temporality beginning in the 1980s in the public sector

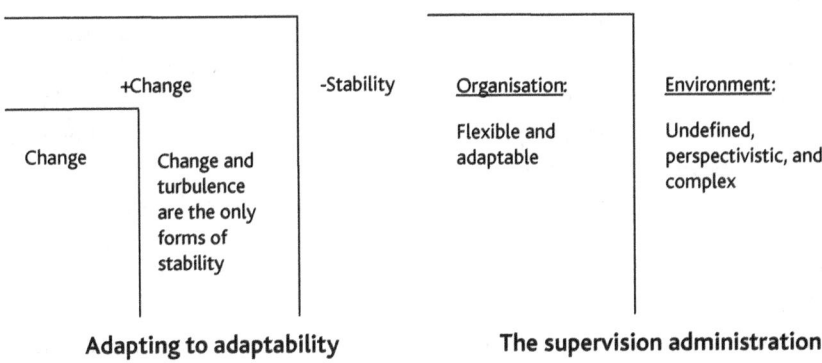

task is to establish expectations about the future with the expectation that all expectations will undergo a radical change (for an analysis of how this question is approached in the economic system, see Esposito, 2012a). Or formulated differently, how to create expectations when you can trust neither experiences of the past nor expectations of the future.

Today, every image of the future represents not only a possibility and occasion for public administration to justify a strategy; it also represents a risk. The idea of adapting to adaptability is given an extra twist with the effort to create organisations that are capable of adapting to something that has not yet even been predicted.

An example of this is a special issue of *Mandag Morgen* (*Monday Morning*) (a leading Danish news magazine) from October 2009 about the future of education. The issue describes how 'specialist competences no longer hold the same lasting value. They have to be continually recreated through new processes because new value is no longer created through the use of existing facts' (*Mandag Morgen*, October 2009, p 14). The quote questions not only a concept of knowledge as stable and lasting; it also cancels references to existing facts as no longer relevant or value-producing. This means that the education system can no longer use existing conceptions of the future to plan the future. Instead, policies and strategies have to be developed based on a conception of the future as fundamentally unpredictable. The same issue of *Mandag Morgen* describes the future as a figure in which 'technologies, which have not yet been invented, are used to solve problems, which we do not yet know' (October 2009, p 14). We are unable to imagine the technologies of the future because we do not even know the problems that they will be designed to solve.

Today's conceptions of the future therefore refer to the future as something that cannot be imagined and described from the perspective of the present. The acceleration of how rapidly premises for thinking about the future (for example, future scenarios or strategies) become rejected result in the notion that the future we are trying to capture is located beyond the future that we are capable of imagining in the present. The public sector shifts its management expectations toward a horizon beyond the horizon. We have, in other words, *the future of the future* (Esposito, 2011; Andersen, 2013b; Andersen and Pors, 2014). The future of the future is the future that you imagine will become visible when the present future becomes the present.

So far we have three layers of operation: administrative decisions about cases (directed by the present past), planning as second-order decisions (directed by the present future), and strategy as third-order decisions (directed by the future present). On top of these three layers we suggest *potentialisation* as a second-order strategy oriented towards the future of the future. Potentialisation, then, is about the futurisation of the future insisting on grasping the horizon beyond the horizon and thereby producing new possibilities not yet expected, not yet imagined, not yet thinkable.

This also has severe effects on the form of the present. In order to look for the future of the future, the present must not be infected by the present past or overly burdened with a specific present future. The future of the future brings with it an extracted present of the present. It is a pure present, an emergent singular moment. It is a totally naked present.

This new temporality is also observable in parts of the private sector. In handling risk problems, Swiss Re writes:

> Risks are a moving target. They are constantly changing or newly developing. That makes it difficult to quantify and judge them. The earlier the insurance industry starts adapting to emerging risks, the better prepared it will be for tomorrow's challenges. Foresight and knowledge sharing across stakeholders are essential to navigate into a future in which change might be the only constant that remains. (Swiss Re, 2013)

Anne Keller, Head of Corporate Citizenship and Art, makes a similar point: 'Swiss Re concerns itself with risk, with assessing the unforeseeable. This uncertainty and the way in which we deal with knowledge calls for employees who have innovative minds, who can look beyond their horizons, are tolerant and unafraid of debate' (Keller, 2013). Swiss Re portrays this temporality in Figure 1.4.

The image indicates that there is not only one horizon, and that in order to understand the future we have to look for the horizon beyond the horizon.

This shift has to do with the fact that the uncertainty of the future is no longer managed simply as a risk but also as a resource. As a matter of fact, the uncertainty of the future has always represented both a risk and a resource for organisations. On the one hand, the fact that the future is unknown makes it difficult to stabilise decision processes. Why choose to do one thing rather than another when we do not know what would be the best choice from the perspective of the future?

On the other hand, however, the uncertainty of the future represents flexibility and possibilities. Because the future is open, it lends itself readily to the effort to create inevitability around a decision in the present. The future presents only limited resistance – it provides the present with the sense of having many different possibilities. However, as we discuss, today's organisations are increasingly expected not only to prepare themselves for, but also make use of, uncertainty and indefiniteness. Elena Esposito has said that the only certainty available to organisations today is to be found in the ability to employ the openness of the future and not in the ability to predict it (Esposito, 2012b, p 231f). The fact that the future may be different than we imagine is used as a means to create welfare innovation.

We can sum up the development of the public sector's perception of time like this (see Table 1.1).

Figure 1.4: Looking beyond the horizon

Source: Swissre.com

Table 1.1: Public administration temporal figures over time

	Organisation navigates according to:	Temporal figure
Bureaucracy	Case management	The present is constructed on the basis of a case-relevant past and an externalised future
Planning	Problem	Adaptation Presentification of the future through planning The future of the present
Adapting to adaptability	Strategy	Adapting to adaptability Contingent images of the future The present of the future
Potentiality	Potentialisation as a kind of second-order strategy Flexibility	Indeterminate future Expecting the unexpected The future of the future The present of the present

Potentialisation

Our thesis is that the efforts of public organisations to manage according to the future of the future, the horizon beyond the horizon, creates a *potentialisation machine*, which fundamentally challenges organisations' way of establishing decisions, priorities and distinctions. By potentialisation we mean the effort to continually transgress existing realities and perhaps even potential ones (Andersen, 2008b; Costea et al, 2012; Staunæs 2011). Potentialisation is about creating possibilities for change beyond the presently imaginable.

We approach this question by showing how it affects and changes three fundamental aspects of organising. First is the fact that temporal aspects of organising are given priority at the expense of factual aspects. Second is the reversal of the relation between order and noise. And third is the effort to render the paradox of decision productive rather than trying to forget and cover it up. This sets the stage for the subsequent chapters and their more empirical inquiries and specific descriptions of the implications of these questions across the welfare society.

Any communication, or any expectation, splits reality into the actual and the potential. Thus, every communication marks something that is brought into the realm of actuality in opposition to a horizon of other possibilities (Luhmann, 1993b). The latter appears as potentiality, in the sense of other possibilities, which the operation in question did not use, but which may become actualised in the future. Thus, the content of the communication is split into the actual, on the one hand, and a series of lines of flight into the potential on the other. Today we make a decision, and this creates a future horizon of possibilities for the continuation of what we are embarking on today.

Interestingly, however, when organisations begin to seek out the future of the future, they simultaneously begin to actualise potentiality! In fact, the organisational objective becomes a transgression of the present potentiality. We see not only the production of concurrent horizons of possibilities each time a selection is made; there is an effort to continually potentialise by exploring the potentiality of potentiality. This is, of course, impossible since each effort to communicate about potentiality simultaneously actualises it, drawing a new distinction between the actual and the potential. But it is precisely this machine that drives the development within the public sector today, the ongoing pursuit of potentiality beyond already actualised potentiality.

The effect is a form of organisation continually stressing and exhausting itself, an organisation that constantly accelerates the production of new possibilities by futurising the future. However, actualising the potential as potential also transforms the future of the future into a future of the present (which the organisation observes as a risky limitation of possibilities). And when attempts to potentialise connect to earlier attempts to potentialise, the organisation unwillingly creates a past of present potentialisation. So it is a tragic movement. The future of the future has to be renewed from moment to moment, and the experience hereby created has to be forgotten in order for the present to be a pure present of the present not infected by any limitations. Only from a pure and naked present can the future of the future be evoked.

Forgetting the past and even the present becomes at least as important as imagining the future. When organisational members become experienced, they are moved to areas where their past has no value. When strategies become well known, they are dropped. As we pursue in later chapters, doing away with structures, routines and taken-for-granted thinking and action becomes an important strategy of forgetting, thus making room for potentialisation.

Prevalence of temporality

The potentialisation machine is connected to a shift of the hierarchy between factuality and time so that time and temporality is increasingly prioritised over factual decisions. As already mentioned, public administration has traditionally been organised around the management of cases and problems. Today, however, factual aspects of welfare become subject to the temporal dimension for purposes of increased flexibility and innovation. The identity of a daycare centre, a nursing home or a school becomes subject to the figure of temporality so the task becomes an exploration of what daycare or schooling might be in the future. Welfare managers are expected to be looking for what schooling, care, health, and so on, may mean beyond the presently imaginable. We might even say that the last bit of factuality is at risk of disappearing. Thus, the primacy of temporality provides welfare managers with the radical challenge of placing their institutions' *raison d'être* at risk in the pursuit of rethinking and innovation.

Noise

When organisations are expected to navigate in accordance with the future of the future, management is no longer seen as a question of providing stability in a changeable world, but as an introduction of an appropriate amount of disturbance and chaos into the organisation. Today, the problem is the inherent tendency to create too much stability, inertia and habitual behaviour of organisations. The fear is that the tendency in organisations to create stability through planning and to stabilise expectations impedes the organisation's ability to continually change and adapt. Management is talked about as a question of challenging the usual patterns of organising and of producing enough disturbance and innovation to keep the organisation in a state of instability – in a state of continual flux. This poses a challenge to our fundamental concepts of organisation.

Since the 1950s, organisational theory has employed cybernetics to describe organisations as the unity of order and noise. Organisations have been viewed as islands of social order surrounded by disorder, chaos and noise, a social order created in and by an organisation's interaction with noise. The driving force behind systemic autopoiesis was the transformation of noise into order. 'Without noise, no system', says Luhmann. In organisational theory, the concept of noise serves a double role as that which, on the one hand, threatens the organisation's fragile creation of order, while on the other, it is also perceived as the driving force behind organisational recreation and reorganisation. Gregory Bateson, for example, writes that, 'all that is not information, not redundancy, not form, and not restraints – is noise, the only possible source of new patterns' (Bateson, 2000, p 416). Thus, cybernetics has used the slogan 'order-from-noise' (von Foerster, 1981, p 17) to describe noise, both as something organisations strive to exclude and limit in order to establish themselves as order *as well as* a source of innovation and change.

In the public sector, the concept of planning and the idea of change as adaptation, which emerged in the 1960s and 1970s, represents an understanding of noise as a threat to organisational order. However, the shift in the concept of time within the public sector toward the notion of adapting to adaptability causes organisations to begin to see noise as life-giving, as a resource for dynamic and development, and as something that is in short supply in the organisation. When public organisations navigate according to the future of the future, we observe a somewhat mystifying phenomenon where the not yet defined, the not yet decided, *noise*, is increasingly perceived as valuable. The undetermined becomes a resource – the less determination, the more possibilities (Andersen and Pors, 2012, 2014; Pors and Andersen, 2014).

Concept 1.2: Meaning dimensions

All communication contains three meaning dimensions although they do not all need to be in play simultaneously. These are:

- *The factual dimension*, which pertains to the selection of themes and objects. These are all structured according to 'the thing' as a particular form of meaning, as the unity of the distinction between this/everything else.
- *The social dimension*, which pertains to the selection of identity. Identity is always structured in relation to non-identity, that is, in relation to distinction between 'us' and 'them'. There can be no 'us' without comparison to a 'them'. 'Us' is only us in its distinction from 'them', but 'they' exist only in 'our' discourse about 'them'. This means that expectations toward 'others' establish the boundary for expectations toward 'ourselves'.
- *The temporal dimension*, which pertains to the selection of what belongs to the past and the future respectively. The present is always stretched out between a past that cannot be changed and a future that has not yet arrived. Time does not move from the past toward the future. What moves is the distinction between past-present-future, that is, the present along with its past and present horizons (Luhmann, 1982a, p 307).

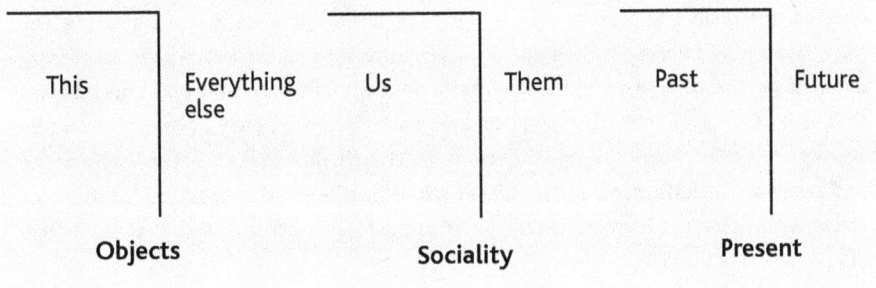

Across the welfare society, flexibility emerges as an ideal and is perceived as the key to more quality for less money. This is precisely about assigning value to the indeterminate. One example of this is the recent lockout by Local Government Denmark (the association of Danish municipalities) of public school teachers. At the centre of the conflict were teachers' working hours. Local Government Denmark's rejection of existing working hour regulations was based on the idea that more flexibility equals a better school. In the school debate, we also see flexibility as an ideal in the critique of 'the tyranny of ones'. What this means is a school that organises its programmes around the formula of one teacher, one grade, one subject, one classroom. The new ideal, by contrast, seeks flexibility in the sense that it rejects decisions that determine, for example, that a particular class has maths instruction at the same time each week, and seeks instead to keep open a range of possibilities for how to organise its programmes. Organising a programme according to a principle of flexible class formation rather than fixed grades, for example, allows the individual school, according to proponents, to better plan in a way that matches the way of learning and present motivation of individual students. From the perspective of an ideal of flexibility, the term grade or class is problematic because it determines in advance the number of students receiving instruction at particular times and in particular places. Flexible class formation, by contrast, is sufficiently open and non-specific to allow possibilities to remain open (Pors, 2011a).

The paradox of decision becomes attractive

Because organisations consist of decisions and are constituted by the way decisions connect with other decisions, they depend on the deparadoxification of the paradox of decision, described earlier.

> **Example 1.2: Indeterminate school architecture**
>
> The ideal of flexibility and indetermination also becomes apparent in the architecture and interior design of public buildings. A manual published in 2009 about the renovation and building of schools and daycare centres describes flexible and alterable architecture. The manual suggests building and designing in a way so that different users can be offered different possibilities. There is a story from a new school where the basic principle was that, 'children learn differently. Some children learn more effectively by seeing, others by hearing or through movement, and others through touch. This means that the school has to be flexible and include many different instructional settings and possibilities in order that children may seek out the best setting for their learning' (Finansministeriet et al, 2009, p 102, own translation).
>
> The architecture and design, however, are not only expected to offer variation. The manual also explains that the rooms and their design should be easily transformed. Moveable furniture, partitions and equipment are seen as the key to flexibility: 'All the furniture in the houses is moveable. Tables, chairs, bookcases and partitions all have wheels, and they are often moved around as a way to facilitate group formation across different classes' (Finansministeriet et al, 2009, own translation). Wheels and partitions allow the teachers to change the size of the rooms. And the sliding doors between the classrooms and walking areas allow these spaces to be transformed into a unified learning environment (Finansministeriet et al, 2009, p 111). Thus, architects are encouraged to support the concept of constant change. By putting wheels on the furniture, installing sliding doors and partitions, the physical spaces can contribute to the swift change in the way activities are organised.
>
> In this way, the concept of potentiality is transported to the realm of architecture. Rooms and spaces are judged on their ability to generate a surplus of possibilities and potentially allow for much more than their uses on any given day. The manual describes how a foyer with stairs can be transformed into many different rooms and meet many different needs, from the student who needs a moment's privacy, to a small group of students or an audience for the annual school play.

Decisions can basically deparadoxify themselves by being allowed to look like necessity. Much management communication can be seen precisely as an effort to deparadoxify. A manager might reference a particular logic of 'competitiveness' or 'demographic development', and in that way make a decision appear a sheer necessity. Similarly, a decision can be communicated as necessary by insisting that it pertains to a particularly beneficial or critical opportunity, which the organisation has to seize. And finally, decisions can be made to look as if others have in fact already made them on behalf of the organisation. Identifying external authorities and assigning particular intentions to them make it seem as if a decision has already been made elsewhere, and that the organisation then has to follow suit.

However, the changing perception of time means that the inherent tendency in decisions to not only stabilise but also create contingency suddenly appears attractive to public administration. The concern is no longer simply how much contingency escapes a decision but also how little, and the possibilities thus lost. Any decision establishes a horizon of potentiality in the form of all the possibilities that the decision did not actualise. Today's decision-makers are increasingly interested in this kind of potentiality – potentiality that is shut down in and by the act of decision. Accordingly, today's public sector seeks out possibilities for accelerating the paradoxes inherent in any decision. It wants to make decisions but does not want to miss out on unused possibilities. Whatever contingency remains beyond the decisions is cultivated in order that possibilities for having made different decisions remain open.

This raises a set of questions to be pursued in subsequent chapters. How are today's welfare organisations more specifically expected to *increase* their internal undecidability? Are there specific *programmes for undecidability*, where organisations programme decisions to simultaneously suspend the role of decisions as the decision premises for new decisions? What does a welfare organisation look like when it constitutes itself as decisions, which prefer to remain undecided? How can welfare organisations adapt to making decisions without excluding possibilities?

Management challenges

Challenges for complexity reduction management

The chapters in this book focus on different areas of the public sector and analyse the specific implications that the expectation machine has for the individual welfare organisation, for public administration of welfare organisations, for the relation between manager and employee and between state and citizen. However, we can already begin to outline the challenges that the expectation machine produces for welfare managers.

The fact that today's public organisations find themselves split between wanting to contain the uncertainty of the future by deciding about it in the present *and* wanting to adapt to external uncertainty by increasing its internal indeterminacy changes the premises for welfare management (Andersen and Pors, 2012). Management becomes a question of how to simultaneously allow expectations about the future to remain open and flexible while also establishing stability and directedness.

The demand for expectations about the unexpected questions our usual conceptions of management and governance. Conventional management and governance are responsible for making decisions in the present about a particular path into the future. A manager's job is to define goals for an organisation – this is where we are today, this is what we are moving toward. Thus, conventional management is about contingency reduction – these are the potential possibilities for future development but we choose to manage according to this specific possibility. With this logic, managers make the future present in the present, that is, they introduce the future into the present as a premise for present decisions. We expect managers to look into the future and interpret our uncertainty about what the future will bring, and to estimate what the organisation ought to do today in order to be prepared for the future. But this management figure comes under intense pressure when organisations begin to conform to innovation and flexibility.

The future of the future brings a fundamental state of schizophrenia to public administration: the administration wants to simultaneously commit to specific future scenarios and allow its conception of the future to remain radically open. It seeks investment in the future but does not want to commit to specific investments. Thus, it seeks to intensify its engagement in the future while maintaining the flexibility to reinvest and redefine. The administration wants to make decisions but does not want to exclude possibilities. The result is the coexistence of conflicting expectations with regard to welfare management. On the one hand, strong managers are expected to reduce complexity for employees by formulating clear goals and providing a sense of direction. And on the other hand, welfare managers are also expected to create and maintain complexity and indeterminacy so that the organisation preserves its flexibility, adaptability and maximum imaginative powers for imagining the future.

The challenge to welfare managers is that the very basic motivational force behind the act of organising – the restriction of contingency via decisions and the linking of decisions to one another – comes under assault. Welfare managers have to work to create unity and consistency in an organisation, which wants to make decisions but does not want to be limited by its own decisions, and wants to reduce contingency as well as produce contingency.

The result is a kind of trembling organisation made up of decisions that try not to be decisions and that offer only undecidability, decisions that continually suspend themselves as decisions. We might even say that welfare managers are expected to develop their organisations through decisions but also to continually introduce an immune system against the tendency of decisions to restrict contingency.

The expectation machine leads to the following challenges for management:

- How may managers prepare organisations for the future without committing them to unnecessarily specific future scenarios?
- How can managers formulate goals and strategies while allowing alternative possibilities to remain open?
- How can managers manage from within the space of continual tensions and conflicts between demands to define the future and demands to open up the future?
- How may managers simultaneously create stability and unity *and* adaptability and transience in an organisation?

Welfare management becomes a question of managing the fact that contingency is both articulated as a risk and a resource. This double dynamic can be seen in the ways in which public sector departments today find themselves caught between a demand for control and documentation and demands for innovation. Welfare managers are required to deliver prescribed results as well as relate to themselves in open and experimental ways to create new opportunities in a time of scarce resources. Public administration is expected to both immunise itself against unexpected outcomes by establishing precise goals, plans, evaluation and supervision as well as venturing into risky experiments whose purpose is precisely to seek out new opportunities in the unexpected and unknown.

The question is whether potentiality administration establishes a new form of management where the potential of future restructuring and rethinking is given all the attention at the expense of present problems and limitations. Does this new form of management commit itself, for better or worse, to constantly seeking out the immanent potential in employees, innovation and reorganisation? Does the effort to create opportunities turn into a programme that is entirely cut off from considerations about the realisation of opportunities? The question is also whether management of potentiality entails a hidden message to public managers, encouraging them to talk about the necessity of innovation but at the same time leave their everyday practice untouched by this rhetoric.

Irrespective of whether one perceives the implications of the new temporal figure in public administration in a positive or negative light, the demand for expecting the unexpected, the penchant for flexible organisation and the pursuit of future opportunities mean that welfare management becomes a question of managing an intensive oscillation between the reduction and acceleration of contingency.

Welfare management becomes the management of hyper-reflexive organisations with respect to how their own foundation – that is, decisions – threatens to unnecessarily tie them down. Such organisations are caught in a self-inflicted expectational double bind, seeking to accelerate the production of future opportunities by making decisions with the awareness that these decisions might threaten to undermine future opportunities.

Reflection 1.1: The future of the future

Ask yourself:

1) How does your organisation perceive the future?
2) How would you describe the way you relate to the future in your organisation? What is the relationship and balance between the planning and opening up of future opportunities in your organisation?
3) What is the role of the past in your organisation?
4) Is there more than one perception of time in your organisation?
5) Are employees required to both seize the present and the future?
6) Are you so focused on the future that you forget to take advantage of experiences and knowledge within your organisation?
7) When was the last time you conducted a systematic effort to gather experiences and knowledge from your organisation
8) How do you take responsibility for the sense of uncertainty that unpredictability often leads to? How do you recreate a sense of security in the your organisation when the future is anything but certain?

TWO

The impossibility of governing society

Is it possible to steer society from a position outside of society? Today's political system acts as if it is, and most radically so when the US for example and shifting partners have been engaged in military actions. Was the Iraq war not an attempt to implement a new social order from the outside? A democracy, at best? Can a bank bailout rescue or change the forces operating in the financial system? One bailout quickly led to another. What are the prevailing ideas when society becomes the object of governance?

We begin our descriptions of welfare management using society as the point of observation. We are interested in the basic conditions for governing society. The first premise for speaking about the public sector and governance is the fact that society is multicentred. Society has become centre-less, and no social system can assume a privileged position from which it controls other social systems in society. Regulatory efforts have to accept that they can only, at best, work as productive misunderstandings.

One of the most traditional conceptions of society, which is often brought up in conversations about management and governance, is the notion of civil government, which took shape in the decades around 1900. The basis of this principle of government is the division of society into three parts: the state, the public (the market) and individuals. Individuals come equipped with freedoms and rights such as property rights, freedom of speech, and so on. Freedom, however, can only be realised in a public social context where freedom becomes restricted. Property rights, for example, can only be realised through a binding commitment toward someone else in the marketplace. This commitment is guaranteed by the state's monopoly on coercion. By being placed a step above everyone else, the state holds the three organisational principles in place (Pedersen, 1996). Thus, the state is perceived to be simultaneously outside society as well as a part of it. And society implicitly means national societies. In the marketplace and society's other public spaces, individuals and organisations can only see aspects of society. They see parts of it. But because of its elevated position, the state sees society as a whole and acts on its behalf. The higher up in the public hierarchy, the better the view, so to say. From this perspective, 'public sector executive' refers to the top of the public hierarchy as well as the top of society. Public sector executives are expected to assume a position from which they not only oversee and represent the unity of the hierarchy at whose top they have been placed; they are also expected to be positioned so high above the skies that they are able to perceive society as a whole. They are expected, to some extent, to be able to represent society in society.

The problem is that this conception does not match the complexity of contemporary societies. It is a product of the legal system in the transition from absolutism to democracy. In order to develop a language that is more accurate of contemporary society, we have to accept a notion of society as functionally differentiated, and account for how this radically affects conditions of governance and management.

Functional differentiation

Niklas Luhmann claims that the prevailing mode of differentiation in society is the result of a development from segmentary differentiation via stratifactory differentiation to functional differentiation (Luhmann, 2013). *Segmentary differentiation* is characteristic of a society that was divided into a number of fundamentally similar sub-systems such as, for example, tribes, villages or families. This placed rather tight restrictions on how complex a society could be. There was a certain level of differentiation of roles such as gender roles, chief and medicine man, but such roles did not assume the character of independent sub-systems. From the time of the Middle Ages, *stratifactory differentiation* begins to take over. Here, systems are differentiated according to the guiding difference upper/lower. Systems describe and identify themselves as one stratum among others, and each stratum establishes fixed positions of status for society's members. Strata include the aristocracy, church, peasants and labourers. This significantly increases the complexity of society and allows for a certain level of labour division among systems. Today's society is characterised primarily by *functional differentiation* where social systems are no longer organised according to a hierarchy. Instead, society consists of a range of different global systems of communication such as the political, economic, art, pedagogical, legal, sports and health. These are communicatively closed around themselves as a result of their self-designated function in society – the economic system is closed around the function of allocating scarce resources, the political system around making collectively binding decisions on behalf of society, the legal system around managing conflicts, and so on (Luhmann, 1977).

All three forms of differentiation still exist today, but functional differentiation is clearly prevailing. For example, bikers and other gangs are proof that segmentary differentiation takes place in our society, and certain families are still organised according to the segmentary principle. Moreover, many workplace lunchrooms have established cliques with fixed seats for people who eat together every day. Similarly, our society still operates with status differentiation. We have economic elites, a political elite, an art elite and an educational elite, although these are neither stable nor socially constituent forms.

We have illustrated the changes in society's prevailing forms of differentiation in Figure 2.1.

The impossibility of governing society

Figure 2.1: Changes in the differentiation of society

Segmentary differentiation	Similar sub-systems, e.g. tribes, villages, and families	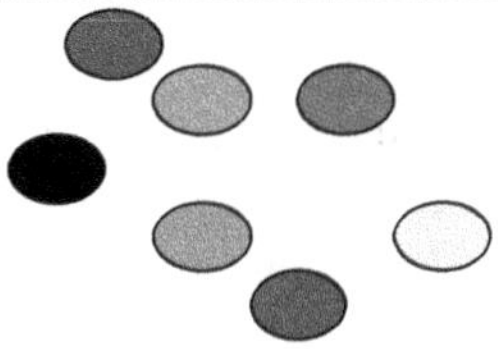
Stratifactory differentiation	Differentiation into dissimilar sub-systems according to the guiding difference upper/lower, e.g. king, aristocracy, peasants	
Functional differentation	Differentiation into dissimilar subsystems, which are distinguished from each other by their function in society. Systems are organized horizontally, e.g. politics, law, and art.	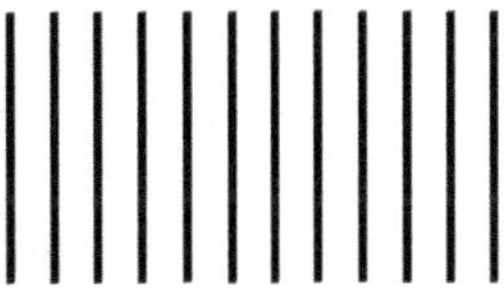

In a sense, the description of society as divided into state, market and individuals, with the state positioned a step above the others, is a description of the functionally differentiated society from the perspective of the stratified society. It represents an attempt to insist on the state's ability to perceive society from the outside, and to reform and govern it from there. A similar insistence on a hierarchical principle can be found in the writings of Pierre Bourdieu, who, despite his view of society as divided into different areas such as bureaucracy, economy, culture, art and so on, which are assigned a certain level of autonomy, remains on the lookout for their hierarchical organisation. Bourdieu talks about the state as constituting a meta-capital, regulating the exchange value between the different forms of capital connected to the differentiated fields (Bourdieu, 1994). We do not believe such descriptions match the complexity of society, and feel that they contribute to a general distortion of governance conditions. It is a distortion, which, in the concept of civil government, exaggerates the possibilities of governance, and, in Bourdieu's description, introduces a kind of governance paranoia by exaggerating the subjugation and repression of certain areas by other areas.

We define *function systems* as social systems that relate to society, are global, and remain functionally closed around themselves in their use of specific media. Function systems are systems such as the political, legal, economic, religious, art and mass media. They are characterised by the fact that they communicate by means of their own symbolically generalised medium: the economic communication system uses money as a medium, the political system uses power as a medium and the mass media system uses information as a medium. The communication media are *symbolic* because they are condensed into singular clear symbols. In the economic communication system, the medium is money and the symbol is coins and bills. Moreover, symbolically generalised media are *general* in the sense that the medium can be used to communicate about anything; it is not tied to specific situations. Anything that can be symbolised with money can be communicated about economically (Luhmann, 1989).

Symbolically generalised media establish *binary codes* for communication. The fact that the code is binary means that it divides communication into plus value and minus value. The money medium, for example, follows the code to have/not have – according to which it is obviously better to have than not to have. The entire world can be summed up with this code, distinguishing between 'what I have' and 'what I do not have'. In connecting to the economic code, everything is perceived in terms of the economy. In connecting to the legal code, everything is understood legally. The codes function like perspectives that exclude each other (Luhmann, 1992a).

Function systems are fundamentally inclusive social systems. In theory, anyone can partake in the communication of a function system. It is not necessary to hold a particular status in order to partake in the economy – one person's money is as good as the next one. But the decision to communicate economically makes the world appear in a particular way.

Concept 2.1: Binary codes

Symbolically generalised media establish *binary codes* that split communication into plus and minus value. Positive value indicates a basic aspiration in the communication. Negative value serves as a reflexive value. When communication employs a binary code, it has to choose either the plus or minus side of the communication.

When communication connects to a symbolically generalised medium, the entire world is perceivable from the perspective of the code. The code divides the entire world in two so that communication has to connect with either the plus or minus side of the code. There is no third value. This also means that two media cannot communicate at the same time. Each of the codes represents its own logic, and a change of code changes the entire content of the communication and possible continuation (Luhmann, 1989, 1992a).

Thus, we can understand society as differentiated into a range of function systems, each with their own symbolically generalised media and their own binary codes or logics, which makes communication between function systems an impossibility. They are different and parallel streams of communication, which function as each other's external environment. We have tried to illustrate this in Figure 2.2, although it does not include all the function systems that exist today. We have organised the function systems on a horizontal line to emphasise that they are not ordered hierarchically and that there is no centre from which society can be represented as a whole. There is no super code capable of uniting the many codes into one perspective.

Figure 2.2: Function systems and their media and codes

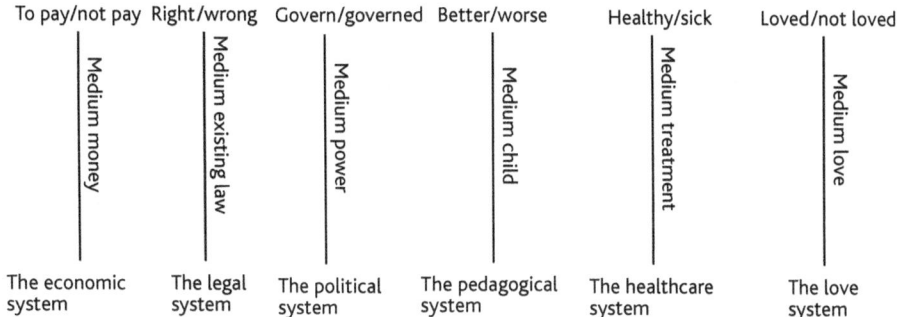

Allow us to elaborate further using a few examples of functional communication to fully clarify this logic.

The legal communication system. The law is linked to a particular medium and a particular binary code. The law's symbolically generalised medium is 'to exist' as in the expression 'existing law'. The medium is symbolically recognised as laws, paragraphs, legal decisions and rules. The code is right/wrong, and being right is obviously better than being wrong. This means that the law as a symbolically generalised medium divides the world into right and wrong. Put together, the code's two sides provide a complete description of the world. Right is always right in relation to wrong, and the distinction is not founded on something outside itself. Thus, the very emergence of the code of law means the expulsion of morality from law. In legal communication, right is right and has nothing to do with justice. This further means that legal communication is founded on a paradox that becomes apparent when the law inquires about its own code – is the distinction right/wrong itself right or wrong? The law's binary code creates certainty that if a person is right, the law is on their side. Uncertainty about the law exists only in forms that can theoretically be alleviated with reference to decisions that are created within the legal system itself (Luhmann, 1989, p 64). Functionally, the legal communication system is closed around the function of guarding against conflict and ensuring stable expectations capable of allowing for specific disappointments. This function finds expression in the desire for social order as the legal system's fundamental value. The fact that legal communication is oriented toward conflicts does not mean that law solves conflicts. When the law observes conflicts, legal communication steps in to transform them into legal questions about right and wrong. This is the only thing the law understands. It is the only thing it can make decisions about. Thus, the function of handling conflicts is a question of having rules in place that allow the law to shift conflicts into the realm of law and make them legal. This eliminates the original 'substance' of the conflict. The act of assigning rights to people is one of the law's most significant tools for the translation of conflicts into legal questions. Without property laws, for example, a conflict between neighbours cannot be considered by the law, and once it has been included under the law, everything that is not relevant for the determination of right and wrong is excluded. And legal communication can even use the distinction right/wrong to define what can be admitted under the law, for example, which facts count as legal facts (Luhmann, 1992b). The law simplifies conflicts and is incredibly precise about what can be included into the conflict and ignores anything that cannot be formulated in the language of law. Personal motifs and interests, for example, are irrelevant to conflicts about purchases if these cannot be discussed in legal terms as preconditions.

The pedagogical communication system. According to Luhmann, the general symbolic communication medium in pedagogy is 'the child' (Luhmann, 1993c). The creation of the very distinction between child and adult is linked to a specific historical development. At different times in history, children were perceived as small adults (Ariés, 1973). The modern conception of the relationship between child and adult develops in the 1700s and disperses the idea of a child as whatever they are born to be. Instead, the child is now viewed as mouldable. What a child becomes is perceived as dependent on the environment that moulds the child. This results in the familiar distinction between nature and nurture, which is basically a discussion about the child's plasticity – how much can a different upbringing and education contribute toward the fate and identity of the individual child? The perception of the child as mouldable establishes conditions for pedagogical communication in which one does not communicate with the child, but where the 'child' allows itself to become representative as the symbol of an educational effort. The child becomes a symbol by means of which communication takes place. The child is the *medium* to be *shaped* by pedagogical communication. The question of the end result of this moulding depends on the specific pedagogical programme. The moulding can be about compliance, morality, creativity, academics or something entirely different. The fact that the child as a medium is a *generally symbolic communication medium* means that there are no restrictions on the kinds of knowledge that can be imprinted onto the medium. Theoretically, the child can be moulded into anything: a tyrant, an artist, an environmentally conscious citizen, and so on. The fact that the medium is *symbolic* means that the child functions as the symbolic and recognisable expression of the medium – the object of communication. The symbol is, however, variable and can be replaced with student, pupil or course participant (and hence is independent of biological age). Regardless of the specific symbol, the distinction remains: child/adult ≈ mouldable/moulded. The binary *code* connected to the child is better/worse in terms of learning (Luhmann, 1989, pp 100-6). In pedagogical communication, everything is observed from this perspective. Everything is perceived with a view to perfection. Thus, it is a *corrective code* in relation to which one can either connect to the code's positive preference value – for example, by considering ways in which the child/pupil/student/course participant may improve – or to the code's reflexive side – for example, by reflecting on reasons for lack of improvement despite the introduction of cutting-edge pedagogical methods. The code is, of course, also employed in ongoing evaluations and tests of the child's competences: pass/fail, strengths/weaknesses, etc. In any case, pedagogical communication is always a question of correction with a view to perfection. The pedagogical function system is closed around the function of teaching and educating. However, from the perspective of other systems, the contribution of the pedagogical function systems is the selection of individuals according to formal qualifications and competences.

The care system. In the care system, the symbolically generalised media is *care*, and the code is to help/not help. When a client appeals to the care system, the appeal might land on either the help or not help side. Only the care system is in a position to decide whether or not there is a need for assistance, and in order to reach this decision, the care request has to be diagnosed. This also means that the reservoir of possible diagnoses in the care system decides the production of care needs. And the definition of a diagnosis is, of course, an internal element within the care system. From the perspective of the care system, problems in the external environment are undefined until the care system has established a diagnosis, that is, has decided whether and to what extent a need for assistance exists. Problems that a potential client from the system's external environment might bring to the care system and present to a social worker are considered undefined care needs. No action can be taken in response to undefined care needs. Through internal diagnosing in the system's communication, an undefined care need can be transformed into a defined need for care or a defined non-need for care. From here, the care system can intervene methodically (Moe, 1998). Thus, problems do not exist in advance as care needs in the system's environment. The system itself produces the problems to which it then responds, and its capacity for problem production depends on its ability to diagnose. In addition, the care system may increase its communicative reflexive capacity by reintroducing the code to help/not help back into itself. This allows the care system to communicate about forms of help as non-help. The system can, in other words, choose not to provide assistance in relation to a diagnosed need for assistance if it believes, for example, that the assistance might turn the client into more of a client. In this way, the care system is able to differentiate its internal operations in endless distinctions between help, non-helpful help and help for self-help.

The mass media system. The code of the mass media system is information/no information, and information represents the system's positive directive value. The system is continually directed toward publicising information, but in order to be able to do so, the system must know how to distinguish information from non-information. Non-information, therefore, is the system's reflexive value. The distinction between information and non-information, however, does not present itself spontaneously. There is no place from which that distinction can be made. This introduces a fundamental paradox into the mass media system since the information that something is non-information is itself a form of information (Luhmann, 2002b, p 28). One of the ways in which the mass media seek to deparadoxify its code is through exemplary news criteria such as 'breaking news', 'conflict', 'norm violation', etc. In addition, the code of the mass media system contains another paradox that appears in the temporal dimension of its communication and functions as the motor of the entire system. The paradox consists in the fact that as soon as a mass medium has separated information from non-information and has publicised it, information ceases to be information. Information cannot be repeated without losing its status as information. This means that the operations of the mass media compulsively transform information to non-information with the result that the system continually makes itself obsolete, forcing it to engage in new operations that distinguish between information and non-information. The preference in mass media for information above non-information means that the function of mass media is the ongoing creation and handling of irritation (Luhmann, 2002b, p 123).

Mass media are closed around the function of irritating society's other systems, thus increasing the irritability of society as a whole and its ability to handle information (Luhmann, 2002b, p 123). From the perspective of society's other systems, the contribution of the mass media is that they provide a shared backdrop. The mass media system guarantees a generally socially accepted present, which other systems can then assume in their own selections (Luhmann, 2002b, p 124). However, the shared reality provided by the mass media does not function as a consensus. The shared reality is constructed through the invocation of thematic issues such as 'the financial crisis', 'Greece's debt problem', 'global warming' and 'piracy'. These thematic clusters work as structural coupling between the function systems by simultaneously providing a shared reality, which everyone can refer to, as well as being sufficiently elastic and diversifiable to assume different meaning in different systems. 'Piracy off Somalia's coast' is assigned a specific meaning in the economic system as increased transport costs and the creation of a new insurance market. In the political system, however, piracy is seen as the sign of a weak government in Somalia, which then calls for international collaboration. And in the conflict and security system, information about developments in the piracy situation serves as the cause of different security-related responses such as the arming of civil ships and the deployment of warships for purposes of surveillance. And finally, in the legal system, piracy leads to discussions of jurisdiction and possibilities for prosecuting in countries outside Somalia. Again, the central point is that information continues to lose value in the mass media system. This forces the mass media to continually reproduce certain themes or to simply abandon them when information can no longer be distinguished from non-information. In this way, the mass media also contributes the production of time and temporal orientation for the other function systems. Table 2.1 sums up the most important modern function systems.

Table 2.1: Society's function systems

Function system	Medium	Code (+/–)	Function
Political system	Power	Govern/governed	Ensure collectively binding decisions
Scientific system	Knowledge	True/false	Seek new knowledge
Economic system	Money	To have/not have	Scarcity management
Pedagogical system	The child	Better/worse in terms of learning	CV classification
Mass media system	Information	Information/non-information	Produce irritation
Legal system	Law	Right/wrong	Caution against conflict
Moral communication	None	Respect/disrespect	Increase conflicts
Art system	The work of art	Art/not art	Observe the world
Health system	Treatment	Healthy/sick	Keep death at bay
Care system	Care	To help/not help	Inclusion
Intimate communication	Love	Loved/not loved	Articulate the highly personal
Religious system	Faith	Immanence/transcendence	Exclude contingency

Today's society is differentiated into a range of function systems, each with their own symbolically generalised medium and their own binary code or logic. This makes it impossible for communication between function systems to exist. To each function system belong certain values, which constitute the systems' blind spots and which allow them to blast into the future with very limited resonance capacity. The systems do not belong to any hierarchy, and there is no centre from which society as a whole can be represented. Each system creates its own comprehensive view of society. Thus, we have a political worldview, an economic worldview, a religious worldview, and so on, but no unity of these views. Society represents a multiverse rather than a universe, and we cannot locate ourselves outside the function systems in order to judge whether power is better than faith, or love is better than money. There is no super code. The only unity in society is functional difference.

> **Example 2.1: Knowledge is polycontextual**
>
> Each social system assigns itself a function, but to another system that function is observed as performance. What operates in one system as a function appears as a performance to another external system. The scientific system assigns itself the function of producing reliable knowledge. Knowledge is the system's sole purpose. To other systems in the scientific system's external environment, knowledge is at best a performance, which serves as support for the other system's internal operations. To the pedagogical system, knowledge can be perceived as competences to be acquired through teaching. To the political system, knowledge is used as ammunition in the political debate. To organisations, knowledge represents premises for decisions. To the economic system, knowledge represents a commodity
>
> | System | Knowledge perceived as performance |
> | --- | --- |
> | Organisation | Decision premises |
> | Politics | Political ammunition |
> | Love | Irrelevant except for meta-communication |
> | Education | Competences |
> | Health | Diagnostic tool |

Function systems as mutually dependent

In a functionally differentiated society, no system can replace another. Politics is no replacement for economy. Knowledge cannot replace religion or law. Economy does not work in the place of love. This does not mean that function systems operate independently of each other, quite the contrary. The mutual dependence among systems increases because the functions are not substitutable. Because of their inability to substitute each other, they become both a burden and a support for each other (Luhmann, 1989, p 110). Function systems rely on certain services from each other. Thus, a flourishing economy is productive for the political system, and in turn, a well-functioning political system is conducive to a healthy economy. However, even the strongest economy does not replace politics. Collectively binding decisions do not result from economic communication. Similarly, issues often spread from one function system to another. A collapsing real estate market creates pressure on the political system. However, a booming economy may also create problems for the political system because it is forced to make collective decisions to increase the workforce, level of daycare services, or to alleviate pressure on the environment. The healthcare system is in a constant process of improving its diagnostic skills. This creates expectations with respect to increased treatment, and increases the demand for resources for the healthcare system, which puts pressure on both the political and economic system. The education system depends on the scientific system, whose knowledge production is observed as competences for students to acquire through education. But the scientific system's ongoing internal differentiation into disciplines, cross-disciplines and sub-disciplines is not only a service to the education system. It challenges its disciplinary categories and causes a content overload, compelling the education system to develop new ideas about disciplinary advancement.

> **Concept 2.2: Integration**
> A society can be said to be integrated when it tolerates internal differentiation. A society is not held together by a sense of community or consensus. The more difference a society is able to tolerate, the higher its level of integration. Demands for unity threaten rather than strengthen a society's level of social cohesion. Similarly, society's integration is reduced by one system's effort to serve as the role model for the others.

In a functionally differentiated society, therefore, the different systems become increasingly dependent on each other. They cannot communicate with each other. They can observe each other and be influenced by each other, but they cannot govern each other in the sense of operating within each other. They are resigned to serving as external environments for each other. As such they can function as noise for each other. However, it is always the system itself that internally decides how to assign meaning to another system's 'noise'. This means that to the extent that there is a certain causality in play in the way that one system affects another system, it is the affected system that decides the specific nature of the causality by making itself sensitive to its environment in a particular way.

Hyper-reflection

Is it really true that society's function systems are as radically separated as we claim? Don't we observe a tendency to mix logics and codes? Is it not the case that solutions to many welfare challenges are precisely articulated as cross-disciplinary efforts and cohesion? What about current efforts to think holistically across systems?

Below, we describe the way in which function systems have become hyper-reflexive about their dependence on other systems, but how efforts to create cohesion and connections across different logics paradoxically add to the differentiation of society rather than minimise it.

What interests us is a relatively new reflexive discourse within the function systems. The function systems begin to reflect on their systems boundaries. They begin to see what they are as an undesirable obstacle to what they want. They begin to articulate a desire to be something other than what they are.

For example, we can observe in the war system a desire to be perceived as socially constructive, which naturally includes engaging in peace-making efforts, but which brings about the paradoxical idea of democracy- and peace-making wars. But at the same time, the war system reflects on its own boundaries. It knows that democracy and peace are not achievable by means of military operations, that they are dependent on a variety of other circumstances: security, education, employment, hopes for the future, and so on. At the same time, it is difficult for

Example 2.2: Society's failure to handle environmental and climate issues

We do not have a social system specifically responsible for managing environmental concerns. All function systems negatively affect the environment and climate, but no system is able to represent the environment as a whole. Even worse: no system is in direct contact with the environment that surrounds and sustains us (Luhmann, 1989).

The only way for society to take environmental concerns into account is through communicative articulation of ecology and the environment, but this articulation can only articulate the environment within the restricted functionality of each of the function systems. The education system can educate about ecological food production. And the mass media can turn environmental events into news and thereby try to irritate other systems into also communicating about environmental and climate-related issues. However, the closed nature of the function systems entails a systematic ignorance of the environmental conditions of society as such. The economy can turn environmental questions into an economic problem and debate whether or not it makes economic sense to invest in preventative measures against environmental disasters. Thus, no function system directly concerns itself with the environment as a whole, and each of the function systems can only communicate about environmental and climate-related question from the perspective of its own code.

What this means is that society's ability to relate to the environment depends on the difficult and fragile interplay between function systems. This interplay is complicated by the fact that each of the function systems operates with its own temporality. Each systems develops its own ways of creating momentum, attention, technological opportunities, and so on. The production in the mass media of descriptions of issues related to climate change do not necessarily coincide with the scientific system's development of technological solutions to those issues, or with the political system's efforts to build support for or create consensus around a given decision or agreement.

As United Nations (UN) climate summits never fail to make clear, building political consensus among a great number of nations with different political interests is often a protracted and complicated process out of sync with the scientific developments afforded by the scientific system. Scientific communication struggles to understand why, despite technological advances that allow for a variety of interventions, political agreement cannot be reached about the deployment of technological possibilities. And the political system wonders why the scientific system is unable to unambiguously produce the certainty of prognoses with which the political system may try to convince sceptics. And in the meantime, islanders in the Pacific are experiencing rising water levels every year as they watch their islands literally disappear.

Does this mean that no organisation fights for climate and environmental issues as a whole? Not necessarily, but their efforts depend on the different function systems' attempt to relate to nature from the perspective of their respective codes. Organisations are compelled to internally manage the differences between different function systems. Nature is always nature for an observer and organisations are constantly facing dilemmas such as either observing a windmill farm from the perspective of a local environmental conservation effort, and hence as destructive of local flora and fauna, or from a global perspective as a step in the right direction toward sustainable energy production.

Thus, society's relationship with its natural environment is complicated by the fact that function systems remain fundamentally closed off to anything but their own interests. The systems' different ways of handling environmental issues is more indicative of their past and present efforts to create political support, technological innovation or news value than about an interest in the environment. Is it at all possible to bring the function systems into sync? Luhmann asks the question: how does our society deal with the fact that we are fundamentally unable to manage our ecological environment?

Concept 2.3: Planning

No society so far has been able to recognise itself, that is, to choose its own structures and to use them as rules for admitting and dismissing members. Therefore no society can be planned.... Planning society is impossible because the elaboration and implementation of plans always have to operate as processes within the societal system. Trying to plan the society would create a state in which planning and other forms of behavior exist side by side and react on its other. Planners may use a description of the system, they may introduce a simplified version of complexity of the system into the system. But this will only produce a hyper complex system, which contains within itself a description of its own complexity. The system then will stimulate reactions to the fact that it includes its own description and it will thereby falsify the description. Planners, then, will have to renew their plans, extending the description to include hyper complexity. They may try reflexive planning, taking into account their own activities. But, in fact they can only write and rewrite the memories of the system, using simplistic devices which they necessarily invalidate by their own activity. (Luhmann, 1982b, p 132)

the military to simply leave it to other systems to create the conditions of its new goals and objectives. From the perspective of the war system, the pedagogical, healthcare and care systems are hopelessly unfit, within the context of war, to provide the necessary services for peace. The Danish Department of Defence, for instance, wanted not only to engage in military operations in Afghanistan, but also to establish a dialogue with civilians. Initially, it tried to create strategic partnerships with private non-governmental organisations (NGOs), but they were not interested in such a partnership. So the Department created its own 'civil society institutions', which even received funding from the Danish foreign aid budgets. The Department wanted to assume responsibility for relief assistance and foreign aid – weapons in one hand and tools for building schools in the other. However, construing foreign aid as an element within its system means that foreign aid becomes coded within the war system as 'security by alternative means'. And it changes the nature of the war: war is perceived and pursued as the building and destruction of schools, hospitals, and so on. Part of the war strategy becomes to prove the evils of the enemy by showing their destruction of the schools built by the Danish military. And schools and hospitals are built in locations where the military needs to show a humanitarian face rather than in places with the greatest need for help.

We see a similar trend domestically when national security is designed to look like welfare policies. The Danish Security and Intelligence Service (Politiets Efterretningstjeneste, PET) is involved in many welfare-related political discussions and formulates policies and methodological guidelines in relation to deradicalisation programmes (national security policies that want to be perceived as care).

Today, the healthcare system has begun to consider the way in which both individual health and 'public' health depend on a variety of aspects that fall outside the traditional boundaries of the healthcare system. It develops visions for greater public health and life expectancy, but knows that these objectives depend on circumstances that are not directly health-related. The health of individuals depends on their habits, lifestyle and culture, which further depends on their education, work, family and housing, which further depends on the status and development of the economic system, political, care and education systems. But the healthcare system is a system whose fundamental function is to provide treatment on the basis of diagnoses under the guidance of the code healthy/sick. And this form of coding has the particular twist that it contains more possibilities for connectivity on the sick side than on the healthy side. A diagnosis describes a deviation from health. As Foucault argues in *The birth of the clinic*, medical language cannot define health in positive terms. Health means distance from death (Foucault, 1989). The healthcare system treats sickness, not health. However, today's healthcare system wants to be something other than what it is – it wants to promote health. But the systems that decide the general state of health in society are not the healthcare system. Therefore, we see a healthcare system that also wants to be educational, instructional, preaching, caring, normative and legislative.

We see new self-descriptions within the function systems defining 'pure' systems logics as lacking and transgression as capable of capturing extraordinary and synergetic energies. Function systems become hyper-reflexive in the sense that they reflect on the boundaries of their own coding and on their fundamental reliance on other systems for the achievement of their own objectives. Being hyper-reflexive means developing programmes for how to temporarily suspend their own code and make room for others (Andersen and Sand, 2012).

Ultimately, therefore, the hyper-reflexivity of the function systems merely exaggerates the differences between the systems, although we do observe a form of structural corruption among systems. As an example, it becomes exceedingly more difficult for NGOs to provide assistance in Afghanistan once aid has been included as an aspect of military operations. Does the world distinguish between a school built as part of a military strategy and a school built as part of a care package? What is it that causes the function systems to become hyper-reflexive? What does hyper-reflexivity provide an answer to?

> **Example 2.3: Boots that do not want to be a commodity**
>
>
>
> 'I am not a commodity!'
>
> The image on the left shows the tag on a pair of boots. The text reads: 'This product was not designed to have any special look or function. It was created to have a self-identity and suit the free spirits. Wear it anyway you want, but do not have any special care with it.'
>
> It is a product that does not want to be a commodity. Or rather, in order to become the commodity it wants to be, that is, authentic, it has to reject its status as a commodity. In this case, this paradox creates a certain awkwardness that the company deals with through humour. Thus, the text ends with the words, 'May the force be with you.'

We believe hyper-reflexivity to be a response to three growing challenges. First, society's increasing differentiation, which consists not only in the general differentiation of the function systems, but also in the increasing differentiation and specialisation of the sub-systems within the individual function systems. This causes the systems to become increasingly dependent on each other at the same time as these dependencies become more and more difficult to manage. Second, the question of simultaneity is radicalised, making it increasingly difficult to manage by means of planning. As already mentioned, all systems are compelled to act simultaneously. In the past, systems handled this through the creation of images of the future, that is, by seeing the future as the space of possibility. The challenge is that function systems have become conscious of the problem of simultaneity. They know that the future they see is not actually the future but an image of the future based on experiences of the past. Function systems are increasingly aware that the future that the systems perceive is a future of the past. Thus, it becomes risky to trust the future. This is why we speak today of living in a risk society, where the very act of reflecting on risk is risky. Finally and third, speed in society has increased, not least with increased media dissemination via the internet and email, which further adds to both the problem of simultaneity and the problem of differentiation. As noted in Chapter One, transience has become a fundamental condition.

Table 2.2: Reflexivity of the function systems

Function system	The fold of the code	Hyper-reflexive self-descriptions
Pedagogical system	Learning to learn	Wants to assume the character of play and leisure. The idea is that this increases learning motivation
Political system	The power to empower	With the notion of empowerment, power of communication no longer presumes the freedom of the powerless but seeks to produce the powerless as free in the image of the powerful The EU's internal market is a political system that describes its unity in terms of economy Voluntary policies are suggestive of a state that wants to be a civil society
Care system	Self-help help	Wants to be caring and diaconal
Economical economic system	Paying for payments	The commodity has to cancel itself as a commodity to achieve value
Healthcare system	Preventive lifestyle	Health-promoting programmes indicate a desire to turn treatment into the promotion of 'the good life'
Mass media system	Informing about information	News journalism strives for the same level of freedom as art, and desires the same authenticity as artworks
Art system	Art about art	Art communicates through the creation of artworks that can be seen by an audience. Modern art seeks the coincidence of work and audience through artworks that define the work as the very meeting of art and non-art, eg street art
Security system	To distinguish between risk and danger is a risk itself	Wants to be seen as caring and as helping radical elements to become free

The penchant for transgression in the function systems might serve as a response to the combination of growing interdependence, increasing demands for speed and growing mistrust of one's own predictions. The systems find themselves in a situation in which there is pressure to communicate and act quickly, but where any sensible choice of communication and action depends on the actions of other systems. The systems increasingly experience their interdependence. The individual system increasingly makes its own operations dependent on the operations of others. This produces a combination of forced choice and necessary delay. However, only the present is real. There can be no delay. Choices have to be made now, but the sensible thing would have been to await the choice of others.

The basic definition of communication is that a message creates a horizon of connectivity. The message itself is not communication but becomes communication once new communication connects with it. This connection further establishes a horizon of connectivity that does not become communication until it connects with other communication, etc. Communication has to either accept or reject communication opportunities – either it connects or it does not. These are the only two options. This does not mean, however, that different communication systems cannot seek out other possibilities. Most people know the challenge posed by the question, 'Do you love me?' You are in trouble if you answer 'No', but 'Yes' also presents certain problems since the next question is 'Why?' – and it is both difficult and risky to prove love. In such cases silence can be a strategy. Silence does not necessarily mean to decline communication; it can be a form of connectivity that reduces the formation of a new horizon of connectivity.

We may consider whether the hyper-reflexivity of function systems is indicative of a strategy not unlike silence, as a way to manage transience and dependence in the functionally differentiated society. Hyper-reflexive function systems can operate without making choices in order to communicate both/and. Education is both work and not work (play and activities). The product is a commodity and not a commodity (because it is authentic). Hyper-reflexivity is a way to generate productive uncertainty in a context where certainty is risky. It is important, for example, that educational communication is not rejected to reveal unmotivated students. Better to plan an activity that is successful if the students take to it but not a total failure if they do not since they are merely rejecting a voluntary chance to play. The fondness in the function systems for transgression becomes a way to manage complexity without reducing it – that is, a way to push it in front of them. In other words, hyper-reflexivity functions as an immune system in the function systems when their communicative autopoiesis is threatened in the regime of transience.

Simultaneity

In the functionally differentiated society, everything happens simultaneously. The economic system makes transactions at the same time as the political system is making decisions, science analyses, and the media informs. The systems do not wait for each other. Here, too, the functionally differentiated society is fundamentally uncontrollable. The political system makes a temporal distinction between policy formation, planning and implementation, and imagines that the systems react to similar reforms. But the systems that the political system seeks to control do not wait for political decisions. They constantly operate retroactively in relation to their own operations. When the political system moves from planning to implementation, the governed systems already find themselves in an entirely different situation than at the time of planning. Consider, for example, in a Danish context the reforms designed to increase the workforce in response to many years of financial growth. By the time the political system had managed, through welfare commissions and endless discussions, to generate a collective understanding of the necessary interventions, the financial boom had long since been replaced by the financial crisis. Nevertheless, the political systems insisted on carrying out the reforms despite rising unemployment rates. The political investment in terms of compromises and consensus was too great for the system to simply abandon the reforms despite the fact that conditions had changed. Hopes were instead placed on future growth, which the reforms could then be a response to.

> **Example 2.4: Pedagogy beyond the classroom**
> In Danish schools today, there is a growing focus on children's learning as the most important driving force. Schools are expected to provide organisational flexibility so that the learning process is not always governed by timetables, lesson duration and structure. In fact, the inverse is perceived as desirable. Moreover, new pedagogical theories describe how children learn differently, and how children learn in all social contexts: in groups, through conversation, and in collaboration with other children and adults.
>
> Thus, in the pedagogical system we observe an increased awareness of the limits of teaching in its traditional conception – in a classroom, with a fixed curriculum, **lessons** of a certain duration. Traditional pedagogical limits such as curriculum, lesson duration or the physical boundaries of the school are no longer seen as sufficient for the successful unfolding of pedagogy. The school in isolation is perceived as inadequate, and pedagogical communication envisions hybrid constellations where learning can merge with play, dinner or swim practice, for example.
>
> This means that schools are encouraged to organise themselves around the assumption that learning transgresses boundaries between lessons and break times, between school and home, between school, daycare and an afterschool programme, and between school and voluntary organisations.
>
> One school in Copenhagen, for example, works with a concept according to which learning is something that happens 24 hours a day, seven days a week and in all social situations. Informational material sent out to parents describes how the school aspires to 'work on students' planning of their own work outside "normal" school hours and outside school premises – the so-called 24/7 model ("learning 24 hours a day, seven days a week").' Pedagogical hyper-reflexivity means that pedagogical institutions are expected to maintain a certain level of scepticism about themselves as an appropriate place for learning.

> On the one hand, the hyper-reflexivity of pedagogy marks a gesture toward non-pedagogical rationalities, but at the same time it also indicates the intensification of the pedagogical rationality. From the perspective of hyper-reflexive pedagogy, all situations can be observed as potential learning. Precisely in order to create more learning, pedagogy seeks to challenge its own boundaries and play itself out in relations between children and parents, in children playing at the playground, in activities in the local football club, etc. Reflecting on one's boundaries becomes a new form of potential limitlessness.

Challenges to social governance

What does this mean for the possibilities of governance in the welfare society? How does one govern in a polycentric functionally differentiated society? How is it possible to ensure integration in a society that can be characterised as a multiverse rather than a universe?

A fundamental governance condition is the fact that one system cannot govern what another system does and what it assigns meaning to. Governance decisions in the political system cannot determine what goes on in the pedagogical system. There may be sound reasons for a minister to abandon the idea of group exams without there being any pedagogical advantages to this, which will in turn compel the pedagogical communication system to explore new ways in which to continue practices that it finds pedagogically necessary. Activation requirements in the social services law are assigned particular labour market value in the political system and in the central administration of the Danish Ministry of Social Affairs, but achieve an entirely different social-pedagogical value in the care facilities that put the law into care-related practice. Here, activation can mean watering the plants (Hansen, 2006).

Our first diagnosis can be summed up with the following list of challenges for governance:

- How is it possible to govern society when there is no top from which society as a whole can be governed? How can society be governed without a centre?
- How can society be governed when society cannot be represented within society, when any attempt to represent the whole is relative to the perspective of the observing function system?
- How can we trust governance when the different function systems are flying blindly into the future with limited resonance capacity and with compulsory inconsideration toward each other?
- How can the political system govern when it has no control over whether its communication is continued as legal, mass-mediated, scientific, moral or something entirely different?
- How can we coordinate and plan when everything happens simultaneously?
- How can we govern a multiplicity of systems that are operationally closed, impenetrable *and* hyper-complexly dependent on each other?

- And with respect to our enormous ecological challenges, how can society adapt to its ecological conditions when it is fundamentally unable to adapt to its external environment, and when the external environment is always confined to being an environment for a system?

As promised in the Introduction, we do not provide any easy answers. How to respond to a paradox if not by means of another paradox? And yet, we can provide certain insights.

First, we reject the idea that there is any one place from which society as a whole can be governed and planned. It would be nice if the political system could perform the job of the banks more proficiently than the financial system. But it cannot. It would also be tempting to let the free market and economic system replace bureaucratic support systems and public assistance programmes. But in the functionally differentiated society, one system cannot serve as the model for another. Politics cannot function as a model for the economy. The free market cannot serve as a model for politics and care. This kind of substitution merely destroys the capacity for self-governance within the systems, and thus reduces the possibilities for handling complexity.

We have to relinquish the ambition of governing *as if* society can be the object of planning. It cannot. There is no 'outside' of society, and none of society's individual function systems can serve as the model for the rest of society without catastrophic consequences for society's and our reproduction of our shared welfare.

Today, we can trace at least four tendencies to use one system as the model for the rest. One of these can be referred to as *state centrism*. Here, society's many problems are addressed to the political system, which is then expected to deliver satisfactory solutions. This form of state centrism can be found in left-wing parties that have traditionally shown more confidence in political governance than in free market self-governance. However, state centrism can also be seen on the right in plans for comprehensive top-down changes to the healthcare system or political redesigns of the public school – all in the name of the free market. Finally, state centrism often appears in the form of political populism when a welfare scandal has caught wind in the media. A child has suffered abuse and the authorities failed to detect it, or a treatment that causes serious side effects has been systematically prescribed without the intervention of health authorities. In such cases, political parties compete in the effort to propose changes that will ensure that such things will never happen again. They give promises of perfect governance, which they are essentially unable to keep, and which often and more damagingly result in top-down governance that undermines self-governance.

The second tendency is *economic centrism*. Here, society's many problems are addressed to the market. However, the market cannot make collectively binding decisions, teach, distribute care, etc. Politics does not serve as the model for the economy, but the market also does not work as the model for politics and care. The privileging of any perspective in a hyper-differentiated society produces totalitarian effects. Its only effect is the destruction of the capacity for self-governance in the systems, and this reduces the capacity for handling complexity. An economic centrism portrays society as choices between state and market, and hence disregards all other function systems such as education, science, law and health.

The third tendency is *aesthetic centrism*. Art is at times perceived as a system that can provide authentic social critique, experimentation, non-instrumental approaches and creativity. Art, play and aesthetics, from the perspective of such centrism, is perceived as the only practice in society that serves no interests beyond its own. Thus, art, play and aesthetics are perceived as more authentic than the rest of society, and this authenticity is the source of the radical nature and revolutionary potential of art. Despite our reverence for art, however, art is not located 'outside' the functionally differentiated society. The efforts by artists to formulate new social models also cannot serve as a model for other systems. Art is unable to create new scientific knowledge or make collectively binding decisions. And like the other systems, art would reduce the capacity for self-governance in other systems if it were to serve as a model for these.

Finally, we observe a tendency today toward a certain *religious centrism*, where religion is seen as a foundation on which society can rest. We are not only thinking of different versions of totalitarian Islam, but also conservative Evangelicalism as we know it today, particularly in the US. However, such religious centrism also manifests itself in Europe as, for example, in a Danish context, when a certain breed of Danishness is held up as the stronghold of its cultural foundation. On the most basic level, function systems have no foundation beyond their own self-

---

Concept 2.4: Monocontextualism vs polycontextualism

Any observation has a blind spot. Observers see what they see but cannot see what they do not see. Any observation of the world is always framed by a particular perspective or gaze, which allows an observer to see, but which also entails a systematic blindness. When observing, one does not see the perspective through which one observes. This is a condition of all observation, all analysis, all thought, and all communication. Nothing exists that does not rely on an observer. Everything is something for an observer. We distinguish between a monocontextual and a polycontextual view of the world as two different ways of dealing with the fact that we always observe from a particular perspective.

In a *monocontextual view of the world*, the observer sees what they see. The world is expected to be what it appears to be. The observer is a first-order observer.

In a *polycontextual view of the world*, observers still see what they see, but with the built-in awareness that what they see will be perceived differently by other observers. Thus, they are second-order observers in addition to being first-order observers. This does not imply the ability to see the blind spot of their own observation or to see what other observers see, but it implies insight into the existence of many different observations, into the fact that the world is observer-dependent, and into the fact that one observes from a particular perspective into which one never achieves complete insight. Thus, polycontextualism implies a view of the world that takes into account that what is observed by one observer probably looks different to another observer.

reference. They do not rest on a culture outside themselves. Thus, any attempt to claim a cultural or religious foundation is out of sync with the complexity of society.

In a general sense, therefore, governance has to contend with its own boundaries. It has to base its action on the fact that it is up to the governed systems to decide how governance makes sense. Governance has to acknowledge that it has to make sense within the governed systems.

The distinction between monocontextualism and polycontextualism as two different worldviews is significant for the discussion of governance in a complex society (Luhmann, 2012, p 13). Polycontextualism represents the necessary foundation for governance today, when one system can no longer dictate processes in another system. Monocontextual management disregards the fact that different systems can only observe governance attempts from their own perspective. Monocontextual governance therefore runs the risk of being rejected as an irrelevant and distracting element by the systems it seeks to govern. Sometimes, less governance produces a greater effect.

Polycontextual governance, on the other hand, is organised in a way so that it can be observed as meaningful from the perspectives of other systems. It is designed to allow for contingent perceptions of it. Accordingly, polycontextual welfare management affords its objects of governance different possibilities for connectivity. It is a form of management that strategically takes into account the fact that there is no way to pre-emptively and precisely determine the way that the governed systems will react to its governance and translate it into their respective perspectives.

Reflection 2.1: Society's differentiation
Ask yourself:

1) Which systems prevail where you work?
2) What are their codes?
3) Which systems depend on each other in relation to your area of expertise? How?
4) What are some of the productive and unproductive misunderstandings between systems that you know from your work?
5) Do you sometimes expect things of a system that it cannot live up to?
6) Which system do you tend to hold up as a model for other systems?

THREE

From bureaucracy to potentialisation

What does it mean to govern within the public sector in a way so that its multifaceted activities and elements are coordinated horizontally? How is it possible to maintain a form of hierarchical unity as the complexity in the public sector continues to grow? Does increased reliance on self-governance also increase the capacity for handling complexity? How does one govern self-governance? And what does it mean to govern while simultaneously encouraging the governed bodies to think along and develop their own innovative solutions?

Today, freedom and self-governance are perceived as highly effective governance strategies. Local autonomy and independence are seen as vital resources for central governance efforts. The hope is that by governing through independence, public administration can increase the speed of adaptation of individual units and their ability to take local responsibility for issues in the welfare state. The hope is also that local freedom will generate possibilities for finding and reaping the potential inherent in the exploration and rethinking of what quality means in specific situations for individual citizens.

In this chapter we explore the relation between governing and governed bodies in public administration today. We show how the formal hierarchy in public administration has been transformed, first into *supervision administration* and subsequently into what we refer to as *potentiality administration*. Today's public administration frames the relationship between governing and governed bodies in various and cryptic ways. Trying to govern subordinate units and institutions through independence means that any attempt at governance entails the risk of limiting institutions' capacity for self-governance. And when the governed bodies are governed in accordance with their ability to rethink welfare services and welfare organisation, any attempt at governance risks limiting the possibilities for innovation by dictating particular understandings of problems and solutions.

In order to more precisely define the conditions of welfare management, we explore the way that the public sector has changed its internal organisation throughout the 1900s up until today. We show how the central administration department has gradually discovered the disadvantages of governing by means of unambiguous hierarchies and central planning. The question is how relations between state, municipality and welfare institution have radically changed concurrently with attempts to gain the benefits of self-governance and self-adaptation. And how this may have created a fundamental schizophrenia in the public sector that now permeates all governance relations. What we look at in this chapter is the history of the hierarchy and of conditions of power.

Generally speaking, the history of public governance over the past century can be divided into four periods: formal bureaucracy, which emerges at the end of the 1800s, sector administration, which appears at the end of the 1950s, supervision administration, which gradually develops around the beginning of the 1980s, and potentiality administration, which emerges around 2000 (Andersen, 2005; Andersen and Born, 2000). Each of these periods defines in its own particular way the relation between governance and self-governance. It is important to note that the development is cumulative. Thus, sector administration adds itself as a principle to bureaucratic administration, and supervision administration adds itself to sector administration without causing the previous order of administration to disappear. All four forms of administration coexist today – sometimes harmoniously so, and at other times in a relationship of competition or conflict.

Table 3.1: Forms of administration

	Form of governance	Object of governance	Limit of governance
Formal bureaucracy	Regulation/control	Civil servant conduct	Civil servant self-control
Sector administration	Planning	Individual administrations	An administration's capacity for translating central input into decentralised output
Supervision administration	Supervision	Organisational autonomy	Organisational independence and strategic capacity
Potentiality administration	Potentiality	Organisational exploration of innovative possibilities	Organisations' ability to risk and rediscover themselves and their potential

Power

The ability to define and describe governance depends on the definition of a concept of power. Power represents the specific language of public administration. Power provides a power-superior with the position to impose on a power-inferior the complex burden of interpreting their wishes and recommendations. Thus, it is up to the power-inferior to translate the general or abstract communication of the power-superior, and to adapt it to their particular context and specific actions. An example could be if the Danish Ministry of Science and Higher Education instructed a university to develop a communication programme, but without further specifying its ideas and visions for the project. The university, then, is not only given a specific task, but also the task of defining the task itself, and has to concern itself throughout with what might have been the Ministry's intention, and specify the task in response to such considerations, well aware that it is never possible to achieve certainty about the intention of those in power.

The most likely scenario is that there never was a clear intention, and that the proposal that the university delivers functions as a proposed intention for the power-superior, who in the end can always claim that the proposal does not match the Ministry's intentions. As this example illustrates, power presupposes the freedom of the power-inferior. Modern power increases freedom for both power-superiors and power-inferiors. In public management, coercion is always present as the alternative to power as sanctions, but as soon as a power-superior makes use of sanctions, the complexity of the situation returns to the power-superior who is suddenly forced to show their intentions and thus place a limit on their freedom. In other words, when someone wields power as coercion, power quickly becomes inflated (Luhmann, 1990, pp 155-8).

> **Concept 3.1: Power**
> Power is the medium for political communication. As a form of language, power divides the world into power-superiority (governing body)/power-inferiority (governed body) in relation to which it is evidently better to be in the position of superiority. Power functions by shifting complexity from the position of power-superiority to the position of power-inferiority. Power is exercised when the power-inferior is unsure of the intentions of the power-superior and hence self-governs based on interpretations of the possible intentions of the power-superior. Power is not the same as coercion. In fact, power presupposes a lack of coercion. Coercion represents the outside of power – that which power communication refers to but can never be identical with. Because coercion functions by subjecting someone to a specific action and requires the perpetual presence of the coercive figure, coercion drastically restricts possibilities for action for both the power-superior and power-inferior (Luhmann, 1990, pp 155-7). By contrast, power functions by governing in relation to the freedom of others. In fact, the greater the capacity for self-governance, the greater the overall power potential.

The point is that in public administration, the power-superior always governs in relation to the self-governance of the power-inferior. Governance is always and cannot be anything but self-governance. Public administration can be described as hierarchical chains of power relations, for example, from minister via head of department, office manager, welfare employee to citizen. Within each relation, governance takes place only when the governed body possesses the freedom and capacity for self-governance. And yet the relation between governance and self-governance has changed radically over the past century. And this history challenges our understanding of public management.

Governance can be defined as the act of minimising a difference. Budget management, for example, is about minimising the difference between a budget on the one hand, and expenses and revenue on the other. Likewise, goal steering seeks to minimise the difference between goals and activities. Thus, governance begins with the formulation of a difference, which then has to be reduced. And this is where governance challenges begin, since only governed bodies – not governing ones – can reduce the difference. This turns all forms of governance into a form of meta-communication: communication about the communication of the governed bodies. The governed system alone decides whether governance will take place. Governance only takes place if the governed system observes the meta-communication of the governing system and defines it as the premise of governance. The governing system cannot itself minimise the difference but can only make it available to the governed systems. Thus, the governing system always depends on the ways in which the governed system assigns meaning to the communication of the governing systems and its definition of the differences to be reduced.

Below we outline the history of public administration through descriptions of central events. Such a presentation of the history of the public sector will obviously be hugely reductive, but it allows us to provide a clear sense of the story about the emergence of supervision and innovation administration.

Formal bureaucracy

Formal bureaucracy based on the idea of the constitutional state dates back to the mid and late 1800s. We can trace the gradual development of a formal bureaucracy, a division into different offices for different jurisdictions and administrative responsibilities. Formal bureaucracy is a form of public administration, which makes decisions about individual cases based on the legal framework of existing legislation. Formal bureaucracy functioned as a case management machine with carefully defined areas of responsibility and guidelines for case management as well as clearly defined areas of competence and archiving methods. This ensured both a certain level of external control of case management and knowledge accumulation as well as the development of a predictable case management practice through ongoing comparisons of current cases, with decisions arrived at in previous and similar cases.

Max Weber pointed at a number of characteristics of modern bureaucracy. First of all, 'There is the principle of official jurisdictional areas, which are generally ordered by rules, that is by laws or administrative regulation' (Weber, 1978, p 956). His second characteristic is, 'The principles of office hierarchy ... in which there is a supervision of the lower offices by higher ones' (Weber, 1978, p 957). This means that the source of authority is based on delegation (Mommsen, 1974, p 76). Weber attributes to the formal bureaucracy technical qualities such as 'precision, speed, unambiguity, knowledge of the files, discretion, unity, strict subordination, reduction of friction and of material and personal cost' (Weber, 1978, p 973). All in all, he thinks that bureaucratisation 'offers above all the optimum possibilities for carrying through the principle of specialising administrative functions according to purely objective considerations' (Weber, 1978, p 975). Or, as Wolfgang Mommsen articulates it: 'Bureaucracy of necessity recognizes everything it comes into contact with according to strictly "instrumental-rational" principles' (Mommsen, 1974, p 64).

The development of formal bureaucracy is conditioned by a stronger legal basis for administrative activities, including an unambiguous legal constitution of its practice in the form of administrative records. The development and differentiation of administrative law is a foundation for formal bureaucracy in the public sector, where administrative law is basically understood as the description of the activities of the state with respect to the different functions of the state, and a doctrine of the order of the executive power and its activities with respect to the different functions of the state.

What constitutes the formal bureaucracy is the operation of the *administrative decision*. In formal bureaucracy, an administrative decision is defined as: 'a unilateral statement by an administrative body of specific and legally binding content' (Andersen, 1924, p 22ff). This is what public administration does. It makes unilateral decisions, which are binding for the involved parties without the parties' involvement in the decision. Unilateral means that the administration holds the sovereign power of decision. It requires neither consent nor agreement from hierarchically subordinate parties, for example, a citizen or business affected by the decision. Thus, administrative measures are defined in contrast to contracts, which are defined as *bilateral statements*. As a bilateral statement between parties, a contract is not valid until the parties agree on the relationship of obligations to which they subject themselves. A contract represents a voluntary restriction of one's freedom. Thus, the constitution of administrative law is based on an exclusion of the contract as that which administrative law is specifically not. And this marks a line between two different legal standards: administrative law and civil law. It also marks a legal division of society into state and society. Whereas a contract represents a bilateral statement between equal parties, an administrative measure represents a unilateral statement within a hierarchical leader-subordinate relation. Administrative law defines the administration as a hierarchy within which power can be legally exercised in the form of administrative measures in accordance with specific rules.

In a formal bureaucracy, governance means controlling administrative measures and the objects of governance, that is, individual offices and officials. The condition of governance and control is the self-discipline of individual officials. Thus, even though formal bureaucracy can be described as chains of power relations and hierarchical subordination, the premise of governance remains self-governance throughout. But self-governance takes a particular form in the formal bureaucracy: as self-discipline. Thus, any power's capacity limit is established through the ability of individual officials to independently act in a systematic, consistent and disciplined way while referring upward in the hierarchy regarding definition of cases, objectives, decision-making procedures, legal basis, and so on (Condren, 2006). In this way, the biggest governance challenge in the administration of formal bureaucracy is the minimisation of the difference between rules on the one hand, and the practices of administration officials on the other, and to ensure that such practices reflect the rules. As part of that effort, public administration can refer to itself as a hierarchy and as a hierarchy of hierarchies, a figure typically seen in organisational diagrams (see Figure 3.1).

Figure 3.1: Hierarchical self-description

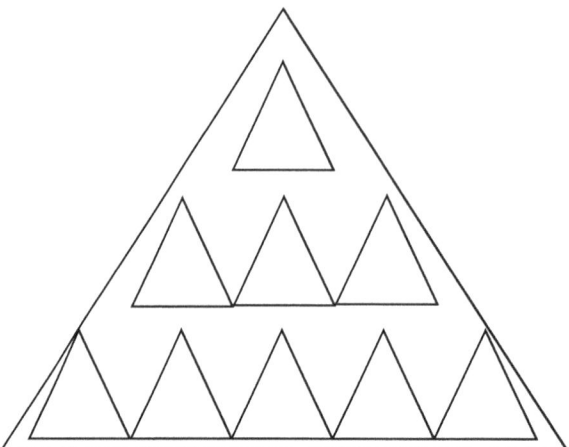

The fundamental bureaucratic paradox is that this system has to apply general rules to all specific cases and unique situations. Because bureaucracy operates by means of rules, its only response to individual cases is to generalise, universalise and formalise.

As formal bureaucracy develops and grows, this becomes increasingly problematic. How can the system act when reality is changing faster than the rules are able to adapt? How can the system act when rules develop shoots and become confusing and perhaps even contradictory to each other? How does the system act when the complexity of the law no longer corresponds with the complexity of society? Internal complexity gradually grows to the point that it can no longer be formalised away.

Sector administration

Responding to the difficulty of handling complexity within public administration and forging greater compatibility between the speed of change in public administration and society respectively, a new form of administration emerges as ideal in the late 1950s and is slowly institutionalised in the 1960s and 1970s. The governance efforts of *sector administration* are focused on the coordination of a swarm of public sub-activities into a comprehensive sectorial perspective. We see the development of vertical sectors for labour market policies, social policies, tax policies, educational policies, and so on. Each sector is organised around a particular set of governance problems, so that a sector represents a problem-driven administrative pillar. Many rules are combined into so-called framework laws, and the various sectors are given planning authority. The prevailing form of governance in sector administration is planning, and the limit of the public sector's planning capacity is defined by the ability of the different planned sub-administrations to respond predictably and uniformly to planned input so that their output turns out as planned.

The lead-up to the new sector administration is the development of a new ideal form of administration. The ideal administrative form in formal bureaucracy was administrative decisions based on clear and delimited legal premises so that decisions remained objective and predictable. Sector administration adds to this an ideal about a coherent coordination of all parts of public administration. The central governance question is how to create coordination among sectors and handle the new internally produced complexity within public administration.

What tricks off this shift are repeatable experiences of being out of sync in law reforms. In a formal bureaucracy change often involves a change of law, and following democratic legal procedures takes a lot of time. You might begin the process by constituting a policy commission that has to analyse the problem and come up with a report. Then the civil servant in central government has to formulate suggestions to a new law. Then you have the discussion in parliament that might lead to a new law that finally has to be implemented. It is articulated as a problem that updating the legal basis for individual programmes cannot solve adaptations, because such adaptations become obsolete before they can begin to take effect. Instead, hope is invested in administrative reform designed to ensure the ongoing coordination and planning of individual programmes on the basis of a comprehensive sectorial perspective.

Thus, the administrative challenge is to re-establish a comprehensive vision and coordination, which increased complexity in the public sector had undermined. The proposed solution is central planning as a way to ensure coordination within sectors, and this produces a shift in public administration from case management to problem-solving.

Often the arguments for reforming a formal organised administrative area into planning sector make use of a particular narrative framing the problem. This narrative has four steps: (1) originally there was administrative unity and a clear and unambiguous hierarchy of rules; (2) developments leading to greater administrative scope and complexity have resulted in administrative divisions; (3) thus unity is lost and is replaced by imbalances and coordination problems; and (4) unity is to be restored through planning and the coordination of public administration into sectors.

Public administration becomes organised into separate sectors and central administration develops its planning capacity. Whereas formal administration was hierarchically divided into offices with clearly delimited legal competencies designed to make decisions about particular types of cases, the new sectors are defined instead as different policy areas such as education, workplace environment, labour market and taxation. The sectors do not make decisions about cases; they are problem-directed and establish premises for subsequent case management by defining and prioritising problems. They operate as a planning *superstructure* added to a formal administration. And planning can be seen as second-order administrative decisions. Planning means to make decisions about premises for subsequent administrative decisions.

Sector administration supplements the hierarchical self-description with input-output models according to which the governed administration is perceived as a black box, which translates resource and personnel input into output as social services. The model can be illustrated like this (see Figure 3.2).

Figure 3.2: Self-descriptions of planning

The problem, however, is that the administration's sectorisation produces its own complexity and generates new forms of public administration unmanageability. The intention behind the sectors was that they would solve the problem of growing complexity and unmanageability caused by years of administrative budding. Planning was intended to ensure vertical coordination within a sector, that is, so that all educational activities in the education sector were coordinated through educational planning that reflected analyses of educational needs in society. The idea was that the position at the top of the vertical governance chain would afford a holistic perspective, which is why planning competences would be located there. However, as the sectors develop and multiply, a certain 'sector egotism' emerges. Individual sectors only concern themselves with their specific areas of interest and expertise. The sector for environmental policy, for instance, focuses solely on the external environment and is unable to see how some of its measures might solve problems in the external environment while creating new problems for the working environment. Analysis causes individual sectors to discover new needs – and hence to demand increased resources. Everyone demands more resources. Such demands produce growth in the public sector, which in turn cause socioeconomic balancing difficulties. The public sector begins to push out the private sector. It becomes increasingly clear that the sector-based vertical mode of planning has to be supplemented by horizontal planning, including horizontal expense policies. Thus, planning breeds more planning.

This form of public administration working though planning systems differentiated in both vertical and horizontal sectors might be illustrated like this (Pedersen, 1996, p 296) (see Figure 3.3).

The consequence of these developments is planning of planning of planning, and in the 1970s, the planning discourse reaches its evolutionary limit. It turns out that planning simply leads to more planning, which increases complexity and lack of methodology in public administration. Reducing complexity also means producing complexity.

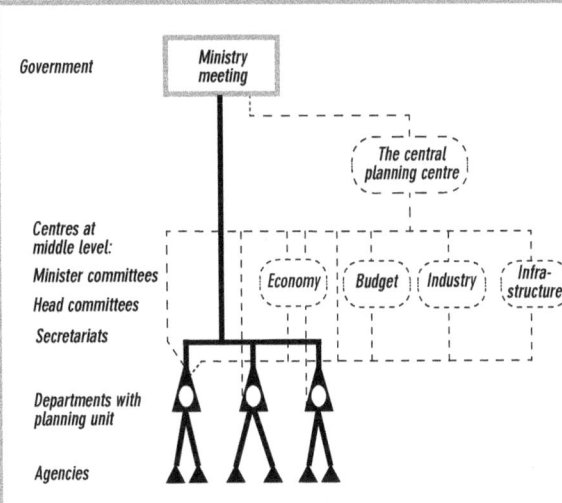

Example 3.1: Report 743 about central administration planning

Report 743 from 1974 represents the culmination of Danish planning optimism. The ambition was 'comprehensive and general planning which would provide a framework for more concrete and specialised planning.' However, it was not considered possible 'to develop one comprehensive plan for the growth of the entire Danish society.' The idea was a state composed by a range of sectors that corresponded to different problem areas such as vocational training, universities, working environment, pollution, etc. The sectors would develop five-year *vertical* plans, that is, plans within the sector pillar. In addition to the sectorial planning system, four planning centres would be constructed and operate as superstructures for the planning of the sectors' planning.

Such centres would develop 10-year horizontal plans. One would be a centre for expense policies; another centre would be for infrastructure. Above the four planning centres would be yet another central planning centre, which would plan the planning of the planning centres in 15-year increments. One such centre became a reality with the Budget Department, and the Ministry of Finance remains to this day the most planning-enthusiastic institution in Denmark.

Figure 3.3: Sector administration

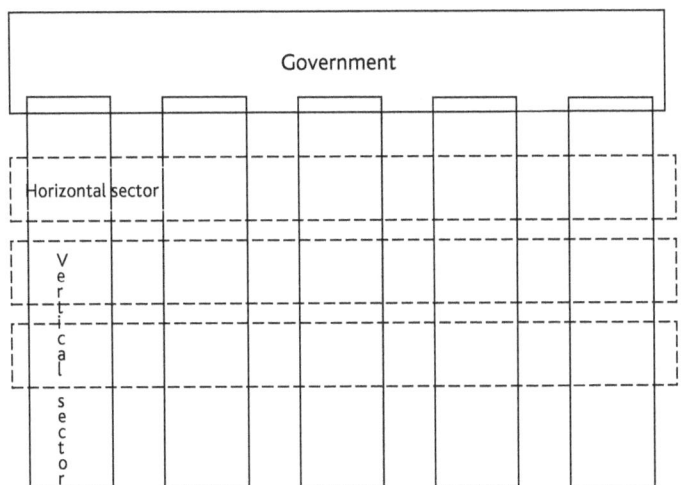

Supervision administration

The unlimited faith in planning finally breaks down from the late 1970s, and new public management (NPM) emerges as the new discourse. It simply becomes increasingly difficult to collect and process the information necessary to maintain planning systems, and gradually we see the popularisation of rewards systems for departments that actively subscribe to adaptability rather than departments that passively subscribe to prevention with regards to expense management.

With NPM a new ideal of adaptability appears in public administration and administrative policies focused on lifting restrictions on the self-adaptation of individual departments. This takes the form of an explicit turn away from planning policies and an outline of a horizon for new administrative policies. In the UK, the report, *Improving management in government: The next steps* presented by the Prime Minister's Efficiency Unit in 1988 (Jenkins et al, 1988) stresses a commitment to contractualisation as well as corporatisation (see du Gay, 2009, p 375; see also Corby, 1993; Freedland, 1994). This means that public service providers are constituted as essentially corporate managerial entities capable of being separately accountable for their own budgets. Subsequently, new administrative policies for the entire public sector are established that aim to increase the sector's ability to adapt by reorganising its boundaries. Instead of coordination from above through planning, the focus shifts to coordination from below through individual institutions and their capacity for self-adaptation and change management. Traditional boundaries are perceived as impediments to change. These new trends challenge the boundary between public and private, for example, through different types of privatisation initiatives, contracting out the import of management technology to the public sector from the private one (Bogdanor, 2001; Campbell, 2007; Vincent-Jones, 2007). And they challenge the boundary between public administration and the citizen, for example, through programmes of service orientation, self-governance, rule simplification and debureaucratisation (Vincent-Jones et al, 2009).

The emergence of the supervision state coincides with a growing focus on change and adaptation as a value, which is above politics (Newman, 2005a, 2005b). The political should not stand in the way of changes within public institutions, which is why institutional independence has to be protected against political interference. Politicians have to acknowledge certain change-related concerns and enter into dialogue with institutions rather than employ the formal hierarchy. In turn, greater demands are placed on the institutions that can no longer defer responsibility with references to the political system (du Gay, 2009, p 373; see also Armbrüster, 2005).

Example 3.2: A new perspective on the public sector

A report by the Danish Ministry of Finance from 1993, *A new perspective on the public sector*, articulates these questions more directly than most other documents on administrative policy. The report concerns efforts to limit political interference in the administrative decision-making process. The report states:

> Political accountability is a premise in the public sector. But this fact does not have to manifest itself in *direct* political management. Direct political management is appropriate in the development of political goals and as a way to ensure implementation of political decisions. Across most of the public sector, however, political governance stands in clear opposition to demands for quality. Governance in the public sector needs to be more general and broadly applicable. It would be appropriate to supplement or in part replace political governance with other forms of governance. (Danish Ministry of Finance, 1993, p 90, own translation)

The question is addressed from several different angles. First, by means of a temporal distinction:

> Traditionally, the public sector has organized itself around the idea that politicians hold a comprehensive view and can govern all details of the public sector. This is no longer a valid premise, and changes to the public sector have to take this into account. Instead, the central focus should be the public institutions whose leaders and employees deliver the services and quality that citizens and businesses expect.... Governance can no longer rely on hierarchical and centralistic solutions but has to rely on principles of dialogue and collaboration. (Danish Ministry of Finance, 1993, pp 6-7, own translation)

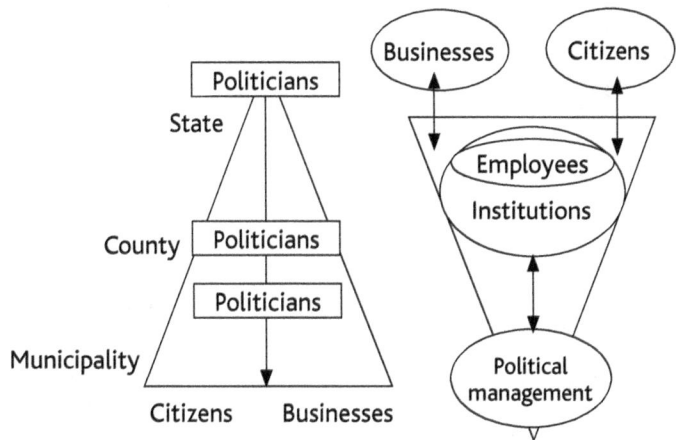

The report by the Ministry of Finance uses the above illustration to show the changes to public governance and adds: 'The hierarchical model which has traditionally dominated the public sector is replaced by a model based on dialogue between state and municipalities and between politicians and institutions. In this model, politicians no longer engage in detailed management' (Ministry of Finance, 1993, p 11, own translation). The report describes this as a natural development in relation to which the Ministry of Finance merely serves the role of facilitator in its reversal of the entire hierarchy so that future political governance finds itself at the bottom, and so that the relation between politics and administration are marked by dialogue rather than authority.

Example 3.3: Quality – putting the institution at the centre

One example is a report on quality. 'Citizens are entitled to quality. But quality is not created through decisions or laws and rules' (Danish Ministry of Finance, 1993, p 55, own translation), says the report. Thus, the right to quality is, in some respects, seen to be above the political. It is a right, which it is implied, should not be violated but which also cannot be secured through politics. The report goes on: 'The responsibility for this [quality] belongs to individual institutions. Today, individual institutions have to *engage in dialogue with politicians* to specify achievable goals within the given framework and *engage in dialogue with service users* to clarify their needs and expectations' (Ministry of Finance, 1993, p 56, own translation and emphases). The report provides the following illustration:

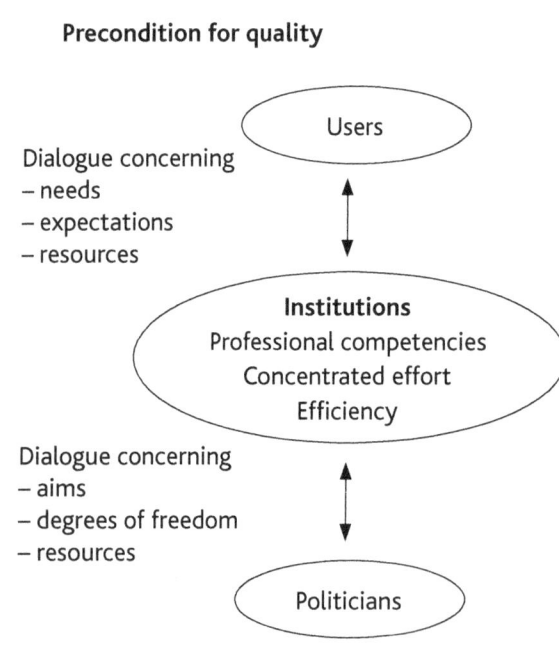

Dialogue becomes the chosen form of steering. The question is, what is dialogue here? When politicians are initiating dialogues with the institutions about aims, autonomy and resources, it is not just a dialogue; it is a unilateral call for a mutual relation. The same goes for the relations between institution and user. It is the public institutions that address citizens as users, and unilateral, they frame a dialogue in order to steer the users' needs and expectations.

Often dialogues are followed by 'internal contracts', but

> these are not usual contracts constituted by full voluntary agreement, as in the market. Instead they are a unilateral statement demanding mutual agreement. The internal contract becomes a steering media used to 'autonomise' the institutions making them responsible for managing their own 'quality' and 'strategy'. Internal contracts are contracts within a hierarchy. Simultaneously they communicate: 'Do as I say' and 'Be autonomous'. They are a tool for allowing larger complexity in public administration in the form of institutions managing themselves, and at the same time being able, with authority, to claim formal unity and control.

Thus, to sum up, supervision administration gained ground in the early 1980s, and is driven by the idea of a public sector that would be adaptable on all levels. Coordination and development are ideally created from below by individual institutions that take responsibility for their own development and their position in a greater whole. The biggest governance challenge is to effect, from above, coordination and adaptation from below. The object of governance becomes the adaptability of individual institutions – the ability of individual institutions to relate to themselves through governance and strategy. This turns governance into supervision (Willke, 1992, 1997). It becomes a question of providing support and guidance for self-management and strategy development (see also Miller and Rose, 1992; Rhodes, 1997; Dean, 1999, 2007; Pierre and Peters, 2000; Kooiman, 2003). The limit of this form of supervision is the institutions' capacity for self-management. So supervision becomes about building up capacity of self-management, that is, management of self-management.

Whereas formal bureaucracy focuses on 'the case', and sector administration on 'the problem', supervision administration is strategically oriented towards 'the future'. The definition of problems is no longer a given, and neither is their adherence to specific sectors. It all depends on the specific strategy for the future. Strategy building, then, entails ongoing reflection with respect to criteria for what is considered important and prioritised problems. Where sector administration speaks of problems and solutions, supervision administration speaks of future challenges and possibilities. To supervise self-managing institutions here means to futurise the present supporting the outlook of the single institution. Supervision does not mean seeing the inferior institution as a solution to the superior's problems. Supervision rather means to support the institutions to do their own strategising, encourage them to look into the future horizon themselves, and to take responsibility for defining problems and prioritising resources.

The reversal of the hierarchical organisation of the public sector transforms the identity and self-description of central administration into a unit that supports the struggles of the various institutions in their efforts to provide welfare to citizens. Central administration provides support in the form of dialogue, internal contracts, education, strategy development, information, management tools, reflection tools and much more. Just a few examples – from the private sector, the concept of 'manager' is imported. To be a manager of an institution indicates that the institution is its own system and the manager represents its wholeness. When central administration renames the heads of offices, calling them managers of a different kind, they communicate that the institution should represent themselves and not only act as institutions-in-a-hierarchy. Internal contracts do a similar trick: when the power-superior invites the power-inferior to make a contract within the frame of hierarchy, the power-inferior institution is told to observe itself as an autonomous organisation with self-responsibility. Central administration begins to use a lot of time developing management technologies and leadership tools. These are offered to the institution as a media of self-management. Budget policy is also changed. Now all institutions are given their own budget and certain economic freedom. They are expected to act as if they were economic actors. Again, the whole idea is to supervise the institution to self-management.

In order for this self-description to be functional and for central administration to serve as the supervisory unit for a multiplicity of independent institutions, it has to be rather well developed. These changes to the unity of administration are illustrated below (see Figure 3.4):

Figure 3.4: Supervision administration as self-description

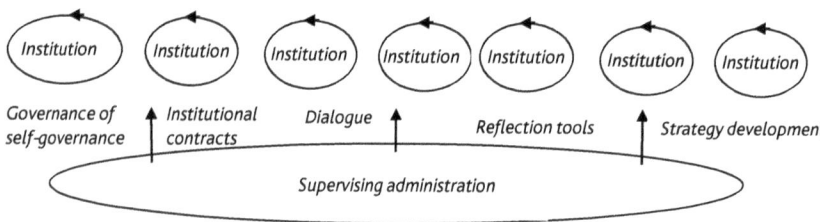

Supervision administration seeks to promote conditions for coordination from below. The task of central administration becomes supporting the capacity for self-governance and adaptability across the public sector (for a similar conceptualisation of public administration developments from hierarchy to supervision, see Kooiman's distinction between 'first-order governance', 'second-order governance' and 'meta governance': Kooiman, 2008; Kooiman and van Vliet, 2000; see also Crozier, 2007).

This shift requires extensive capacity building in central administration, at both state and municipality levels. We often think of centralisation and decentralisation efforts as opposites, but in supervision administration they are not, because centralisation functions as a prerequisite for decentralisation (see also Pedersen and Hartley, 2008). In order to make it possible to govern through self-governing welfare institutions with independent strategies, there has to be a substantial central administration for the development of self-governance tools and budgeting and accounting models, which can provide strategic and relevant information to both central administration and institutions, strategies for independent strategy building in welfare organisations, as well as control and documentation programmes designed to help institutions work more independently. And the inverse is also true – the capacity for self-governance and self-adaptation becomes a prerequisite for the supervision of central administration. The greater the capacity for change and adaptation in individual institutions, the greater the capacity for governance in central administration. Supervision needs to balance the steering effort. Too little steering leads to a lack of capacity building in the institution. Too much destroys self-management. The capacity of individual welfare institutions to self-govern with respect to a range of variables such as budget, quality management, value management, activities, annual plans, staff development, strategic development, team management and so on, greatly improves the quality of the governance dialogues between central administration and the institution.

Evidently, the goal is not just simply to increase capacity for change and strategy building in individual institutions; it is also to manage the way in which the institutions describe and administer their new 'independence'. Central administration develops its capacity for discourse formation and discourse management as a central aspect of its supervision efforts. The Danish Ministry of Finance governs through the communication of socioeconomic analyses and diagnoses, and seeks to create a broad understanding of socioeconomic responsibility. This form of governance communication works horizontally across different ministries and their areas of interest as well as vertically from state level to the regions, municipalities and individual institutions.

Obviously, there is more to this than just discourse management. The effort also involves negotiation systems as well as the governance of public sector economic management systems in general (Jensen, 2012; for a more comprehensive analysis of the history of Danish expense policies, see Jensen, 2003, 2008). Similarly, around the end of the 1980s, the Danish Ministry for the Environment uses the concept of sustainability to construct a definition of environment, ecology and climate issues that similarly cut across traditional sectorial and hierarchical divisions, both horizontally and vertically. The goal is to propagate environmental and climate-related awareness everywhere, and to encourage institutions to include the environment as a central aspect of their strategy (Andersen and Born, 2000). By the 1990s, the Danish Ministry of Health began to formulate horizontal strategies and referred to the population as 'the people's body'. Health was to become a collective concern that was integrated into all public policy, the so-called Health in All policies discourse (Stahl et al, 2006; Greer and Lillvis, 2014). The different sectors no longer simply govern within the frameworks of their own 'governance chains'. They develop horizontal governance ambitions whose 'foreign' perspectives and concerns have to be accepted and integrated by the various departments and institutions as meaningful in order to be successful (Peters, 1998). Whereas formal administration established *formal spaces* (offices and office space) for administrative decisions, and whereas sector administration established *sectorial problem-oriented spaces* for planning and prioritisation, supervision administration seeks to govern through the continual creation of *imagined spaces*, which outline social concerns, broad images of the future and meaning horizons in relation to which decentralised administrative departments and institutions can independently formulate their own problems and strategies.

> **Example 3.4: Invitation to evaluation review**
>
> Many Danish municipal administration departments organise annual evaluation reviews with welfare institutions such as public schools, daycare centres or special education schools. Standard procedure is for a municipal head of department and a few municipal consultants to visit individual institutions and their directors. Together, the group reviews the institution's record of meeting its goals, specific development projects or areas of intervention, economic standing, etc.
>
> We can see such reviews as symptomatic of the way supervision administration operates. They are designed to supervise decentralised leaders. The municipal administration seeks to support the self-management of the decentralised leadership and to develop its strategic capacity. Thus, the reviews reflect a form of supervision that seeks to increase the institutions' level of independence through dialogue and reflection. One municipality, for example, describes the purpose of the reviews as 'establishing the basis for the schools' ability to more actively document and demonstrate the quality of their teaching and pedagogical practice.'
>
> This gives the evaluation reviews a dual purpose. On the one hand, the reviews are meant to support and guide institutional self-governance, management and strategy development, and on the other, they are intended to ensure administrative supervision. The evaluation reviews facilitate mutual dialogue and debate, and also serve as an avenue for the municipal administration to gain insight into potential difficulties within the institutions so that the administration can take action accordingly, if need be.
>
> Thus, it remains unclear whether the reviews take place within a hierarchy or as a bilateral exchange. One municipality writes that, 'the leadership of the school and the municipal school administration get a chance to engage each other as discussion partners.' But it also describes how the municipal representatives report back to the municipal hierarchy.
>
> The reviews mark at once a hierarchical governance relation between municipal administration and institution *as well as* a focus on institutional self-governance. This duality of governance is also reflected in the very design of the reviews. They often take place at the institutions, which assume the role of host with the municipal representatives playing the role of visitor. However, the institutions have been directly instructed to invite the municipal administration to visit in order to engage in mutual discussions. Does the welfare institution or the municipality set the agenda? Who heads the meeting? Who is responsible for taking down the minutes?
>
> The reviews serve as an example of how supervision administration creates ambiguity across public administration about whether the administrative units rely on hierarchical or more bilateral relationships (Pors, 2011b).

Potentiality administration

In the same way that the hierarchy became the source of its own complexity, and that planning-based sector administration sought to respond to this complexity, and in the same way that planning did not simply solve the problem of complexity but also produced new complexity and hence new unmanageability, supervision administration and its emphasis on strategy building on all levels also produces new forms of unmanageable complexity. This weakens the faith in the ability of organisations to strategically self-govern. Two premises are put in question: the strategic fixation of the future of the present, and the organisation as a given agent of change and coordination.

With respect to the strategy premise, it becomes increasingly more difficult to believe in the images of the future around which the strategies are built. Are the strategies future-proof? The concern is that specific visions of the future are not only quickly outdated, but also too restrictive to serve as premises for handling complexity further down in the public hierarchy. And there is an increasing uncertainty about whether the strategy building taking place at the top of the hierarchy serves to reduce, or whether it simply adds complexity to processes further down in the hierarchy. At the same time, doubts are raised about whether the welfare organisation is an appropriate strategic unit to effect change and coordination. Are there not many cases and processes in an innovative public sector that are so particular and specific to fit into the same strategy? The shift from planning-based sector administration to strategic supervision administration, and the inherent ideal of the latter of adapting to adaptability is a shift from coordination from above at the level of the planning system to coordination from below through individual institutions' independent participation in a greater whole through strategy building. Here, the goal of supervision administration is to transform the institution-within-a hierarchy into an independent self-adapting organisation. Today, the new concern is whether strategy at the level of the single organisation may become a structural impediment restricting the space of operation for single and particular decisions and decision-making processes within the organisation.

Coordination is not only a question of individual organisations' independent participation in a greater whole, but also of the interconnectivity of operations both within and across organisations. The ideal is no longer simply the self-adapting organisation, but also the flexible operation. The organisation no longer simply sets the premises and framework for operations but emerges in coordination with operations. The ideal is not merely the adaptable organisation, but an organisation in a state of continual becoming through its many heterogeneous operations, which flexibly and perpetually interconnect from below.

This is related to a blossoming critique of public bureaucracy and its reluctance to take risks in the name of renewal and innovation. As du Gay (2008) has analysed, in the UK, the New Labour government's White paper, *Modernising government* from 1999a, and its related policy documents (Cabinet Office, 1999a,

1999b), places considerable emphasis on the capacity of executive leadership to help change the culture of 'risk aversion' that is considered endemic to the British Civil Service. The White Paper explicitly states that officials must 'move away from the risk-averse culture inherent in government', and that this was to be achieved through removing 'unnecessary bureaucracy that prevents public servants from experimenting, innovating and delivering a better product' (Cabinet Office, 1999a).

> **Example 3.5: The experience manager**
>
> In 2009, the municipality of Århus hired an 'experience manager' in an effort to ensure a good experience for anyone contacting them.
>
> The experience manager describes the function of the job as the effort to rethink service as experience:
>
> > "If we re-imagine public service as experience for citizens, managers need to perceive and manage employees as individuals who make a difference. Good service refers to the service itself as well as someone's experience of this service, which means that individual employee efforts become a crucial factor.... Service understood as experience for citizens requires management to manage from that fundamental premise. It means that organisational goals are not reached through the achievement of certain standards but face-to-face with citizens."
>
> The municipality is assuming the role of potentiality administration. It is no longer simply a question of establishing service goals, but instead a question of constantly transcending established relations between the administration and citizen. Each encounter with citizens is unique, according to the municipality, and does not reflect standard procedures. Quality is perceived as a process and as a product of, sometimes unpredictable, encounters between citizens and officials. These encounters should always aspire to more than mere service. The relationship with the citizen becomes open to play. "We focus on a high standard of service and see ourselves as hosts for our visitors. This concept expresses the relation to the citizen in a simple and clear way", says the experience manager. The municipality play-pretends that the relation between municipality and citizen can be defined as a relation between a host and guest, and this game allows it to transcend expectations about the encounter between the municipality and citizen.

We see the emergence of a new concept of radical innovation, a radicalisation of the adaptability ideal of the 1980s. Whereas adaptability was primarily a question of constructing an administration with organisational adaptability on all levels of the hierarchy, radical innovation is not simply about organisational change but about creating organisations that question themselves, their basic premises and all their practices. Governance is no longer simply a question of developing the most effectively organised nursing home, but also about questioning the very function of nursing homes, care practices and care service assumptions. Radical innovation refers to change processes, which include not only the organisation of welfare, but also the definition of welfare.

Potentiality administration adds itself as an additional layer to supervision administration. This form of administration does not simply support the self-governance of individual welfare organisations; it provides constructive resistance to welfare organisations with expectations about 'thinking outside of the box' and by continually challenging their habits, assumptions and practices. By potentiality we mean expectations about constantly seeking to go beyond what is considered possible. It means to create opportunities beyond the horizon of what was imagined to be possible and imaginable.

While supervision administration would ask a preschool to formulate three goals and write up an annual plan, and would generally work to support the preschool's goal management efforts as a way to help it govern itself and its activities, potentiality administration asks the same preschool to toy with the concept of what a preschool can potentially be. The preschool is encouraged to question what may potentially serve as its central values. It is asked to question the criteria for relevant activities. Thus, potentiality administration supports the effort to dissolve premises even before establishing premises. It encourages institutions to go beyond imaginable, possible and meaningful objectives. In this way, it represents a radicalised form of supervision administration.

Strategy provided a solution to the need to reduce the complexity of future decisions by outlining a specific image of the future. In the supervision state, strategy emerges as a third-order decision. A first-order decision means making a decision about a case (in formal bureaucracy). Then, in sector administration, planning serves a second-order decision. Planning refers to a decision about premises for subsequent decisions. By prioritising problems, the state defines what may subsequently become a case. And supervision administration finally introduces strategy a third-order decision, which defines the references for subsequent problem formations through the selection of images of the future. These decisions all seek to reduce complexity, absorb uncertainty and stabilise contingency. The higher up in the order of decision we get, the more withdrawn the stabilisation of contingency, the roomier the premises established by the decisions, and the greater the amount of unreduced contingency pushed ahead by the decisions. However, regardless of the order of decision, all decisions concern themselves with alternatives, and they all absorb uncertainty inside the administration with respect to existing expectations. The question is how to make decisions about which opportunities to realise on the basis of a horizon of alternatives. Potentiality administration seems to reverse this. In potentiality administration, decisions are almost unrecognisable as decisions. The fourth-order decision of potentiality administration does not simply represent an even more withdrawn form of decision. It is not simply a decision with even less definition of premises for subsequent decisions (of the third, second or first order). It is a decision that does not want to be a decision. It is a decision that does not seek to choose to realise one opportunity from a horizon of alternatives, but instead a decision that seeks to generate a new horizon of possibility from which subsequent decisions may choose. In other words, it is a decision that seeks to create undefined complexity from which subsequent decisions may derive. It can only do this by doubling and re-entering the difference of decision back into itself. To decide means to relate to expectations, and this applies even when the decision in question is one that seeks to dissolve premises and generate a new complexity for subsequent decisions. This kind of decision, which we refer to as a potentiality decision, still has to decide which existing structures and assumptions to dissolve in relation to a horizon of alternative structures and assumptions, which might also have been dissolved (see Figure 3.5).

Figure 3.5: Potentialisation as a fourth-order decision

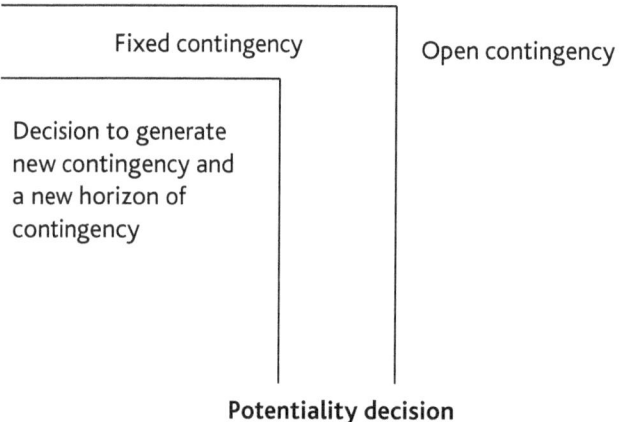

Potentiality administration views structures as problematic simply because they are structures. Structures are a sign of shutdown potentiality (Pors, 2014). This form of public administration wants welfare organisations and their employees to continually rethink their structures and thus create new occasions for decisions and new potentiality. Each moment should remain open and should not be limited in advance. This is clear in the case below about a municipal charter in Aalborg municipality that outlines the intention to 'free up the full potential of the organisation' while refusing to define what 'freedom' means. The charter, we should remember, represents itself a form of structure. It is an administrative potentiality decision about not being restricted by structures. Where the message of supervision administration was 'Do as I say – be independent', potentiality administration sends a more radical message: 'Do as I say – free yourself from every structure'.

Example 3.6: The Freedom Charter

In 2012, the senior services department in the municipality of Aalborg launched a municipal charter encouraging officials, local welfare managers and professionals to think innovatively, let ideas flow, get rid of bureaucracy, and embrace the courage to pursue what makes their work meaningful.

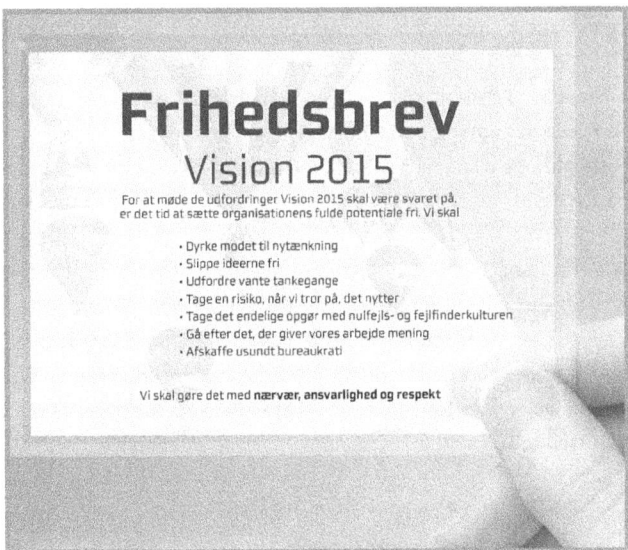

What motivated the charter was increasing frustration over the difficulties of placing citizens at the centre of municipal efforts in a sector characterised by silo structures and professional specialisation. There was general dissatisfaction with the fact that recent quality standardisation and documentation efforts had resulted in disproportionate amounts of bureaucracy. The municipality wanted to encourage more experimentation and a more innovative approach across the organisation, from heads of departments to local home care managers and their employees.

What the document signals is an administrative fantasy about encouraging individual officials to relate critically to the rules and regulations that make up public administration. The hope is that new opportunities will grow from the courage of individual managers to disregard categories, boxes and procedures. A suitable amount of civil disobedience is viewed as a resource, which the municipality is expected to produce, reach for and employ as a means to improve welfare services. Individual welfare managers or professionals are expected to assume a critical perspective on rules, categories and organisational structures, and to take independent responsibility for the management of the functionality and dysfunctionality of existing rules.

> With this kind of charter in hand, the municipal administration can encourage individual employees to create small innovations by taking on certain risks and by targeting unnecessary bureaucracy. However, the status of the charter in relation to the formal hierarchy remains unclear. The municipality's internal network describes the question in this way: 'Each manager is responsible for interpreting the charter. When and under what circumstances is it okay to disobey? There are no guidelines for how to use the charter and there is no definition of what freedom means. Such clarification would violate the very essence of the charter, that is, the freedom to think innovatively.'
>
> The charter can be seen as an indication of the way that potentiality administration produces and distributes dilemmas among units, managers and employees. When and under which circumstances should one disobey? What happens if one takes a chance and fails? Who is responsible in such cases?
>
> The charter lets the municipality have its cake and eat it too. It increases the focus on innovation and seeks to appropriate employees' eye for development opportunities. But at the same time, it allows the municipality to maintain the functionalities of hierarchical and formal structures. The charter does not formally annul documentation requirements. It provides no specific guidelines for where, when or under which circumstances the welfare manager is permitted to suspend existing administrative procedures.
>
> Welfare managers are expected to work within the framework of a hierarchical structure and its formal divisions and at the same time to take responsibility for not allowing those structures to impede ongoing processes, experiments and innovation.

Potentiality administration stresses the importance of flexibility. Decisions should be made to match the possibilities and needs of the moment. Structures should function not as limitations but as flexible tools and components that can be flexibly combined with other tools and components.

A certain level of plasticity must also characterise definitions of quality. Quality management tools, designed in the 1990s to govern and supervise the shift toward organisational independence, have come under increased scrutiny throughout the public sector. Quality management tools work precisely by providing general definitions of quality and quality-producing procedures. This becomes problematic from the perspective of potentiality production because of the risk of missing out on intrinsic potential, for example, in the exploration and consideration of individual citizens' experiences of quality.

Restrictive frameworks must not stand in the way of collaboration within organisations or between organisations. In fact, the prevailing term is 'co-creation' rather than 'collaboration'. And agreements should not be too fixed. The preferred term is 'partnerships', which refers to second-order agreements. Partnerships make promises about future promises. The partners make promises to one another without making promises. They promise to work together to explore the possibilities for future commitment (Andersen, 2008b, 2012a). It is a question of designing flexible premises that are not too restrictive and remain open toward potentiality and virtuality (Staunæs and Raffnsøe, 2014).

These shifts in public administration also find expression in applied architecture and technology, which no longer simply provide functional solutions to given problems. In potentiality administration, architecture and technology are designed to maximise functional equivalence. Not only do they provide solutions to different problems, but they also invite experimentation with different equivalent ways of combining problems and solutions. They potentialise experimental comparisons of non-comparable variations of problem–solution combinations (see Juelskjær, 2011).

> **Example 3.7: Potentiality management in public school reform**
> By focusing on potentiality, governance and management will often be able to spot and generate new possibilities in the spaces between institutions organisations, or by softening the boundaries between welfare institutions and civil society.
>
> A government proposal about public school reform outlines a rethinking of the design and layout of future schools and afterschool facilities as a way to exploit the possibilities of the interface between play and learning: 'The facilities are designed to match the needs of both school and afterschool programming.... This creates a natural connection between educational activities, learning situations, and free time. New possibilities emerge precisely in the space between play and learning' (Finansministeriet et al, 2009, p 80).
>
> The government's public school reform proposal and the 'whole school' initiative can be seen as attempts to improve education by nurturing and capturing potential learning that takes place outside and beyond traditional classroom instruction. For instance, break times throughout the school day are described as contributing to the activity that they provide a break from. Interestingly, the examples provided in the proposal for how a school day may be structured in different grades are remarkably lacking in detail about specific teaching strategies for individual subjects. By contrast, there is no shortage of examples of break-time activities that may contribute to learning, either through semi-academic activities or physical activity, which is considered to increase learning in children.
>
> The proposal tells the story of Jasmin in first grade whose break-time is facilitated by a play patrol that organises games for the children. The games involve a great deal of physical activity in order to ensure that the children's break includes movement. While Mathias, who is in fourth grade, eats his lunch, the teacher initiates a conversation about where different foods come from, and thus extends the lesson on food production to the lunch break. And Frederik, in eighth grade, rides his bike from his school to a local secondary school to participate in a bridge-building programme. The school's cycling contest and points award system, where the class receives points for every kilometre they cycle, turn cycle trips to and from school into

> potential learning situations. The higher grades take turns calculating a variety of statistics in relation to the amount of kilometres each class has logged every week. This also helps ensure that the children use their time outside of class periods to exercise and engage in physical activity, which will optimise their learning process.
>
> The government's public school reform proposal represents an example of potentiality governance embodied in the dream of how break-time, playground time, swim practice and dinner with the family become coordinated elements of children's learning processes (Pors, 2014).

Potentiality administration not only supports self-governance through dialogue, institutional contracts, strategy training and governance tools. The point of departure is not the pre-existence of a certain amount of chaos and uncontrollability within the welfare institutions, which public administration seeks to help bring under control. By contrast, the starting point is too much order and stability. The problem is that what is uncontrollable in institutions remains invisible to them because they are locked into structures that are considered inevitable. Thus, the starting point for central administration in potentiality administration is that leaders do not encounter enough complexity and chaos through which to enact opportunities and change. Thus, potentiality administration provides support primarily in the form of activities and governance tools that contribute to the softening of structures and premises. Examples of such activities and tools are innovation games, processes, labs, co-creation concepts, partnership concepts, institutional speed dating, and so on.

Public administration can be depicted as in the following illustration (see Figure 3.6), where central administration contributes to the softening of structures and the creation of new virtual possibilities for welfare institutions. Central administration provides support in the form of innovation games, future labs, charters, flexible architecture, speed dating, partnership contracts, self-observation tools, responsibility games, and much more. Instead of providing answers, central administration asks questions, and instead of defining frameworks, it asks institutions to reject frameworks and to question everything.

Figure 3.6: Potentiality administration

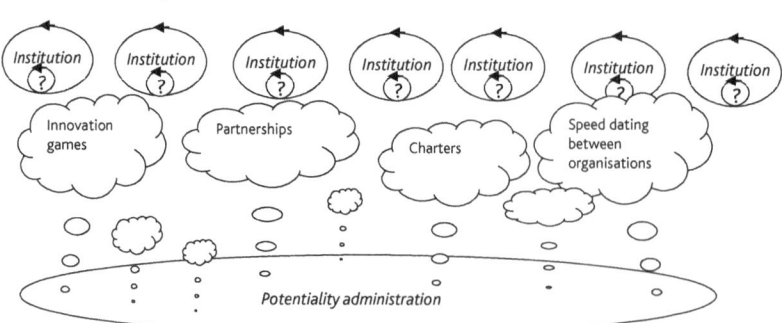

Example 3.8: From reality to ideal and back

The basic premise for this game is to see possibilities in the impossible, which are created over time and thereby made visible to others within the organisation. Participants are asked to fill in the 'win/wip model' (pictured below). They are then divided into groups where they show each other their completed model and discuss questions such as 'What is your organisation's vision for the future?', 'What is the vision among members of your work unit for the unit in five years?', 'Which things were not possible to see five years ago which it is possible to see in your workplace today?' and 'What would it take for you to move your work unit from "what it is now" to "what is possible"?' (Caroselli, 1996, p 263).

The win/wip model

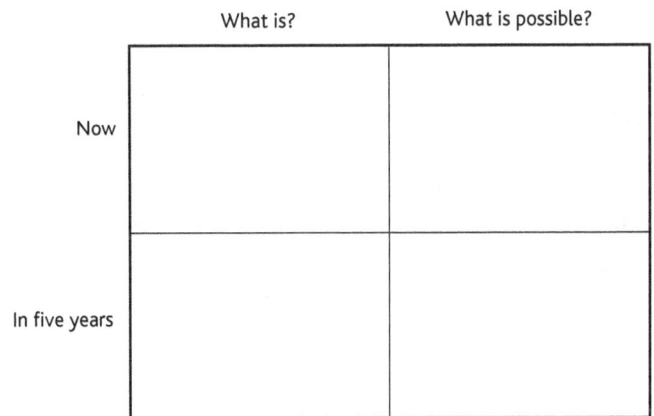

The game distinguishes between present present ('What is now?'), present future ('What is possible now?'), future present ('What is in five years?'), and future future ('What is possible in five years?'). The basic premise for the game is to futurise the organisation. Participants are asked to imagine all the things that will become possible in the future as a way to open up a horizon of possibilities. By supporting dialogue not only about the future that can be seen from the perspective of the present, but also about the future of the future, the game creates a playful reflection of the future as more open and contingent than what can be imagined from the perspective of a specific present. The game stimulates the imagination of the organisation and its employees in such a way as to allow them to transcend a limited concept of the future as a simple extension of the present. It is a potentiality game (Andersen, 2009, 2013b).

Challenges for governance

We have tried to describe the history of public administration in terms of increasing complexity encountered through experimentation with new forms of differentiation, each one adding to the level of uncontrollable complexity and continually leading to new forms of differentiation. Today, we see the coexistence of four different forms of differentiation within public administration: bureaucracy, sector administration, supervision administration and potentiality administration. Each of these forms represents a different way to create unity and internal differentiation, and their coexistence results in a form of hyper-complex public administration. We see the emergence of increasingly sophisticated versions of the relationship between govern/governed bodies. Governance and self-governance interconnect in increasingly paradoxical ways. And with the emergence of hyper-complexity in public administration it becomes increasingly difficult to construct clear, objective and predictable decision premises. It seems that the undermining of expectations as decision premises becomes the method to avoid friction between the different forms of differentiation.

This is a rather radical development. Imagine if Poul Andersen, who wrote his dissertation on sources of invalidity in Danish public administration in 1924, asked the same questions of today's potentiality administration he did back then. What might a source of invalidity represent in the context of an innovations game, a charter or a partnership? That would be a difficult question to answer.

Table 3.2: Summary of developments in public administration

	Governance form	Object of governance	Orientation	Temporal orientation	Operation
Formal bureaucracy	Rules/ control	Conduct of officials	Case	Present past	Decision
Sector administration	Planning	Individual administrations	Problem	Present future	Planning
Supervision administration	Supervision	Organisational autonomy	Future	Future present	Strategy
Potentiality administration	Potentiality	Operations seeking out possibilities	Undefined complexity	Future future	Potentialisation

What does all this mean for the conditions for welfare management? How are conditions for the management of change formed in public administration?

Supervision administration

The mounting independence of public institutions fundamentally changes premises for governance. Governance can no longer simply operate through hierarchies and central planning. This creates a fundamental governance problem, which is how to exercise top management without undermining the decentralised dynamic within individual organisations.

Today, it is apparent that the move to create institutional independence was a radical event. Supervision governance adds new complexity to public administration that increases the possibilities for governance and self-governance. But this rise of complexity comes at a price. Throughout public administration, it becomes ambiguous – an open question – whether institutions operate within an unambiguously hierarchical relationship or a more ambiguous bilateral relationship. Today, our understanding of the relationship between power-superior and power-inferior is always open for negotiation, as is the relationship between governance and self-governance, including the question of which governance tools pertain to various governance relations.

In other words, governance has lost its innocence in the sense that it has lost its ability to be unambiguous (Pors, 2012a). It becomes an inherent part of governance to question its own governance efforts. Occasionally, municipalities or ministries are accused of not governing enough. When Danish public schools fail to live up to international standards, when yet another case of incest sees the light of day, or when a senior citizen has not had their apartment cleaned in weeks, the media call out to politicians to take action. Thus, there are still constant demands for state and municipalities to control, dictate and set clear standards for welfare institutions, but such demands are just as relentlessly accompanied by an avalanche of statements about how control, unambiguous goals, and so on are dysfunctional in relation to the possibilities for institutions and professions to deliver quality welfare services. While politicians and public leaders may try to distinguish between means and ends, and between central policies and local independence, such distinctions are certain to fail when faced with questions about how such distinctions are made and justified. Would a politician not draw the distinction differently than the manager of a nursing home? Perhaps micro-management and quality assurance mean the same thing, only observed from different places?

As a result of the process toward institutional independence, any attempt by the state or municipality to find a formula for governance that does not restrict the independence of institutions risks failure and often generates new complexity. Municipalities can no longer govern schools, for example, on the basis of clear objectives, but have to translate such objectives in a way that is not perceived by the schools as an encroachment on their independence. Thus, demands for increased governance do not result in more governance. Instead, such demands result in a rush of reflection on how to govern without being perceived by governed bodies as a significant limitation to their ability to self-govern.

An additional cost of increased complexity is that governance becomes paradoxical. Central administrations ask themselves: how may top management occasion an institution-within-a-hierarchy to recognise and recreate itself as an independent organisation with responsibility for its own development, strategy and results? How can subordinates be made to perceive themselves as independent? This is the central governance challenge. Therefore, central administration's governance strategy communicates 'Do as I say – be independent'. In the next chapter we discuss how this puts pressure on subordinate institutions. They can never be entirely sure when to do as they are told and when to be independent. One day they are told to behave more independently. The next day they are reprimanded for not following directions. Central administration also comes under increased pressure because of institutional requests, on the one hand, for it to remain at a distance and allow institutions more freedom while at the same time wanting it to be present, interested and continually acknowledge the work of the institutions. In other words, 'Stay away – be interested in what we do'. From the perspective of state and municipal administration, the effort to govern welfare institutions is a question of balancing an institutional desire for freedom and leverage and a reluctance to accept administration interference on the one hand, and institutional appeals not only for supervising support but also clear political messages and decisions on the other.

Supervision management leads to the following governance paradoxes:

- How may top management occasion an institution-within-a-hierarchy to recognise and recreate itself as an independent organisation with responsibility for its own development, strategy and results?
- How to govern with the help of messages such as, 'Do as we say, be independent!'?
- How to govern when the only form of effective governance in relation to subordinate independent institutions is governance that does not resemble governance?
- How to make itself relevant to organisational self-governance when organisations both request freedom and intervention?
- How can top management mobilise willingness to adapt within the institutions without standing in their way and without becoming the authority to which they are adapting?

Potentiality administration

We may say that potentiality administration surfaces as a viable solution to the fact that the three governance logics – rule-based governance, planning and supervision – continue to clash and create problems in contemporary public administration contexts. Potentiality administration is a product of the need to reflect the coexistence of these different logics, and a call for administrative policies that reflect such internal contradictions. Some refer to this as meta-governance

(Jessop, 2003; Kooiman and Jentoft, 2009). It is a call for a new form of governance capable of containing the dysfunctionalities that appear when regulation, planning and supervision collide and create a range of paradoxes and impossibilities for public managers and public administration. It is a call for administrative policies that do not allow themselves to become paralysed by the conflicts between three fundamentally different forms of governance, but instead seek out and exploit the possibilities generated by such conflicts (Majgaard, 2008/09, 2013). However, the problem is that such demands lead to its own governance logic – potentiality governance – which adds itself to the other three and thereby also adds to the complexity and clashes between fundamentally different forms of governance.

Potentiality administration does not relieve but intensifies internal self-questioning in the public sector. It represents a pursuit of forms of governance that do not restrict institutional capacity – not only for self-governance but also for innovation. Potentiality administration seeks to facilitate a form of independence where institutions continually confront themselves by reflecting on whether a given action, service or procedure might be carried out differently, might be rethought. It introduces new contingency into public administration. The mindset is everywhere and always: it could be different.

The central question of supervision administration about how to govern without placing restrictions on the capacity for self-governance is radicalised into a question of how to govern independent welfare organisations on the basis that the object of governance cannot be unambiguously and pre-emptively defined and cannot be controlled by means of conventional governance tools.

On the one hand, potentiality administration represents an intensification of supervision administration because it similarly encourages welfare organisations to engage in critical reflection of their own knowledge forms, functions and organisation. However, where the inherent purpose of such reflexive governance in supervision administration is to consolidate the organisational characteristics of welfare organisations (through formal strategies, goals, self-evaluations, documentation, etc), potentiality management seems to rely on a perpetual call for welfare organisations to risk themselves as organisations by experimenting with their boundaries or by seeing themselves from the perspective of the citizen.

Ironising about itself and its self-description as bureaucracy, potentiality administration accelerates the paradoxes that had already become part of public governance with supervision administration. Public administration communication is no longer only double-tongued in its encouragement of governed entities to be both governed and self-governing, but also with the message: 'Take us seriously and don't take us seriously when we govern', 'Obey by deciding when to obey and when to perform civil disobedience and hence create opportunities for innovation'.

Potentiality administration results in the following governance paradoxes:

- How to govern from the outside in a way that organisations internally produce a surplus of possibilities for themselves from which to choose?

- How to simultaneously govern and recognise the fact that the central contribution of governed bodies is transgressive and partially unmanageable?
- How to govern governed bodies to remain perpetually critical toward the understanding and descriptions by governance of welfare services and the needs of citizens?
- How to govern the capacity and willingness to risk one's identity?
- How to encourage subordinate entities to both obey and to consider the appropriateness of disobedience?

As a consequence of the emergence of supervision and potentiality administration, all naïve trust in governance dissolves. It is no longer possible to dictate simple control over governed bodies because such control always undermines the capacity for self-governance. The capacity for self-control is precisely greater the more freedom the institutions are granted in their handling of information, which they have access to as the ones closest to the citizens.

Ultimately, this means that any leadership in public administration is faced with having to consider how to accelerate or handle such fundamental and inescapable paradoxes in their own governance practice. Administration executives run the risk of perpetually deconstructing their own management space and positions. A few years back, for example, the municipality of Copenhagen worked to strengthen self-administration in its preschools. The heads were expected to act as managers and to take on management responsibilities. But the municipality did not make any changes to the existing regulatory and control systems. On the one hand, the municipality created expectations about self-administration, while on the other, it intervened directly in countless instances and undermined a great number of management initiatives. The same thing happened in the case of a quality reform initiative in 2007. The reform sought to support institutional self-responsibility while defining the language through which institutions were allowed to arrive at it. Independence and bureaucracy coincide in one movement and constitute a strange form of governance, which tends to deconstruct itself from within.

Unfortunately such examples of inexpedient governance are more complicated than merely blaming incompetence on central administration because of its failure to take into consideration the radical implications of its support of self-administrating and self-governing institutions. It is also a question of this taking place within a political democracy with elected politicians operating outside and above administrative departments. Public top management has to perform the role of supervising management in relation to subordinate institutions, and at the same time serve the political system like soft clay in relation to politicians' performance and political leadership. This often results in mixed messages, where central administration one day calls for self-administration from its schools and preschools and the next day interferes on behalf of politicians in specific management dispositions in the institutions.

Public administration is required to function as a medium for political efforts to show political vigour, but has to simultaneously convince welfare institutions to perceive this as a welcome opportunity to reformulate their objectives. This is quite a task. How can public administration use education policies to both allow politicians to appear as agenda-setting for educational development as well as allow schools to see themselves as self-developing? Supervision administration employs tools such as evaluations to make welfare institutions visible to politicians while also making it possible for the institutions to perceive this intervention as self-intervention. In order to govern welfare institutions, the administration has to convince them that self-evaluation is a necessary part of self-governance. But how does public administration convince decentralised institutions of the viability of time-consuming documentation and reporting efforts? How does it develop specific governance and evaluation models that secure political influence without causing the institutions to feel that their independence has been violated?

As a result of the emergence of supervision and potentiality administration, governance can no longer be perceived as planning. With the above challenges in mind, public sector welfare managers and administrators can no longer observe welfare institutions from the perspective of simple planning because it would produce adaptive institutions that would refer responsibility for their development up through the hierarchy. We are familiar with this from general institutional dissatisfaction with municipal decisions. The expectation that institutions be responsible for their own development as independent organisations with independent strategies shifts the perspective of central administration to a second-order strategic perspective. Welfare management becomes a question of unfolding second-order strategies designed to support the first-order strategies of the welfare institutions. Being a second-order strategist is about opening up space and possibilities for the first-order strategies of the welfare institutions. It is about making the institutions see the differently possible in what appears inevitable. It is a question of hacking into the mindset of the institutions and offering new horizons of meaning and the future for the institutions' self-development. From this perspective, disagreement and conflicts are not necessarily something to keep at bay or solve. Instead, it is a question of creating and providing dynamic and productive conflict space.

> **Reflection 3.1: Potentiality administration**
> Ask yourself:
>
> 1) What is the relationship between governance and self-governance in your organisation?
> 2) Have you taken any initiative toward developing capacity for independence in your organisation?
> 3) How do you communicate, 'Do as I say' *as well as* 'Be independent'?
> 4) To what extent do you accept responsibility for the fact that such double-bound communication can be perceived as dysfunctional by the governed bodies?
> 5) How do you encourage people under you to think 'outside of the box'?
> 6) Do you sometimes lose sight of the value of stability and continuity in your eagerness to create innovation?
> 7) Do people who work under you sometimes think of you as 'hot air' when you try to push them toward more of a helicopter view?
> 8) Does your organisation's leadership tend to become closed around itself and lose attention to specific everyday problems in the organisation?

FOUR

Welfare organisations as infinite potential

What does it take to innovate and reimagine welfare services? What would it mean to raise the quality of welfare by placing individual citizens and their needs at the centre of welfare efforts? How do we reap the benefits of new welfare technologies? Each of these questions defines the welfare organisation as the solution to problems in the welfare state. The individual welfare organisation becomes the site where questions of lacking adaptability and innovation can be solved. We accumulate more and more expectations about what individual welfare organisations are supposed to deliver. And we perceive more and better institutional management as the solution to countless problems. The question is, however, how are specific management conditions in a nursing home, a secondary school, a group home or a rehabilitation facility affected by public administration ambitions about potentiality governance? What does it mean to manage a welfare organisation in which management is restricted by central rules and regulations, has to implement central planning, is supervised in its effort to create an independent profile, *and* is required to reimagine and innovate welfare services?

We discussed in Chapter Three the way that public administration has evolved from a formal bureaucracy via sector-based administration to supervision and potentiality administration. That historical narrative is about the need to maintain unity and a comprehensive vision while managing increasing differentiation and complexity in public administration. It tells the story of shifts and twists to the relationship between governing and governed bodies, and the emergence of a form of governance whose objective increasingly becomes the capacity for self-governance among governed institutions.

In this chapter, we turn the question on its head and view the problem from the perspective of the individual administrative institution. Governance of self-governance creates an institutional double bind. As objects of governance, they are required to follow directions from above. As self-governing bodies, they can only follow directions from above by not following directions from above and only taking directions from themselves. Therefore, we want to look at how organisations can operate while taking into account such various and complex expectations about independence and subordination respectively.

We distinguish between an institution's self-reference and external reference in its decision-making processes. Everyday institutional life includes countless minor and major conflicts about whether to make decisions with reference to the organisation itself or to the municipal or national hierarchy that the organisation is part of. How, for example, can a daycare facility explain to its staff its decision, despite limited resources, to purchase a more expensive microwave oven instead of a cheaper brand because the former is included in a municipal procurement contract and the latter is not? As most welfare managers will attest to, managing a welfare organisation is very much a question of coordinating decisions based on local interests with the demands and expectations placed on the organisation by politicians and central administration. How can the timing in the institution's own development projects be synchronised with municipal or national development efforts? Managers of welfare institutions are responsible for ensuring that ongoing conflicts between the individual institutions and municipal or national agendas do not undermine institutional development or the commitment of their employees.

We perceive the question of institutional independence not simply as a question of freedom from obligations dictated from above but as a more complex interplay between self-reference and external reference in the organisations. We distinguish between 'the innocent institution', 'the professionally responsible institution', 'the strategic organisation' and 'the potential organisation' as four manifestations of the relationship between self- and external reference.

Figure 4.1: The growing independence of welfare institutions

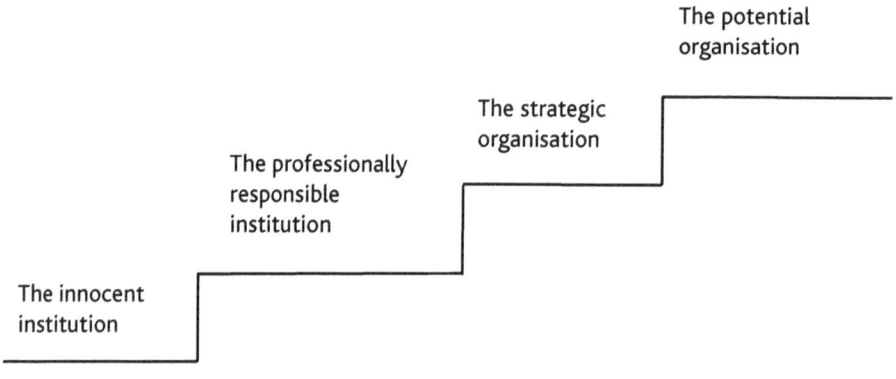

Innocent institution

Welfare institutions within formal bureaucracy primarily operate through external reference and define themselves according to their allotted position in the hierarchical structure. The very concept of 'institution' means being defined by a structure outside the institution itself. An institution performs a function that is defined from outside itself; it cannot define itself. An institution is not an independent system but an element within another system. We refer to this concept of institution as *innocent institutions within a hierarchy* – institutions that always justify their actions with reference to authorities hierarchically located above them, such as the law and politics. In this context, acting responsibly means to live up to formal expectations and obligations. Innocent institutions only make simple decisions whose decision premises have been defined from above. They possess basic self-reference through their upward external reference to the hierarchical structure.

Professionally responsible institution

Sector-based administration shifts the balance between self- and external reference in the direction of increased self-reference. Institutions still operate through external reference with respect to their overall objectives and the specific tasks they are designed to perform, but they operate through self-reference in terms of the means and methods they choose to employ in their effort to solve the given problems and to achieve their given objectives. Thus, they are assigned independent professional responsibility for how to fulfil their externally given objective. We refer to this form of institution as the *professionally independent responsible institution*. The professionally responsible institution does more than make simple decisions based on established decision premises. Even though it remains at the lower end of the planning and governance chain, and even though it is perceived from the outside as a black box trivially translating input into output, the given objectives leave a wide and contingent space of decisional possibilities for the institution to manage internally and independently. The institution needs to interpret its objectives in the context of its own professional framework. The objectives are not always entirely well defined, and the institution has to respond to possible conflicts among objectives. It has to prioritise its objectives – some things are more urgent than others, and some things need to be done before others. Different equivalent means–end calculations need to be compared. Thus, the institution has to decide on a number of premises in order for it to make decisions, which extends its independence beyond basic self-reference via external reference to hierarchically established premises. The professionally responsible institution is professionally *self-reflexive* via external reference to a planning system of predefined objectives and questions. It is independent in the sense that it relates to itself professionally. Goals and resources are established from above, but the institution is granted a certain amount of freedom with respect to prioritising, methodology and means. This level of independence enables the governing body to think in terms of input and output in relation to the institution. Acting responsibly in the professionally responsible institution means assuming substantial responsibility for the satisfactory handling and solution of relevant problems as they relate to the general objectives.

Strategic organisation

The introduction of supervision administration creates yet another shift in the balance between self- and external reference. Institutions become self-referential both in terms of goals and means. Supervision administration challenges the institutions to independently establish and govern themselves. External reference exists merely in the form of required documentation of institutional independence by means of strategies for the internal management of a range of potentially conflicting goals, methods, problems and solutions. Thus, the institutions are now perceived as *strategic organisations* and are required to formulate their own goals and strategies, including strategic reflection of their professional area of knowledge (Newman, 2005b). Strategy functions as a third-order form of decision. The innocent institution made basic decisions in relation to which all decision premises had been established in advance. The professionally responsible institution made prioritisation decisions as the final link in a planning chain, where planning is defined as a decision about premises for subsequent decisions (a second-order decision). Strategy, then, functions as a third-order decision, where the welfare organisation makes decisions about its future and in doing so establishes premises for prioritisations in the present. The strategic organisation reflectively relates to its objectives and hence to potential conflicts between different professional competences through external reference to a future, which it seeks to stabilise and use as organisational premise, but which simultaneously represents a horizon of possibilities.

An institution represents, as already mentioned, an element within another system. An organisation, by contrast, represents an independent system that creates its own elements and has the capacity to programme and reprogramme itself by defining and redefining its purpose. The strategic organisation, in effect, creates a strange and paradoxical constitution of the welfare institution as organisation (the element as system). An element of the system becomes defined by the system as its own system, externally defined to create itself as self-defined. Extending across all institutional levels, given objectives are no longer established by the system. Daycare institutions, for example, are now required to provide a business plan, complete with independent goals and strategies for achieving their goals. They are expected to document their independence and accountability. This can be seen as the final dissolution of the original unity of the hierarchical structure, which is now replaced by a form of polycentrism consisting of a multiplicity of – at least in theory – independent welfare organisations, which are expected to act independently but which nevertheless remain lodged within a hierarchical structure that refuses to look like one (Newman, 2004; Pors, 2012a, 2012b).

Example 4.1: The preschool curriculum at Sunflower

One of the ways in which Sunflower, a preschool in a Danish municipality, is being governed is by being obliged to formulate its own strategies and prioritisations. Sunflower outlines its mission statement on its website in the following way:

> Sunflower's educational mission statement:
>
> We want our programme to provide a warm and safe place for children, a welcoming place for parents to visit, and a pleasant place for our staff to work.
>
> We work to ensure:

- That the preschool is experienced as a comprehensive whole where we are considerate to one another
- That children are surrounded by responsible adults
- That each child feels recognised and valued
- That the children learn to become aware of themselves, their feelings, wishes and needs, and also learn to be considerate of others
- Conditions for making friendships and space for emotional relations between children
- That the children participate in making decisions
- That we prioritise children's independent play
- A balanced relationship between play and learning experiences such as activities, field trips, singing and music, etc
- That we pay attention to experiences we have here and now
- That we maintain and develop children's interest in and love of nature.

Our educational activities base themselves on the individual child and versatile development.

The website also includes reflections on the plan's status as a strategy:

> As the plan indicates, our presentation of the curriculum should not be perceived as direct planning but as a guiding framework for our day-to-day activities. We use it as a point of departure to focus our educational efforts to ensure that they meet the developmental needs of the individual child. Our annual evaluation of our program subsequently accounts for the methods we have applied in our day-to-day activities with the children. (Vingesuset, 2015, own translation)

Potential organisation

Potentiality administration radicalises expectations placed on welfare organisations about their required independence. It is no longer sufficient to be self-referential with respect to means and ends. Organisations are expected to demonstrate their independence through flexibility and perpetual change. Whereas the strategic organisation achieves independence by establishing organisational structure such as goals, annual plans and self-evaluation systems, the potential organisation achieves independence by showing that its own organisational structures do not limit its capacity for innovation or change.

The potential organisation does not create quality through specific definitions of quality or by planning how to quality assure and document the delivery of actual services. Instead, it considers the necessity of flexible planning in order to be able to reorganise and reconsider when it observes that the needs of an individual user require a different service than the planned one. Whereas the strategic organisation achieves independence through the consolidation of an organisational self, capable of maintaining its focus and directedness, a potential organisation recognises that organisational structures are unable to adapt to unique situations and that the organisation runs the risk of missing out on potential opportunities (Pors, 2011a). The potential organisation relates to itself as a process (Pors and Ratner, 2013).

Example 4.2: The potential organisation as an amoeba

The H.C. Andersen School in the municipality of Odense serves as an example of a welfare organisation that has organised itself in a flexible way in order to provide each individual student with the best and most suitable learning conditions. The school aims to seize emerging – and sometimes unexpected – opportunities for learning. On its website, the school writes: 'The flexible school is an amoeba organisation, capable of orienting itself according to registered needs.'

The school describes itself as an amoeba. This metaphor suggests an organisation that is able to continually change and does so in order to provide students with different forms of learning and learning environments. The student body is rather mixed – many of the students come from difficult backgrounds and struggle with learning. Thus, the school has had to think differently about teaching and organising. It has developed a concept about successful teaching as the ability to operate with varying and flexible learning environments. The website explains:

> We operate with learning environments such as "the auditorium", "the study nook", "the lab", "the open room", etc. Based on this, successful teaching becomes an amoeba-like concept because our students are different and enjoy and benefit from very different learning environments with respect to content, methodology,

organisation and structure, and because learning criteria have to be continually updated as new knowledge becomes available.

The school works with different forms of organisation such as 'the lab' or 'the study nook' and different principles for arranging groups of students (see below), which can be employed depending on which learning style is deemed the most productive by the teaching staff in collaboration with students and with reference to nationally established collective goals.

The school's intention is to create flexible and emergent forms of organisation. As the figure below shows, the school has decided that each day is to begin with a morning assembly. The rest of the school day, however, can be constructed and organised around different organisational possibilities. These might include cross-disciplinary projects or joint teaching in large groups, but can also include smaller groups created according to different principles such as learning style, interests or level of achievement. Thus, organisational structure such as, for example, timetable planning, cannot simply be decided on once or a few times a year. Rather than being established in advance, the organisational setting is dynamic. Still using the amoeba metaphor, the school writes:

> Thus, the school tries to see it self as an amoeba, flexibly and self-reflectively meeting the challenges it encounters, both from within its own environment and from the surrounding world. It would be very difficult to produce specific proposals for how a weekly schedule might look before establishing specific goals. And there also can be no pre-existing structure....

This organisational form makes special demands on the staff. School staff members have to be capable of continually changing their practice in relation to observed needs in students and the organisation:

> The professional didactic deals with contingency by handling and understanding feedback, which paves the way for dynamic and amoeba-like teaching situations, capable of adapting to challenges and conditions from the external environment as well as the internal community.

The 'amoeba organisation' represents a good example of the potential organisation. The metaphor coins the organisation as the essence of transformation, an organism capable of emerging in many different ways and able to adapt to and exploit possibilities that arise (Pors, 2011a; Juelskjær et al, 2011).

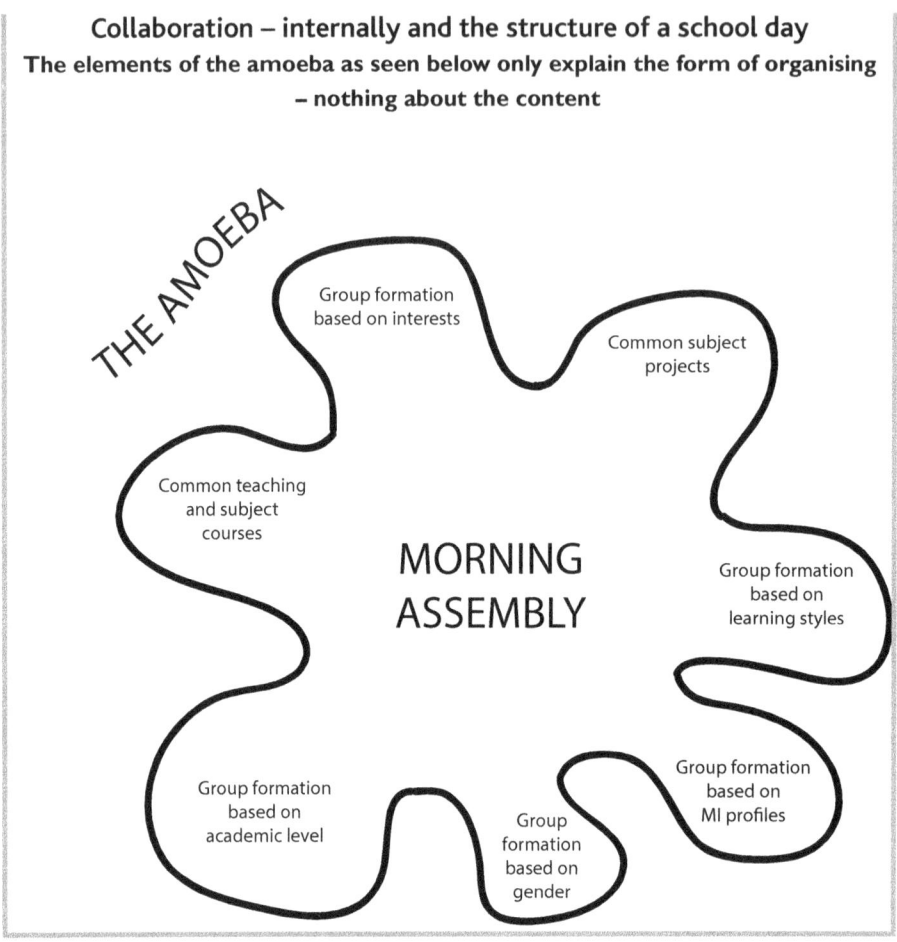

The potential organisation further radicalises the relationship between self-reference and external reference by requiring the self to reflect itself as other. Thus, the potential organisation does not accept someone as independent simply on the basis of the documentation of personal goals. The self cannot be self-evident. The self is expected to relate to itself as potential by questioning itself, playing with itself and experimenting with itself. The potential welfare organisation becomes independent by risking itself, dissolving fixed structures and creating flexible and multiple self-descriptions.

The appeal to create potential organisations applies to more than internal organisational structures. Potentiality administration directs welfare organisations to demonstrate their independence by risking the boundaries between themselves and other welfare organisations. Today, potentiality administration is used in welfare organisations to promote ideals about the centrality of the citizen, coherent user processes and user-driven innovation. Thus, organisations are also expected to be able to emerge as coherent organisational processes across formal organisational boundaries. Organisations in the elderly care sector, for example, are expected to work collaboratively so that clients will not have to notice and relate to the formal organisational boundaries between kitchen, home care, visitation and training unit. The potential organisation is expected to take advantage of the fact that certain situations benefit from a cross-organisational organisational identity. Concepts such as 'coherent user processes' or 'interdisciplinary learning' become central objectives that the organisation strives to deliver. Thus, the individual organisation operates with self- and goal descriptions that exceed the ones that correspond strictly with the formal organisation. The potential organisation can contribute different perspectives on its own boundaries and the boundaries of its responsibilities. Thus, the potential organisation is also the organisation of the operation: depending on the specific situation or project, the organisation can describe its boundaries in different ways.

In other words, the potential organisation achieves independence not only through the consolidation of itself and its boundaries, but also by risking its own identities and by seeking the potentiality of alternative selves, images of the future and boundaries. The potential welfare organisation has to be able to constantly produce itself as contingent. Whereas the innocent institution made basic decisions, the professionally responsible institution made priority decisions, and the strategic organisation made decisions about its future reference, the potential organisation makes decisions that decide without ruling out alternatives. The organisation operates via second-order strategies in the sense that it both stabilises expectations and seeks to keep them open. The organisation becomes self-reflexive about itself as streams of recursive operations and sceptical about any form of structure.

Function of noise

We can also describe the process of institutional independence in welfare institutions from a slightly different perspective by looking at the function of 'noise' at the different stages. We define noise as the surplus of meaning produced by a system's operations. Organisations that make decisions continually produce noise in the form of alternative decisions that could have been made (Pors, 2011a). The innocent institution perceives noise as a problem and strives for a one-to-one relation between the decision that the institution makes and the given decision premises. Noise indicates unpredictability, and unpredictability needs to be negated. The professionally responsible institution confronts noise as vagueness of objectives, which allows the institution a certain level of freedom with respect to prioritisation and interpretation. And it produces its own noise in the form of unused alternative solutions. The strategic organisation confronts noise as a world in constant change. It does not see that its external environment is an internal construction in the organisation in the same way that it also does not see that noise emanates from its own activities. Noise becomes a self-created imperative for change. The potential organisation perceives noise as a scarce resource and a source of renewal and change. Noise is potentiality! Where there is no noise, there is the risk of stagnation and unmoving structures. The concern is whether there is enough noise from which to establish order (Pors, 2014).

> **Example 4.3: A 'good meal' and the need for 'remote management'**
> In collaboration with her kitchen staff, a head kitchen manager in a Danish municipality had worked intensely to improve the food served to clients in the municipal elder care programme. She had worked to ensure that the food was more appealing and of higher quality, and the kitchen sought to rethink and improve everything from calorie count to packaging. However, despite these efforts, studies tracking the users' BMI showed that they remained malnourished.
>
> The kitchen manager believed that the meal situation was as significant for whether or not the elderly clients ate enough as the food itself. However, the municipal structure and the fact that the kitchen was located many kilometres from the nursing home where the food would be consumed meant that the manager and her staff were completely disconnected from the nursing staff and the meal situation. The manager wanted to address this problem and the frustrations and feelings of isolation experienced by her unit. She wanted a closer proximity with the way the nursing staff handled the meal situation. Her first initiative was to survey users' experience of the meal situation. She asked herself: have we, at any point, asked the users about their views on what constitutes a good meal? She went on to visit a nursing home and a care centre café and observed the meal situation. The observations provided her with a much more nuanced understanding of how meals took place and the factors that influenced users' experiences of their meals. She became aware of the challenges facing the nursing home staff with respect to ensuring that the meal situation lived up to the kitchen's requirements. It turned out that factors such as table placement and seating arrangement were significant for the clients' experiences of the meal.
>
> Subsequently, the manager conducted training for the nursing staff, placing special emphasis on nutrition and the importance of a 'good meal'. The training was designed to support an interdisciplinary collaboration between the kitchen and nursing staff. The training provided an opportunity to go beyond disciplinary boundaries and to build interdisciplinary collaboration to improve the meal experience for the nursing home clients.
>
> A good meal is an example of how to conduct quality management in situations where quality is created in the interfaces between organisational boundaries. The kitchen manager's response to the problem was to conduct 'remote management'. She was interested in the conditions underlying the nursing staff's effort to contribute to a good meal, and began to manage the situation through training and increased collaboration.

Concept 4.1: Noise and organisation

> This cannot be emphasized strongly enough.... To this extent the meaning process lives off disturbances, is nourished by disorder, lets itself be carried by noise.... (Luhmann, 1995, p 83)

> ... the "order from noise" principle ... require(s) the cooperation of our demons who are created along with the elements of our system, being manifest in some of the intrinsic structural properties of these elements. (von Foerster, 2003, p 13)

Demons within an organisation are the undecided elements of decisions, which John Caputo has termed the 'ghosts of undecidability'. Undecidability, not perceived as excess but instead as the concomitant byproduct of any decision and decision premise, constitutes the organisation's serving demons. An organisation does not need noise and disturbances from outside in order to change. Decision communication produces its own noise based on which order is to be achieved. It is engaged in the continual production of its own inner demons of expectational uncertainty – a pursuit that generates still more demons.

Table 4.1: Institutional forms

Institution	Operation	Form of independence	Function of noise
Innocent institution	Decision	Self-reference via external reference to hierarchy	Noise appears as vague premises and is produced as unwanted unpredictability
Professionally responsible institution	Planning	Professional self-reflection via external reference to planned objectives	Noise appears as vague goals that allow the institution a certain level of freedom to interpret and prioritise
Strategic organisation	Strategy	Reflection about goals and hence about possible conflicts among disciplines via external reference to a future, which is sought fixed and serves as the organisational foundation	Noise appears in the shape of an external environment in constant flux
Potential organisation	Potentialisation	Reflection of the self as other. The self cannot be self-evident but is expected to relate to itself as potential by questioning itself, playing with itself and experimenting with itself	Noise appears as a scarce resource and a source of renewal. Where there is no noise, there is the risk of stagnation and rigid structures

Challenges for management

What does all this mean for welfare management? How does the growing independence of institutions and potentialisation have an impact on the management of a nursing home, a daycare institution or a hospital?

In Chapter Three we discussed the way in which public administration is fundamentally constituted as a hierarchical organisation, operating through administrative decisions in the form of unilateral statements. The *unilateral* character of such statements is precisely what distinguishes administrative decisions from private contracts, which are *bilateral* (the parties need to agree before an agreement can be said to have validity). The shift in the direction of supervision administration is rather radical in relation to this definition. Why? The changes we describe through the lens of increased institutional independence can be seen as a folding of the distinction between unilateral and bilateral.

The innocent institution is defined unilaterally within the hierarchy. The professional institution is unilaterally assigned a goal, which is linked to specific professional competences and with limited independence with respect to means. There is an element of mutuality between administrative hierarchy and institution within a unilateral framework. The strategic organisation is established by means of a unilateral invitation to mutuality. The bilateral nature of the relationship is unilaterally defined through the unilateral demand placed on the institution to be independent. Thus, it is not simply a question of a continuum between governance and self-governance as a gradual shift toward more self-governance and less central governance. Instead, it is a fundamental element of governance to continually communicate both governance and self-governance. Central administration remains on the unilateral side of the distinction between unilateral administrative decision and bilateral contract. This increases the inner complexity of bureaucracy and establishes specific governance paradoxes. The most important paradox facing the strategic organisation from above is the administrative request to 'Do as I say – be independent'.

The emergence of the strategic organisation establishes the following paradoxes for welfare management:

- How does an organisation create itself as independent when independence has been issued as an order by the hierarchy?
- How does an organisation create meaningful change on the basis of paradoxical governance that says, 'Do as we say, be independent'?
- How does an organisation demonstrate independence vis-à-vis an administration that both wants and does not want to be a hierarchy?
- How does an organisation accept a unilateral invitation to bilateral development?

Complexity is further increased by the fact that each specific institution is always constituted as a formal institution, professionally responsible institution, strategic organisation and potential organisation. From situation to situation, each specific institution may experience having to switch between these four constitutional forms. Thus, each institution has to be able to act in accordance with four – rather mutually antagonistic – sets of rules. Moreover, many situations will appear ambiguous and unclear, and will invite continual oscillation among the forms.

Today, politicians and the public sector expect welfare organisations to utilise their independence to dissolve boundaries between themselves and other welfare organisations. This threatens the purchaser–provider split model that establishes clear boundaries between the budgets of individual welfare organisations, and it threatens administrative hierarchies that establish internal organisational management relations and do not immediately allow for the head of one organisation to manage employees in another. The potential organisation is expected to challenge boundaries through its processes and solutions, but collaboration among welfare organisations is often organised according to purchaser–provider split models that are based on the absolute separation of the organisations' budgets and accounting.

The shift from the innocent via the professionally responsible toward the potential organisation creates the following welfare management paradoxes:

- How to create a meaningful organisational identity on the basis of ambiguous and conflicting demands about being an innocent, professional, strategic and potential organisation?
- How to formulate goals and strategies while keeping alternative possibilities open?
- How to manage an organisation while striving for maximum flexibility for individual operations further out and down in the organisation?
- How to both govern in accordance with a strategy and encourage everyone, in the name of innovation, to question pre-existing assumptions, including the most basic function of the institution?
- How to manage an organisation while striving to dissolve its structures and become pure process?
- How to communicate both the minimisation and acceleration of contingency?
- How to create possibilities for the connectivity of decisions without defining in advance the criteria for connectivity?

In concrete everyday situations, the complex task of being both innovative but also capable of documenting, assigning responsibility and ensuring the achievement of goals falls to the practitioners of the welfare state. In terms of potentiality, possible future resources are always already part of the description of an organisation. Negotiations between politicians and administration on the one hand, and individual welfare organisations on the other, include two languages: the language of the actualised and the language of the potential. This can sometimes lead to rather curious conversations. When actuality and potentiality become interwoven and perhaps appear equally realistic, decisions are sometimes made about spending cuts based on expected optimisation of resources such as, for example, rehabilitation efforts within eldercare services. In other words, there is a risk of reaping the expected benefits of potential outcomes years before they become actualised.

Thus, during times of an increased focus on resource efficiency, the question is whether the ideal about flexibility, innovation and potentiality management can be used to legitimise untimely spending cuts. Inherent in these ideals is the assumption that additional potential can always be found in people (provided they develop better/more), in the breakdown of boundaries (for example, through expectations about learning at home or on the playground or at school), or in new organisational forms. Do such ideals create a situation where welfare managers or professionals are unable to argue against spending cuts without being perceived as not being innovative enough? Might not politicians and officials call for unjustified cuts based on the argument that individual units need to create more value through flexible design, better use of employees, breaks, as well as the inclusion of citizens, relatives and volunteers? With an eye for the worst-case scenario, we wonder if these new expectations with regard to innovation can be used to legitimise unreasonable spending cuts based on the perceptions that if only the administrative units would become sufficiently innovative, questions of resources would become secondary.

> **Reflection 4.1: The growing independence of welfare institutions**
> Ask yourself:
>
> 1) How do you deal with equivocal expectations? That is, how do you simultaneously show your independence and your obedience?
> 2) Do you confront central administration with a similar dilemma by simultaneously demanding more freedom as well as more attention and recognition?
> 3) Do certain situations place your organisation in the position of being called out as an innocent, professional, independent and potential organisation?
> 4) How do you make sure to keep your administration at close proximity as well as at arm's length, depending on your specific needs?
> 5) How do you manage to operate with different organisational self-descriptions which all define the limits of organisational responsibility differently?
> 6) How do you ensure that the governance paradoxes facing your organisation are not simply transposed onto individual employees who are left to handle them on their own?

FIVE

Searching for possibilities between disciplines and codes

How do individual welfare organisations choose and prioritise conflicting interests? Any manager of an institution knows that important decisions require the interplay of different rationales. Ideally, economic, political and professional interests come together to form a perfect union, but this does not always happen. How can welfare organisations create and maintain a focus on central responsibilities when they are also expected to accommodate a wide range of other interests? What, first of all, constitutes the central responsibility for a daycare centre of a group home today? What level of professionalism does the potential organisation require of professionals? And how does that affect management conditions?

Here, we pursue the same question that we introduced in Chapter Two, that is, the relationship between differentiation and unity, but we focus on the way in which this question presents itself for the individual organisation. Is it better to manage a multiplicity of interests on the organisational level than on the level of society? Is it easier to represent the unity of society in an organisation than on the level of society?

A municipal preschool has to balance a set of interests. A preschool is a care institution, whose job is to establish a sense of security for the children in its care. But it is also an educational institution with responsibility for the children's development. The 'same child' is not the same child observed from the perspective of the two different codes, and there are no guarantees that the challenges the institution seeks to provide the children with from an educational perspective coincide with the sense of security that the care perspective strives for. Moreover, a preschool also serves as the provider of children to elementary schools, which make general non-individualised demands on the preschool's educational goals. A preschool has its own budget and is subject to strict prioritisations, and during budget revision or when applying for extra funding, it needs to master the act of packaging educational goals into economic arguments. In addition, a child's sense of security does not begin or end in preschool. The preschool's options are determined by how well the children's families function. 'Collaboration' with parents is important. However, 'collaboration' involves a series of asymmetrical interests and concerns: perhaps the family wants maximum attention for their own child, perhaps they expect that collaboration means joint decision-making in and about the institution, or perhaps they take a service approach ('Can I pick up a little later today, I have a meeting...'). The preschool, on the other hand, might – in the name of collaboration – adopt an educational perspective on the family ('Perhaps you should pick Jonah up a bit earlier? It is important to prioritise your children while they are young'), or a care perspective (in order to care for the child one has to care for the family). And in certain cases, it might even choose a legal perspective if the care and educationally based conversations with the family lead to enough concern that it triggers the preschool's obligation to report the information to social services.

Our thesis in this chapter is that over time, the individual welfare organisation connects to a growing number of function systems. This increases the internal complexity of the welfare organisation. An increasing number of codes and functions come into play at the same time and in the same cases, and there is increasing openness as to the specific ways of linking the different functions. Gradually, the reservoir of codes comes to be perceived as a resource in itself, as a contribution to the continual contingency of how to ask and respond to welfare questions.

All this undermines the self-evidence of the function systems' delivery of factual premises for the organisation. There is a fundamental difference in the constitutional conditions of organisation systems and function systems. Function systems are constituted on the basis of the factual dimension. They remain open in relation to the social dimension – who can participate in the communication of the function system – but they remain closed in relation to the factual dimension – how to speak about a case, whether to speak in medical, legal or economic terms. Organisations, by contrast, are constituted on the basis of the social dimension through membership. Only those who are granted membership can participate in decision communication. Everyone else is excluded. But organisations are open in relation to the factual dimension. An organisation's structural link to a function system enables the organisation to observe the communication of the function system as a service in its capacity of factual premises for decisions. However, once the self-evidence of the link between organisational system and function system is put into question, it becomes similarly more difficult for organisational systems to produce a factual basis for their decisions.

Developments in legal programmes determine constitutional conditions for the relationship between organisation and function systems. Therefore, we start by showing how legal changes allow for new forms of structural coupling between organisations and function systems. This means that we are going to pre-empt a more extensive description of the history of the law, which we return to later, in Chapter Nine. Here, we limit ourselves to a reasonably rudimentary distinction between four legal forms, whose development overlap, and each of which sets particular legal conditions for structural coupling.

The cumulative changes within the law from formal law via substantial law to reflexive law and hybrid law also represents a gradual pulling back of the law that opens up non-legal considerations within individual public organisations. This opening toward non-legal concerns immediately enables professionally responsible welfare institutions to not act exclusively in relation to the law in their internal practice but also in relation to other function systems. These are function systems such as scientific, health, educational, care service, sports, art, war and many

Concept 5.1: Organisation vs function systems

Organisations are systems that constitute themselves through decisions. When decisions make decisions, they form a symbolically generalised medium based on one of society's function systems. This can be the medium of economy, which is money, or the medium of the legal system, which is 'existing law'. The choice of medium colours and codes the decision in a particular way. When a decision is made through the medium of money, it becomes an economic decision about paying or not paying, and the whole world is viewed from that perspective.

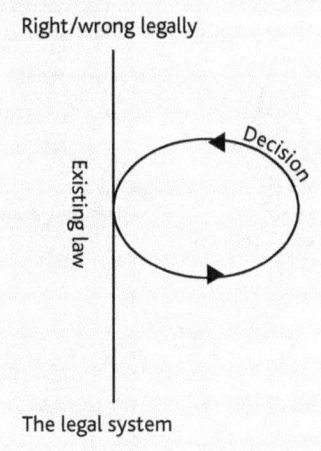

The legal system

others. And as already mentioned, each function system communicates in its own code. Our thesis is that, over time, individual administrative organisations become influenced by different codes. Along with bureaucracy and formal law comes the *formal institution*, which is primarily governed by one code, the code of law. With sector administration and substantial law we get the *homophonic organisation*, which links up to one additional function system via a legally defined objective, which decides the organisation's function and logic. A legally established objective regarding education, for example, connects schools to the educational function system. Supervision administration and reflexive law bring along the *heterophonic organisation*, which is capable of formulating multiple objectives and thus connects to many different function systems. There is no way to prescribe in advance in the heterophonic organisation the application of specific codes, and the weighing of heterogeneous concerns serves as a continual challenge to this form of organisation. The problem is that the functionally determined interests must be weighed against each another, but there is no code for this weighing. And finally, along with potentiality administration and hybridity comes a radicalisation of the heterophonic organisation. Instead of seeing the prioritisation and weighing of different codes as a problem, it now becomes possible to see function systems as an open reservoir through which the organisation can experiment with itself and its form. It is an organisation that continues to explore the potential inherent in function systems for asking questions, defining cases, describing the organisation, formulating strategies, etc. It is a *communication-seeking potentiality-generating organisation*.

Table 5.1: Toward the heterophonic and communication-seeking organisation

Administrative form	Legal form	Complexity of codes	Decision challenge	Self-description
Formal bureaucracy	Formal law	Formal 'innocent' institutions are primarily coded legally	Legal decisions	Legal self-description via external reference
Sector administration	Substantial law	Homophonic organisations are legally linked primarily to one other function system in addition to the law. This system defines the organisational objective	Legal estimation that allows for a professional perspective from a particular non-legal system	Monofunctional goal-oriented self-description
Supervision administration	Reflexive law	Heterophonic organisations in which the law opens up toward a multiplicity of social systems. The organisation becomes a site where many codes are weighed and clash under particular conditions	Balanced prioritisation of a multiplicity of concerns, each of which belong to its own systems logic without the possibility of a comprehensive view	Multiple functional self-descriptions without fixed ranking
Potentiality administration	Hybrid law	Communication-seeking potentiality-generating organisations in which the law and organisational prescriptions for practice compel an ongoing exploration of the organisation's potential, given different forms of coding. Complexity is no longer simply something to be reduced but something to be produced. Complexity means possibilities	Ongoing communicative exploration of the potential and sites for decisions generated by the availability and development of differently coded perspectives	Multiple hybrid self-descriptions that can be played with strategically

Example 5.1: From homophony to heterophony in Danish foreign aid
The year 1962 marks Denmark's first foreign aid act, called the Technical Partnerships with Developing Nations Act. It set out clear objectives and means for Danish foreign aid. The goal was to increase living standards. The Act defined means primarily as technical support, state-sponsored loans, and later on, an industrialisation fund designed to promote investment in developing countries. Thus, it represented formal, legalised foreign aid.

In 1971, a new Act was passed entitled the International Foreign Aid Partnerships Act, which replaced the 1962 Act. Unlike the 1962 Act, this Act was goal-oriented. It stated: 'The main objective behind Denmark's national foreign aid is the formation of partnerships with the governments and authorities of developing countries that support their efforts to achieve economic growth as a way to help ensure their social progress and political independence in accordance with the UN treaty, mission, and founding principles as well as the promotion of mutual understanding and solidarity through cultural partnerships.'

The objectives were defined in broad and somewhat ambiguous terms, but the primary concern was to have a definition that allowed for concrete means and problem–solution models to be developed over time. This allowed for a much more complex perception of issues and problems. As part of the effort, the government founded the aid organisation Danida as a professional organisation. In our context, Danida can be seen as a primary homophonic organisation, which, based on the law, forms the code help/no help, and continues to develop new problem–solution models.

From 1988, new semi-legal regulation of foreign aid was introduced through aid work strategies adopted by the Danish parliament. Examples include 'Strategic planning' (1988), 'Strategy 2000' (1994), 'Partnership 2000' (2000), 'Security, growth, development' (2004), 'Freedom from poverty, freedom for change' (2010) and 'The right to a better life' (2012). Such strategies queried the premises of Danish foreign aid by continuing to introduce new perspectives, visions, angles and concerns into the field. Rather than proposing specific problem–solution figures, they developed an indefinite number of concerns such as sustainability, democratisation and human rights concerns, which are expected to be included in Danida's future problem–solution models. For example, in 'Partnership 2000': 'Danish foreign aid works to fight poverty by focusing on sustainability through poverty-driven economic growth. Equal participation by men and women in the development process, environmental concerns and respect for human rights and democratisation are critical to the fight against poverty and also remain independent goals for the development process. Thus, gender concerns, environmental concerns and democracy concerns are all interdisciplinary considerations in the Danish foreign aid efforts.'

Development no longer simply means helping, but also educating, creating security, empowering women, etc. Danida is expected to juggle countless different codes in its projects. As an organisation, Danida is pushed in the direction of a heterophonic and communication-seeking organisation, expected to perform the impossible, that is, both integrating

> heterogeneous interests and concerns as well as exploring the development potential of different codes. What kind of development potential does a democracy perspective generate? A gender perspective? A sustainability perspective? (own translations).

Formal institution

As already discussed, the formal institution works primarily through external reference. Its premises are all legally defined and function as an external framework for the institution.

The formal institution considers substantial questions to be political. Within the formal institution, substantial discussions are assumed to reside within the political system whose compromises result in formal law, which unambiguously conditions the administration's decisions. It needs no other concerns beyond purely legal ones. The legal code holds the monopoly on the organisation's self-description and on the generation of premises for decisions and rulings.

This does not mean that the institution represents a trivial machine, blindly calculating legal decisions. But it does mean that the complexity facing the decision is primarily legal in kind so that different complexes of law, legal cases, legal facts, precedent, and so on, partake in a hermeneutical interpretation and prioritisation aiming to achieve a comprehensive legal perspective.

It also does not mean the total exclusion of non-legal considerations. But it does mean that to the extent that non-legal considerations are included (for example, in the form of expert knowledge about specific case aspects), it happens in accordance with legal procedures, and non-legal observations are not included as decision premises until they have subsequently become the object of legal interpretation as legal facts. The law holds primacy over non-legal perspectives. This can be illustrated in this way (see Figure 5.1).

Figure 5.1 shows how a formal institution, establishing itself through decisions, is legally connected to the legal system. This connection does not turn the formal institution into a sub-system under the law, but the connection means that decisions form the law as medium. Thus, organisational communication is coloured by the law and the decision is legally coded, whereas the law and the organisation remain each other's external environment. They are only tangentially linked so that a decision is simultaneously an operation within the law and within the organisation but also an operation in each of them.

Figure 5.1: Formal institution

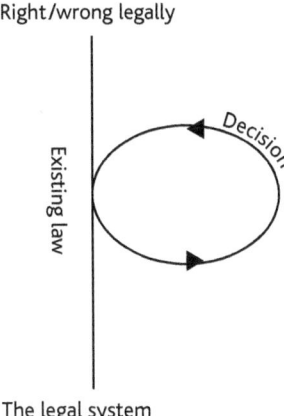

Homophonic welfare institution

The institutions we now call our welfare institutions date back to the 1960s. Their formation rests on the fact that each of the individual institutional forms (schools, universities, hospitals, nursing homes, etc) is associated with one particular function system in addition to the law. They are therefore not just sub-administrations; they are also something else. Within the pedagogical function systems we see the gradual development of a number of highly specialised institutions such as preschools, primary schools, secondary schools, vocational training, business schools, maritime schools, nursing schools, and so on, which are all designed to shape the pedagogical code and professional competency, albeit from the perspective of their own educational programme and objective. In the care system, we see similar differentiation into different institutions, each with their own care-based objective, for example, nursing homes, orphanages, assisted living facilities, unemployment benefits, foster care, drop-in centres, and so on. In the healthcare system we see the formation of organisations such as hospitals, medical clinics, dental clinics, eye specialists, X-ray clinics and health visitors. These lists can be extended to all the function systems.

These institutions have all been established based on a specific programme with specific objectives in relation to a specific social system. We might refer to these institutions as homophonic welfare institutions because they are guided by one specific professional competency, one perspective, one general concern, one function, one code and one given objective. This differentiation of welfare institutions in their adherence to different social systems can be illustrated like this (Andersen, 2003b) (see Figure 5.2).

Figure 5.2: Homophonic welfare institutions

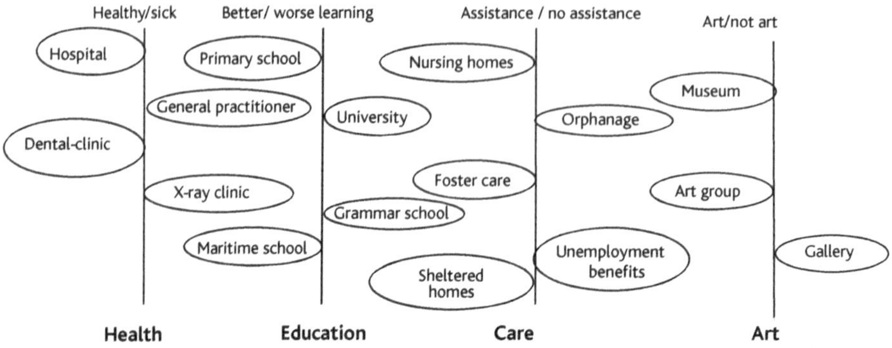

Health	Education	Care	Art
Healthy/sick	Better/worse learning	Assistance / no assistance	Art/not art
Hospital, Dental-clinic, General practitioner, X-ray clinic, Maritime school	Primary school, University, Grammar school	Nursing homes, Orphanage, Foster care, Sheltered homes, Unemployment benefits	Museum, Art group, Gallery

We should stress the fact that the homophonic organisation is also legally constituted. However, the law does not prescribe behaviour, only objectives – what we refer to later as the substantial form of law – such as caring for elders who can no longer care for themselves at home (nursing home), or preparing children for school (preschool). Once an objective has been established, the law assigns primacy to a specific function system in the context of a specific organisational programme. In preschools, the law assigns primacy to pedagogy in its adherence to a programme concerning school preparation. To say that pedagogy holds primacy in preschools means that pedagogy becomes the primary code through which communication, decision and management take place. Pedagogy functions as the prevailing language through which the preschool class describes itself, its environment and its practice. And from the perspective of this pedagogical self-description, the law is seen as merely a frame.

Thus, the homophonic organisation is also a formal institution, which employs goal-oriented law to constitute the organisation in its adherence to one particular function system. The homophonic organisation works with a *double code* – a legal discourse as well as a welfare function-oriented discourse, where the law functions as the formally constituent discourse, which simultaneously withdraws by defining a goal that implies that the organisation connects to a particular primary function system.

The development of the homophonic organisation also produces sub-fields within social studies, which provide scientifically elaborated language for individual organisational forms. There is research specialising in educational institutions, in hospitals, art organisations – and everyone claims that their particular institutional object is of particular interest and entirely beyond comparison with other institutions. Schools are something unique and cannot learn from hospitals, which are also described as unique, etc. Thus, social studies contribute to the formation of the function-driven homophonic welfare organisation by confirming and cultivating its self-image.

One of the first people to do research in this field was the US sociologist Talcott Parsons, who, in the 1950s, began to explore the unique qualities of the school, the university and the hospital. Parsons believed that organisations are basically classifiable in relation to a primary function, which they are organised around, and which always references a specific function in society. He distinguished between organisations oriented to (1) economic production (private companies), (2) political attainment of goals (government agencies), (3) integration (courts and political parties), and (4) pattern maintenance (cultural institutions, churches, schools). Thus, from the perspective of this logic, private companies are described as guided by economic rationality with a focus on the maximisation of economic productivity and the minimisation of economic costs. Similarly, military organisations are described as oriented toward technical efficiency with the primary goal of maximising power in a given area. And universities are described as primarily oriented toward the maintenance of patterns through two parallel goals: education and research. The function of universities in this context is described as 'expressive' rather than 'operative' (Parsons, 1956, 1971; for a similarly function-based description of the school, see also Hills, 1976).

The homophonic organisation provides us with typified organisational self-descriptions, which emphasise individual organisational types as the answer to problems related to a particular function system. The school provides an organisational answer to the challenge of organising instruction marked by interaction in classrooms. The political party represents an organisational answer to how to organise in a political democracy, where the challenge is to survive ongoing shifts between being in opposition and in power. The defense system represents an organisational answer to how to organise during periods of peace while remaining perpetually prepared to engage in a war situation.

The homophonic organisation has a primary connection to a function system, which is functionally supported by the law. This also pertains to a primary codification of the organisational communication, which expresses itself through monofunctional self-descriptions in organisations – self-descriptions – which, as we said, are also reflectively elaborated through research. In theory, the organisation may connect to other codes under particular communicative circumstances, but such connections never fundamentally challenge the organisation's basic self-description. By contrast, we might say that the unambiguous and unilaterally coded self-description makes it possible for certain organisational themes to unproblematically code themselves differently and even become internally organised as sub-systems within the organisation (for example, financial offices at a university, a dental clinic at a school or security personnel at a welfare office).

The homophonic organisation connects organisation and function system without rendering the organisation a sub-system within the function system. A school perceived as an organisation and a school perceived as an instruction are two different systems. The school as an organisation makes decisions, which can serve as the premises for instruction, but the organisation does not perform an instruction. Instruction provides instruction. In turn, instruction does not make decisions. Decision and instruction represent two different streams of communicative operations, which are brought together in the school but which never coincide. Instruction serves as communication in the educational system and is therefore not part of the school as organisation but functions only as a significant *external environment* for the school. The school connects decisions and instruction but also has to ensure that they do not destroy each other. As an organisation, the school can decide that there are certain decisions it cannot make. An interesting question is when the school as organisation ends and the school as instruction begins. Or, more generally, how is the relationship between organisation and function system regulated? This is both a practical and management-related question for any welfare institution.

A number of welfare institutions manage the relation between organisational system and function system by way of concepts such as 'methodological autonomy', 'professional autonomy' or 'academic freedom'. In public schools, for instance, teachers' methodological autonomy has meant that it is difficult for the school as an organisation to make pedagogy an object of decision. Pedagogy represents the teachers' contextual judgement of what is needed. Similarly, the scientific system would argue that research is not an organisational practice but precisely a scientific practice. From this perspective, a university administration merely functions as an expensive framework. However, the fact is that the placement of the dividing line between organisation and function system depends on the observing system. Boundaries always mean two boundaries. The organisational system and the function system each have their own boundary with the external environment. From the perspective of the university as organisation, research merely represents a means to a particular goal, which has either been established by the university itself as decision or by the political system. From a scientific perspective, generating new knowledge is a goal in itself. A director of municipal children and youth services might want it both ways. They might argue that teachers have methodological autonomy, but school principals are responsible for the pedagogical leadership at the school, and as a municipality they are responsible for ensuring that what takes place in the schools reflects the municipality's educational policies.

As we have seen, challenges pertaining to how to manage the relationship between law, organisation and function system make themselves felt in the homophonic organisations. However, such challenges are rarely addressed to the individual organisation. Instead, they are often articulated as questions of professional autonomy and are handled via collective agreements between labour unions and municipalities. In conjunction with homophonic welfare organisations, the professions emerge as organisations designed to protect professional autonomy for teachers, doctors, nurses, researchers or social workers. They argue that the professions represent specific values that need protection. Thus, in the literature on professions, we can trace an ongoing conceptual effort to delimit professions from non-professions. Only real professions are entitled to professional autonomy. Doctors, academic researchers and lawyers have been recognised as members of established professions for a very long time. It has been much more challenging for nurses, social workers and teachers to achieve the same recognition. And the jobs of hair stylists, home care workers, cleaning personnel, office workers and others have been referred to mostly as occupations or trades, but never as professions.

The criteria have changed historically, but a central tenet has always been that a profession lays claim to a specific knowledge field (for example, medicine), a specific education (for example, medical school), specific autonomous professional values (for example, protect human life and relieve pain), which have defined the job as more of a personal calling than a simple obligation, which does not require personal involvement and judgement (Parsons, 1939; Weber, 1946, 1994; Luhmann 2006).

Despite the fact that the law allows goals to open up for organisational connections to other function systems, these invited non-legal perspectives might at times conflict with the legal perspective. This poses yet another challenge: how to weigh legal and functional professionalism against each other. In homophonic organisations, this question finds expression within legal communication with concepts and principles of judgement. Judgement is the legal term for the individualisation of a legal decision within the boundaries of the law. The law distinguishes between arbitrary judgement and legally based judgement. Arbitrary judgement is perceived as an illicit way to individualise because a set of non-legal considerations are used to justify a decision without legal grounds and explication. By contrast, a judgement is legally based if it includes a professional judgement, whose open and explicit nature serves as the basis of the possibility of legally discussing the objectivity of the judgement (Koch, 1982; Andersen, 2008a).

Thus, we see the emergence of certain management and governance challenges with the homophonic organisation and its double coding despite the primacy of one code:

- Where can the boundary between organisation and function system be drawn? And is there any way to regulate the boundary when it is always defined from within the individual system?
- How can a welfare organisation make decisions that can simultaneously be perceived as a meaningful framework for 'work' within a particular function system?
- How does one distinguish between a professional decision and a legal decision?
- How can law and non-law be weighed against each other? And should the weighing itself be legal or non-legal?

Heterophonic organisation

The past 15 years have further intensified the level of complexity of these questions. As welfare institutions have grown into independent and strategic heterophonic organisations, establishing their own goals and objectives so that they, in a sense, become self-programmed, they are assigned and assign themselves an increasing number of differentiated goals and functions. The goals often coincide with the institutional connection to a particular social system, for example, when Danish public schools are expected – in addition to providing educational programmes in writing, maths, languages, and so on – to train students in democracy, healthy lifestyles, responsible sexual habits, ecological awareness, etc. The schools are still organised around pedagogical competencies and language, although the ever-increasing differentiation into sub-programmes make it seem as if other social systems relate to the school system in a parasitical manner. This puts a strain on educational professional competence. Today schools are expected to cultivate more than simply pedagogical interests. They are expected to contribute to cultural integration, to coordinate their development with policies established by the parent school board, to integrate and build partnerships with parents, to pre-empt psychological and social issues by monitoring their students' social behaviour and to share their concerns with the police and social services, etc. Some municipalities have employed social workers whose job is to visit the schools and manage and prevent social problems, for example, by observing parent-teacher conferences. Thus, schools are expected to tackle concerns and interests, many of which go much beyond the logic of pedagogy. Schools become linked to the care system. This potentially turns school leadership into much more than pedagogical leadership. Many schools find themselves facing the dilemma of insisting, on the one hand, that school leadership is a strictly pedagogical effort and hence rejecting non-pedagogical considerations (or interpreting them pedagogically), and, on the other, taking on the large amount of external expectations and accepting pedagogy as one among many other considerations to be taken into account in a school setting, which means that school leadership is no longer simply pedagogical leadership but an orchestration of pedagogy that includes a number of non-pedagogical concerns that are not necessarily compatible and in relation to which pedagogy may not hold primacy.

Similarly, today's hospitals don't simply diagnose and treat diseases. They also prevent and educate the public about disease. They provide guidance about lifestyle choices and how to relate to food, exercise, sex, drugs, etc. And it is often the case that the focus of such guidance is not only the patient but also the patient's family and relatives. Hospitals are expected to provide existential support to incurably ill patients. Psychological support and grief therapy have become an integrated part of their responsibility. Hospitals are required to have the capacity to embrace health, care, education and diaconia (caring for each other).

Parts of society's welfare responsibilities have been outsourced to voluntary organisations or private companies whose focus also includes making a profit, advertising and other activities. Thus, when the Danish company ISS wins a municipal outsourcing contract for municipal home care, the company can no longer simply describe and govern itself in accordance with an economic logic. It also has to describe itself as a care institution using the language of help/no help. It has to describe itself as a political company, participating in negotiations about the future of eldercare, and it has to accept being perceived by the political system, from the perspective of govern/governed, as implementing political decisions.

Today's social services departments do not simply consider the needs of their clients on the basis of legal discourse about right and wrong from the perspective of their clients' rights. They also need to provide help to self-help from the perspective of a discourse on care. In addition, their decisions should also ideally be observable from the perspective of education as support toward job market relevant self-development. Finally, each act of support has to be observable as a good investment from the perspective of economy (Andersen, 2007b, 2008a).

> **Example 5.2: Heterophony and outsourcing of meals to seniors to ISS catering in the municipality of Lyngby-Taarbæk (described in depth in Andersen, 2000)**
>
> In 1990, the service company ISS offered to conduct a no-cost analysis of meals for seniors in the municipality of Lyngby-Taarbæk. The company's analysis indicated potential rationalisations and public cost cuts if the municipality were to outsource its kitchens. In 1992, the municipality decided to go ahead with the outsourcing contract. ISS catering won the contract and took over the municipal kitchens at the beginning of 1994. The shift did not, however, go smoothly. The staff had barely started to wear their new ISS uniforms and drive the new ISS cars when seniors and family members filed the first complaints with the municipality about the food and food delivery services. As the complaints continued to roll in, political conflict spread.
>
> Here are a few illustrations of the intensity of the conflict. Before 1990, the social services committee had never discussed the provision of meals for seniors. In 1995, the 12 scheduled meetings in the committee all included the provision of meals to seniors on the agendas. Before 1992, the committee on ageing and disability had never discussed the provision of meals for seniors. In 1995, it was an agenda item at 10 meetings. Before 1992, the local media had never written about the provision of meals to seniors. In 1995, 16 articles appeared in local newspapers. The opposition repeatedly demanded explanations from the mayor about the case. The municipal council included ISS performance on their meeting agenda. The media reported from the meetings. A research company, Vilstrup Research, was hired to conduct an objective analysis of user satisfaction with the provided meals. The media portrayed the report as indicative of conflict, and of failure of governance in the municipal council. The municipal council appointed a test eating committee consisting of prominent members such as the social services manager. The committee visited different nursing home kitchens each week to try the food and reported back to the social services committee, which put ISS on each of their meeting agendas and led to demands for more control. The case rolled on.
>
> ISS ultimately concluded that the heavy media coverage of the catering case in Lyngby-Taarbæk was threatening to undermine the image of the entire ISS group, and subsequently chose to pull out of the contract. The question is, how did a well-planned outsourcing project get so out of hand? One answer might be that it had to integrate many different communicative codes, which easily leads to conflict. There were at least three codes in play in the case of ISS in Lyngby-Taarbæk.

First, the codes of the political system: govern/governed and government/opposition. The municipal outsourcing of responsibilities to ISS represented a management decision, which meant that ISS was subsequently perceived by the municipal administration as one among many other implementing units, that is, as governed – the municipality governs, ISS is governed. The political communication system entails an ongoing struggle to assume the position of governing power, and this struggle divides the world into government and opposition according to which all communication is designed to win government rule (in a municipality this would mean the mayor's office and the majority in the municipal council). An often-effective strategy in this process is for the opposition to try to expose the government as ineffective. This was the strategy employed by the minority in Lyngby-Taarbæk which was also further supported by the fact that the municipality was receiving monthly reports from the consultancy firm IMM about ISS failures to comply with the contract terms. The opposition naturally interpreted such failure to comply with a failure of governance on the mayor's part. Subsequently, the mayor then had to demonstrate vigour and governance power by reprimanding ISS in a way that was visible to the opposition, as if ISS was a subordinate and disobedient administrative organ.

Second, the case involves the economic code, to have/not have. ISS is primarily connected to the economic code. To the company, assuming responsibilities for municipal kitchens did not represent a governance decision, but first and foremost an economic decision, indicating that it would be financially beneficial to ISS and the municipality to have ISS run the kitchens. From this perspective, outsourcing means that ISS takes over the kitchens. They are given the authority to manage them. The subsequent scolding of ISS by the mayor and the municipal administration as if they were being governed simply made no sense to ISS. The company did not see itself as a part of the municipal hierarchy but as an independent organisation. To ISS, the complaint only makes sense as a disagreement over payment, not as the rebuke of a subordinate.

Finally, the case involved the code of mass media: information/non-information. From the perspective of the media, the Lyngby-Taarbæk case represented a goldmine of stories. It comprised an abundance of conflict. And because it was easy to perceive the local events as a symptom of national controversies about outsourcing, the future of the welfare state and corporate greed, the local news story was quickly transformed into a national new story, which accelerated general interest in the case.

At the same time, nobody consciously reflected on the fact that the case involved many different communicative codes. Communication about the case was marked by a monocontextual idea of the world as identical with its appearance. There was no awareness of the existence of other observers who held other perspectives and to whom the case appeared differently. The effect of this was that internal contradictions were transformed into an independent conflict system with a life of its own, irrespective of the conflict participants. None of the involved participants were in control of the conflict, which meant that no one was able to either bring it to an end or give it direction. Instead, the conflict consumed increasing attention from all involved parties.

Thus, almost all welfare institutions are placed in a situation in which they are required to weigh at least three or four different considerations: their 'original welfare function', the law, economy and one additional welfare concern.

In conclusion, our diagnosis is that many welfare organisations have become heterophonic in the sense that they no longer simply connect to one primary social system. The traditional homophonic organisation holds one primary connection to one social system. Its professional competences and specialised language remain stable in its self-description and self-programming. The shift from organisational homophony to heterophony means that an increasing number of organisations no longer limit themselves to one primary connection to one social system.

The relation between organisational system and function system is defined by contingency, and one of the effects of the shift toward heterophonic organisations is that this contingency becomes visible within the organisation. An organisation can be said to be heterophonic when it connects to several social systems without a pre-defined concept of a primary connection. Thus, heterophonic organisations always comprise a multiplicity of interests, functions and professional competencies and do not operate with a horizon of premises for the regulation of choice of connectivity. Heterophonic organisations contain a surplus of possible perspectives on any given situation and question. Whenever their perspective on specific interests changes, so does the way they perceive problems and possible solutions. A hospital, for example, may be approached by a patient who is so severely overweight that it poses a health risk to that person. From the perspective of medicine, solutions may include surgical reduction of the stomach. But from the perspective of pedagogy, a solution would be to educate the patient about daily eating and exercise habits, and to teach the patient to prepare and eat food in new ways. From the perspective of the care system, the patient may be seen as a person with low self-esteem, and possible interventions could be creating an opportunity for the patient to achieve a sense of accomplishment in their life (Knudsen and Højlund, 2012; Knudsen, 2012b; Højlund and La Cour, 2015). Each perspective shifts the boundary of what is perceived as public administration and what is not, and thus also changes the organisational game board. We could say that welfare institutions have developed a strategic approach to their function, professional competencies and objective. They are compelled to continually ask questions such as: what will a hospital look like in the future? What is a museum, a school, a university, a defense system, a social services administration? And depending on the answer, different modes of connection to social systems become central so that the interface between public administration and society has to be continually interrogated (Andersen, 2003b, 2008a, 2008b; Villadsen, 2008; Andersen and Born, 2007a; Rennison, 2007a, 2007b; Storm, 2010; Roth, 2012; Thygesen and Andersen, 2012; Rodger, 2013; Andersen and Knudsen, 2014; Knudsen and Vogd, 2015; Schirmer and Michailakis, 2015).

From the perspective of the organisation, heterophony means the availability of a growing number of media to a growing number of organisations. Not only are these media available to communication about specific functionally delimited themes but also to the overall organisational self-description. A heterophonic organisation cannot choose to 'departmentalise' its connections to a number of function systems to only concern sub-systems in the organisation. Therefore, the heterophonic organisation is also characterised by its continual effort to create a primary coding. Or in other words, the organisation has to continually make decisions about its choice of communication medium, and the specific medium required for the continuation of the decision communication can never be decided in advance. Such decisions are crucial since the symbolically generalised media operate by means of binary codes, which initiate their motivational and reflexive values. Each time a different code is chosen, the perspective on the decision, the organisation and surrounding world also changes. Thus, the heterophonic organisation is characterised by clashes between incompatible values and by the fact that no single value can capture and represent the unity of the others. Any attempt to install a super-value only adds to the polyphonic complexity. A super-value would quickly fall to the level of other values and would only add yet another connection to another function system with a new medium and new code. The basic strategic problem for the heterophonic organisation is to create and recreate its own horizon of premises.

If we observe the heterophonic organisation from the perspective of the individual function system, the effect is a loss of obvious relevance. When an organisation changes from homophony to heterophony, it causes the previously primary function system that served as the basis of the organisational self-

Figure 5.3: Heterophonic welfare organisation

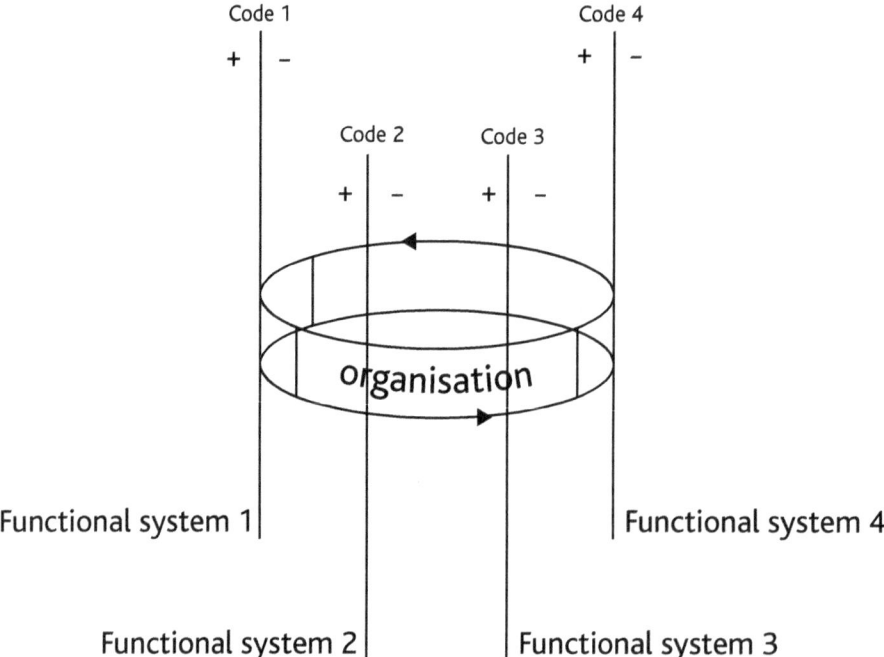

description to no longer remain obvious. It suddenly finds itself competing with other function systems and runs the risk of being excluded at the expense of another function system, for example, if an economic interest is given more focus than a care interest in a social administration, or if a preschool prioritises a learning objective above a care consideration. In public debates this question has been framed as the displacement of core competencies and concerns, particularly by economic considerations. There is no longer a given structure for how to base an objective premise for a decision. This means that an objective premise cannot be established without exposing the underlying exclusion of alternative interests and objective considerations.

One might assume that this would put the manager of a public institution in the position of having to decide which codes the institution should form in particular situations, and hence which concerns to address. However, for that to be possible there would have to be a place within the institution from which the manager could observe the organisation and its codes from the outside. Such a place does not exist. Management always takes place by connecting to a particular code and the problem remains the same as on a societal level: there is no place within the organisation from which to represent the organisation as a whole, since the organisation appears differently depending on whether it observes itself from the perspective of the economic code, the legal code, the code of care, etc (Andersen and Born, 2007a). If an organisation is observed from the perspective of law, one sees a formal structure. If the organisation is observed from the perspective of pedagogy, one sees projects. Observing the organisation from the perspective of economy causes one to see a long-term exchange, etc. Thus, in a sense, the heterophonic welfare organisation is a stranger in its own house. Its self-description has multiplied and it has to be simultaneously one and many. Its institutional identity traits are under partial erasure.

Table 5.2: The relationship between communicative code and possible organisational self-description

Code	Organisational image
Right/wrong	Perceived as a formal structure, as a hierarchical frame for decisions and competencies
Better/worse educationally	Perceived as a project and a resource container. References to pedagogy allow for considerations of the role of the individual within the project
Loved/not loved	Seen as an emotional and physical reproduction unit similar to families or other primary groups. The reference to love opens up an expressive space: a shift from society to community
To have/not have	Appears as a long-term exchange, a reduction of transaction costs and a reference signalling resourcefulness, both internally and externally
Power-superior/power-inferior	A sovereign domain for the organisation of decisions and political reference signals decision-making capacity

Assuming the validity of this diagnosis, we are left with the following management challenges:

- What does management mean in the absence of a super-code for weighing the value of the various codes against each other and when any attempt to constitute a super-code simply leads to the import of yet another interest, which does not preside above but adds itself to the many existing interests?
- If management means the ability to represent the unity of the organisation, what does management do when the organisational unity continues to change depending on the specific code?
- How does one avoid leaving the prioritisation of incompatible interests up to personal whim because of the lack of objective criteria?
- How can decisions be evaluated when the criteria for evaluating changes depending on the code?

Communication-seeking organisation

The shift from the heterophonic organisation toward the communication-seeking organisation can be described primarily as a shift from heterophony as a challenge in relation to the prioritisation of incompatible interests to heterophony as an organisational resource for the production of possibilities. From the perspective of the communication-seeking organisation, function systems can be seen as an open reservoir through which the organisation can experiment with itself. This organisation constantly explores the potential of the different function systems in order to articulate questions, make a case, describe the organisation, formulate strategies, and so on (see also Knudsen and Højlund, 2012). This is the *communication-seeking potentiality-producing organisation*.

The emergence of this new form of organisation takes place at the same time as what we, in the first diagnosis, described as the growing tendency in function systems toward a model of hyper-reflection between the systems and something else; for example, pedagogy that seeks to both value learning and play power that seeks to empower, health treatment that prefers to be health-promoting, etc. From within the individual function system's communication about its internal affairs, we see the articulation of the dependence on other function systems, whose characteristics remain undefined, complex and multiple, meaning that individual function systems describe their reliance on other function systems, but do so in an indefinite and ambiguous way. This reliance is described as open, complex (dependent on many factors) and multiple (not only reliant on one function system but many). Thus, for example, when pedagogy makes use of play, learning is made to depend on the social and psychological atmosphere in which learning takes place, on the children's background, level of integration, parents' background and employment status, etc. The communication-seeking organisation is perceived as the response to undefined, complex and diverse dependencies among function systems that seek to be what they are not and cannot be.

The call for a communication-seeking organisation can, as an example, be seen in Danish governments' health programmes since 1999, where non-health-related perspectives are incorporated as a way to support health-promoting efforts. The first sustained formulation of this model can be found in the government's public health programme from 1999: 'The public health programme is designed to ensure political accountability for effectively prioritising and coordinating preventative efforts across sectors, administrative levels and competencies. For that reason, it stresses collaboration in areas where we currently see grey areas for accountability' (Sundhedsministeriet [Ministry of Health], 1999, p 6, own translation; for a more in-depth analysis of the programme, see Højlund and Larsen, 2001). This approach means that heath policies have to be defined as horizontal and cross-sectoral. Instead of working through their own institutions, health programmes are compelled to try to implement their policies through other institutions, public and private. The document points out four so-called prevention environments through which the public health programme must be implemented: primary education, the workplace, local communities and the healthcare system. In relation to primary education, the document says: 'Primary education must serve as a health-promoting environment and provide students with tools to promote their own health and the health of others' (Sundhedsministeriet [Ministry of Health], 1999, p 8).

The result is that it becomes increasingly difficult to delimit health issues. The government's idea manual for its public health programme illustrates the complex figure this way (see Figure 5.4).

Figure 5.4: A model for health in a social context

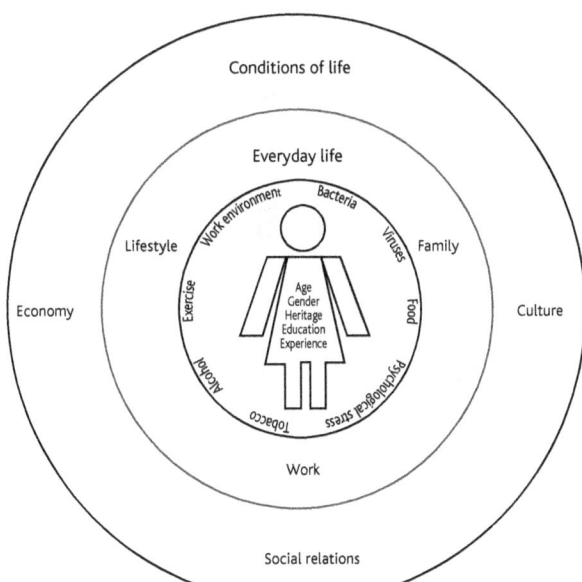

The model indicates the difficulties of delimiting health issues. The health of an individual is seen as an effect of immediate health risks such as tobacco, alcohol and diet. These are the effect of specific daily routines including family, work and lifestyle, which is further affected by broader conditions in society – social, economic and cultural.

This means that the healthcare system acknowledges the necessity of non-health-related perspectives. Individuals are expected to assume a greater responsibility for their health although communication from the Danish Ministry of Health suggests that the willingness and ability to assume such responsibility depends on the individual's level of education, employment status, family situation, economy, culture, and so on. This raises a new question: how can the healthcare system insist on personal health responsibility while acknowledging the complexity both of individual health and of the person's capacity to take responsibility? Is it possible to insist on health responsibility knowing the individual's general health may benefit more if they disregard their health and focus on finding employment? These are the complexities that health organisations now have to respond to. Health organisations are expected to seek out the most effective codes for the production of possibilities in relation to a given problem.

A number of new buzzwords emerge together with the communication-seeking organisation: interprofessionality, relational coordination, relational bureaucracy, collaborative professionalism, social capital, core competencies and core task. They all call for flexible organisational couplings of different communicative codes and functions. 'Interprofessionality' as an example is articulated as a method for bridging and integrating professions with a focus on the individual citizen. Danielle D'Amour and Ivy Oandasan explain it like this:

> In the same manner that disciplines have developed, so too have numerous professions, defined by fragmented disciplinary specific knowledge. Each profession owns a professional jurisdiction or scope of practice, which impacts the delivery of services. This silo-like division of professional responsibilities is rarely naturally nor cohesively integrated in a manner, which meets the needs of both the clients and the professionals. The notion of interprofessionality is useful to direct our attention to the emergence of a more cohesive and less fragmented interprofessional practice. This does not imply the development of new professions, but rather a means by which professionals can practice in a more collaborative or integrated fashion. This distinction separates interprofessionality from interdisciplinarity. (D'Amour and Oandasan, 2005)

Jody Gittell is the driving force behind another leading concept, namely, 'relational coordination'. She defines it like this:

In contrast to the traditional bureaucratic form of coordination that is carried out primarily by managers at the top of functional silos, relational coordination is carried out via direct contact among workers at the front line, through networks that cut across functional silos at the point of contact with the customer. Relational coordination thus improves performance of a work process by improving the work relationships between people (shared goals, shared knowledge, mutual respect) who perform different functions in that work process, leading to higher-quality communication. Task interdependencies are therefore managed more directly, in a more seamless way, with fewer redundancies, lapses, errors, and delays. (Gittell, 2011b, p 402)

Emphasising 'Communicating and relating for the purpose of task integration', Gittell draws the organisation as built up around the single citizen, as here, where patients re put at the centre of a flexible network of professionals (Gittell, 2011a) (see Figure 5.5).

Figure 5.5: Patients at the centre

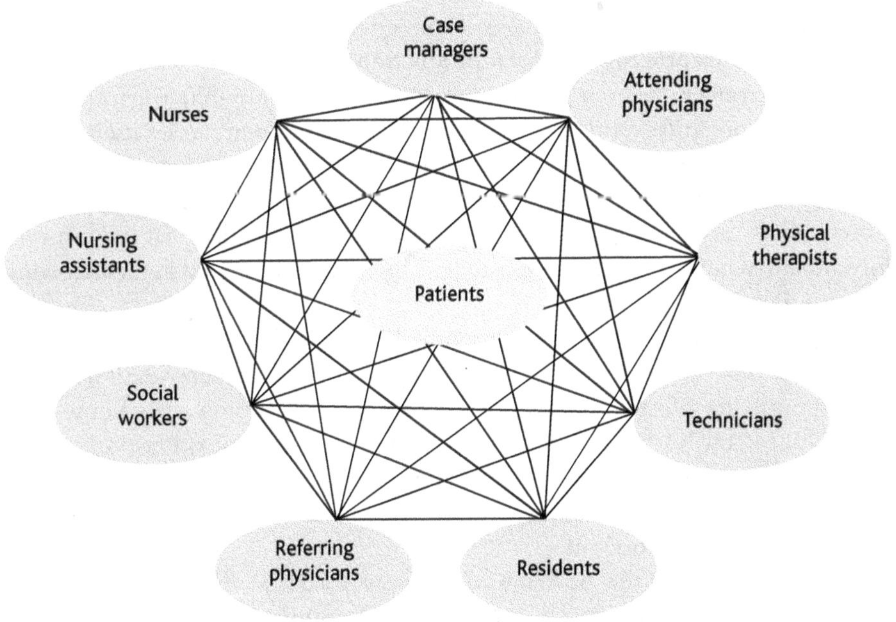

The citizen is installed at the centre as the empty nodal point, wherein a number of perspectives has to be integrated in distinctive ways, from case to case.

In Denmark, the equivalent buzzword is 'core task'. This theme has matured over the last 10 years, as more and more local governments reorganise their welfare institutions with a point of departure in the concept of 'core task'. The basic idea is that public organisations should not be organised around functions but around the core task.

This could appear as a way of reducing the growing complexity of the public sector. However, it is, in fact, quite the opposite. The concept of the core task makes it possible to produce even more complexity by inviting in ever more professional perspectives in relation to welfare production and tasks.

In a discussion paper entitled, 'Core tasks for and with citizens', the concept of core task is defined in the following way: 'the main task of a given organisational unit is to create long term effects.... The core task is not the same as the specific tasks and services ... it need to be abstract and detached from the concrete work tasks and services' (Teamarbejdsliv og Center for Industriel Produktion [Team Work Life and Centre for Industrial Production], 2014, p 3).

Which question is the core task an answer to? The core task is defined so that it indicates a common orientation yet sufficiently abstract to allow for the differences of different professional perspectives. As is written in the same discussion paper: 'In almost every area the core task demands different professional approaches and different functions.... Collaboration between the different professional groups and functions is necessary. It is therefore important that all professional groups and functions figure out how they contribute to the core task and not least how they collaborate' (Teamarbejdsliv og Center for Industriel Produktion [Team Work Life and Centre for Industrial Production], 2014, p 3).

With the concept of core task we get an image of the public organisation as an emergent organisation that only in a forthcoming way organises itself around the core tasks. The core task can only function as a core task if it is empty, that is, without a core. The ideal is a fluid organisation without a lasting structure. Every single task needs its own organisation, which in a relational fashion calls forward different professional perspectives. This is often illustrated in the following way (see Figure 5.6).

In Figure 5.6, the core task is at the centre. Professionals are to constantly search for possible contributions from the different professional perspectives. It becomes the responsibility of each member of the organisation to offer their knowledge and skills, to collaborate and to invite in and make space for other professional groups. The outside of professional collaboration is marked as an ever-changing context of citizens, technology and politicians, which means that the core task must repeatedly by rethought.

What characterises the descriptions of core tasks in contemporary public organisations is that they reach out for their 'constitutive outside' that cannot be determined, controlled or governed. In schools the core task is no longer teaching, but learning and development. In elderly care, the core task is no longer simply service delivery, but efforts to help the individual regain an independent and meaningful life. Teaching can be seen, controlled and assessed, but learning and development are not immediately visible. What occurs in the mind of the individual pupil is hidden and cannot be controlled from the outside. Schools can teach, but learning only happens in the consciousness of the individual.

Figure 5.6: The core task at the centre

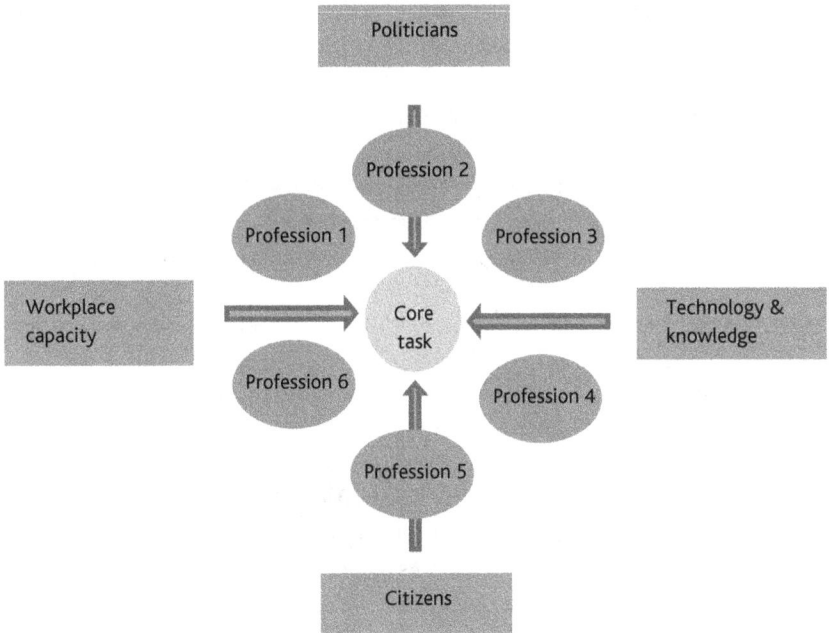

Source: Reconstructed from a presentation conducted by Team Work Life (see also Albertsen et al, 2012)

Similarly, service delivery is visible and can be controlled, but the quality of life and the social relations of the individual remain outside the reach of organisational control. What happens when some core goals are defined so that they cannot be seen, assessed, controlled and achieved? Perhaps the tragic of such definitions of the core task is also productive in that it forces the public sector to constantly search for new potentiality in observing a problem from other perspectives (see the municipality of Holbæk Kommune, 2014). It seems that indeterminate descriptions become functional when public organisations are to juggle a not yet defined and delineated multiplicity of perspectives and codes (Müller and von Groddeck, 2013).

> **Example 5.3: The hash conversation**
> 'The hash conversation' is a dialogue concept that was published in 2005 by the Danish Committee for Health Education. It is designed for use by professionals in a variety of welfare organisations that work with young people. It is a highly nuanced and complex concept, and its purpose is described as 'providing youth with more nuanced and flexible perspectives on smoking hash in order to assist young people in creating positive changes for themselves.'

The concept emphasises that there are different perspectives on hash, and that this should be a basic premise for professionals seeking to have a conversation about hash with young people. The observer-dependence of hash use is illustrated by means of two statements about hash by two different health professionals. "I don't believe it is appropriate to use the word 'treatment' in the context of hash", a prevention consultant says. "Hash cannot be abused." A manager of a treatment facility has a different view: "I take hash usage very seriously. Hash is much more dangerous than heroin and cocaine." Thus, the fact that hash is observer-dependent does not simply refer to a distinction between professionals and clients, but rather to the existence of different perspectives from which hash can be considered.

The concept clearly references three different codifications of hash: a *pedagogical coding*, which is about shifting the approach to hash among young people, a *medical coding*, which is about the health effects of hash, and a *care coding*, which is about how to help young people overcome social problems, where hash is merely one aspect among many others. Moreover, the concept stresses the importance of having an 'open and equal dialogue', meaning that all three forms of coding have to function in a restrained way. Pedagogical communication should not lecture. Medical communication should not be perceivable as treatment. And care communication should not be patronising. As noted, 'it is not a question of treatment but of having a dialogue based on trust.' And further, 'the adult should be able to have a discussion based on exact information and knowledge without railroading the young people with emotional prohibitions and raised fingers.'

This means that the conversation and its premises have to be established from within the conversation. The conversation becomes communication-seeking. The specific code it uses is determined by what creates openings in the conversation. Because it can never be taken for granted that the young person will connect to the conversation, the concept does not define premises for the conversation but establishes methods for seeking out communication potential. Thus, the codes represent a repertoire rather than fixed premises. The baseline is that change is a question of the young person's self-change. What the conversation offers young people is a space for reflection and articulation.

The concept contains different techniques for seeking out communication. One of these is called 'The structure of the conversation'. It crosses two continuums in a diagram: the horizontal axis goes from hash use to problems, and the vertical axis moves from the general to the specific. The idea is to seek out communication opportunities with young people by switching between the four positions in the diagram, for example, by switching between talking about general information about hash and the specific experience of the young people. The important thing is to avoid statements such as 'Because this applies to another, it also applies to you'. Instead, the conversation model should be: 'This applies to many – how is it in your case?' Another inquiry technique uses a figure with two intersecting circles. One circle is named 'hash use'; the other is called 'problems'. The intersection of the two circles is called 'exploration'. The point is that the relationship between hash usage and problems cannot be given prior to the conversation: 'the intersection is the object of a shared exploration

> and discussion. It is important to not have any unambiguous truth before the discussion.' Thus, the conversation explores the possibilities and boundaries of the conversation. A third exploratory technique invites the young person to describe their relationship to hash usage using a diagram with four spaces: benefits of continued use, disadvantages of continued use, benefits of quitting, and disadvantages of quitting. These three techniques are employed to continually keep communication open, alive and under investigation for communicative opportunities, and to ensure its ability to move freely among the many perspectives. The evolution and continuation of communication is prioritised above the specific choice of perspectives and codes.

Whereas the heterophonic organisation causes the function systems to enter into a form of competition with one another when the organisation weighs heterogeneous interests against each other, the communication-seeking organisation represents an even more radical development. First, the it can be connected to more potential function systems because it continually scans its environment for possible connections. But more significantly, it is not merely a question of prioritising interests but of exploring communication potential and alternative definitions of the problem–solution relations. And the organisation expects not only that the function systems make themselves available, but also that they reduce the risk of connectivity by continually making dis-connection possible – not unlike the above hash talk example, which does not establish an automatic connection between diagnosis and treatment, or social problem and social intervention. It is not simply a question of competing informational contributions to the organisation's decision machine, but a further complication of the process of establishing factual premises since the organisation refuses to choose between them. It rejects fixed decision premises because it wants to avoid reducing communicative potentiality and wants to afford each operation the opportunity to explore premise effects before establishing premises. In this way we might say that factuality is incorporated after the decision has been made. Factual premises should not be permitted to inhibit the communication-seeking operation.

The communication-seeking organisation adds further challenges to the heterophonic organisation:

- How to seek out communicative possibilities without a localisable position 'outside' the communication from which to observe it?
- How to take responsibility for communication (the organisation) and control it without prescribing the premises for which interests to favour?
- How can a welfare organisation govern without standing in the way as impractical (monophonic) decision premises for decision processes, which continue to seek out communicative possibilities and alternative decision codes?
- What are the conditions for organising when the relation between decision premises (the choice of codes) and decisions are temporarily inverted? Does

this make of the organisation a subsequent rationalised self-description, assigned to decisions after they have been made?

Figure 5.7: Communication-seeking organisation

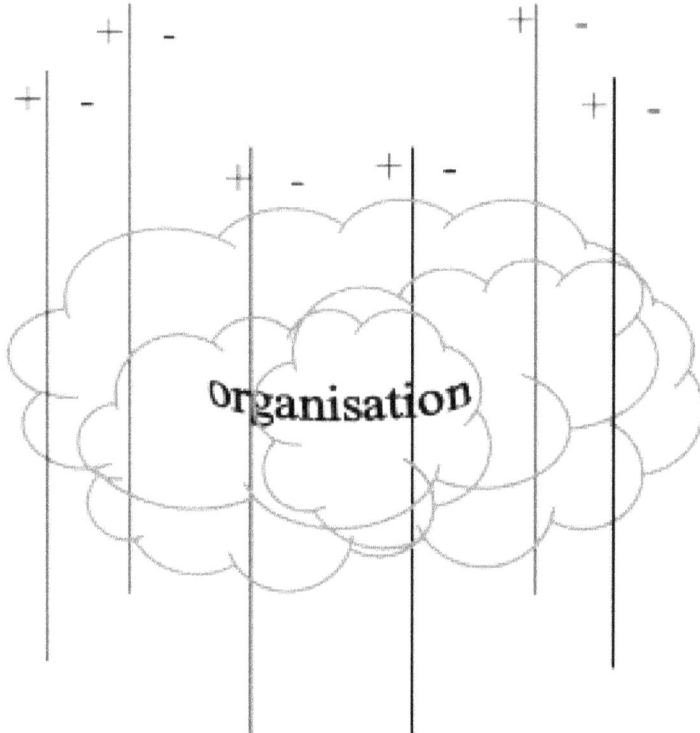

The shifts that take us from the formal to the communication-seeking organisation change the relationship between welfare organisations and their specific professional competencies. Today, a psychiatric ward can no longer maintain a natural or unambiguous relationship to treatment. Similarly, a daycare facility can no longer conceive of its mission solely as caring for children. Welfare organisations are continually engaged in exploring the ways in which their professional competency can be aided by other professional competencies, and how their professional knowledge and capacity serve as part of the solution to problems in other fields.

As described, in recent years there have been increasing calls for welfare organisations to focus more on their core responsibilities. It has been described as a return to the origins, to what really matters, to the original professional areas of expertise. However, the problem is that it is no longer possible to conceive a return to a simple idea of welfare organisations as constructed around a singular professional competence whose content is given and known. The debate about the centrality of core responsibilities might be surfacing today *precisely because* we have irrevocably lost the ability to have an uncomplicated relationship to the concept of core responsibility.

In the context of eldercare services, the ideal of focusing on the citizen has been articulated as the opportunity for professionals to rediscover their professional core values after a decade of focusing on quality in terms of allotted minutes and descriptions entered into documentation systems. Care workers are finally permitted to return to their education and make use of their central competences: caring for and helping citizens in need. Similarly, central actors in the area of education such as Local Government Denmark, the central organisation for Danish municipalities, the Danish Ministry of Education, the Danish Union of Teachers and the union for elementary school principals have called for learning to serve (again) as the dominant driving force in education policies, planning and management. This ambition is put forth as an effort to cut back bureaucracy and hence to respect the primary objective of education, which should not be tainted by what has been criticised as an 'economy of voyeurism', meaning a system in which onlookers (politicians and administration) make the decisions.

And indeed, these shifts do signify a resuscitation – or at least a reference to – a traditional and familiar pedagogical concept of care and learning, which is that learning takes place not only in the classroom but also in every other context of a child's life. However, the fact that politicians and administrative professionals now base educational policies on that basis signals a shift. It means that what had previously served as the object of political governance, which in the case of education meant the school as an organisation providing educational services in the form of lessons, is suddenly perceived as insufficient in itself and has to be revitalised by providing educational services in the form of play, activities, collaboration with afterschool programmes, etc. It represents, on the one hand, a renewed interest in the professional competences of the teacher, but at the same time, also signals an opening toward a radical renegotiation of how to mark the boundaries between teachers and social education professionals, or how to determine the distribution of roles between teachers and volunteer organisers of swim teams, etc. Although it would appear that renewed focus on the school as a place of learning would represent a return to core values, it ultimately results in a new sense of ambiguity and an obvious need to redefine the concept of teacher and of social educator.

This also means that the language of core task effectively transforms conditions of accountability in welfare organisations. Although the idea of core responsibility seems to present itself as a means to make the professional knowledge and judgement count in decision-making, in fact it dissolves or at least postpones the possibility of professional accountability. When welfare organisations are expected to create themselves as communication-seeking organisations, professional judgement serves as a means to test and produce possibilities rather than as premises for decision-making. The question emerges: how can responsibility be assigned when that which is to be taken responsibility for can only be identified, described and delimited after the professional decision has been taken?

Thus, when the public sector today calls for a renewed focus on *core values*, it is precisely because welfare organisations have irrevocably lost the possibility of an unambiguous and simple conception of their core values and responsibilities.

> **Reflection box 5: The communication-seeking organisation**
> Ask yourself:
>
> 1. Which codes exist in your organisation? How is the choice of code decided?
> 2. What happens to 'the case' when the code changes? How does this transform the space of decision?
> 3. Which conflicts occur in your organisation?
> 4. Do you sense a hierarchy of codes, so that one code (for example, economy) dominates the others?
> 5. How do you feel about the force of exclusion inherent in the insistence on a specific code?
> 6. How do you discuss and manage the balancing of incompatible interests?
> 7. Do heterophonic demands in your organisation challenge professional autonomy or professional accountability?
> 8. Do you view certain codes as opportunities and others as limitations and necessities? How does this affect your management space?
> 9. How do you juggle codes so as to not miss out on communicative opportunities, for example, at meetings?

SIX

From contract to partnership

We have described the gradual differentiation of society. We have shown changes to notions of temporality in organisations due to 'the logic of adaptability'. And we have provided a description of the disassembly of hierarchical structures in the public sector and a development in the direction of a rather complex potentiality-seeking public administration dependent on independent welfare institutions that continually question themselves. Finally, we have described a shift from homophonic to communication-seeking organisations.

Such shifts also include radical changes to the conditions of possibility for horizontal relations among welfare institutions. Today, we have a great number of independent welfare institutions – public, private and voluntary – each with its specific programmes and strategies. At the same time, each individual case involves numerous welfare institutions. In certain cases, the involvement of welfare institutions can be arranged successively (for example, one institution refers a citizen, then the citizen is sent to another institution for treatment, and finally the citizen is sent to an institution for rehabilitation). However, in many cases the case requires simultaneity among institutions. An at-risk child changes school. The change of school and the question of the successful integration of the child activates a number of different institutions, which are designed to support the child in different ways while still pulling in the same direction – the psychologist from the counselling centre, the municipal social worker, the police officer from the social services collaboration unit, a health professional, youth workers and teachers, and, of course, the school principal. The orchestration of the many institutions also involves a great number of heterogeneous interests and logics from different function systems. And because each case is considered unique, there are no clear standards for which institutions to bring together and how to connect or not connect the various interests and considerations.

Altogether, we see a simultaneous increase in differentiation and independence, increasing dependence across function systems and welfare organisations, as well as increasing needs for flexibility. The question is, how can increasingly complex dependencies among welfare institutions be managed? How can mutual expectations among welfare institutions be created when the premise is constantly shifting expectations? How can collaboration among welfare institutions be built when the collaboration has to include sufficient plasticity to be formed in many different communicative media?

At the heart of these questions, we find the concept of contract and contractualisation. In this chapter we focus on how the developments pursued in former chapters rely on and produce certain forms of contractualisation. More specifically, we argue that with the emergence of the supervision and potentiality administration we also get new forms of contractual relations in the public sector. What happens is a re-entry of the form of organisation into the form of contract so that we get so-called trust-related partnerships (Stelling, 2014) that function as potentialisation machines.

Somehow the concepts of contract and the contractualisation of the public sector could have been the core theme of this book. Since the 1980s, almost all relations in the public sector have been transformed by some sort of contractualisation (Vincent-Jones, 2006). Heuristically, the trend of contractualisation can be put into a matrix like this (see Table 6.1).

Table 6.1: Typology of contractualisation

	Internal	External
Individual	Management contracts Performance contracts Competence contracts	Citizens contracts
Organisational	Internal contracts	Contracting out Outsourcing Public–private partnerships Partnerships

Individual-internal contractualisation. For quite some years, the trend has been to introduce contracts as a steering technology in relations between the organisation and the individual employee. The organisation makes one-year contracts with the managers about their managerial objectives. Performance interviews between manager and employee often take a point of departure in performance contracts including task and objectives, but also goals and commitments concerning the single employee's personal self-development (see more about this in Chapter Seven).

Individual-external contractualisation. Since the 1990s, public administration has made contracts with the single citizen. Unemployment administration begins to make employment-seeking contracts with unemployed citizens. Social workers make integration contracts with immigrants including themes of education, language learning, jobseeking and parental skills (see more about this in Chapter Eight).

Organisation-internal contractualisation. Since the mid-1980s, power-superior institutions in the public sector have made contracts with power-inferior institutions, sometimes about results and objectives and at other times about strategic developments. They might be internal contracts between ministries and agencies or between municipalities and the single welfare institution (as discussed earlier in Chapter Three).

Organisation-external contractualisation. Since the beginning of the 1980s, we have witnessed privatisation and marketisation where the public sector uses private entrepreneurs. The processes have often taken the form of contracting out or of public–private partnerships. However, a quite different form of external contractualisation is long-term and trust-based partnerships that have more strategic, innovative and project-oriented goals rather than simple service delivery. These partnerships might be between public organisations and private companies, but they might as well be between public organisations from different sectors or between public and volunteer organisations.

In most cases, contractualisation does not simply mean that the hierarchy (state) is substituted or supplemented with contracts (market). In most cases the form of contract undergoes radical transformations, thus changing the very rules of the game of government and public administration. Beginning with the difference hierarchy/contract, the transformations basically go in two directions (we follow here Gunther Teubner's brilliant works – see Teubner, 1988, 1996, 2000).

In the first form of transformation the difference hierarchy/contract is re-entered into the hierarchy, thus producing a kind of hierarchical organised contract. Hierarchy indicates unilateral statements. Contracts, on the other hand, indicate mutual relations. The re-entry produces contracts in the form of a unilateral call for mutuality. For example, a power-superior administration may invite the power-inferior citizen to make a contract with the administration, saying 'You can either collaborate with us and say yes to our offer of a dialogue and a mutual contract or we will unilaterally make the decision for you.' Another example might be internal contracting communicating, 'Do as we say – be autonomous', as discussed in Chapter Three. We might call this hybrid transformation of the contract 'hierarchical contracts'.

In the second form of transformation the difference hierarchy/contract is re-entered into the contract, making a kind of self-organised contract. Here the mutual agreement includes an organisation of its own in such a way that the contracts are simultaneously a result of contracting between autonomous organisations and a result of autonomous processes within the contract itself. The contract includes procedures for how to change itself. Long-term partnerships are the typical example here. They are more agreements about shared future-orienteered projects than agreements on simple transactions. Partnerships re-enter the form of organisation into the form of contract by developing the contract into a second-order contract that makes promises about future promises. Gunther Teubner calls this 'controrgs' (Teubner, 1996, 2002) (see Figure 6.1).

In the following, we primarily look at the development of the second form of contratualisation, the so-called 'controg'. Our focus is the emergence and implications of long-term trust-based partnerships. Such partnerships are central to the argument of this book because they create a particular machine of potentialisation as an answer to the question of how to manage relations between mutual autonomous welfare institutions belonging to different sectors of society, how to form symbolic medias from different functions systems and how to meet the demands for radical flexibility.

Figure 6.1: Two forms of contractual hybrids

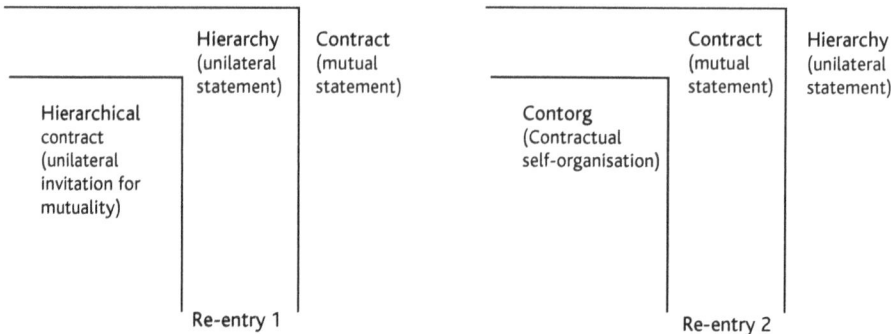

General observations about the contract as a bilateral form

We can observe a contract as the unity of obligation and freedom (Luhmann, 1981, p 249). A contract communicates about bilateral obligations. It is a promise about the exchange of obligations. However, the communication of obligation always presupposes the freedom of the contract partners. A contract negotiation might not explicitly articulate the partners' status as free subjects, but this status is nevertheless always presupposed, since freedom is a precondition of the partners' ability to commit themselves. Being forced to do something is not a contract. Force does not produce obligation, and hence obligation makes no sense without freedom. Obligations both limit and presuppose freedom. Or, as Durkheim notes: 'The only undertakings worthy of the name are those that are desired by individuals whose sole origin is this free act of the will. Conversely, any obligation that has not been agreed upon by both sides is not in any way contractual' (Durkheim, 2013, p 158). Thus, a contract represents a voluntary limitation of one's freedom.

However, a contract also always represents multiplicity, since the bilateral obligations are always perceived differently by the contract partners. Derrida argues that,

> ... you can only enter into a contract ... if you do so in your own tongue. You're only responsible, in other words, for what you say in your own mother tongue. If however, you say it in your own tongue, then you are still not committed, because you must also say it in the other's language. An agreement or obligation of whatever sort – a promise, a marriage, a sacred alliance – can only take place, I would say, in translation, that is, only if it is simultaneously uttered in both my tongue and the other's.... There is no contract possible – no social

> contract possible – without a translation contract, bringing with it the paradox I have just mentioned. (Derrida, 1988, p 125)

In other words, contracts can only maintain their unity by being a multiplicity. Obligation has to always be read by the free subject. Otherwise the contract is no longer the 'voluntary limitation of one's freedom'. This means that obligation must be read in the language of the contract subject. And since there is more than one contract subject, the contract in turn becomes a meeting place for those languages. If one of the languages forces itself on the others as the unambiguous interpretation of the obligations, the contract ceases to be a contract. A contract is a meeting place for languages, which, qua their encounter, double the mutual obligation.

In systems theoretical terms, we might say that a contract functions as a structural coupling between communication systems that are otherwise closed to one another. As operatively closed systems, they must assign meaning to the contract in each their own way. But at the same time, the way in which one system perceives the contract as meaningful also has to make sense to the other involved systems. One system's interpretation has to be recognisable as obligation by the other system. The paradox, in other words, is that a contract needs to be both one and many at the same time. A contract between communication systems has to function as a collective contract as well as a contract for the individual system. A contract can only maintain its unity by also functioning as a multiplicity (Teubner, 1998, 2000).

The fact that a contract is both one and multiple means that it serves as a shore on which languages meet but do not merge. A contract is precisely not a collective. It can never represent a collective with a shared language and horizon since this would cause the very distinction between obligation and freedom to collapse. The form and multiplicity of a contract presupposes that the concept of the collective functions as the form's constitutive outside, that is, as the thing a contract can never be and up against which a contractual relationship is always defined.

In sum, a contract is the voluntary limitation of freedom, it is always multiple, and it functions, by way of its multiplicity, as a structural coupling of social systems. Over time, the forms of limitation and multiplicity have evolved with the result that the contract's function as structural coupling has become increasingly complex. We go on to draw a distinction between four different forms of contract that construct limitations in somewhat different ways and that have thus come to function as the answer to different functions of coupling (Teubner, 1988). We use the concept programme to describe the way in which limitation is articulated in contracts. We use the concept regulation to describe the different notions of regulation that apply to the different forms. The coupling function describes the way that the contract enables coupling between function systems. Order refers to a contract's internal complexity (see Table 6.2).

Table 6.2: Forms of contract

	Programme	Regulation	Coupling function	Order
Formal contracts	Conditional orientation	Behaviour	As structural coupling, a contract functions as a realisation machine so that specific events within a system can be captured as specific opportunities for the realisation of operations within another system	First-order contract (a promise)
Material contracts	Oriented toward purpose	Goals and results	The contract as structural coupling still serves as a realisation machine but more systems can be coupled and allow for greater autonomy	
Reflexive contracts	Procedural orientation	Interests	The contract as structural coupling allows for prioritisation of what cannot be prioritised. The contract establishes conditions for paradoxical collaboration	Second-order contract (a promise about subsequent promises)
Partnerships	Oriented toward potentiality	Possibilities	As structural coupling, the contract functions as a potentiality machine, which continually explores the possibilities for new collaboration	

Formal contracts

Formal contracts are programmed in accordance with conditional norms, which means that the obligations and promises agreed on by the contract partners are conditional and based on a set of if/then logics: if you deliver x, then you receive y. This also means that formal contracts represent commitments based solely on behaviour and actions – 'If you act in this way, I promise to act in this way'. The contract puts the organisation under obligation to take certain action. Or, put differently, formal contracts make certain reservations in relation to potential conflicts about promised action.

As coupling between organisations, a formal contract represents a specific kind of decision within individual organisational systems. A formal contract is an organisational decision to make some of the organisation's own decisions dependent on decisions made by another organisational system with regard to a specific question. Thus, as an organisational element, a contract functions as a decision premise that connects the organisation from within to operations in another organisation, that is, a decision that 'if organisation B behaves according to the contract, then we will also act according to the agreement'.

In order for the formal contract to serve as coupling between organisations, at the same time the contract has to be assigned economic and legal significance. Thus, the formal contract not only connects organisational systems; it also connects the legal and economic systems. Or more precisely, it is the coupling of economy and law that allows for the coupling of organisations. As the coupling between economy and law, the contract has to be able to be read and translated economically and legally in a unique way. In the legal system, communication uses the code right/wrong. From that perspective, a contract represents a promise, and as a promise the contract enables the law to judge an agreement conflict between organisations and to assess who is right and who is wrong. Communication in the economic system uses the code to pay/not pay, and from that perspective a contract is not a promise but an exchange between organisations, which is conditioned by payments.

While law and economy can provide the contract with internal meaning, they can also provide meaning for each other's readings of the contract. When the law observes economic communication about economic exchange, the law productively (mis)understands this communication as if it represented an exchange of promises. And when the economic system observes the law and its contractual promises, it simultaneously observes promises economically as transaction costs (Andersen, 2013a). This relationship can be summed up like this (see Table 6.3).

Table 6.3: Contractual coupling of law, economy and organisation

Communication system	Code	Contractual translation	Mutual observations of contractual observations
Legal	Right/wrong	Promise	Exchange as an exchange of promises
Economic	Pay/not pay	Exchange	Promises as transaction costs
Organisational	Decision	A decision to accept one's dependence on a specific organisation in the environment	The organisation is observed in economic terms as a nexus of contracts. The organisation is observed in legal terms as a formal organisation constituted by law

The formal contract and its specific mode of coupling law and economy allows the contract to function as a realisation machine for potential exchanges among organisations. If one organisation produces a surplus of nuts and bolts, for example, but in turn experiences a shortage of money, while another organisation has enough money but lacks nuts and bolts, then contracts create conditions for realising possibilities for exchange.

Material contracts

Material contracts also regulate the relationship between organisations. They make it possible to assign an organisational system greater freedom in the way that it fulfils its contractual obligation toward the other organisation. They replace conditional programmes with statements of purpose. Statements of purpose consist not of if/then sentences but of purpose/result sentences. The partners commit not to behaviour but to the fulfilment of specific goals and results, and this allows the contract partners greater methodological freedom in relation to

Example 6.1: The formal contract, 'a text between the lines'

In the early 1960s, Professor Stewart Macaulay carried out a series of empirical studies of contracts. He saw contracts as a nexus in a stream of communication participants:

> Those who negotiate the deal are often not the people who draft the written document recording it. Still others must perform the contract. This opens the possibility that, for example, a firm's lawyer may have different assumptions and expectations than its purchasing agents, sales people, and engineers. Strategy may be involved too. If I want a clause that says if event X takes place, then consequence Y will follow, you may demand something in exchange that I do not want to give you. When I anticipate this, it may be better to avoid raising the issue in negotiations and hope that the matter can be resolved if event X ever takes place…. In short, there are many reasons that the paper deal will fail to capture the real deal. As a matter of fact, there is a "text between the lines". (Macaulay, 2003, pp 46-7)

What Macaulay means by 'real deal' is 'both those actual expectations that exist in and out of a written contract and the generalised expectation that a trading partner will behave reasonably in solving problems as they arise' (Macaulay, 2003, p 46, note 6). With his contract-legal study, Macaulay opened up for investigation the formation of expectations in contract communication, both during the creation of a contract as well as in a contract's many communicative afterlives.

In 1963, Macaulay used a series of interviews to show that people who are tied to different organisational roles (salespeople, finance people, purchasing agents, lawyers and attorneys) conceive of a contract in entirely different ways (Macaulay, 1963a). Businesspeople are more likely to trust a man's word, even when a transaction involves significant risks. Lawyers, in turn, complain about this attitude. Macaulay quotes a lawyer from one of his interviews: 'Often businessmen do not feel they have "a contract" – rather, they have "an order." They speak of "cancelling the order" rather than "breaching our contract"' (Macaulay, 1963b, p 61). Another businessman says: 'You can settle any dispute if you leave the lawyers and accountants out of it. They just do not understand the give-and-take needed in business' (quoted in Macaulay, 1963b, p 61). Businesspeople and salespeople prefer a word for a word. They 'often do not, exhibit great care in drafting contracts, pay much attention to those that lawyers carefully draft, or honor a legal approach to business relationships' (Macaulay, 1985, p 467). Lawyers, attorneys and budget management people focus more specifically on contract writing – lawyers and attorneys because a contract pre-empts conflict; budget management people because a contract from their perspective functions as a management tool in relation to processes in a large organisation.

the fulfilment of the contract. The contract establishes goals and results but leaves open methods and means.

Material contracts can still be seen as machines for the realisation of potential collaboration and exchange between mutually independent organisations. However, they function as the regulation of a more complex relation, which typically also means that the contract is not only a coupling of law and economy. Typically, these contracts incorporate a third function system in accordance with the purpose stated in the contract. If, for example, the contract pertains to a set number of knee surgeries, the objective is specified but the specific method of surgery is kept open. The contract then incorporates the healthcare system as an independent professional perspective.

Reflexive contracts

Reflexive contracts amplify the contractual complexity even further by seeking to pre-empt the formation of conflict between contract partners in a contractual situation where the partnership is much too complex to be described in if/then sentences and also too indefinite to be described by way of clear goals and results. Thus, reflexive contracts provide a model for establishing commitment in cases when the purpose of the collaboration remains ambiguous. In reflexive contracts, conditional programmes and goal programmes have been replaced by procedural programmes, which indicate the interests reflected in the collaboration. Moreover, reflexive contracts outline procedures for how to prioritise conflicting interests.

Like material contracts, reflexive contracts can be seen as machines for the realisation of potential collaboration and exchange between mutually independent organisations. However, as structural coupling, reflexive contracts open up to still more function systems. The specification of interests to be reflected in the collaboration indicates the different function systems that the contract seeks to bring together through structural coupling.

Partnerships as second-order contracts

Partnerships as a form represent a break with the three previous forms. Formal, material and reflexive contracts can be seen as realisation machines. Organisations realise their freedom and property by entering into contractual obligation-based relations with others. Partnerships, on the other hand, are machines of possibilities. They contain the inherent potential to continually produce new possibilities for the partners and their mutual relations. Partnerships may produce new partners, new visions for the future, new and development concepts, new collaborative themes and interests.

What turns partnerships into machines of possibility rather than realisation machines? The fact that they are of the second order. Partnerships, simply put, represent promises about the fact that the partners will enter into a contractual relationship in the future. Whereas first-order contracts are about promises, second-order contracts pertain to promises about promises. Partners of second-order contracts promise each other to promise something in the future. Thus, partnerships are designed to manage the fact that all aspects of a promise exist in a state of perpetual change.

> **Example 6.2: Patient-oriented hospitals**
> In 2002, the Danish company ISS and Hørsholm Hospital formed a partnership agreement pertaining to all non-clinical service functions at the hospital (Hørsholm Sygehus [Hospital], 2002). This is the drawing the hospital produced to represent the partnership:
>
> The drawing consists of three circles. The inner circle lists responsibilities such as cleaning and patient food. The second circle defines service as flexibility, dialogue and behaviour. And the outer circle represents the partnership and establishes a context for how to perceive and carry out services and tasks. The partnership is described using words such as 'shared responsibility', 'collaborative projects', 'shared company culture', 'shared values', 'mutual respect', 'loyalty', etc. An arrow points from the centre out of the figure with the headline 'Project Partnership' and the sub-titles 'attitudes', 'values', 'measurement' and 'dialogue'. The arrow emphasises the fact that the partnership is perceived dynamically as an evolving entity – the content of the partnership can change over time.
>
>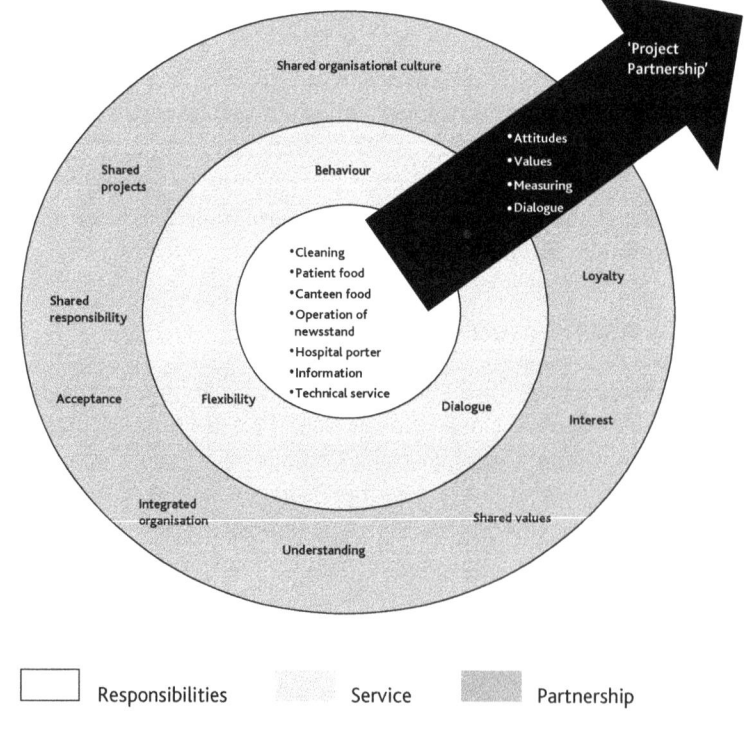

> The general tender conditions of the partnership tell us a few things. First, the fact that the partnership is based on a general vision in which the hospital is perceived as 'patient-focused'. Second, the service catalogue in the tender documents is rather striking: 'As a point of departure, Appendix 1 does not describe how to carry out the services covered in the request for tenders but rather which types of services are needed and which output is expected. Thus, since the partnership contract establishes itself on a mutual desire to develop new visions and models for the delivery of specific services, we encourage bids that include suggestions and ideas for such models as well as potential future solutions, to the extent that this is possible' (Hørsholm Sygehus [Hospital], 2001a, p 5, own translation).
>
> It might seem logical that the final contract would then specify the services clearly and unambiguously. However, this is not the case. The contract service catalogue states that, 'descriptions deliberately provide little detail' (Hørsholm Sygehus [Hospital], 2001a, p 5, own translation). As an example, the contract section covering food production and delivery specifies requirements as 'reasonable possibilities for menu choices and choice of different types of diets (Regular diet, Super diet, Vegetarian diet and a no pork diet).... In collaboration with the hospital, contract partners are responsible for ensuring ongoing modifications to the selection of diet and food types in response to new types of patients, demographic shifts and other gradual changes to nutritional requirements.... The provided food should at all times meet existing recommendations for Danish institutional food delivery and the nutritional policies of Frederiksborg County.... Food production must include a certain amount of organic products' (Hørsholm Sygehus [Hospital], 2001b, section 3, p 9, own translation).

Partnership agreements are contracts that incorporate the logic of transience. Whereas the shifts in contractual programmes from formal via material to reflexive contracts are about an increased capacity to manage still more factual complexity, the transition to partnerships is a question of managing temporal complexity. Partnership programmes are potentiality programmes. They are programmes for the potential of a given collaboration, that is, for the development of collaborations rather than their actual realisation. What stands out in partnership documents are not if/then sentences or the definition of goals and procedures. Instead, they are characterised by a great number of indefinite promises and open images of the future. Partnerships are about committing to future commitment (for a more in-depth analysis of partnerships, see Andersen 2008b, 2012a).

Whereas first-order contracts relate to promises, second-order contracts relate, as we have already mentioned, to promises about promises. But a promise about a promise has a radically different social standing than a promise. A first-order promise presupposes a social order, legally and otherwise. A promise given in a first-order contract refers beyond the contract itself to the law as social order. Partnerships, on the other hand, represent the notion of an emergent social order. A promise about a promise is about establishing an order for future collaboration. It is a question of creating conditions and premises for subsequent promises. This changes the definition and possibilities of the temporality, factuality and sociality of obligation in the contract.

Temporality. The formulation of future horizons becomes essential in partnerships. The temporal dimension of first-order contracts has to do with the presentification of the future. A first-order contract gives a promise in the present about a future commitment. We might say that it works to establish the future of the present. A second-order contract, by contrast, indicates a horizon for how the partners will collaborate about new potential future commitments in the future, that is, not only the future of the present but also the future of the future. Future horizons do not indicate promises about specific future action. They are also not prognoses about specific future needs according to which action can be planned. Future horizons are images of what a future collaboration might look like, including entirely new responsibilities and visions. Future horizons represent expectations about future expectations about the collaboration. A promise about future horizons and visions is a promise about a premise for subsequent promises. Second-order contracts thus pertain to the way in which the stabilisation of mutual expectations takes place with the expectation of changing expectations.

Factuality. First-order contracts are typically concerned with specifying delivery on the factual dimension. Second-order contracts shift primacy to the temporal dimension because the object of exchange is possibilities of exchange. Thus, a partnership is not about the case or the facts in themselves (issues, responsibilities, deliveries) but about the commitment to a particular perspective on cases and facts that do not yet exist. In partnerships, factuality appears in a state of deferral. Instead, the social perspective and its continual maintenance become central.

Sociality. Finally, partnerships differ radically from first-order contracts on the social dimension. First-order contracts presuppose that contract partners remain independent agents. This means that the focus of first-order contracts is the mutual obligation in relation to participants' freedom to limit their own freedom. However, in partnerships this is less obvious. What an organisation promises in a partnership is to create itself in the image of the partnership in order to remain a relevant partner, both now and in the future. Thus, on the social dimension, a partnership becomes a promise about a collaboration in which the partners evolve together and independently. It relates to the obligation to create oneself as a free and independent partner for the partnership, an obligation toward freedom in the image of the partnership.

Table 6.4: Shifts in dimensions on the first and second order

Dimension	Contract	Partnership
Temporality	Presentification of the future	Presentification of future presentifications of future
Factuality	Specification of deliveries	The indication of factual perspectives on the development of responsibilities that are still unknown
Sociality	Contract partners are presupposed	Partners commit to create themselves in the image of the partnership

> **Example 6.3: Partnerships about quality living services at a nursing home**
> The municipality of Kolding made the decision to organise the building of a new nursing home as a public–private partnership. The goal was to include and make use of the innovative capacity and thinking of private actors, particularly in relation to new welfare technologies. They were asked to propose a comprehensive solution to the building, renting and operation of the facility as well as caring for residents over a contract period of a minimum of 20 years.
>
> Early on, the municipality began to fear that the potential to involve private actors might be restricted by the municipality's many detailed requirements, expectations and standards with respect to building and design. In fact, the municipality discovered that the overwhelming amount of specific demands, which quickly accumulated during the writing of the tender documents, did not leave any room for private actors to be innovative.
>
> The concern was that the municipality's design standards were standing in the way of allowing new welfare technology, which might be developed in subsequent years, to be used. The municipality worried that its capacity for imagining future possibilities was too limited. And worse yet, that their detailed descriptions of and standards with regard to everything from the height of the window sills, distance between outlets, etc, would further restrict private actors and prevent them from applying innovation and developing new solutions. Moreover, the municipality worried that the detailed building and design standards might shift the focus away from the immaterial values that represented the real objective of the whole project. Perhaps the municipality was not the true expert on the subject of quality senior living?
>
> Following such considerations, it became an important challenge for the municipality to limit its need to pre-emptively specify, make explicit and dictate. The municipality asked itself: which attitude gets us further? And it came to the conclusion that being open and accommodating prompted market actors to engage in new collaboration, develop new welfare technologies and reflect on how to improve overall quality of life.
>
> In the end, instead of publishing several hundreds of pages of tender documents, the municipality put out a 12-page pamphlet with everyday stories about a good life at a nursing home. 'Using real-life stories and narratives,' the pamphlet 'describes different aspects of

> the life and practice, which Kolding municipality wanted its future nursing home to reflect.'
>
> These everyday stories came into being through a process of inclusion in which residents, employees, relatives and representatives from the local community 'explored' daily life at the existing nursing home facility. A three-day event brought together these different groups to give them a sense of what life in a nursing home was really like.
>
> This story is an example of a municipality confronted with and reflecting on the many disadvantages of a traditional contract and its decision to engage in long-term partnerships with market actors. The object of exchange was deliberately kept undefined in an effort to make it the object of ongoing development. The municipality refrained from proposing pre-defined solutions and put in the effort to express its needs via evocative stories about a desirable model for senior living. The municipality explicitly stated that the pamphlet was meant to serve as an inspiration and not as a list of requirements. Instead, the only requirement was the willingness of the private actors to commit to a 20-year partnership based on ongoing dialogue, collaboration and development. Prospective partners were not able to propose solutions to a small part of the contract or lack interest in a commitment to the ongoing development of nursing practices, care and services in collaboration with the municipality.

Partnerships continually explore new potential promises and collaboration by incorporating different and shifting perspectives from the function systems into the partnership vision (Lüdecke, 2015). Thus, in a partnership, there is no pre-determined model for how to connect specific function systems. Instead, partnerships scan the potential inherent in the connections between different function systems. Which potential innovative possibilities arise if we adopt a care perspective on our collaboration? What if we adopt an educational, religious or aesthetic perspective? Partnerships ensure a frame for productive disagreement and clashes between heterogeneous codes and expectations. Thus, partnerships connect at least four different function systems and continue to explore the possibility of adding more. And additionally, they represent second-order connections with built-in reflection and dynamism. From the perspective of the law, a partnership represents not only a promise but also a promise about a promise; from the perspective of economy, not only an exchange but also an exchange of possibilities for exchange (a potential market); from a political perspective not only a mode of implementation but also a way to do politics; from the perspective of the service system not only the provision of specific services but a development programme for future services.

Partnerships should therefore be perceived as functionally equivalent of contracts in cases when the conditions for first-order contracts disintegrate. They represent a functionally equivalent response to disintegrating conditions. Partnerships stabilise expectations in anticipation of shifting expectations. First-order contracts refer via

Table 6.5: Partnership observed by different function systems

Function system	Code	Partnership
Legal system	Right/wrong	Promise about promising
Economic system	Pay/not pay	Exchange of possibilities for change
Political system	Govern/governed	Constitution: decision of decision
Service-related system 1	+/− Performativity	Programme for service programming
Service-related system 2	+/− Performativity	Programme for service programming
Service-related system X	+/− Performativity	Programme for service programming

external reference to conditions that precede the contract and are considered stable. Partnerships refer via self-reference to conditions defined by the partnerships and which are never perceived to be stable, since partnerships only exist in their actual manifestation. Thus, partnerships are not merely second-order contracts but also a second-order social order, which exists only in its becoming. As Maas and Bakker write, 'partnerships ask for "unfrozen circumstances", in which dynamic, social spaces and fluid forms can be examined as long as necessary' (Maas and Bakker, 2000, p 198).

Challenges and paradoxes

These partnerships establish new paradoxes and challenges for contractual collaboration. The fundamental paradox is that a partnership is at once an agreement and not an agreement, which both desires commitment while seeking to maintain unrestricted and unconditional freedom. This paradox is managed, as mentioned, by means of the constant deferral and displacement of the promise: a promise about a promise.

However, there is another side to this paradox, which is that it signifies a process of contractualisation wanting to transform itself into a community (Andersen, 2012a).

This represents a paradox because the distinction obligation/freedom precisely constitutes the contract as the opposite of community. As mentioned earlier, freedom also means the freedom to give this obligation an afterlife through its translation into the 'language' of individual contract partners. The ambition to become a community entails the desire to establish a shared language among organisations. This would dissolve the very form of contract and cancel out the difference between obligation and freedom.

The new partnerships strive to constitute that which functions as the contract's constitutive outside. They strive to establish contractual obligation in relation to the one thing contracts cannot mandate obligation in relation to. Moreover, such paradoxes obviously also raise the question of who is in a position to define a shared language.

Figure 6.2: The contract that wanted to be community

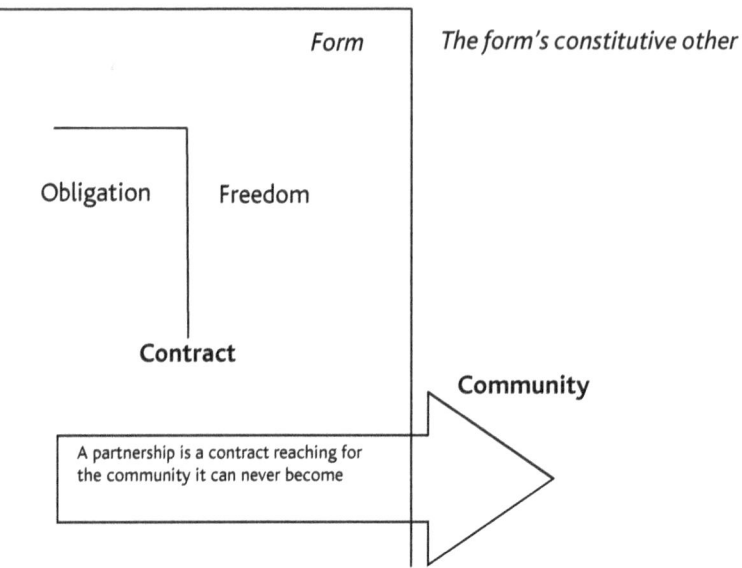

A whole series of challenges emerge in the wake of the creation and development of collaborations between welfare organisations:

- How can restrictions be established that remain unrestricted?
- How can mutual expectations be stabilised in anticipation of shifting expectations?
- How can differentiation and flexible couplings of perspectives and interests be combined?
- How can an organisation that increasingly consists of a multiplicity of partnership-based projects, moving across both internal and external formal boundaries, be managed?

Supervision and potentialisation of partnerships

Our concluding remarks in this chapter address changes to the role of central administration when welfare organisations increasingly become intertwined via a partnership relation with other welfare organisations across boundaries traditionally separating public, private and voluntary spheres (La Cour and Højlund, 2012). How does one manage an organisation that increasingly consists of a multiplicity of partnership-based projects, moving across both internal and external formal boundaries?

Anders La Cour and Holger Højlund have proposed the idea of polyphonic supervision of partnerships to describe how a number of alternative communication media are made available to a third party seeking to function in the role of supervisor of partnerships. They argue that, 'the chosen code establishes very different conditions for individual partnership forms by showing partners how to construct images of each other within the partnership' (La Cour and Højlund, 2008, p 221, own translation). Moreover, they stress that, 'inconsistency and internal contradictions perpetually lurk as a risk for any supervision which seeks to apply several codes. However, polyphony also represents flexible possibilities for making oneself relevant as supervisor within a broad range of different partnerships' (La Cour and Højlund, 2008, p 222).

Table 6.6 below represents an expansion and elaboration of a similar table in La Cour and Højlund (2008).

Table 6.6: Polycontextual partnership

Code	Construction of the partnership	Construction of partnership partners	Supervision of partnership creation
Power-superiority/power-inferiority	Constitution: decision of decision	Partners are construed as independent decision-capable actors	Delegation of authority and autonomy
Pay/not pay	Economic alliance based on exchange of possibilities for exchange	Partners are construed as homo economicus participating in a long-term economic alliance	Communication of vision and strategy. Investment in the partnership
Better/worse educationally	Mutual learning process, exchange of knowledge and experience	Partners are construed as oscillating between the positions of teacher and student	Facilitation of the framework for partnership creation. Guidance and coaching
Right/wrong	Promise about subsequent promises	Partners are construed as legal subjects with similar interests	Conflict mediation, procedural rules and mandatory reflection
Loved/not loved	A vertical or horizontal 'marriage' for co-evolution	Partners are construed as lovers, blind to each other's flaws and shortcomings	Create space for partners to allow each other to give to each other
Help/no help	A collective of mutual compassion	Partners are construed as dependent on each other's help and care	Care for partners' care for each other
Play/reality	A community of serious playmates	Partners are construed as playmates	Organise partnership-creating games such as team building and speed dating

To the extent that welfare organisations come to depend on each other across public, private and voluntary lines, across horizontal sector lines such as health, education and care, and across different management hierarchies such as state, region and municipality, management becomes a form of supervision and potentialisation of partnership formations that take different forms depending on the choice of code. Partnership is a transient form of agreement, seeking to both restrict and remain unrestricted. The effect of this is that the management of partnerships necessarily becomes the management of transience. It is a form of management forced to serve as a parasite on fragile partnerships that never are but always exist in a state of becoming. This form of management is, by extension, itself rather fragile, because, despite its support of speed dating, its delegation of competences, its coaching, mediation, and so on, it is unable to create and maintain, not to mention control, the partnerships.

Reflection 6.1: Partnership creation

Ask yourself: questions for managers of collaborations

1. Which collaborations do you participate in?
2. What is the nature of your collaboration? Is it based on a first- or second-order agreement? Do you have an agreement or an agreement about an agreement?
3. Which codes clash in the partnership?
4. If you work with contracts, do they include elements from different contract forms within the same contract? How do they work together?
5. Do you believe that you and your collaborators are engaged in community building? Do you think everyone perceives 'the same' community?
6. Are you sometimes disappointed that your collaborators end up having different expectations?

SEVEN

The playful employee

How can employees be managed to become innovative? How do public managers establish expectations for employees to self-manage when expectations to the organisation constantly change? How can managers establish expectations when all that can be expected is the unexpected?

The acceleration of expectations for individual welfare organisations to create innovation and change also affect the relation between organisation and employee. As a manager, it is no longer possible to unambiguously represent the unity of the organisation and use that as a platform from which to define and delegate responsibilities. The manager is forced to manage in response to employees' self-management and hope that the sense of unity, which the manager is unable to conceive, might be more accessible for individual employees.

With the potential and communication-seeking organisation, management can no longer be described as the effort to shield employees from a turbulent world through complexity reduction. The hope is precisely that the contingency of individual encounters between welfare professionals and citizens can be used as the springboard for new possibilities and better quality. Complexity is transferred down through the organisation to individual employees because, as they say in the human resource policy in Randers municipality, 'knowledge about the type and complexity of a problem is greatest in the place where the problem arises. Those employees who encounter the problems have the competence and authority to address them' (Randers Kommune, 2009, own translation).

The crux of this diagnosis is changes to the definition of public organisation employees. The idea of continual change continues to challenge the relationship between organisation and employee and results in rather remarkable experiments in the field of employee management. This chapter follows the shifts from formal organisational membership, which traditional bureaucracy offers its officials, via the professionalisation of welfare employees to different forms of *self-enrolment* which today characterise the relation between employees and the strategic and potential welfare organisation. We show how we are currently facing an exceedingly paradoxical management regime, which places more emphasis on employees' self-management while making it more difficult for employees to know if they meet expectations, and which places stronger emphasis on management at the same time as the object of management becomes increasingly more invisible and unmanageable (see Table 7.1).

Table 7.1: Forms of membership

Institutional form	Codes	Membership form	Central themes
Formal/innocent institution	The law	Formal membership Public servant	Factuality Objectivity Predictability Formal qualification
Professionally responsible institution (sector administration)	Different professional codes (eg, health, care, pedagogy)	Double membership of profession and organisation	Continuing education Balance between specialist and generalist
Strategic organisation (supervision administration)	Pedagogy Love	Self-enrolment via self-development Self-enrolment through anticipation of the organisation's needs	Lifelong learning Competency development Personal engagement Authentic love of work
Potential organisation (potentiality administration)	Play	Playful reinventions of forms of membership	Imagination Contingency

Formal membership and the semantic of the public servant

With formal law, bureaucracy and the formal (innocent) institution also comes formal membership, which regulates the relationship between organisation and employee. Formal membership appears at the same time as the semantic of the public servant, the first semantic to define the relationship between public administration and employee as precisely a relation between *organisation* and *employee*. Up until this point, public administration was not considered an actual organisation, and the relationship was articulated instead as a relationship between state (politics) and government official, according to which the government official was perceived as a particular position and order rank within the political system.

The semantic of the public servant emerges in the beginning of the 20th century and produces a number of catch phrases for the description of the ideal public employee: 'fidelity', 'loyalty', 'diligence', 'discipline', 'formal qualification', 'predictability in decision-making', 'objectivity' and 'legality.'

The concern is to create a predictable, calculable administration in which employees make objective, impersonal and fact-based decisions (Condren, 2006). This administration emphasises the importance of establishing the rank of public servant by public administrative measure, striving for lifelong employment so that the employee maintains independence in their decision-making. The argument is that decisions made by public administration officials, as opposed to private organisations, have to be made in accordance with neutral and objective criteria rather than according to questions of profitability. One of the designers of the Danish Public Service Act of 1919, Kristian Hansen Kofoed, equals administrative measure with state interest and contractual appointments with the egotistical management of special interests. Administrative measure represents 'peace and order'; contract represents 'disorder and destabilisation':

But with a rapidly changing staff whose members still consider whether or not a change of employment would improve their circumstances, the conditions for developing and nurturing strong public servant traditions will not be present.... [If contracts were introduced] we would abandon and lose the benefits of the present system with respect to stability and solidity. (Kofoed, 1928, pp 1-17, own translation)

Danish Professor of Administrative Law, Poul Andersen, speaks to the same question in 1926, when he notes that, 'moreover, this administrative measure has the effect of ensuring the public servant a legal status with respect to personal matters, that is, with respect to salary, retirement, standoff pay, working hours, etc, a status whose specific content is defined by law but is not created or established individually' (Andersen, 1926, pp 78-84, own translation). As Kofoed notes, the status of the public service should be regulated by the interests of society and not by the special interests of individuals. The interests of society and the state as expressed by law is the place from which the public servant is observed.

Concept 7.1: Formal membership
Membership represents the unity of the different *generalised motive* (*roll*) and *person*. A decision establishes an organisational role and a specific person becomes linked to that roll. As generalised motives, rolls reside above the personal and situational. The generalisation of motives ensures the impersonal quality of membership. Thus, membership entails a *zone of indifference* between organisation and individual, which marks the organisation's indifference to personal feeling and motives. Membership defines the personal as irrelevant to the organisation (Luhmann, 2000a).

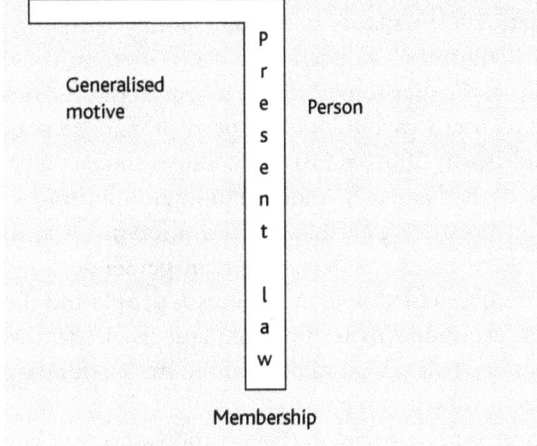

The medium of the formal membership is 'existing law'. This means that decisions regarding membership are coloured by the code legal/illegal. The relationship between role and person is described in terms of rights and obligations. Thus, membership in the formal organisation is a matter of legal decisions, typically supported by a personnel policy practice, which establishes personnel rules and regulations, and hence anticipates conflicts that can subsequently be settled according to the code legal/illegal.

The semantic of public servants establishes a concept of formal membership linked to the medium of law. The explicit grounding of public employment in public and administrative law, as opposed to private law, means that the relation organisation/employee is defined as a unilateral hierarchical relationship of superiority/inferiority rather than a bilateral contractual relation. The public servant plays an organisational role, and access to this role requires formal educational qualifications. The ability to fill the role is linked to expectations about diligence, loyalty and obligation. These expectations emphasise the *actions* of the public servant rather than their *thoughts* or *feelings*.

Membership of public sector administration and the professionally responsible institution

By the end of the 1950s, state administration begins to focus on the lack of people skills among management-level state employees. For the first time we see the emergence of the term 'employee' in public administration, and state offices are now described as groups of *people* who need to function as an effective work unit. This leads to a need for continuing education for managers and leaders. In Denmark, the report *Continuing education for academic public servants in the central administration* from 1960, published by the so-called Public Administration Committee (Forvaltningsnævnet, 1960), places personnel policy questions on the agenda, and recommends continuing education as the answer to these questions. Seminars on leadership and other topics are used to introduce state-level managers to psychological and socio-psychological aspects of management and leadership (see Andersen and Born, 2001, p 58). This also coincides with the 1963 opening, on a trial basis, of the Danish School of Public Administration (Forvaltningshøjskolen) and its conversion to a permanent institution in 1965, an event that helped stabilise and ensure a steady offering of management-related training programmes. The beginning articulation of employees as people and the inclusion of psychological and social conditions as important aspects of effective work processes indicate the early steps toward a softening of the strict boundary in the formal membership between roll and person.

In the 1970s, sector administration, with its focus on coordination among policy fields, initiated a debate about the need to maintain a balance between being a specialist and a generalist. Greater flexibility and mobility was called for at the top level in public administration departments. Top managers should no longer simply focus on their own office or department and its particular set of interests or concerns, but direct their focus toward the sector as a whole. Higher up in the hierarchy, the idea of planning compelled state leaders to not only be specialists within a sector but to become generalists with extensive cross-sectorial familiarity and knowledge. This shift affected the shaping of employees' generalised motives, which was no longer just based on facts and professional knowledge but also on willingness and ability to assume a more comprehensive perspective of the state. State employees were now expected to assume responsibility for a comprehensive whole that exceeded their particular formal organisational and professional field.

As already described, public sector administration brings along the professionally responsible institution, which significantly increases the state's awareness of the many welfare professions. Individual institutions discover themselves as professional institutions with an inherent competence to choose their own means and methods to solve given problems and achieve given objectives. This gives the institutions an independent professional responsibility. It means that the professionally responsible institution opens up the legal membership to influence from different professions. Membership is still established by the law, which defines employment requirements, but it is also shaped by its association with different welfare professions. An elementary school teacher is formally an employee of the state but would still be expected to nurture their association with the teaching profession and seek out professional development there. The institutions are responsible for creating conditions for their members to solve problems in a professionally (pedagogically, health-professionally, social-professionally, etc) satisfying manner.

This is reflected in the development and stabilisation of professional knowledge. In 1958, the Danish School of Educational Studies appointed its first professorships in pedagogy, and in 1963, the Danish parliament decided by law to make the Danish School of Educational Studies responsible for developing and utilising the School's research with a particular focus on the interest of the state. Under the auspices of unions, union membership publications and at seminars at the School for Social Work or the Danish School of Educational Studies, welfare professionals were given the opportunity to familiarise themselves with the latest research and to engage in professional debates. Thus, membership of a professionally responsible institution is both a question of seeing oneself as part of the state hierarchy and as part of the profession from which one procures knowledge in order to make better professional decisions about means and methods in the everyday operations of the institutions.

Thus, the sector administration and the professionally responsible organisation represent the first tentative reconfigurations of the difference between role and person. Employees begin to be considered as people, and social and psychological aspects of the workplace become objects of management. The leaders of the state are expected to assume greater responsibility for the state as a comprehensive whole, and not only for the restricted professional field covered by their own offices. And teachers, social workers and other welfare professionals are given increased access to knowledge, training and professional development through the stabilisation of the professions. We might say that their formal public employment is supplemented with their membership of a profession, and that the latter does not contain the same distinct separation of role and person.

From formal membership to self-enrolment

The emergence of supervision administration and the strategic organisation in the mid-1980s, however, constitutes a radical transformation of the membership form in the direction of what we call 'self-enrolment'. The call for ongoing change and strategic self-adaptation significantly challenges formal membership. It is no longer sufficient for membership to adapt slightly over time, and in light of this, fixed formal membership forms are now seen as impeding change. Suddenly, that which served as the function of formal membership – that is, establishing stable impersonal roles – is now viewed as a conservationist dysfunction. Formal membership impedes the organisation's adaptability and is now replaced by a membership form that similarly has the characteristics of always being able to be something else (du Gay, 2009).

The formal institution employed decisions about formal membership as a way to assume full responsibility for the inclusion and relevance of individuals in the organisation. This becomes highly problematic in the strategic organisation. If the organisation is to be in a state of continual change, placing responsibility for individual employees' roles entirely with the organisation becomes much too rigid and protracted. The question that arises from the mid-1980s is: how can an organisation create the conditions that allow individual employees to assume responsibility for their own inclusion into an organisation that is constantly in the process of becoming something other than what it is?

This question prompts a new model of membership, which we refer to as the *membership of self-enrolment*. The membership of self-enrolment doubles up on formal membership. It says: 'We have decided that you are a member on the condition that you continually self-enrol by creating yourself and your role in the image of the organisation's needs.' The role of the employee becomes to define and redefine their role on behalf of the organisation.

This shift in the direction of self-enrolment challenges the law as the medium of membership since it makes little sense to formulate personal self-motivation as obligation. It is difficult to speak in legal terms about a person's self-motivation. As a result, since the mid-1990s, organisations have been searching for alternatives to the law as the medium through which to formulate self-enrolment.

Self-enrolment in the sign of pedagogy

From the mid-1980s, we see the development of a new ideal for public employees with concepts such as 'self-improvement at work', 'lifelong learning', 'responsibility for own development', 'talent', 'competence reviews', 'profile analysis', 'coaching' and 'adaptability'. These are all catch phrases that remain immune to criticism. How does one argue against lifelong learning (Costea et al, 2007)?

Such catch phrases are a testament to a pedagogical coding of the membership of self-enrolment. In pedagogical communication, 'the child' functions as the symbolically generalised communication medium (Luhmann, 1993c). The child represents a not yet fully formed human being, open to being shaped through upbringing and education. The end result of this process of formation depends on the particular pedagogical programme, for example, compliance, morality, creativity, factuality or something entirely different. The child as medium follows a particular binary code: better/worse in terms of learning (Luhmann, 1989, pp 100-6). In pedagogical communication, everything is observed from that perspective. Everything is observed from the perspective of the aim of perfecting the child in relation to the learning goal.

When the membership of self-enrolment is formed in pedagogy as a medium, it does not simply result in a situation in which the manager is given the role of teacher and the employee the role of student. Instead, it is required of the individual employee that they observe themself through the lens of pedagogical language. And the manager serves as the coach, supervising the employee's self-relationship. Competency reviews, membership profiles, competence agreements and so on are designed to support employees' efforts to observe themselves pedagogically as a formable 'child'. In competency reviews, employees are expected to present themselves as a formable resource and to present a plan for how to develop this resource. The manager does not take the position of the teacher by suggesting specific training programmes, but facilitates and coaches a process through which employees independently formulate goals for their own development. Each employee therefore becomes the designer of him or herself as medium: educator and child in one (Andersen and Born, 2001; Andersen, 2007a)!

Pedagogical self-enrolment creates a number of implications for pedagogical communication as well as for membership. Theoretically what happens is that the distinction generalised motive/person is doubled and folded into itself on the motive side of the distinction. This results in a personalisation of the generalised motive! Now, the generalised motive is defined as personal self-motivation: the generalised motive establishes the expectation that the person who becomes linked to the motive will independently define the generalised motives as if the motive was motivated by the organisation. We have tried to illustrate the shaping of the medium of pedagogy by the figure of self-enrolment here (Andersen, 2013b) (see Figure 7.1):

Responsibility for self-development

When membership is coded pedagogically, individual employees are assigned responsibility for ongoing self-development. 'Employees,' writes the Danish Ministry of Finance, 'must assume responsibility for their own development. Employees should not leave it to management to take care of their professional

Figure 7.1: The shaping of the medium of pedagogy by the figure of self-enrolment

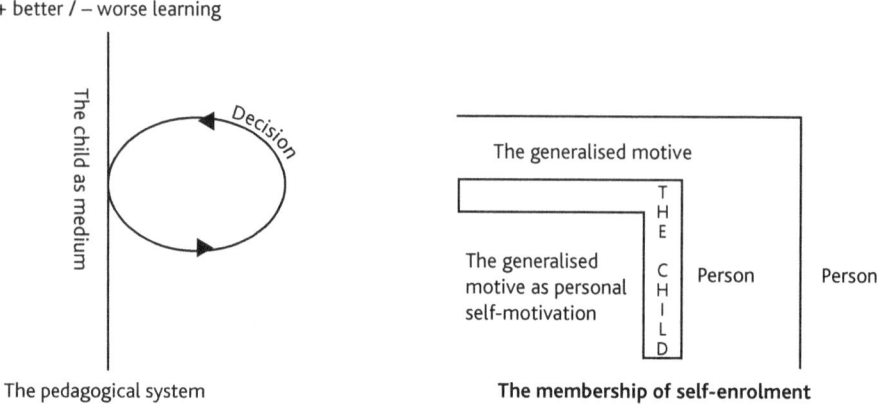

and personal growth. The individual employee has to actively consider possibilities and needs for self-development in order that she or he is equipped to meet new challenges and new demands for competencies' (Danish Ministry of Finance, 1994, p 18, own translation). The Ministry stresses self-responsibility for own competence development and for tuning one's competence development to the needs of the organisation and the job market. The adaptability of the organisation is linked to individual employees' personal competence development: 'Competence development and learning opportunities create flexibility in individual employees and in the institution. Therefore, competence development represents the most important driver of adaptability' (Danish Ministry of Finance, 1995, pp 195-6, own translation). Individual employees are made responsible for their own self-development in order to ensure the adaptability of the organisation. The workplace, in turn, is responsible for providing competence reviews so that it might assume responsibility for employees' ability to assume responsibility for themselves and for the organisation.

This establishes employees' willingness and capacity for self-development as also the premise of job security and stability. The Danish Administration Department writes in 1987: 'Job content is changing with increasing speed, and security for individual employees is now perhaps more related to the ability to "keep up" professionally and personally in relation to the continually growing demands of the job' (Christensen, 1987, p 20, own translation). Local Government Denmark writes: 'The new security is based around the individual.... This increases demands for individual initiative and enterprise' (Kommunernes Landsforening [Local Government Denmark] and KTO, 1995, p 48, own translation). And the Ministry of Finance writes: 'Through continued development and qualifying activities, the individual may increase his or her security, both in relation to the workplace and in relation to the job market as a whole' (Danish Ministry of Finance, 1994, p 18, own translation). The condition of organisational membership, therefore, is the ability to anticipate the competences that will be in demand in the future, and to continually develop in relation to those.

Competence as capacity for self-development

This particular linking of the concept of 'competence' with the concept of 'adaptability' causes the concept of 'competence' to lose its referential self-evidence. Within formal membership, competences were given formal competences such as, for instance, a higher education degree. However, it is no longer possible to unambiguously establish what counts as a competence. 'Knowledge,' writes the Ministry of Finance, 'no longer has extended shelf life' (Danish Ministry of Finance, 1998, p 25, own translation).

The concept of competence is emptied of any content except its self-reference: being competent now means to engage in competence development. Thus, employees are primarily perceived as the potential for self-development. The most important competence is the ability to see oneself as unfinished. The challenge is how to maintain oneself as a 'child' in order to endlessly extend the possibilities for shaping and reshaping oneself. This means that unlearning becomes as urgent as learning. Too much professional identity leads to conservationism and threatens the maintenance of oneself as medium. Experience and strict professional identity function as an impediment rather than a resource. As stated in a Danish television show about unemployment: 'Throw away your CV!' The essential thing is no longer what you know, but your potential for development (Costea et al, 2006).

From mastery of external knowledge to mastery of one's self-relation

The invitation to employees to constantly develop themselves constitutes a particular perspective from which employees can view themselves. This perspective is the code of pedagogy, better/worse in terms of learning. However, since the most important aspect is no longer to learn something specific but to be learning, this perspective indicates a doubling of the code, that is, it is not only a question of being better or worse at something, but a question of being better or worse at adopting the perspective better/worse in relation to oneself, meaning being better or worse at establishing new learning objectives, better or worse at continually developing oneself, challenging oneself, reimagining oneself. The central competence is no longer related to the relation between employees and an external object as an object of mastery but to employees' relations to themselves and their mastery of this relation. Thus, pedagogical correction comes to equal the correction of one's self-relation! Employees are asked to see themselves and their personalities as something incomplete, perpetually in need of further development.

As a result, the classification of employees according to competences can no longer be decided once and for all but has to be tested throughout the entire employment process. And the responsibility for this process is shared between employer and employee. From the perspective of pedagogy, it is the employee's most significant responsibility to explore their own relevance to the workplace and to use these insights to subsequently correct their self-development. This, in

> **Example 7.1: Self-development, 'a house of mirrors'**
>
> In 2004, an OECD report concluded that Danish schools lacked an evaluation culture. The recommendations in the report suggested that developing a stronger evaluation system would serve as 'the most significant single intervention in order for other initiatives to be successful,' but the specific definition of such an evaluation culture was less clear. Initially, the report caused politicians to propose a set of national tests that would measure students' academic performance. However, the conversation quickly shifted to seeing the problem as an indication of public school teachers' reluctance and inability to evaluate their own teaching (see Pors, 2009). In order for the school to change, teachers would need competence development.
>
> The Danish Ministry of Education went on to launch a web-based evaluation platform designed to disseminate knowledge about and methods for developing an evaluation culture. Many of the platform's methods and tools focus on the development of individual teacher or collaboration among teachers. For instance, a team of teachers is described as 'a learning space where individual teachers are able to reflect on their development goals and competences – an opportunity to reflect on their own practice.' Teachers are encouraged to use dialogue tools and classroom observations as a way to use each other for purposes of self-exploration, asking questions such as: 'How do I react?', 'When do I shut down?'
>
> Thus, the evaluation process is defined as a question of the ability of individual teachers to reflect on their own possibilities for development and growth. Teachers are encouraged not only to observe themselves but also to observe the way they observe. One of the platform tools encourages teachers to pay attention to whether 'particular difficulties or strengths in the observer's own teaching practice make the observer more susceptible to focus on similar characteristics in the observed teacher.'
>
> Perhaps not surprisingly, evaluation emerges as the observation and evaluation of a teacher's performance. However, evaluation is also seen as the capacity for self-reflection. The concept of evaluation capacity refers precisely to this form of second-order observation, where a teacher's capacity for self-reflection is made the object of reflection (Ratner and Pors, 2013). And finally, evaluation is also articulated as a third-order observation with the idea of a 'training pedagogy' for evaluation capacity. The evaluation portal describes a recurrent problem in the schools as 'the lack of a specific training pedagogy for the development of evaluation capacity.'
>
> Efforts to introduce and develop an evaluation culture in Danish public schools based themselves on a specific image of successful employees as those who continually and actively

> manage their self-relation and self-development. Competent employees are described as those who come into view for themselves by continuing to take a step back and observing their own observations. Employees' self-relation becomes a house of mirrors where teachers engage in an indefinite process of incorporating new elements of the self as objects of reflection and development (all quotes are from www. evaluering.uvm.dk, own translation).

essence, is the condition of membership when self-enrolment takes place through pedagogical coding: an expectation about individual employees' perpetual self-examination of their ability to allow themselves to be challenged and to develop for the benefit of the organisation.

Self-enrolment in the sign of love

But the strategic organisation does not only code membership pedagogically. The problem is not only how to speed up organisational competence development; increased adaptability can also be achieved by affording employees a greater level of strategic responsibility. In the late 1980s, it was seen as a problem in the public sector that, 'employees show only limited initiative in relation to the general situation of the institution and focus primarily on individual cases.' Management was asking for their employees' 'input into and responsibility toward the institution's overall task performance' (Administrationsdepartementet [Administration Department], 1987, p 2, own translation). 'The ideal,' writes the Ministry of Finance in its report *Welfare tools*, 'is no longer the responsible but the *"responsibility-seeking employee"*' (Danish Ministry of Finance, 1995, p 179, own translation, emphasis in original).

The concept of the responsibility-seeking employee is an indication that public organisations are beginning to observe employees from the perspective of the medium of the love system: passion (Andersen and Born, 2001, 2007b, 2008; for an example from a private organisation, see Bramming and Johnsen, 2011). Theoretically, love communication serves the function of articulating the 'highly personal'. Intimacy, in this context, is 'when more and more domains of personal experience and bodily behaviour become accessible and relevant to another human being and vice versa' (Luhmann, 1995, p 224). Highly personal communication in the love system is constituted by means of the binary love code loved/not loved according to which it is preferable to be loved rather than not loved (Luhmann, 1986, pp 18-33).

The code loved/not loved makes membership of an organisation a question of seeing the organisation as one's 'significant other', meaning that the organisation is perceived as the thing around which one's entire worldview revolves. In the same way that it is expected from the perspective of love communication that a person includes the significant other in everything they do, membership becomes a question of *anticipating the organisation's needs* (Andersen and Born, 2001; Andersen,

2013b). Love may intensify communication by renouncing communication to a large extent with the expectation that the lover will anticipate the needs of the other. The dynamic is based on the notion that no explicit requests or pleas will be needed. Love communication assumes the ability to anticipate each other's wishes without articulating them. In fact, it would be an admission of failure to have to ask the other person for something (Luhmann, 1986, p 26). Love communication can be summed up as shown in Table 7.2.

Table 7.2: Love communication

Love code	Loved/not loved
Universality of the love relation	Inclusion of the partner in the consideration of all life situations
Love and world	Love represents the internalisation of the systematised world relation of the other
Love and anticipation	Love can intensify communication by renouncing a great deal of communication. It relies on anticipation
Symbolism of love	Action is chosen not for its concrete effects but because of its expressive symbolic meaning
Command of love	Allowing the other to give

The shaping of the membership of self-enrolment in the medium of love affects the membership in several ways. Like the pedagogical coding, the love coding doubles and folds the difference 'generalised motive'/'person' into itself on the motive side of the difference. The personal self-motivation aspect of the generalised motive is further intensified in the love coding. It is no longer simply, as in the pedagogical membership, a question of competence development, but of including one's personality and personal engagement in an effort to create oneself in the image of the organisation. Employees are expected to act as if their organisational roles and responsibilities serve as the expression of personal motives and engagement. The shaping by self-enrolment of the medium of love can be illustrated like this (see Figure 7.2).

Responsibility for engagement

The codification of the membership of self-enrolment in the love code means that the communicative rules of love apply in the decision of membership. We are not claiming that employees actually have feelings of love toward their workplace, but simply that we note the emergence of organised games that employ the love code, and where one of the requirements of the game is to show one's love of one's workplace. Initiative and engagement become new catch phrases (Chapman, 2006; du Gay, 2008). The Danish Ministry of Finance, for example, writes that, 'it is by virtue of enterprising employees who want to grow and engage and who have the capacity for swift adaptability and flexibility that the state will be able to meet new challenges and create the best solutions for the benefit of society as a

Figure 7.2: The love code formed by self-enrolment

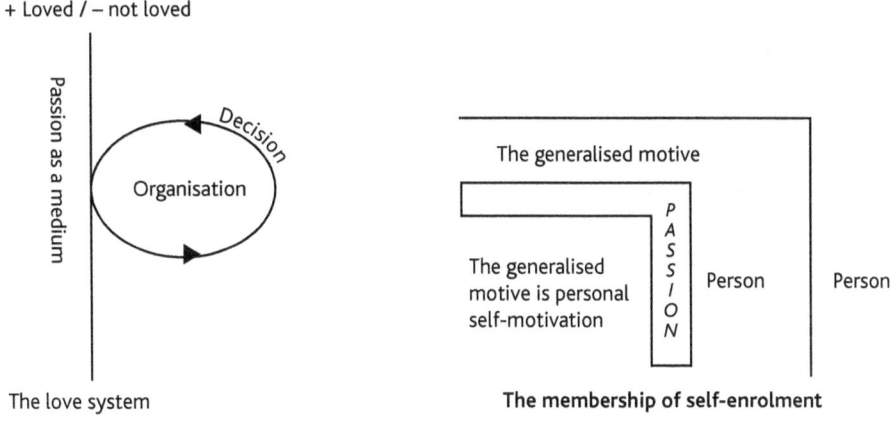

whole' (Danish Ministry of Finance, 1998, p 6, own translation). Engagement is a precondition for taking responsibility. Only engagement makes it possible for the individual to actively construct what responsibility means in relation to the institution without a mediating superior. Engagement indicates the employee's attempt to relate to the organisation's goal and not only their individual cases. As the Danish Administration Department writes in 1987: 'The individual needs to see his or her function from a comprehensive perspective and not merely as the sum of individual cases' (Administrationsdepartementet [Administration Department], 1987, p 8, own translation). However, engagement represents an internal relation within the individual that is not observable from the perspective of the organisation. This is why the words 'engagement' and 'initiative' often appear together in presentations about employee and personnel policies. *Initiative represents the external observable side of engagement.* Contrary to the concept of civil servant, engaged individual responsibility manifests itself in the organisation and not in the form of following orders or as the fulfilment of obligation, but precisely as an independent initiative that has not been requested.

The objective behind these efforts is to create partnerships between organisations and employees in which institutions represent a shared responsibility: 'Public employees and managers assume shared responsibility for the development and growth of the institution and of employees' (Danish Ministry of Finance, 1995, p 179, own translation). It sounds almost like wedding vows when the Ministry writes: 'Institutions and employees must engage in mutual development' (Danish Ministry of Finance, 1995, p 179, own translation).

The asymmetry that ultimately remains between manager and employee appears to consist of the difference between *giving*, on the one hand, and *providing the opportunity to give*, on the other. 'The organisation' and 'management' are responsible for providing employees with the opportunity to give. The Danish Ministry of

> **Example 7.2: Employee personality as a resource in the municipality of Århus**
>
> The municipality of Århus hired an 'experience manager' with the intention of creating a focus on the citizens' experience in their encounters with municipal services (see also Chapter Three). Rather than thinking of welfare as output, the municipality wanted to perceive welfare as an experience. This affects the way the organisation views its employees. The municipality writes: 'If service is output, the manager will perceive employees as a function responsible for delivering a service.' However, the text goes on, 'if public service is reconceived as an experience for citizens, the manager is compelled to view and manage employees as people who make an individual difference. Good service, then, becomes the result of a service as well as the experience of this service, which in a significant way turns the personal effort of employees into a central factor' (Dall, 2011).
>
> The focus on experience management frames the competences of individual welfare professionals not only as a question of professional knowledge and experience; instead, 'employees become a resource – not only by virtue of their hands but also the mind and heart behind them.' The experience manager states:
>
> > "Instead of viewing difference and personality as challenges, the manager needs to see the force hidden inside employees who do not only use their professional knowledge but also their personality to achieve clear goals."
>
> Thus, today's welfare organisation views their employees' professional knowledge and function not simply as resources but also as a superficial exterior that hides other and more important resources – people with hands and minds:
>
> > "Bringing citizens' experience into focus as the point of departure for the organisation brings people into play. It calls for responsibility rather than control, for management rather than administration and power of differentiation rather than cohesion. Instead of continuing to reach for new resources, the question is how to employ existing resources in new ways. Behind functions are people – and our job is to set them free – hands and mind."
>
> As a result, employee personality emerges as a value in achieving and delivering better welfare. Management is a question of bringing employees' personalities into play (Dall, 2011).

Finance writes: 'It is a question of a much broader commitment for both employee and institution, where competence, flexibility and responsibility are exchanged in return for opportunities for development and challenges' (Danish Ministry of Finance, 1995, p 179, own translation).

Seeing the 'whole employee'

If management is a question of providing employees with the opportunity to give themselves fully, and if employee engagement is a condition of organisational performativity, then the private and personal have to be redefined as positive elements in organisational communication. It is no longer enough to describe the private as a necessary backdrop and a potential impediment to getting the job done. If what is desired is personal engagement from employees, the organisation has to show an interest in ensuring ways in which the job can be meaningful for the individual:

> The personnel policies are designed to ensure that each job description aims for the greatest possible level of meaningfulness.... It is not enough that one's workplace and job hold a strong outward image if one does not personally feel involved in contributing in a positive way to the institution's achievement of goals.... However, it is also important that employees do not feel as if they are being reduced to professional individuals but also feel welcome and appreciated with their particular personality and peculiarities. Respect and appreciation are not only a matter of praise and positive mention but also equally about criticism – constructive criticism.... Each individual is taken seriously as a person and as a professional. (Administrationsdepartementet [Administration Department], 1987, p 6, own translation)

Here we see no zone of indifference between organisation and member but, on the contrary, *intense interest in the personal*. We see an organisational interest in the 'whole employee': 'The whole employee serves as a frame for the many initiatives designed to ensure that employees thrive and feel engaged, responsible and motivated in their work' (Danish Ministry of Finance, 1998, p 31, own translation). And the 'whole employee' includes not only all aspects of the person in the work setting but also the employee's life outside the organisation: 'Those employees who are able to combine their work life with life outside their workplace in a satisfying way are often the happiest, most engaged and productive employees....

Example 7.3: The whole flexible employee

The following case is taken from the municipality of Hedensted, and is an edifying tale loosely based around employee narratives as a way to illustrate the municipal personnel policy, which also includes a 'life phase'-based policy. The municipality stresses that 'not all employees have the same needs – and definitely not at the same time.' Therefore, 'it is important that both employees and managers remain flexible in the effort to support each other.' This is the story.

Dog's first sick day

Each morning, while the coffee is brewing and with the sound of the radio playing in the background, I take a moment to sit down with my laptop to get a sense of what my day looks like. This gives me a chance to reflect on the day while I prepare the kids' lunches. Once the children are up, everything is about them. One morning, there was an email from a new employee. It had been sent just after 5am and the subject heading read, 'Sorry, sick dog!' I read the email that said: 'Unfortunately I have to take my dog, Tinka, to the vet because she has been sick all night. I sincerely hope to be able to get to work a little later in the day and catch up since I am supposed to write the minutes from the MED meeting, which have to be sent out tomorrow. If not, I'll have to fit it in tomorrow morning and ask that today be considered a vacation day.' I smiled at the computer, not because I am familiar with the troubles of dog owners – in fact, I am allergic! No, I was smiling because I could sense that the email had been written with a mix of concern and sense of responsibility. The concern was obviously primarily about the dog, but it was also concern about how I might receive this kind of 'sick note'. We had been working for months to implement a new structure in the administration. Many of us had new employees, managers, colleagues and responsibilities. And Tinka's 'mom' and I did not yet know each other very well. However, I could see that she did whatever she could to make ends meet, and I was sure that the reason for her email was that her dog really was sick and needed urgently to see a vet. What would my response be? Or should I even be responding to her email at 6am? She might no longer be at her computer. And if she were, she might think of me as the kind of manager who works around the clock. I finally made up my mind and wrote: 'I hope Tinka feels better soon. I appreciate your concern for the MED minutes. Get back to me when you know how everything works out.' I spent most of the day going to different municipal meetings, and when I arrived at the office, I was told that Tinka's 'mom' had called. The dog had stepped on an old metal splinter, which of course hurt, but had also developed a fever. The vet had cleaned the cut, bandaged up the paw and prescribed medication, which would make her feel better in a few days. It was my wife's turn to pick up the children from school so I was able to spend a few quiet hours by my desk that afternoon. Just after 4pm, the concerned dog mom suddenly appeared in the door to my office holding a sullen-looking black lab. 'Oh, this must be Tinka…', I said. 'Yes, all bandaged up and pumped full of antibiotics. She was not feeling well enough to be left at home alone, so I decided to bring her along. She can help me write those MED minutes. But I will still be taking a vacation day today.' 'Well,' I said, 'if you and Tinka finish the MED minutes for us to send out tomorrow, why don't we just call today "dog's first sick day."'

[Thus], the relationship between employees work life and other aspects of their lives must be included in performance review and personnel policies overall' (Danish Ministry of Finance, 1998, p 32, own translation).

Considering the organisation in everything one does

Passionate codification means that employees are expected to constantly make themselves the object of the organisation's love by anticipating the organisation's needs. Employees today are expected to adopt the organisation's worldview. They are expected to align the organisation's interests and goals with their own interests and goals. And in places where the organisation has not yet developed an explicit worldview, it is expected that employees anticipate one by actively imagining what the organisation's take on something might be. Thus, the organisation becomes the employee's 'significant other'.

Being in a love relationship with one's workplace entails considering the organisation in any situation, including, for example, the family's planning of who drops off and picks up children from school next week, or agreements about whether or not to check emails after the children have been tucked in bed at night. Loving self-enrolment means that employees are responsible for including and considering the needs of the workplace in the planning of their family life and vice versa.

Feelings of doubt about whether or not the organisation reciprocates one's love serve as the dynamic of the membership of love. When employees doubt the organisation's love, they are compelled to continually anticipate the needs of the organisation, projects and colleagues. From the perspective of the organisation, this is the whole point of this form of membership: to create employees who are hypersensitive to the organisation's needs without having to articulate these needs to employees. It is an endless spiral: when has an employee anticipated enough needs? This is an inherent tension in the membership of self-enrolment when the code is loved/not loved. Bauman elaborates: 'The job is never finished, just as the stipulations of love and recognition are never met completely and unconditionally. There is not time to rest on one's laurels; laurels are known to wilt and fade in no time, successes tend to be forgotten a moment after being scored, life in an organisation is an infinite succession of emergencies.... This is an exciting and exhausting life; exciting for the adventurous, exhausting for the weak-hearted' (Bauman, 2008, p 130).

Postponed membership of self-enrolment

The strategic organisations of supervision administration entail a radically different form of membership than the one offered by the formal bureaucracy or in the professionally responsible organisation. Formal membership disregarded any personal motivation for employment. The membership of self-enrolment, by contrast, blurs the distinction between personal and public with the expectation that employees' personal motives are both irrelevant to the organisation but also what everything is about. The organisation's motive becomes the personal motivation of employees. Employees are expected to be personally motivated to self-motivate as if their motivation were that of the organisation. In the code of pedagogy, self-enrolment becomes a question of being self-motivated to develop the competences that the organisation is going to need. And in the code of love, self-enrolment becomes a constant question of making oneself loved by the organisation. In other words, a constitutive part of the role (the generalised motive) is to be responsibility-seeking and self-motivated – to engage in an ongoing process of self-creation and development of one's organisational roles and projects (for pay as codified intimacy, see Rennison, 2007c).

In the codes of pedagogy and love, self-enrolment is something for which employees have to continually qualify by continuing to shape and form themselves according to what might be considered valuable for the workplace. This means that employees never quite achieve the status of full member. Membership always lies ahead, and they always drag a bit behind. They are always on the way to becoming members. From the perspective of the pedagogical code, there are always new competences needed to match the direction that the organisation is taking, and employees are expected to always further develop their capacity for and openness toward competence development. From the perspective of the love code, employees can always show more unrequested initiative as a way to show their love of the organisation. Love communication works within a self-constituted hierarchy according to which initiative ranks the highest and operation and completion rank at the bottom (see Pedersen, 2011). This hierarchy has the potential to significantly accelerate an employee's responsibilities and workload. Employees prove their membership at meetings and in performance reviews by proposing new ideas for projects and tasks. However, the ideas require planning, implementation and completion, which might take months. Showing up to strategy meetings saying that they are busy finishing projects and therefore cannot contribute new ideas does not generate productive energy and dynamics. And employees risk not being given a role in the projects that are going to shape the organisation in the future – which is why employees often initiate and get involved in many more projects than they can actually fit in.

Self-enrolled membership can lead to emotional rollercoasters. Membership is always a future and unachieved goal – which has to be actively pursued – and the requirements for achieving membership remain obscure (since employees are expected to develop competences with a view to unknown future demands and to anticipate what remains unarticulated in the organisation). However, showing initiative entails risks since its central function is to represent employees' understanding of 'what we share'. Thus, the rejection of an initiative simultaneously serves as a rejection of an employee's vision of and for the organisation, and hence the shared ideas and values the employee believed the relationship to be based on. Having an initiative turned down is the same as being told one is not loved. This means that the membership of self-enrolment can be exceedingly fragile because employees may feel that their organisational affiliation is put in peril with the rejection of a single idea.

Potentialised membership

Pedagogical and love-coded self-enrolment is a good match for the strategic organisation and its efforts to be in a constant state of change. Self-enrolling employees do not wait for their superiors to tell them how to progress, but anticipate the organisation's needs before it utters them. This makes it possible to increase the speed of the organisation. However, passionate membership still entails a conservationist risk because the relation may become marked by security and loyalty and anticipation a matter of routine. With the potentiality administration and its penchant for redefinitions of roles, for boundaries and for images of reality also comes concern over how to prevent membership from becoming too established. Perhaps employees have remained in the same job for years, know their colleagues and always choose to collaborate with the same people. Managers seek to prevent employee relations from ceasing to evolve because everyone believes they know each other's competences and what each individual has to contribute. The emergence of the potential organisation increasingly brings into focus the risk of employees having grown too close to their organisation and therefore having lost the ability to observe the organisation and be observed by it in fresh ways.

As we have described it, the potential organisation is also the communication-seeking organisation. Thus, it is difficult to point to a single code as the primary mould for its membership. A central dynamic of the communication-seeking organisation is precisely to leave the choice of code open. Experimenting with viewing employees from different perspectives creates opportunities. The organisation seeks to make strategic use of the different images of roles and responsibilities provided by the different communication forms. However, one form or code seems particularly well suited for the potentiality administration's predilection for contingency: play. Organisational games and a playful approach to membership open up for different perceptions of the relationship between organisation and employee. Play is used to literally introduce more imagination into the relationship. The language of play is precisely about imagining the otherwise possible. Using play as communication form and the imagination as communication medium create a frame for seeing the employee as someone who is included because they play with the idea of inclusion.

The use of play as an 'icebreaker' emerged in organisations back in the 1980s. However, at that time, play served the relatively simple purpose of creating a positive atmosphere in situations where strangers were required to work together and to boost energy following a long meeting. From the 1990s, play began to be seen not as a break from work that provided renewed energy but as an aspect of work (for a more comprehensive historical analysis, see Andersen, 2009, 2013b; Costea et al, 2005, 2006). Play and work are not each other's opposites. As work in the potential organisation becomes a question of rethinking and innovation, play moves into the sphere of work (Costea et al, 2007). We see the emergence of a concept of 'serious play'. Or, as two Swedish management writers note:

> On a cognitive level, serious play stimulates people to imagine new possibilities and learn from new challenges. On the social level, serious play engages people in storytelling processes that allow them to make sense collectively to changes to their environment. On the emotional level, serious play encourages people not to fear change but rather to embrace it and maintain an open attitude of acceptance and responsiveness. (Statler and Roos, 2002, p 2)

As a communication form, play functions as a special kind of doubling machine. Play splits the world into a world of play and a world of reality. The real world is where signs and actions represent what they say they do. In the world of play, by contrast, signs and actions are objects of play: 'These actions in which we now engage do not denote what those actions for which they stand would denote' (Bateson, 2000, p 180). When children play-fight, they continually draw a distinction between play-fighting and actual fighting, and this distinction relies on the fact that the fight refers to a fight but does not refer to what a fight would normally mean. The division of the world by play makes apparent the contingency of reality – the fact that it could be different. Or, as Dirk Baecker notes: 'In play, socialness is experienced as what it is, namely as contingent' (Baecker, 1999, p 103). Play duplicates the social, so that the contingency of social reality becomes visible through play. According to Bateson, objects of play are always categories, boundaries, differences or frameworks. Play makes communicative distinctions visible: '[Play] discovers where the lines are and learns to cross them' (Bateson, 1955, p 151). To engage in play also means that the player divides themself into one who plays and the person outside the game. As a participant in play, they have to accept not only seeing contingency in the world but also to view themself as contingent. The 'playing self' places brackets around the 'real self', which allows for players to pretend to be all kinds of things without having to answer to these roles once play time is up: 'I was merely playing CEO'. However, playing CEO – being something one is not – opens up for a new set of eyes with which to view oneself: 'Perhaps I could be more CEO-like?' Playing with the self makes it possible to spot the contingency of the constitution of the self.

Imagination is the symbolic medium for play as communication form. Play thrives on the tension created by putting into question something that is considered self-evident. It brings energy to the game. And imagination is construed as the source of the ability to imagine contingency in play. It is, in other words, a medium suitable for exploration not only of the actually possible but also the conceivably possible, and perhaps even the inconceivably impossible. Imagination is used when seeking to go beyond the limits of possibility. Self-

Concept 7.2: Play

Play draws a distinction between play and reality, but only play itself can decide that, 'this is play – out there is reality – pay attention to play.' Play can only be played forth. The outside of the difference play/reality is constituted by the distinctions established by social systems when they communicate. According to Bateson, we always play with categories, lines or frames. In one of his examples a child plays archbishop: 'The child is playing at being archbishop. I am not interested in the fact that he learns how to be an archbishop from playing the role, but that he learns that there is such a thing as a role. He learns or acquires a new view, partly flexible and partly rigid, which is introduced into life when he realizes that behavior can, in a sense, be set to a logical type or to a style.... One can learn about a line which will be between archbishop and "not archbishop", or play that line.... [Play] discovers where the lines are and learns to cross them' (Bateson, 1955, pp 149-12). Dirk Baecker formulates it in this way: 'In play, socialness is constituted by ways of reflection onto itself as the other side of itself. In play, socialness is experienced as what it is, namely as contingent, roughly meaning that it is neither necessary nor impossible, or again, given yet changeable. Play in general reveals the form of the social by which the play infects the world' (Baecker, 1999, p 103).

Figure 7.3: The medium of play shaped by self-enrolment

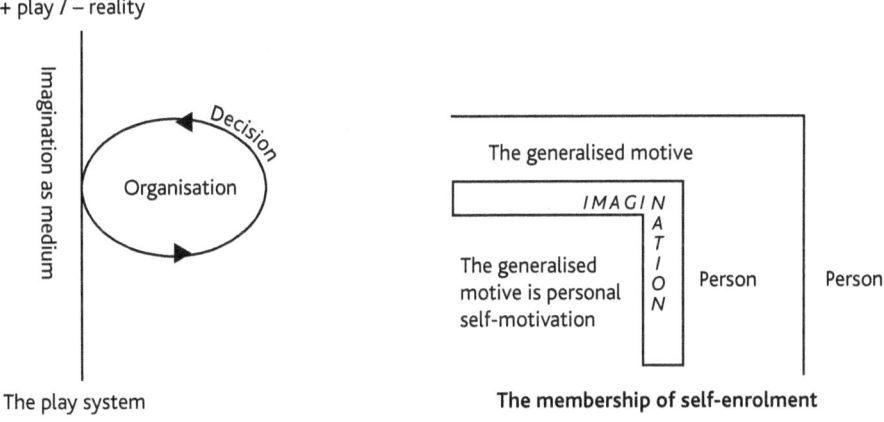

enrolment shaped by the play code and using imagination as symbolic medium creates employees capable of 'playing' with themselves and with social relations within the organisation.

Play and radical change

The potentialised organisation perceives play as a way to create radical change. It is not a question of specific or planned changes but of enabling the organisation to navigate unpredictability. In management studies, Pat Kane explains that, 'we need to be energetic, imaginative and confident in the face of a unpredictable, contestive, emergent world' (Kane, 2004, p 63). In a short article from 2002, Matt

Statler and Johan Roos write: 'Playing seriously helps organisations prepare for the unexpected' (Statler and Roos, 2002, p 1). According to Charalampos Mainemelis and Sarah Ronson, play is the cradle of creativity and serves as a way for the organisation to combat instrumental and rigid thinking. They argue that, 'the role of play ... is to help organisations maintain more flexible and more sophisticated forms of consistency by encouraging their members to occasionally experiment with possible realities, behaviours, or identities' (Mainemelis and Ronson, 2006, p 117).

Play is described as a way to encourage employees to experience unpredictability in a positive way. Statler and Roos write: 'We find that serious play encourages people to prepare themselves for the unexpected by constructing new knowledge, sharing meaning with each other, and maintaining an open, poised, and curious attitude towards change' (Statler and Roos, 2002, p 2). Moreover, play is also seen as a way to allow employees to play with their organisational membership: 'We play the way we are, the way we could, or could not be, and through our engagement on play it shows us what we choose to do, not what we have to do. Sometimes, however we get so caught up in our play that it leads us to change who we are: we call this transformation' (Linder et al, 2001, p 13). Pat Kane formulates the link between play and self-development like this: 'The player at work is a fully "potentialized" worker' (Kane, 2004, p 84). Accordingly, play is conceived as something that opens up a horizon of development possibilities for individual employees. Herminia Ibarra and Jennifer Petriglieri distinguish between identity play and identity work, and argue that, 'identity play aims to explore possible selves' (Ibarra and Petriglieri, 2010, p 11). In identity games, employees flirt with alternative 'selves'.

The goal of self-development is not a specific definition of self: 'The target identity is multiple, unspecified or unknown' (Ibarra and Petrglieri, 2010, p 16). Identity play is exploratory: 'When engaging in identity play ... people may rehearse a variety of possible selves, without necessarily seeking to adopt any of them on a permanent basis ... this play enables them to evaluate possible selves and separate fantasy from reality' (Ibarra and Petriglieri, 2010, p 17).

The shift from play identity to work identity is marked by the shift from flirtation with many 'selves' to a commitment to the realisation of a self (Ibarra and Petriglieri, 2010). Thus, what we have is a semantics built on expectations about employees who relate to themselves as a multiplicity through playful exploration of alternative selves. It is not simply an expectation about self-development – that is, the continual development of a self – but about viewing one's central

Example 7.4: Playing with employees and their future

The game *Possible Predictions* is about playing with alternative futures. The introduction to the game describes the process of beginning to reflect on and describe the future as an important step toward creating a desired future (Jones, 1998, p 164). Participants are given a piece of paper divided as shown below into the categories 5, 10 and 15 years. One participant writes their name on the paper and passes it on to the next person, who writes down a prediction about the person in 5, 10 and 15 years' time. The paper is then folded so that the next person can make their predictions without looking at previous predictions. The predictions should be positive and reflect positive qualities about the person in question. Ultimately, all participants end up with a piece of paper with everyone else's prediction about them. Thus, the game offers participants a multiplicity of positive predictions about their future. The game concludes with a discussion of whether participants would have made similar predictions about themselves, if anything came as a surprise, and whether or not participants are inspired to realise certain predictions (Jones, 1998, pp 164-5).

5 years	10 years	15 years

The basic idea behind *Possible Predictions* is that dreaming about the future inspires different perspectives on the present. Playing with ideas about the future opens up new ways of perceiving it. And this allows the present to appear as contingent – as holding different possibilities. In other words, the game uses the contingency of the future to create contingency in the present.

In the game, the only limit to the creation of new possibilities is the limited imagination of individual players. The game is designed so that participants are not restricted by the limitation of other players (which is why players are asked to fold the paper). At the same time, the game also encourages individual players to become aware of the limitations to their own images of the future by confronting them with the multiplicity of other players' images of possible futures.

The final stage of the game introduces a tension between play and reality. Participants are asked to state which predictions they plan to actually realise. Thus, the game not only creates play and imaginative freedom, but also a sense of commitment to decisions.

worldview as contingent and as the object of alternative configuration, redefining the possibilities of thinking the very concept of development.

Play as an acceleration of pedagogical and loving self-enrolment

In the potential organisation, play operates as a form of acceleration of the logics of both pedagogy and love. While pedagogy responds to demands for adaptability by encouraging employees to relate to themselves as competence and to answer supervised questions about their strengths, weaknesses and learning objectives, play encourages playing with the very concept of competence. From the perspective of pedagogy, lifelong learning is the model for creating change. Play adds to this perspective the contingency of concepts such as competence and qualifications, and stirs employees' imagination in terms of the possibilities for radical change. In play, imagination, rather than willpower or talent, serves as the ultimate limit of self-development, which means that in economic terms, imagination becomes a scarce resource. Imagination becomes the ultimate scarce resource when the focus is self-development and change. If employees are unable to imagine an alternative future, no amount of willingness, engagement or competence development capacity will do.

Similarly, play can accelerate loving self-enrolment. Love responds to demands for adaptability through expectations about employees who anticipate the organisation's needs. However, whereas the language of love entails the risk of turning anticipation into a matter of routine, and the risk that social relations become marred by fixed mutual expectations and ideas about collaboration, colleagues, etc, play as a management tool specifically targets the effort to unthaw frozen relationships, both in terms of social relations and self-relation. Thus, play creates opportunities for playing with relations and possible relations and with the possible needs of the organisation, or with project goals, with teams, with what it is that brings us together and what separates us, so that we might again anticipate the organisation's needs without getting stuck in routines.

In short, it is a question of introducing imagination into workplace relations. Play may strengthen an organisation's human resources by stimulating employees' ability to imagine each other, that is, increase the possibilities for employees to view each other as knowledge resources and collaborators. The connection between the play semantic and the love semantic finds explicit expression in parts of the play semantic, not least in Sandelands' work on organisational change. Sandelands' basic point is that play strengthens and develops love: 'Play is founded upon love' (Sandelands, 2010, p 77). Hence, the point of departure is the organisation as love and partnership relations among employees. And play is assigned a special function: 'Play is a way that love grows and develops' (Sandelands, 2010, p 77). This happens by introducing imagination into the love relationship: 'Play is the form that love takes at the boundary between fantasy and reality where new social arrangements arise to take the place of old social arrangements' (Sandelands, 2010, p 72). Sandelands sums up: 'Play is new love being born or an existing love being renewed' (Sandelands, 2010, p 80). And Pate Kane writes: 'People at play are more present, more engaged, more passionate and better performers' (Kane, 2004, p 84).

Example 7.5: He is super-competent, but…

The following is a case we have borrowed (with permission) from Susanne Ekman's book *Authority and autonomy. Paradoxes in modern knowledge work*. The case is from a large Danish publishing house. Susanne Ekman interviews and analyses a manager who describes the difference between two of his employees:

> Luke was an experienced editor who had been in the business for years. According to his boss, he was both competent and conscientious, but despite those qualities, he was not his favourite. He tried to explain why: "He is also fucking competent, but he's more like a classical editor, because everything you tell him to do, he does right. He's good at everything in writing. He's creative with his language, in the sense that it works great with everything he does, whether it's back cover text or whatever he might be writing. And he has a good sense of what needs to be done and when he can't do it alone and therefore has to ask me, for example, for help or support. He's a fucking good editor." And yet the boss feels like something is missing. And this 'something' is initiative or innovation: "He doesn't challenge me. I'm the one who has to say to him: 'Now you should do this or that.' And then he's fucking great at it, and you think, 'Damn, good going!' But he doesn't take any initiatives on his own." However, Camilla does. And the boss admits that she is his absolute favourite. He smiles when talking about her: "Camilla, on the other hand, takes all sorts of weird initiatives where some of them are like … where you go: 'Come on Camilla, that's too far out.' But I mean, it's just so funny, so you just get so much fun out of it. And maybe every tenth time you go: 'Wow, that just too fucking cool!… None of the other editors … challenge me. Camilla does, because she's so weird". (quoted in Ekman, 2012, p 197)

As we can see, the highly developed ability to carry out specific tasks is not enough to impress the manager. He wants more – and specifically the ability to challenge. He wants an employee who makes proposals and continually challenges models of work. And the employee needs to be the one who takes the initiative in order to deliver development possibilities for the possibility machine. The result is a set of specific expectations about social interaction in the workplace (Ekman, 2012). Thus, the good employee is someone who continues to surprise the organisation by coming up with ideas and suggestions that no one else has imagined. Membership of the organisation is achieved by exploding the boundaries and definitions of relevant information and communication in an organisation.

Voluntariness and reality bans

In the play code, self-enrolment is something one plays into existence. Playful membership continually explores possibilities for alternative conceptions of the self and of membership. The playful membership potentialises the self and also potentialises different possible memberships, that is, a surplus of possible connections and ways in which to self-enrol. This means that playful membership plays with different models of membership, and this is the way to become a member. This form of membership entails questioning membership itself, and multiplying and virtualising it rather than clarifying it.

A fundamental feature of play is its voluntary nature. One cannot be ordered to play. Or at least, no play would result from such an order. In the self-enrolled shaping of play, the premise of voluntariness becomes the expectation that employees view their participation as voluntary and therefore forego any use of external reference to any authority outside the game. Participants are barred from claiming that they are only playing because they have been ordered to do so. They have to at least play *as if* it were voluntary.

Play also entails a requirement about complete dedications, which is very similar to the engagement requirement in love communication, although in a sense it is even more unconditional. Love does not preclude a certain distanced strategic reflection of one's love declarations. All love communication entails a strategic aspect, which is about how to express oneself in a way so that one continues to be loved. This is different in play. The doubling of the self into a self and a playing self is precisely designed to allow players to leave their selves outside the game in order to be able to fully dedicate their playing self to the game without any conditions. Quoting once more from Pat Kane's *Play ethics*, the conception of the ideal relation between play and engagement is that play 'opens up the infinite possibilities arising from full engagement of heart, body and soul' (Kane, 2004, p 86). This seems like a lot to expect from employees. Moreover, it functions in the organisation as a rather exclusive machine, which considers employees' working conditions, work responsibilities and work roles communication-irrelevant unless they become objects of play, and even then, they only have relevance on the self-created conditions of the game. We might say that play institutes a rather severe ban on reality. Employees might be invited to participate in a game that focuses on their images of the future. Colleagues and superiors are literally playing with their future, and they are compelled to play along and are only considered good playmates to the extent that they refrain from using references to reality such as 'I don't feel like it', 'My experience is...' or 'That's not possible because...'. They are bound to unconditional participation in the game, which also includes an unconditional faith in the fact that the game is unrelated to reality. It simply represents a playful experimentation with possibilities for alternative manifestations of social realities. We use our imagination and demand of participants that they believe it when we tell them that nothing happens in 'the real world' while we are playing. Our faith in the separation of the virtual and real worlds is assumed

– just because we are toying with new work constellations at the office does not mean that one necessarily has to switch teams when play time is over.

Management challenges

What are the more specific implications of all this for welfare management? How does one manage self-enrolled employees? And what does it mean for today's public employees that their membership is (also) defined by self-engaged proposals for their roles and responsibilities in the organisation? What are the implications for employees of the call for them to potentialise themselves by imagining alternative roles for themselves in the their organisations?

The addition to formal membership in the shape of the three forms of self-enrolment changes conditions for management and employment in a fundamental way. An indication of this is the changes we have seen to the concept of responsibility. In formal membership, it was the manager's responsibility to describe and delimit the responsibilities of employees. With pedagogical and loving self-enrolment, responsibility becomes something that individual employees seek out. Responsibility represents a self-relation, not an external reference to a superior. Responsibility is not something employees are assigned; it becomes something they take and something they are responsible for seeking out. It becomes their responsibility to figure out what is responsible. Particularly in the case of loving self-enrolment, employees become responsible for an ongoing reformulation of their responsibilities in ways that the organisation has not requested. Playful self-enrolment further accelerates and intensifies responsibility. Employees become responsible for surprising the organisation with potential forms of responsibility, which no one could have imagined prior to their participation in the game. It becomes the responsibility of employees to make themselves available to the organisation as a horizon of potential employees – to create themselves as a surplus of possibilities.

What further complicates matters is the fact that these different forms of membership – along with their particular forms of responsibility – are in play at the same time, which means that we can never truly know which one is the most significant in a specific situation. The historical development of these membership forms is not consecutive, so that one replaces another. The formal membership of bureaucracy still exists in the form of employment contracts and the legal rights and responsibilities of any employment situation. Thus, the pedagogical and loving self-enrolment forms of the strategic organisation as well as the playful self-enrolment of the potential organisation represent possibilities for communication about membership that are always available to the relation between employee and organisation. We have tried to illustrate this in Table 7.3.

In the same way that today's welfare institutions have to navigate between being a formal, professionally responsible, strategic and potential organisation, relations between managers and employees are similarly shaped by the difficulties of deciding whether membership communication takes place in a legal, pedagogical,

Table 7.3: Form, function and effects of self-enrolment

Code	Form	Function	Effect
Right/wrong	Formal membership assigned through organisational decision	Stabilising expectations about employee expectations	Constitution of organisational memory
Better/worse in terms of learning	Self-enrolment through continual self-development. Participation is a matter of constantly trying to achieve relevance to the organisation in its becoming	Selection based on capacity for self-selection	Self-infantalisation Self-correction of personality
Loved/not loved	Self-enrolment through anticipation. Participation relies on capacity to make oneself loved and to install the organisation as the 'significant other'	Relinquishing and relieving organisational communication by allowing employees to anticipate the organisation's needs through a highly personal connection to the organisation	Constant struggle to make oneself loved Zone of intensity Stress due to the lack of end to the production of expectations
Play/reality	Self-enrolment through play. Plays with the idea of membership and this constitutes membership	Visibility of social contingency in the self-relations of employees and in all social relations within the organisation	Self-denial Reality-denial Virtualisation and multiplication of membership

loving or playful code. It can be difficult for employees to figure out which expectations apply. At times, being a successful employee means carrying out given tasks in a professional and timely manner. Other times, being successful means approaching the manager with an entirely new configuration of the task itself. In playful membership, such tension is even considered productive because its inner dynamism is precisely the difficulty of deciding whether or not something is, in fact, an organisational decision or just part of a game. A team of employees may be asked to play with the idea of which future tasks the team might take on. Initially, the team is told not to worry about what is realistically possible, but to give free reign to their imagination. However, when the game ends, they are still asked to choose some of the possibilities that the game produced as something they will commit to.

The same management paradoxes that applied to the relation between public administration and welfare organisation also apply to the relation between managers and employees. Employees are faced with the complex problem that the organisation tells them to 'Do as you are told' while also requiring them to 'Be independent'. Self-enrolment represents a fold in the formal membership so that the hierarchy persists. When employees are asked to self-enrol, they are told to be independent. And employees can never be sure when to show independence and when to obey orders. They operate within ambiguous expectations where anything they do may at any time prove to be the wrong choice.

Managers, in turn, are left with the challenge of working with employees who request complete freedom in their work while also seeking recognition and approval by an authority. Employees seem to be saying: 'Allow me complete freedom!' and 'Recognise me!' The manager is subject to the same complexity, inversed. Employees who accept the organisation's call for independence through continual self-development, engagement and play will return the expectation as paradoxical demands on the manager. The experience of the manager will be ambiguous communication from employees who want complete freedom, including freedom from managerial involvement and surveillance, as well as a more appreciative manager who constantly recognises and responds to their work (see Ekman, 2012).

Self-enrolment also creates a problem of visibility. How does the organisation know when an employee has, in fact, self-enrolled? The manager wonders: 'Does she mean it? Is her engagement real? I see that she is working hard and seems engaged, but does she have any real sense of what is going on?' And the employee asks similar questions: 'Do I like being here? Is it the work I like, or my colleagues? Do this job and this organisation allow me to be who I want to be? Is my self-enrolment real?' Membership that depends on self-enrolment creates a paradoxical situation in which the organisation's criteria for measurement can be stated explicitly, but the question of whether these criteria are met remains implicit and thus invisible. There is no such thing as definite proof of such things as love or playful self-denial. There is no way for the organisation to know whether or not the self-enrolment of its employees is authentic. Thus, managers look for *signs* of self-enrolment, and the emotional expressions of employees become such signs – the organisation is emotionalised. But people can lie about their feelings, and this pushes the organisation toward a state of trembling and borderline paranoia. The organisation has made itself dependent on the emotional lives of its employees, something that it can neither control nor see. Hypocrisy lurks.

However, a manager might also fear a situation where employees are *too* authentic in their self-enrolment. This is one of the problems addressed with the notion of *work–life balance*. On the one hand, we see the call for complete engagement, but on the other, organisations concern themselves with whether or not their employees have a life outside of work. We might say that the force of self-enrolment is so strong when the medium is passion that the organisation runs the risk of over-inclusion of individual employees along with the concomitant responsibility for the lives of those people. Over-inclusion refers to a situation in which a psychic system allows a specific social system to dominate its entire contact with reality, which prevents inclusion into other systems (Stäheli, 2003). Organisational over-inclusion entails the risk that individual employees can no longer serve as a critical innovative force for organisational processes, and in the long term, most burn out if all they do is work. The idea of work–life balance can be seen as the organisation's immune system designed to regulate over-included employees. Today, it is the manager who says to the employees: 'Get a life!' With seemingly limitless work, organisations may find themselves in a situation where they are responsible for defining employees' internal boundary vis-à-vis the organisation.

Finally, there is the issue of how to fire employees with whom the organisation has tried to establish intimate relations. Like membership itself, the act of firing someone seems to split itself into a formal dismissal and a 'loving' one. The first one follows and stresses legal procedures. The latter focuses on the emotions of the remaining employees and on the fact that being laid off can be seen as a chance for the laid-off employee to find a better partner who will better support their effort toward self-realisation. Somewhat caricatured we might say that self-enrolled employees who face possible lay-offs become responsible for recognising when or if they have become stuck in a job and ought to look for a new partner to rekindle their self-development process.

We have tried to list a set of central management paradoxes within the context of the membership of self-enrolment:

- How to simultaneously manage in accordance with employees' capacity for seeking out responsibility while also reaping the benefits of keeping the definition of responsibility open?
- How to communicate to employees: 'Solve the problem you've been assigned *and* rethink the basic premises and ideas behind the problem'?
- How to simultaneously allow employees complete freedom and also provide daily recognition?
- How to both manage in accordance with personal engagement and prevent employees from identifying so heavily with the organisation that they no longer contribute anything new?
- How to fire an employee whose responsibility has, for the duration of the employment, included responsibility for self-enrolment?

While it can be difficult to point to specific causes of stress, we see some clear links between self-enrolment and stress. Today, there is most often no clear and transparent framework for individual public sector employees. And a great number of employees report feeling stressed. When welfare institutions are expected to live up to exceedingly complex expectations, which perpetually change, the expectations directed at individual employees become similarly complex, and it can be difficult to understand and manage one's responsibilities. The problem is in no way only related to time constraints and the difficulty of getting to everything. It is, in fact, difficult to fully know what 'everything' entails, including prioritising tasks and responsibilities. Many welfare workers feel that, while they work long hours, they struggle to find time to do the work that they believe is their actual job. Social workers, nurses and educators experience having very limited time to practice what they consider their core professional function.

In the formal and professionally responsible organisations, stress could be perceived as the effect of a disagreement between organisations' expectations and an employee's work capacity. Stress was viewed as the result of an employee's failure to live up to organisational expectations. Today, stress is about self-stress. From the perspective of the love codification of organisational membership we might propose the thesis that stress is related to the fact that organisations expect their employees to independently create and anticipate the expectations that serve as the basis of their efforts. Stress refers to a disagreement between the expectations that an employee has taken on, on the one hand, and the expectations that the employee had expected to further anticipate, on the other. Stress then becomes an expression of insecurity about whether or not an employee's love is reciprocated, and whether or not they have the capacity to be loved at all. Have they absorbed enough expectations?

This pressure is not helped by the fact that most employees partake in a number of different management relations, projects, partnerships, etc. The 'significant other' whose needs employees are trying to anticipate is a many-headed creature, and employees can never feel sure about which head is watching their actions as either loving or un-loving. Whose recognition, ultimately, expresses the organisation's love? Who should employees try to woo to win the love of their organisation? When the organisation codes its membership passionately, it simultaneously renounces the possibility of an authoritative centre from which requirements and expectations flow. Employees partake in many specific relationships. An employee may have one manager or several. They have colleagues. They participate in a handful of projects with different circles of participants. There are customers and different points of contact with citizens. Whose love are they trying to win, and when have they received sufficient confirmation of love by the many different faces of the 'significant other'? This is a fundamental challenge of self-enrolment that each individual employee is faced with.

Some would argue that the cause of stress is incompetent managers failing to understand the seriousness of the question. But the problem is that it is incredibly difficult for today's managers to prevent and mitigate stress. Self-enrolment not only causes stress; it also undermines a manager's ability to reassume the responsibility that has become too overwhelming for an employee or group of employees. A manager cannot simply take over specific tasks from stressed employees without running the risk of hurting their feelings by preventing them from contributing their love offering. Additionally, organisations that formulate stress management policies addressing the need for employees to 'learn to say no', ensuring employees that, 'perhaps expectations are not as great as you believe,' are actually not removing expectations from the shoulders of their employees but rather producing a new layer of expectations by not only expecting employees to create their own self-expectations, but also expecting them to know their limits and to be able to say 'no'. Even if an organisation tries to make expectations less diffuse, it may create an even more complicated expectational landscape where individual employees become additionally responsible for using their 'no' to show their love of the organisation. Thus, stress management policies might actually accelerate the expectational spiral rather than mitigating it. Finally, it can be very difficult for a manager today to relieve employees since a majority of the tasks employees engage in have not been assigned by a manager but stem from projects that employees participate in with other colleagues in teams, which might even work across different departments and workplaces. It is often near impossible for a manager to have a strong sense of the work portfolio of individual employees, and employees often assume new responsibilities and tasks without the manager's knowledge. Thus, even when a manager directly orders employees to work less, employees do not perceive this as an actual possibility, since following the manager's order would mean letting down a number of collaborators both within and outside the organisation. Assuming responsibility in one project might mean to disappoint in another, and so employees become responsible for disappointing in a responsible way. Self-enrolment creates tough conditions for stress management.

We introduce two reflection boxes below. The first is addressed to managers, the second to employees. But we think that most welfare practitioners will find relevancy in both. The strategic and potential organisations contain a multitude of ad hoc relations between manager and managed, which distinguish themselves from the formal hierarchy. The majority of management relations can be described as both unilateral (hierarchical) and bilateral. Any manager is also an employee. And any employee is also a manager – perhaps project manager, or at least self-managing, with responsibility for themself as well as relations to the external environment via colleagues and citizens.

Reflection 7.1: Management of self-enrolment

To the manager, ask yourself:

1. How do you view your employees? Which codes do you connect to when viewing them?
2. Are you always aware of times when the code shifts and what this means for what you see and the rules that apply?
3. Do you place your employees in paradoxical situations where living up to certain expectations implies not meeting other ones? How do you deal with asking the impossible?
4. Are you gendered in the way you see your employees?
5. Do you allow your employees to distinguish between the professional and personal?
6. How do you manage emotional communication and the intimisation of work?
7. What is your attitude toward stress? What do you think of as the cause of stress?
8. Which expressions of emotion do you recognise as signs of authenticity in your employees? Engagement? Depression? Aggression?

Reflection 7.2: Employee self-management
To employees, ask yourself:

1. What is your ideal for your professional life and for yourself as an employee?
2. Which code shapes your ideal, and which paradoxical expectations do you become entangled in?
3. How do you view your colleagues and manager? What gives shape to your expectations? Is it humanly possible for your colleagues and manager to live up to your expectations?
4. How do you communicate your feelings? How do you view the feelings of others? Do you assume responsibility for your feelings?
5. Are you caught up in a tragic pursuit of intensity and feel unhappy when work becomes routine but also when it becomes infinitely challenging?
6. Do you think your work ideas match that of your colleagues?
7. Does your workplace prevent you from carrying out what you consider the most important aspect of your job?
8. Do you have a strategy for how to deal with the complexity of your life and the many different expectations you face? How do you decide which expectations to meet and which ones to disregard? And how do you handle disappointment?

EIGHT

Citizens as a resource

This chapter represents our final exploration and focuses on the relationship between *public administration* and *citizen*. Our claim is that the self-relation of citizens becomes the object of public welfare management. Increasingly, citizens and the activation of their resources are seen as the key to improving the welfare society. The differentiation of society plays a central role in this process, since the way in which public administration perceives citizens depends on the function system it connects to.

Several questions guide our exploration. First is the way in which citizens come into being as potentiality. Second is the way in which the function systems become increasingly more dependent on citizens. And third is the way in which personal responsibility is assigned new form and function. This chapter, in other words, addresses the challenges that arise when managers and professionals are expected to assume responsibility for citizens' ability to assume responsibility for their own and others' quality of life.

The citizen in the image of public administration

The way that public administration views citizens has undergone significant changes over the past century, from the citizen as legal subject via the citizen as the recipient of services to the active fellow citizen. This historical development does not simply fall into separate and consecutive periods, but develops as layers (Dean, 1995; Cruikshank, 2004; Andersen, 2007b). We have summarised it in Table 8.1.

Table 8.1: Forms of citizenry

	Governance technology	Object of governance	Limit of governance
Citizen as legal subject	Law and legally defined services	The citizen's formal sphere of action	Private sphere
Citizen as recipient	Instruction Counselling Decisions Action plan	The citizen's material sphere of action	The citizen's motivation to receive help
Citizen as active fellow citizen	Shared perspective Dialogue Citizens contract	The citizen's self-governance	The citizen's capacity for self-reflection and choice of freedom
Citizen as potentiality	Explore through conversations Social party games Aesthetic tools	The citizen's contingent self-relation	The citizen's imagination and self-images

From legal subject to active fellow citizen

The *citizen as legal subject* has a long history. Roughly speaking, the development of the past 300 years represents a movement from rights as something individuals were required to apply for and to justify by means of status. Rights represented one among many other personal privileges called the bourgeoisie. Gradually, rights became universalised: first, with the granting of rights to men of a particular age, status and wealth, then men of any age, then women, and today, rights are granted to the individual from the moment of birth. At the same time, rights become divided into economic, political, personal, etc. The granting and universalisation of individual rights creates a form of governance according to which anything that is not explicitly prohibited by law is permissible. The object of regulation is the formal constitution of the citizen. At first, individuals are constituted as free sovereign legal subjects through the granting of freedom rights. Subsequently, legal limitations to individual action are established through regulation of the possibility of individuals to apply their freedom rights. The private sphere so to speak defines the limits of governance and regulation.

The *citizen as recipient* comes into being with the sectorisation of the welfare state. This development means that the citizen is granted social rights and obligations in relation to a number of issues, and is made aware of this. Gradually, the regulatory relationship is flipped so that it is no longer only public administration that regulates the formal constitution of the citizen. Instead, public administration begins to define it as an obligation for citizens to know and request the administration's fulfilment of their welfare rights. We might say that the social welfare state regulates not only citizens' formal constitution but also their material constitution, as citizens are offered a variety of services such as assistance, healthcare, education, etc. The focus of public administration is to diagnose a problem (for example, an illness or social problem) and to prescribe a service that matches the problem. The welfare system sees it as their job to deprivatise citizens' problems by objectivising, defining and mitigating them in an objective and professional way. This leads to the development of a number of problem-oriented management technologies, ranging from the instruction and counselling of citizens about how to solve the problem, via decisions about treatment or interventions, to individual action plans where the welfare administration makes decisions about the premises that will decide any further action.

With the citizen as recipient offered a number of welfare services, public administration begins to show an interest in their motivation for accepting the services of the welfare state. Is their motivation sufficiently strong? Do they need more counselling? Whereas citizens as legal subjects were assumed to be motivated to create and decide their own lives, the notion of citizens as recipients raises the question of whether or not citizens have sufficient understanding of their problems to take appropriate action. As a legal subject, the citizen is perceived as 'bonus pater' and is assumed to possess a certain measure of rationality and self-interest. Therefore, no further interest in the citizen's self-relation is necessary, and the focus remains on legal demands for specific services. However, with the concept of the citizen as recipient, public administration begins to wonder if citizens really possess adequate understanding of and insight into their problems. It might be necessary to explain why a certain medication needs to be taken regularly, or to explain the diagnosis that the professionals agree on so that the citizen understands why they must accept certain services. Thus, the welfare administration still presupposes a fundamentally motivated citizen. The citizen might just need a better explanation and understanding of the larger context of the problem.

The *citizen as active fellow citizen* emerges along with the supervision state (White and Hunt, 2000; Lister, 2001; Stevenson, 2003). Implicit in the notion of active fellow citizen is the expectation that one is not simply a citizen *in* society but also *for* society. While expectations pertaining to a good legal subject are about self-discipline in relation to a formally defined space of action, expectations placed on active fellow citizens are about practising one's freedom by taking responsibility for oneself, for one's family *and* for the development of the collective. Only when citizens employ their freedom to benefit the state by assuming responsibility for themselves and their surroundings are they viewed as free and sovereign. Thus, the object of governance is citizens' relationship to their own self-relation. From the perspective of public administration, the relationship with citizens is a question of shaping selves capable of shaping themselves and their own paths. Citizens are supervised into choosing themselves as free in a way, which is also recognised by the system as responsible. Freedom becomes an obligation, so to speak (Rose, 1999). In light of this, public administration begins to view its previous governance technologies with a certain amount of scepticism. Previous governance technologies all focused on problems. The ideal was to observe a case in itself, separate and objectified from the citizen. The notion of the active fellow citizen makes this model problematic, and welfare administration feels like it is appropriating citizens' problems by claiming to be able to objectively define their problems. The ideal about citizens who assume responsibility for themselves and govern themselves calls for citizens to 'take ownership of their problems', as it is often referred to. This is not possible in a system where the professional holds the professionally sanctioned right of definition. 'Instruction', 'counselling', 'decision' and 'action plan' become problematic technologies because they are established around the state as active subject and citizens as passive object (Andersen, 2007b). The challenge now is to balance the asymmetry between the state as the defining and acting subject, on the one hand, and citizens as passive recipients of assistance, on the other. How, for example, might treatment and education become a shared responsibility and a shared effort for both professionals and citizens without undermining the status and knowledge of professionals and dissolving their professional responsibility and authority?

We see the development of a number of new governance technologies directed at citizens, designed to try to take on this challenge. This is like having your cake and eating it. Among such technologies is 'Shared Perspective', a technology designed to allow professionals to objectively analyse a problem while also incorporating the worldview of the citizens. 'Shared Perspective' is described as a way to combine the views of the professional and the views of the citizen in order to create a shared perspective. It seeks to make the citizen claim ownership of the problem while allowing the professional to use their knowledge to shape the problem. At the same time, action plans become more dialogue-based so that they function as shared plans for welfare administration departments and citizen. However, it is obvious that *dialogue as governance technology* is not simply dialogical. The public sector's invitation to dialogue between state and citizen relies on a unilateral monological invitation to bilateral dialogue. The function of this dialogue is double empowerment – to empower the citizen in relation to the case *and* through self-relation, and to empower the administration by inviting the citizen to a dialogue about self-relation – something that otherwise resides outside the administration's scope of operation.

Over time, a contract dimension adds itself to the dialogue technologies. These *citizens contracts* have a special quality, both because they continue the paradoxical and asymmetrical form of the dialogue technologies by serving as a unilateral call for a bilateral agreement, and because citizens contracts do not simply presuppose the citizen as a free and powerful contract partner but are about the citizen's commitment to their self-relation, including an inner dialogue about the relationship between obligation and freedom (Yeatman, 1997, 1998; Andersen, 2004, 2007b, 2008a, 2012b). Contracts have since become a regulatory strategy designed to promote citizens' ability to choose, and to be independent and self-regulating (Sullivan, 1997; Lewis, 2002). It has also been argued that the

Concept 8.1: From power to empowerment

The code of power divides the world into power-superior (governor) and power-inferior (governed). Power is exerted when the power-inferior self-governs based on interpretations of the possible intentions of the power-superior. The question of empowerment arises when the power communication senses that its expectation about self-governance will not be met, and that the exercise of power in itself has an undermining effect on the self-governance capacity and self-confidence of the power-inferior. This turns empowerment into power communication, which sees itself as liberating. It is power that refuses to be itself. Empowerment functions through a duplication of power. The difference between governor and governed is copied and re-entered into itself so that the object of governance becomes the self-governance of the governed. The form of power becomes power over the self-relation of the governed. This is only possible if the power-superior views the power-inferior through the distinction powerless/empowered. Only if the power-superior perceives the governed as powerless can they be transformed into empowered subject by the power-superior. In other words, the production of empowered citizens presupposes their initial production as powerless citizens. Since only the power-superior can draw the distinction between powerful and powerless, empowerment becomes a question of freeing the power-inferior in the image of what freedom means to the power-superior. This is why, as Barbara Cruikshank has described (2004), empowerment always pivots on the line between liberation and totalisation. The totalising element has to do with the exercise of power inherent in the act of defining someone as powerless, without an independent will, and definitions of when someone appears and can be recognised as powerful, independent and wilful.

peculiar mix in social work contracts of legal and disciplinary forms of power might work as a way of protecting the administration against public law (Nelken 1987), and some have warned that the administration and citizen run the risk of watering down and damaging the weave of norms that normally apply in relation to contracts (Vincent-Jones, 2000).

The notion of the active fellow citizen creates a radical shift in the public sector's expectations with regard to the motivation of the citizen, who is no longer assumed to be motivated. Welfare administration questions the very existence of a motivated self who can be addressed. And worse yet: it begins to question

---

Example 8.1: Citizens contracts

In the early 1990s, citizens contracts were introduced as an experiment in the field of social work in Frederikshavn. In that context, the journal *Socialrådgiveren* (*The Social Worker*) reflects on them:

> Gone are words such as case manager and clients. Now everyone is an employee working in a shared workplace – the activity department. Those who were previously called clients are asked: What do you know and what do you want? Once they have figured this out, they are hired, and if they don't meet the contract terms, it comes out of their paycheck. The social workers don't want to steal their clients' problems – they need to take responsibility for their lives. But it can be difficult to be tough and a "yes" is often easier than a "no". (*Socialrådgiveren*, 5/92, p 3)

Clients are referred to as employees in the hope that this will encourage them to recognise themselves as such. They are asked to see themselves as employees who voluntarily enter into a contract with the workplace and take responsibility for missed work. The contract serves as a disciplinary measure for inculcating responsibility and for 'living within one's means'. The reason behind the administration's withholding of pay is not that they did not receive any services for the money – they are not concerned with output. But if the administration continued to pay employees, it would mean that they were 'stealing their clients' problems'. The deduction in pay is for the clients' own sake; it is a way to respect them. Thus, the contract is perceived as a way to support inner willpower in the client from without.

Ten years later, the municipality of Karlebo is discussing contracts with its citizens. Head of child and family services Niels Dueholm comments in an interview with the Danish newspaper *Jyllandsposten*:

> We are looking into the possibility of making deductions in the welfare cheque for families with children who engage in criminal activities. A contract may include a provision stating that the child is not allowed in a particular public space past 10pm. If the family is unable or unwilling to follow this simple requirement, it can result in cuts to the welfare cheque.... A family contract may also include provisions about the family sharing a meal at least once a day and talking about

> the events of the day. The goal is to speak about what the child is doing and might help restore the parental role. (*Jyllandsposten*, 8.9.02)
>
> Contracts are viewed as a technology for the creation of families who take responsibility for their own lives. Thus, the contract is not simply perceived as a way to force the family to behave in a certain way, but as a tool to strengthen the family and to allow it to be free and independent.

whether the existing issue is actually the issue it has diagnosed, or whether the issue is merely a symptom of the lack of motivation in the citizen. Previously, when the citizen was perceived as recipient, a person's alcoholism was seen as precisely that, an alcohol problem. However, in the context of the active fellow citizen, the alcohol problem is seen as a symptom of a much more comprehensive problem about the person's lack of inner self-motivation and capacity for self-management. All problems suddenly relate to the inner motivation of the citizen.

The administration begins to distinguish between citizens' manifest motivation and their latent motivation. Manifest motivation is the motivation explicitly articulated by the citizen, and latent motivation refers to the citizen's unarticulated and unrecognised inner motivation. When the administration observes a lack of manifest motivation in the citizen, the distinction between manifest and latent motivation ensures that the administration cannot simply note that the citizen is unmotivated and therefore refuse to provide assistance. The notion of invisible latent motivation allows the administration to work with the citizen's self-motivation. The goal is to transform latent motivation into manifest motivation, and only the manifestly motivated citizen is granted the right to self-govern since self-governance presupposes a self-relation. And the latently motivated citizen is precisely characterised by being out of touch with their positive inner core.

Today, the active fellow citizen has been given an even more radical twist with the notion of *the citizen as potentiality*. It is no longer simply the citizen's self-governance that serves as the object of public administration, but the potential for the self-relation to become something it is not yet. This means that the administration is looking for possibilities to develop the citizen's capacity for self-management through an ongoing exploration of how citizens might think differently about themselves and their opportunities. The citizen is seen as potential: as the representative of hitherto unknown possibilities for both the citizen and the administration. The activation of the potential of individual citizens to be learning, increasingly self-sufficient, more responsible, independent, and so on, is articulated as the path to greater quality of life for the individual. In education, we see the development not only of goals and policies for teaching, but also of different ways for children and young people to maximise, develop and make use of their potential. And within eldercare, policy development no longer simply relates to care and services but also to the potential for individual citizens to become more independent and to take responsibility for their own quality of life. Additionally, public involvement and the effort to consider the perspective of citizens are increasingly seen as opportunities for public administration and for welfare institutions to effect change and innovation. With tools such as 'citizens journey' (a study of the way citizens experience different public institutions and services), interviews with citizens or short anthropological studies of the life-world of individual citizens, the administration seeks to gain a better understanding of the unique motivations, resources and ambitions that drive individual citizens. The hope is that greater knowledge of people will lead to improvements and cost reductions across welfare services. The responsibility of the administration and welfare organisations, in other words, becomes a question of increasingly allowing the potential of citizens to be brought into play. The focus on citizens' potential is seen both as a way to ensure greater quality of life for the individual as well as a way to revive public administration, through user involvement in innovation processes, for example.

In the context of human resource management, Bogdan Costea, Norman Crump and Kostas Amiridis describe what they refer to as 'the potentiality principle' (Costea et al, 2012). They argue that human resource management contains an ideal about human beings as always capable of further development, and that human beings always hold an immanent potential, which needs to be conjured, released, liberated and mobilised (Costea et al, 2006, 2007). A similar vocabulary seems to be in play today in the development of expectations about citizen-centred governance. In the light of the history we have described, of the relation between citizen and public administration, it might seem surprising that the citizen, who in the capacity of legal subject was precisely defined as outside the public sphere, has today been positioned so explicitly as an object of inclusion whose resources should be mobilised, almost like an employee. When citizens are described as legal subjects, the private sphere marks the limit of public regulation. However, today it has become an established truth that the involvement of citizens as participants in the production and delivery of welfare and better use of citizens as resources can create better welfare. Expectations abound, today, about the benefits of mobilising citizen resources toward greater independence as well as the optimisation of citizens' desire to learn and volunteer to contribute to the welfare society.

When the citizen is described as potentiality, the limit of governance is not only citizens' capacity for self-governance but also their capacity for self-exploration and the discovery of how alternative manifestations of the self, alternative narratives about the self, contain new possibilities for self-potentialisation and subsequent self-realisation. It is a question of cultivating the ability of citizens to imagine themselves. It is not simply the self-governance of citizens that serves as the object of public administration but the contingency of the self-relation. With the citizen perceived as potentiality, the administration no longer assumes that hidden behind the non-manifest motivation of the citizen is one positive core of latent motivation. There is no 'core self' – not even a latent core. Instead, the self is perceived as a relation – for example, a narrative relation – that comes

Example 8.2: From welfare to self-worth – and new expectations of professionals

The municipality of Kolding has formulated a vision for the welfare services of the future entitled 'Self-worth is more than welfare'. This vision is based on the observation that the need for welfare continues to grow because of an ageing population with high expectations of public services while the economic foundation is under pressure. The municipality writes:

> Kolding is a self-worth society. We give back opportunities and authority to people who are capable. We believe that a framework of shared values, citizenship and voluntary efforts strengthen the individual as well as society. We believe that self-worth is more than welfare. People want to do it themselves – for life. With the self-worth society we provide room for them to do so.

The vision relies on the notion that every citizen holds a potential, which means that the state should tread carefully when granting and providing assistance, and focus instead on motivating citizens to take care of themselves. Rather than automatically granting assistance and service in response to diagnoses, the municipality seeks to see citizens as hidden resources who can help themselves care for themselves. The municipality describes finding and nurturing the potential of citizens as its most important job:

> In the same way that a nursery prunes a tree in order to encourage new growth, we prune away various disservices and allow people's self-worth to grow. We reject a certain way to see people. We believe that all human beings hold resources and potential that might contribute to their ability to manage their lives and that people fundamentally want to be independent. We want to help them achieve that. (chair of the Social Committee in the municipality of Kolding, quoted in *Mandag Morgen*, 24.10.12)

In the self-worth vision, a reasoning where certain diagnoses automatically leads to certain services is problematised. Instead, the municipality expects its employees to work flexibly and, depending on the situation, disregard conventional procedures and seize opportunities to allow citizens to become more independent. The path to increased independence and the ability and desire among citizens to care for themselves is described as a process of loosening the desire and demands to provide care and assistance:

> What happens when we let go of our need to control and accept that the path to success is not always straight? When we inspire courage in citizens who will have to increasingly care for themselves in the future? They grow – right in front of our eyes. Not everyone sees it. But we do. We watch them strengthen their souls.

into being through the act of self-relation, including self-relation as relating to others. Motivation arises when a relation relates to itself. This relation is always contingent. Self-relation is never singular; the self is multiple. One always has contingent narratives about oneself. Thus, it is no longer a question of bringing out the latent self and making it manifest. The self-relation of citizens is contingent, and this contingency must be brought into the open in order that citizens may choose themselves. Developing an eye for the existence of several narratives of oneself and several 'voices' allows the individual to relate to such voices and perhaps shift their internal power relation. Thus, the contingency of the self-relation represents potentiality for both citizens and the administration. It is as question of strengthening citizens' experience of contingency. Citizens become polyvalent and can be observed differently by different systems and observed differently by themselves. And these different perceptions of the citizen are viewed as a valuable resource. The development can be summed up as shown in Table 8.2.

The movement toward viewing citizens as potentiality has a number of implications for welfare organisations. First, it poses a challenge to the relationship between citizens and professionals. When citizens are viewed as unique and are activated as the co-creators of welfare, professionals can no longer simply deliver

Table 8.2: Forms of citizen governance

	Governance technology	Object of governance	Limit of governance	Citizen's motivation
Citizen as legal subject	Law and legally defined services	The citizen's formal sphere of action	Private sphere	The citizen is viewed as bonus pater, whose inner motivation is assumed
Citizen as recipient	Instruction Counselling Decisions Action plan	The citizen's material sphere of action	The citizen's motivation to receive help	The citizen's motivation is assumed but must be supported with explanation and knowledge
Citizen as active fellow citizen	Shared perspective Dialogue Citizens contract	The citizen's self-management	The citizen's capacity for self-reflection and choice of freedom	Motivation is divided into manifest and latent, and manifest motivation cannot be assumed
Citizen as potentiality	Explore through conversations Social party games Aesthetic tools	The citizen's contingent self-relation	The citizen's imagination and self-images	Motivation is viewed as an emergent phenomenon related to the contingency of the self-relation

the professionally correct service. We take a closer look at this question by asking how the roles made available by welfare function systems for professionals and citizens change. Second, the understanding of citizens as potentiality leads to a proliferation of responsibility for welfare. The administration has to develop competences such as expanding the capacity of volunteers to take responsibility for helping citizens to take responsibility for their own learning, development, quality of life, etc. We explore the way in which the welfare society becomes increasingly dependent on citizens' willingness and ability to assume personal responsibility for their own and others' welfare, and the challenges this creates for welfare management.

The citizen as the audience of function systems

Shifting our point of observation from the relationship of public administration/citizen to function system/individual allows us to perform a significantly more nuanced analysis, and in particular, it affords us a more tricky insight into the ideal that we normally refer to as 'focus on the citizen' or 'individualisation.' Indeed, a closer look shows that the other side of individualisation always means that the systems assume the right to define the meaning of individuality.

First, the basics. Over time, the individual function systems establish roles that serve purposes of both inclusion and exclusion. Roles provide psychic systems with communicative possibilities of connectivity within the function system. Roles allow function systems to establish admission criteria for communication and to define some as communication-relevant in particular ways. Roles make it possible for function systems to address specific psychic systems and to recognise them as people within the system while blocking out other roles that would otherwise be available to these people. The health system, for example, addresses someone as doctor, and thus makes that person communication-relevant within the health system. However, at the same time, the role of doctor blocks out other roles that a person as a psychic system fills in other social contexts, such as mother, wife, volunteer, consumer or athlete. Thus, in relation to function systems, roles define the communication *relevance* as well as communication *irrelevance* of the psychic system – both inclusion and exclusion. A doctor who has to make a decision about whether or not to continue treatment of a very sick patient might include aspects that are outside strictly medical considerations, such as personal sympathies, hope, etc. The role of doctor blocks out all non-medical consideration as communication-irrelevant. Thus, despite the fact that an individual is sure to think about the non-medical aspects of a situation, a doctor, qua their role as a doctor, is unable to present such considerations to the medical teams as the basis of their decision.

In historical terms, function systems operate with two different kinds of roles: *performance roles* and *audience roles*. Performance roles relate to conditions for performing within the systems whereas audience roles only provide a role in the form of the system's external environment. We all know this distinction: actor/

audience, doctor/patient, social worker/client, journalist/reader, politician/voter and teacher/student. Anyone who is not involved in the operations of a specific function system (for example, diagnosis and treatment in the role of doctor) remains central to the system as audience or public for the function systems (for example, patients in need of examination and treatment, relatives of patients, etc). All function systems provide particular audience roles (Stichweh, 1997, p 97). The audience role serves as the system's image of who populates its external environment, and the audience is only allowed very limited role scripts. The audience functions as a parasite on the system in the sense that it does not perform in relation to the operations of the function system. Patients do not constitute the healthcare system and function primarily as observer of and observed by the system. This does not mean that the audience is insignificant. As observer, the audience contributes by being observed by the function system, for example, when political parties reference 'public opinion' and see themselves as representatives of it. Or when the audience of the healthcare system organises in competing patient associations, which all demand special attention and prioritisation. In such cases, the audience makes itself felt as an external environment that the system is forced to consider. This is of particular significance in many welfare systems such as healthcare, education and care in which audience roles are differentiated and organised in organisations that constantly compete and fight for attention. Thus, we distinguish between *performance roles* as that which afford the person who fills the role the opportunity to be observed as a contributor to the system, and *audience roles* in which a person is not recognised in the communication as individually performing, but which still serve a central role as external environment for the function systems.

Each function system produces its own performative roles as well as its own audience fiction. And each audience fiction establishes its own horizon of expectations for the citizen. The healthcare system sees a patient, the education system sees a student, the care system a client, etc. Teachers and students enters a classroom well aware of the existing set of expectations and rules for acceptance that apply in the communication, for example, the fact that the teacher asks questions and the student answers them. Seeing a doctor activates a different horizon of expectations. The doctor also asks questions, but the patient knows that these questions do not serve the function of testing their knowledge, and is an attempt by the doctor to gather information that can serve as the basis of a diagnosis. The different audience fictions allow the function systems to approach citizens in a functionally relevant way, including the effort to compel citizens to contribute to their communication and practice. Audience fictions stabilise citizens' expectations in relation to the encounter with the doctor, the teacher, the social worker, etc. Thus, individual function systems are associated with a set of different citizen figures.

With the notion of the active fellow citizen comes a strange doubling of the audience roles that the function systems employ. Active fellow citizens, as we have described them, create themselves as free and assume responsibility for themselves and their fate by taking on the collective whole. However, this self-relation looks different from the perspective of different function systems. The definition of active fellow citizen means something entirely different in the care system, the education system, etc. What remains the same is the expectation that individual citizens relate proactively to themselves through the codes and languages of the systems. One is expected not only to relate to the doctor, teacher or social worker on the system's premises, but also to create oneself in the images of the systems. In addition to previous audience fictions about the role of student, patient, etc, we now also *get second-order audience fictions* (Andersen, 2013b). Second-order audience fictions encourage citizens to see themselves from the perspective and code of the function systems. And the individual function systems develop fictions about the self-relation of citizens. What takes place is a re-entry of the distinction performance role/audience on the side of the performance role. The excluded mass audience is now included as performing, which leads to individualisation. The student is expected to contribute to their own learning and ceases therefore to be one among many in the classroom since the individual student, in addition to the collective goals of the class, possesses their own learning goals. The patient is expected to participate in their diagnosis and treatment. Clients are expected to help themselves. The consumer is expected to contribute to the production of the product and become a co-producer. This means an individualisation of the audience that further allows the client, student and patient to be granted a certain status of person within the function system.

Self-supporting clients are addressed as at the mercy of the function system. Citizens are expected to be able to observe themselves from the perspective of the system. However, the systems do not afford citizens a general observational competence, which would allow them to communicate their broader view of the system. Citizens have to see themselves through the lens of the system but are not permitted to look at the system as such. They are expected to contribute to their own learning, including seeing themselves pedagogically, but if a citizen tries to direct the pedagogical perspective outward toward other students or the teacher, they are perceived as aggressive, as getting involved in someone else's business. Citizens are invited to self-perform as a stand-in for the system, but this invitation does not include performing in the system! Thus, the construction of the active fellow citizen is a bit like Alice in Wonderland – both inside and outside. The active fellow citizen becomes a *monster*, symbolically joining what cannot be joined: system and environment. Active fellow citizens are invited to come inside on the condition that they remain outside (Knudsen, 2010). This shift from first-order to second-order audience fictions is summed up here (Andersen, 2013b) (see Table 8.3).

With the notion of the citizen as potentiality, citizens' contributions become increasingly significant. Citizens are not invited into the systems as an act of compassion. Function systems communicate about how their performances rely on the performance of citizens. Education is most successful when students take responsibility for their own learning. Social work runs the risk of failure and being

Table 8.3: First- and second-order audience roles

Function system	Code (plus/minus)	Folding of the code	Performance role	First-order audience role	Second-order audience role
Pedagogical	Better/worse in terms of learning	Learning to learn to learn	Teacher	Student	Responsibility for own learning
Political	Power-superiority/ power-inferiority	Power to empower	Politician	Citizen	Active fellow citizen
Care	Help/no help	Help with self-help	Social worker	Client	Self-supporting client
Healthcare	Healthy/sick	Preventive lifestyle	Doctor	Patient	The healthy citizen
Economic	Pay/not pay	Pay for others' payments	Producer	Consumer	Political consumer and the consumer as co-producer

seen as patronising if clients are not involved in the process. From that perspective, citizens represent potentiality for the system. However, such potentiality only becomes a realisable possibility if citizens see themselves the same way. Thus, function systems view their own audience fictions as both figures of inclusion and exclusion. It is problematic for a function system if its catalogue of audience fictions is not seen as attractive to citizens. It is a problem if a patient refuses to take responsibility for their own health or if a client shows no willingness to change their situation. *The production of contingency within the audience fictions becomes a strategy for inclusion.* Or, in other words, from the perspective of the function systems, it is of the utmost importance to have a variable collection of audience fictions so that very few turn down the opportunity to play an active role.

It would be a problem for the education system, for example, if the performing audience role about assuming responsibility for one's own learning is not perceived as accessible and attractive to all students. What if a student prefers to play football or computer games or finds it more attractive to daydream? In such cases, the role 'responsible for own learning' would produce communication irrelevance in relation to the student's rather than communication relevance. It could be that 'responsibility for own learning' was perceived as the role of teacher's pet for the few who always and conscientiously do their homework and who are always rewarded with good grades. The inclusive ambition inherent in the notion of 'responsibility for own learning' ironically runs the risk of producing exclusion in relation to those students who do not see it as possible or attractive to assume the role. Semantics about different forms of intelligence and learning styles multiply the possible meaning of 'responsibility for own learning'. The role of student is made contingent and indefinite so it becomes easier to assume the role and to shape it – even as someone who struggles to get homework done. Responsibility for own learning can also apply to someone who is a 'touch and feel' child. As Helene Ratner writes: 'Theories about many different learning styles and intelligences *pluralize* the classroom to allow for *individual* students to have their own learning style' (Ratner, 2013, p 131, own translation, emphasis in original). Based on the theory of learning styles developed by Dunn et al (1992; see also Dunn and Dunn, 1993, 1999), the book *Fokus på læring 3.0. Om læringsstile i hverdagen* (*Focus on learning 3.0. Everyday learning styles*) distinguishes between different aspects that might affect the learning of an individual: perceptual, psychological, environmental, physiological, emotional and social. The book then goes on to distinguish between a number of preferences within each of these aspects – preferences for learning styles held by individual students. Furthermore, the social aspect can be divided into preferences for learning on one's own, in pairs, smaller groups, larger groups, with a view to expertise or for variation. Finally, individual preferences are judged according to a scale ranging from strong, moderate, neither-nor, moderate and strong. This allows for a great number of possible combinations, each of which represents a specific learning style. Students might prefer a learning style that makes room for personality traits such as being very auditory, highly sensitive to sound, analytical, a morning person, not very self-motivated, requiring structure or preferring to work in pairs (Lauridsen, 2012). The recognition of different learning styles is a way to increase possibilities for inclusion. It provides a multiplicity of ways in which to recognise students as communication-relevant. It also means the dissolution of the classroom as a given unit, and teachers can no longer base their instruction on established notions of good pedagogy and didactics because these will always be relative to the learning styles among students. Moreover, the discourse on learning styles becomes so highly complex that it produces new risks of exclusion. In order to be recognised as someone who takes responsibility for own learning, a minimum requirement is the ability to describe one's learning style.

A similar focus on contingency in the audience roles can be seen in several other welfare-oriented function systems. The care system, for instance, now works with personality typologies, something that has otherwise been employed primarily in the context of recruitment and staff development, including, for example, Myers Brigg's Type Indicator and the Enneagram Test. The Enneagram Test distinguishes between nine personality types: reformer, helper, achiever, individualist, investigator, loyalist, enthusiast, challenger and peacemaker. In social work, these typologies are used 'to start a dialogue with them about what works for them and to support clients in their effort to discover their own path towards self-sufficiency' (Gjesing 2010, p 20, own translation).

New professional roles

The changes in audience role in the direction of second-order and contingency also challenge what it means to be a welfare professional. The performance roles in the function systems (doctor, teacher, social worker, nurse, educator, etc) undergo a revision in order to give room for a performing audience, and the performance roles come to depend on the audiences' self-contributions. As the anthology *At skabe en professionel* (*Creating a professional*) shows, all welfare function

Example 8.3: 'The lens captures the beauty of the addict'

An edition of the journal *Socialrådgiveren* (*The Social Worker*) includes coverage of a photography exhibition by social worker Jannie Bertz whose photographs show a different image of drug users than the ones people typically associate with life on the street. Three clients from a rehabilitation centre in Kolding played the role of supermodel for a day, complete with their hair and make-up done, and dressed in haute couture.

The project was not intended to achieve a specific change or end result. Instead, it was about affording the drug user the experience of a different self-image. The social worker comments: "I wanted to give them the chance to play princess for a day when what they are used to is being viewed as drug addicts."

Thus, the goal was to give the clients a physical experience of a different identity: "You can see how happy Brian looks in the photographs. There is something very beautiful about him. But he can't see that. So my goal is to show him and everyone else."

The project wanted to introduce contingency into the self-images of the clients – to give them a chance to experience themselves differently in a context where they were not unambiguously seen as drug users or homeless. The project focused precisely on the simultaneous existence of several self-images – several possible worlds. Bertz comments: "My original idea was to photograph them in regular clothes. But then it evolved into a 'mix of worlds', in which different perspectives meet and connect."

She also describes how the opportunity to be viewed differently – to experience a different relation between client and professional – could be motivating for the drug users: "Brian stayed clean on the day of the photo shoot. And he has told me that the project gave him the motivation to completely kick his meth habit."

> Instead of action plans with concrete goals and agreements, the experience of seeing themselves differently and establishing new alternative self-perceptions is viewed as a resource for the clients. The objective is to create a sense in the citizen that their self-image could be different. We might say that social policies borrow its method from the realm of aesthetics – in this case, the fashion industry – as a way to create new possibilities for citizens.

systems today are faced with the challenging task of redefining their performance roles in light of the shift to second-order systems. Margaretha Järvinen and Nanna Mik-Meyer write:

> Whereas professionals used to be experts who knew, based on their training and experience, "what was best for the users", and who therefore served the role of active agent in the process of defining goals and making decisions about methodology, welfare state employees have been reduced to "facilitators" whose goal is to place the user at the centre and contribute to his or her self-development and administration of risks. The job of a facilitator or coach is not to solve the problems of citizens but to create the best possible framework for citizens to solve their own problems. (Järvinen and Mik-Meyer, 2012, p 18, own translation)

Helle Bjerg and Hanne Knudsen show how today's public school teachers no longer simply base their teaching on knowledge about their specific subject and about pedagogy, but also on their knowledge of individual students as people. Personal knowledge becomes indispensable when the object of teaching is to allow students to assume responsibility for own learning. And, according to Bjerg and Knudsen, this fundamentally changes the teacher's professional role: 'What is new about this is not that the teacher's personality plays a role in relation to the students. What is new is that the teacher's personality becomes an integrated element in what it means to be a professional' (Bjerg and Knudsen, 2012, p 94, own translation). Thus, the emergence of the notion of 'the performing audience' means that the performance role, as the unity of role and person, is folded into itself on the side of the role so that we get 'the personal performance'. The performance role becomes a question of performing the very relation between role and person. A professional becomes one who does not simply step into an impersonal role but who professionally relates to the role as personal (see, for example, Obling, 2013). Central to filling the performance role is one's ability to come through as a person vis-à-vis the citizen, since the citizen will otherwise not be able to assume responsibility for self-governance in the system's image. Self-management is presumed at both sides of the difference between professional and citizen. If, for example, health prevention is a matter of managing the self-management of citizens, the professional must also have the capacity to self-manage from the perspective of prevention.

This is why we see a strong focus today on the need for welfare professionals to be 'authentic'. We see pedagogical debates about the authentic teacher, care debates about the authentic social worker and nurse, health debates about the engaged and empathetically minded doctor. In 2009, for instance, the journal *Socialrådgiveren* (*The Social Worker*) led a discussion about 'the authentic professional'. The starting point was that people reflect themselves in others and if social workers wanted to help clients achieve greater self-worth, they had to be encountered as authentic people: 'The more authentic we can be as professionals, the more we are "showing the way" for clients to have the courage to be themselves, and vice versa' (Bækgaard, 2009, p 22, own translation). This represents a radical break with the traditional performance role, which was precisely based on a distinction between role and person. Doctors were perceived as trustworthy precisely because they spoke as doctors and not as private people, and therefore represented not just themselves but the entire healthcare profession as such. Authority is a central aspect of the traditional performance role, and is granted through one's ability to serve as the representative of a system. 'Authenticity' is antagonistically opposed to 'authority' since one can only be said to be fully authentic when representing oneself and only oneself. Authority is achieved through external reference to a system one is granted representative status of. Authenticity, by contrast, is achieved through pure self-reference, which produces an identity that is identical with itself. As Jane Bækgaard says of the authentic social worker: 'It is important to take care of oneself as a professional, to work honestly and without restraint and to stay alive on the inside. To feel complete in one's incompletion. To have the courage to be who one is with what is in the present' (Bækgaard, 2009, p 23, own translation). Professional authority, in turn, can only be achieved through disregard for the personal and by serving as a representative of the system by means of education and competences. The shift to the second order and the folding of the difference between role and person into a call for professional personalisation of the role create a fundamental unsolvable paradox within the performance role, because people are required to be both professionally *authoritative* and personally *authentic*. A person can only be an authority by excluding the personal, and can only be authentic by being identical with their self-relation and not simply playing a role. There is no way to appear as authority without losing authenticity and vice versa.

Proliferation of personal responsibility and the emergence of hyper-responsibility

It should be clear by now that the shifts we have described in the relationship between public administration and citizen all point toward a revival of the concept of personal responsibility. Administrations and function systems call for more personal responsibility from citizens. This development is somewhat surprising in light of the fact that society's functional differentiation and establishment of bureaucratic organisations represented a break with regulation through the

Example 8.4: Mentoring work as the prevention of extremism

In 2012, the Danish Ministry of Social Affairs and Integration published the handbook *Relations and mentoring work* (*Relations og mentorarbejde*) as part of an effort to prevent extremism (Ministeriet for Børn, Legestilling, Integration og Sociale forhold, 2012). The publication was a result of a partnership between the Ministry of Social Affairs and Integration, the Prevention Center in the Danish Security and Intelligence Service (PET), the municipalities of Copenhagen and Århus and the Police Department of Eastern Jutland. It was directed at educators, teachers, social workers, residential social workers and employees of the Pedagogical and Psychological Counseling Center (PPR). One tool for mentoring is a so-called diagnosis form. Below is an example of its use:

Risk factors and protective factors	Description and assessment	Potential for chance and action
Personal	D appears intelligent but emotionally inhibited	D is good at reflecting and thinking about social issues. We can use this constructively by including him in new social contexts. A goal could be for D to apply to a folk high school after he completes high school
Social	D thinks of himself as 'anti-authoritarian' and struggles with typical social contexts. He often skips school and does not do any sports or other afterschool activities. He is associated with sub-cultures that 'fight against racism and fascism'. D attends many demonstrations and protests. Usually, these are peaceful events but D has also been involved in quite a few violent confrontations with the police and people that he sees as political opponents. D only has a few actual friends in these groups. He speaks quite a bit about E who appears to be the group's ideological leader and whom he admires	It seems obvious to build on D's positive social engagement. Together, D and the mentor will explore different existing associations and grassroots organisations working with social and humanitarian projects that D might be able to participate in. Additionally, the idea of attending a folk high school might allow D to make new friends and interests
Motivational factors	D seems very directly motivated by 'the case' but is also motivated by participation in a group. He has a substantial need for recognition. He greatly admires E, and would clearly like to have a closer relationship with E	The mentor is in the process of forming a good relationship with D who increasingly shares his thoughts and feelings with him. It seems that the relationship with the mentor could distance D from E and make him less dependent on E

Risk factors and protective factors	Description and assessment	Potential for chance and action
Ideological factors	Ultimately, D has 'good' values. He is against racism, wants to save the environment and believes in local democracy. However, he sees enemies everywhere. He views the authorities and the police as the 'henchmen of capitalism' who oppress society's weakest groups. D finds it difficult to believe that anything can be achieved though traditional democratic channels. He is a proponent of sub-cultures and alternative lifestyles	The mentor should initiate a conversation about the possible future implications of D's ideological involvement and violent activities. The discussion should include peaceful ways to influence society
Obstacles	For the time being, D projects all his feelings and engagement into 'the case'. However, it is obvious that D is unable to find the recognition he wants anywhere but the group – and particularly from E. D is not interested in distancing himself from the group, or going away to school	The mentor should try to reach an agreement with D about visiting a folk high school that works with politics and social issues. The goal is to encourage D to view the idea of folk high school (and hence distance himself from the group) in a more positive light

When the citizen is observed as potentiality, dialogue techniques become technologies for communication-seeking communication. The focus is on finding possibilities for effecting a positive development. The professional is expected to build authentic relationships with individual citizens and thus cultivate citizens' potential for giving their lives the desired direction.

individual morality of the 1700s and 1800s. The functional differentiation of society and bureaucratic organisations meant that society no longer had to rely on personal responsibility. Impersonal function-specific roles took over. And law and morality became separated.

How, then, should we conceive of this new emphasis on personal responsibility? Do we mean something different today when we speak of responsibility? Our argument is that what we are seeing is a new form of *hyper-responsibility*, which means responsibility that moves to the second order (Knudsen and Andersen, 2014). It is an expression of both a sense of powerlessness in the social systems as well as an attempt to control what cannot be controlled: a personal sense of responsibility.

This contains a significant management paradox: the individualisation and personalisation of the many forms of welfare responsibility (health, education, care, etc) can be seen as an effort to relieve both function systems and welfare organisations by making individuals responsible for the system's failure to perform. However, in order to shift responsibility onto the shoulders of citizens, the systems have to assume responsibility for enabling individuals to both see their own responsibility and to live up to it. The welfare systems and welfare organisations assume responsibility for the personal responsibility of the individual citizen without any actual measures of control. This makes them dependent on a new form of uncontrollability.

We begin by briefly summarising the way that the responsibility of the individual citizen has been articulated, and then move on to take a closer look at the legal construction of responsibility as form and its inherent paradoxes. We apply the same historical index as the one we used to describe the history of the concept of the citizen.

The concept of the citizen as legal subject makes a clear distinction between formal responsibility and personal responsibility. Formal responsibility is one that the state and public administration can impose on citizens with reference to the law's definition of obligation and injunctions. That is, formal responsibility is a specifically defined and calculable responsibility, for example, the responsibility to send one's children to school. Personal responsibility resides outside of the state's domain although the administration presupposes its existence. Personal responsibility is precisely personal and hence not a public concern. To personal responsibility also belongs responsibility for choosing to fulfil or not fulfil formal responsibility. The state interpellates citizens to accept different types of formal responsibility, but it is up to the personal responsibility of the individual to fulfil formal responsibility, and if a person chooses not do so, they are presumed to be willing to accept the legal ramifications, for example, a fine.

With the concept of the citizen as recipient, each welfare system develops its own more substantial expert ethics based on objectively justified norms for citizens. We see a differentiation into responsibility for health, responsibility for care, responsibility of education, etc. The state takes responsibility for defining what counts as responsible for the citizen, working through experts who provide advice and guidance. Nutrition policy might serve as an example. In 1936, the Danish Council for Housekeeping published its first pamphlets for Danish housewives. In the period up until the 1950s, the Council mostly wrote advice about how to stretch scarce resources and preparing nutritional meals for the family. Later, it turned into advice about health-promoting meals and mealtimes. The citizen's capacity for personal responsibility was never questioned, only the fact that citizens sometimes lacked knowledge and information that might be useful when taking personal responsibility. Thus, the aim was to strengthen the ability for citizens to be responsible by supplying 'information for citizens'. The advice was typically specific and concrete, such as directions for how to prepare a healthy meal or suggestions to parents about establishing a bedtime routine.

With the concept of the active fellow citizen, public administration begins to question the capacity and motivation of citizens for personal responsibility. The legal distinction between calculable and personal responsibility comes under attack. The new ideal is responsibility-seeking citizens who not only have a responsibility but who also seek responsibility for themselves and their lives, including their families and community. The state takes it upon itself to ensure that individual citizens seek to take responsibility. Thus, personal responsibility becomes a public responsibility at precisely the moment the state seeks to strengthen personal responsibility from without, and hence no longer takes it for granted. The state's responsibility for citizens' personal responsibility is split in two: on the one hand, the economic empowerment of citizens designed to stimulate the rational will and incite responsibility (in lay terms: give and take) – the theory is that when citizens discover the implications for not taking responsibility, their sense of responsibility grows. On the other hand, social empowerment is intended to support the individual's capacity for responsibility by building self-worth and self-reflection. Citizens contracts are precisely designed not as a commitment to a specific action but as a commitment to commitment as such (commitment to freedom also represents citizens' commitment to internal dialogue about the relationship between obligation and freedom).

Finally, with the concept of the citizen as potentiality, the problem is no longer just citizens' willingness to take responsibility but also their ability to imagine and their sensitivity to potential responsibility. It is no longer enough to be willing to take responsibility if one is unable to identify one's responsibility. And it is not enough to simply follow well-established norms for what responsible behaviour entails. Citizens are now expected to take on responsibility for continually seeking out potential responsibility; to be hyper-sensitive to opportunities for taking responsibility, not only for themselves and their family, but also for an undefined collective (Højlund, 2012). In 2008, on the website for the government campaign 'My Responsibility' (mitansvar.dk), Danish Minister for Welfare Karen Jespersen asked the following question: 'Your child's friend is not feeling well because her parents are going through a divorce. Do you talk to the parents about it, or do you feel uncomfortable and hope that the child's teacher will deal with the problem?' (5.19.08, own translation). The problem – and responsibility – here, is the wellbeing of the child's friend, which is affected by her parents' divorce. The minister does not invoke demands, rules or norms, but simply appeals to citizens to expand their sensitivity and capacity for responsibility. She insists on the need for parents to be responsible, but does not explicitly state her precise expectations of them. The entire campaign is designed to encourage citizens to 'take greater responsibility', but it never defines what it means by 'responsibility' (Knudsen, 2010, 2011; Knudsen and Andersen, 2014). It seems to be a general trend for the welfare systems to appeal to more responsibility regarding health, education, work, care, sports, eating habits, family and integration, but without further specifying the responsibility. In her book about the history of parental responsibility, Hanne Knudsen refers to this expectation as *indefinite responsibility* (Knudsen, 2010). The function systems increasingly find themselves in situations where their performativity depends on the responsibility of individual citizens. However, as the systems continue to expand the scope of potential responsibility for citizens to assume, responsibility can no longer be generalised, formulated and defined as rules and guidelines. Thus, public administration begins instead to establish spaces for citizens to collectively develop their sense of responsibility. Open conversations, dialogue games and responsibility games are designed to create social spaces in which citizens may explore and discover potential

Example 8.5: Health in play

In 2007, the Danish Health and Medicines Authority and Danish Veterinary and Food Administration partnered up with the organisation Skole og Samfund (School and Society) to create the game *Health in Play – Dialogue and Collaboration about Health in the Classroom*. The game is designed to initiate a dialogue about health at school and also to formulate agreements about health-related responsibilities with regard to nutrition, exercise, drugs and alcohol, general wellbeing, knowledge and attitudes to health.

The game includes a video presentation, which can also be found on the Danish Ministry of Health's website. The video includes the following statement by the health consultant for the municipality of Gladsaxe, Teresa Dominicussen: 'It is easy enough for the municipality to frame the question of health on its own terms, but it is important that parents and students recognise themselves in the conversation so that their actions extend beyond the school to also include their home life.' The video then cuts directly to a consultant from University College South, Karsten Jensen, who says: 'It does not mean that we all have to live in the same way, that we have the same preferences. It is important to allow room for differences in a diverse society' (own translation) This is the management dilemma to which *Health in Play* seeks to respond to.

Health in Play is intended for use in public schools in the context of parent events, staff development days or programmes for older students. On tables are game boards with three squares entitled 'Agree', 'Somewhat agree' and 'Disagree'. Each of the groups is given a stack of statements, for example:

- 'It is not acceptable that students try alcohol at home'
- 'Exercise and play should be incorporated into more subjects than just PE'
- 'In order to choose healthy foods over soda, candy and chips, students need knowledge, experiences and strong role models'
- 'Parents are their children's most important role models'
- 'Parents are responsible for establishing a strong parent network in their child's class'
- 'Children and teens need to be motivated to live healthy lives'
- 'Children and teens have to learn to take responsibility for their health'

The first two-thirds of the game are made up by a playful exploration of possible responses to the responsibility cards, including the potential action that might accompany the different responsibilities of parents, students and the school respectively. The third part of the game focuses on formulating an agreement about the distribution of responsibilities. Which health responsibilities belong to parents, to students and to the school respectively? Ultimately, however, the agreement's implementation is not subsequently supervised or sanctioned by anyone, so the question of whether the agreement serves as play or agreement is kept open.

Games like this serve as explorations of potential citizen responsibility. They are not about arriving at a predefined sense of responsibility, but about a collective exploration of new

> possible modes of responsibility. Thus, the game addresses citizens as responsibility potential. By allowing parents to play with the concept of responsibility in a non-binding way, they are invited to reinterpret their role as responsible parents (Andersen, 2009).

responsibility. We have summed up the development of the responsibility concept in Table 8.4.

Table 8.4: The articulation of responsibility over time

	Concept of responsibility	Responsibility technology	Form
Citizen as legal subject	Responsibility is split into formal responsibility and personal responsibility	Rules Injunctions	Traditional first-order personal responsibility
Citizen as recipient	Formal responsibility is supplemented with a substantial expert ethics. Personal responsibility is still assumed but is also infused with information and advice	Advice Guidelines Specific directions	
Citizen as active fellow citizen	Personal responsibility is no longer assumed. The state questions the citizen's willingness to take responsibility and seeks to take responsibility for ensuring that citizens take responsibility	Unilaterally organised conversations Empowerment Citizens contracts	Hyper-responsibility: second-order responsibility
Citizen as potentiality	Expectations about infinite responsibility, including responsibility for the constant exploration of potential responsibility	Open conversations Responsibility games	

First-order responsibility

The first two responsibility semantics reference the 'traditional' form of personal responsibility. Here, the expectation about responsibility is always split. On the one hand, responsibility assumes the form of an external call to be responsible in response to rules and injunctions (the first semantic about the citizen as legal subject) or advice and guidelines (the second semantic) or existing norms as large. On the other hand, responsibility exists as an inner drive where individuals are only accountable to themselves. These are two sides of the same difference. We might say that traditional personal responsibility is constituted by the difference between the external and internal drives. Traditional personal responsibility defines being responsible as fulfilling both drives. Jacques Derrida has analysed this discursive form, and shows how it installs a fundamentally paradoxical effect because one can never be said to live up to the expectation about being responsible. He refers to the distinction between an outer and inner call for responsibility as a distinction between 'general' and 'absolute' responsibility (Derrida, 1992b).

General responsibility establishes an expectation about the individual being compelled to justify their actions in relation to expectations in their environment: A person is responsible when they respond to another person and are held responsible in relation to the other. Being responsible means to follow generally accepted rules, norms, advice and guidelines. This quickly becomes problematic since it is difficult to know where to draw the line for one's accountability vis-à-vis external expectations about responsibility. How does a person act in situations with a surplus of expectations about responsibility where they can only fulfil one responsibility at the expense of another?

Or more specifically, what should citizens do when they are not only expected to abide by existing rules and injunctions, but also to be accountable to the broad spectrum of advice, guidelines and instructions provided by the welfare state? Throughout the 1960s, 1970s and 1980s, an increasing number of welfare areas sought to supplement rules and injunctions with information and advice. Citizens were faced with the very real question of how to be accountable to all of it. They were literally faced with a surplus of general responsibility.

Traditional personal responsibility places the answer on the opposite side of the difference, that is, with absolute responsibility (the inner drive). Absolute responsibility is the place from which one relates to general responsibility and makes decisions. In *absolute responsibility*, one references only oneself. There is no one to ask for advice since that would be a reference to the general responsibility, and hence to a responsibility outside oneself. Being absolutely responsible means having to take on full responsibility and assuming full responsibility for judging what counts as responsible. A person follows only their inner drive for responsibility. There is no explaining away their choice by referring to general rules; it is a person's decision and it cannot be explained or justified. Explaining oneself means skirting responsibility. Thus, in order to fulfil the expectation about absolute responsibility, a person has to fail to meet expectations about accounting for the rules and advice of the general responsibility.

Ultimately, traditional personal responsibility leads to the paradox that in order to be responsible people have to be both generally *and* absolutely responsible even though the two expectations are incompatible. Indeed, in order to be generally responsible, a person must be absolutely responsible, and in order to be absolutely responsible, they have to be generally irresponsible. This is the impossible communicative logic of responsibility: a person can only be responsible by being irresponsible.

The first two responsibility semantics deal with this paradox by hiding it. Public administration keeps the production of irresponsibility invisible in the expansion – in the name of responsibility – of the amount of rules, advice, guidelines and instructions. The paradox is handled by never addressing the absolute side of the responsibility. Absolute responsibility is marked as 'private' and 'personal', and this marks the end of the conversation. The only conversation is about rules and advice.

Second-order responsibility

The other two responsibility semantics, by contrast, cause the paradox to visibly erupt within public administration. From the moment welfare administrations question citizens' commitment to responsibility, the rules for the communicative logic of responsibility change drastically. The questioning of citizens' willingness to assume responsibility cuts across the difference between general responsibility and absolute personal responsibility by framing citizens' internal drive and absolute responsibility as a public and general concern. The highly personal becomes political. But is this possible? Is it possible to address absolute responsibility without fully dissolving the distinction between general and absolute and hence the very idea of personal responsibility as form? It is indeed possible, but only through a doubling of the form of responsibility so that the general responsibility moves to the second order. Shifting the paradox to the second order does not dissolve it but makes it productive (Knudsen and Andersen, 2014).

Thus, in addition to the traditional personal responsibility constituted as the unity of general and absolute responsibility we see a second-order general responsibility, which is responsibility for exploring potential responsibility. We refer to this second-order responsibility as *playful hyper-responsibility* (Knudsen and Andersen, 2014; Andersen and Knudsen, 2014). It is playful because it does not simply focus on what it means to act responsibly but engages in playful exploration of potential responsibility. The playful aspect can take the form of organised games – by emphasising its status as 'responsibility games'. Such games, intended for citizens, exist today in almost any area of the welfare state (Andersen, 2009). However, the playful aspect might also take a different form that is not marked as play but instead as open dialogue whose form is playful and has no immediate implications. Play targets possible distinctions between general and absolute responsibility. It targets the general responsibility and its potential distinctions between responsibility and irresponsibility, between regulated and unregulated responsibility, between responsible and irresponsible advice, etc. And it targets the question of how absolute responsibility may respond to general expectations about responsibility, which things a person should choose to be held accountable for, and when it is necessary to act irresponsibly in order to be responsible. Thus, in its second-order configuration, responsibility becomes simulated and hypothetical.

Additionally, the *hyper* in hyper-responsibility refers to the effort to create hypersensitivity in relation to potential responsibility. There are no given and prescribed ethics, norms or rules. There is only the invitation to play. These games become responsibility labs. Hyper-responsibility is a transient form of responsibility because it can never become fixed and stabilised. If it were to become stabilised, the very fulfilment of the responsibility would be considered irresponsible. Thus, responsibility is no longer a question of listening to the voice of duty and being accountable. Playful hyper-responsibility is about the potentialisation of responsibility. The attention to potential responsibility is more important than fulfilling a given or prescribed responsibility and the central capacity is to be able to imagine potential responsibility.

The shift from first-order to second-order responsibility actually also influences how law defines and observes citizens' formal responsibility. Going second-order changes conditions for first order responsibility. Helen Reece has investigated the changes in British family law and its definition of 'divorcing responsibility', arguing that in family law from the late 1990s,

> ...the ideal individual is neither fully responsible nor fully irresponsible. Instead, he adopts the following approach to responsibility: he has a sense of, addresses, considers, undertakes, takes, takes into account, takes seriously, recognises, acknowledges, faces, faces up to, faces up to fully, has regard to, looks to, shares, accepts, meet, deals with, fulfils, and discharges. In essence, there is no action that the individual must take or refrain from taking in order to be responsible. He exhibits the degree of responsibility that he has reaches be his attitude towards his action. (Reece, 2000, pp 69-70)

Figure 8.1: Hyper-responsibility as form

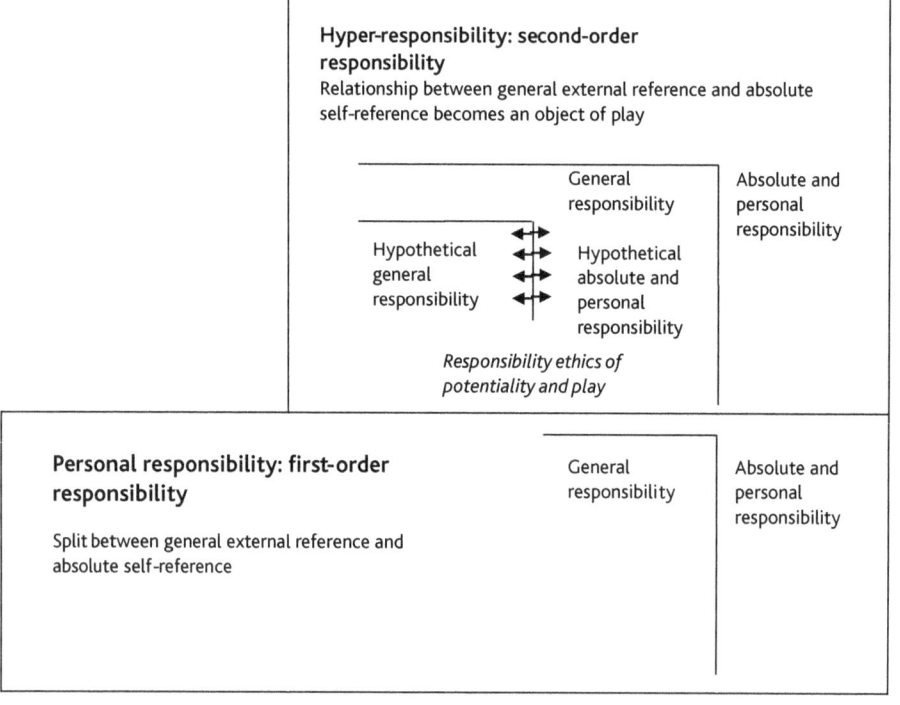

Reece concludes that in present law 'The responsible post-liberal individual is judge, not by what he does but by how profoundly he has thought about what he does' (Reece, 2000, p 70).

Hyper-responsibility is like a discursive game because it values the potentialisation of responsibility above the realisation of responsibility. It does not recognise someone as responsible by their actions but by their engagement and involvement in citizens contracts, dialogues and responsibility games. In order to be recognised as responsible in a second-order context, a person must participate in these simulation games and demonstrate their willingness to identify potential responsibility.

Challenges for citizen management

These shifts within the relationship between public administration and citizen turn the citizen's self-relation into an object of management. But they also establish a rather paradoxical framework for public administration and the professionals who come face to face with citizens.

- How can the administration encourage citizens to recognise themselves as active responsibility-seeking citizens?
- How does the administration know if it is, in fact, governing when the goal is to commit citizens to an internal dialogue about obligation and freedom that remains invisible to the state?
- What does governance mean in the context of a fundamentally invisible self-relation?
- How can the administration be controlled when it is forced to govern according to non-documentable premises?
- How can public administration both govern according to the self-relation of citizens and also protect their freedom and inviolability vis-à-vis the state?
- How can one inquire about power when managers and the administration believe that they do not exercise power but simply empower citizens?
- How can personal responsibility be called for without deconstructing it by making the personal public?

With the emergence of second-order responsibility, a central challenge becomes to combine or oscillate between the two forms of responsibility. On the one hand, the emergence of second-order responsibility represents a radical change in the communicative logic of responsibility. On the other hand, we might ask what the implications are for first-order responsibility, which, after all, remain in force. Second-order responsibility and its ongoing potentialisation of responsibility supplements first-order responsibility, but first-order responsibility is about the conditions for the realisation of responsibility. And there is no compulsory combination of the two orders. The second order simply exists as a responsibility to explore potential responsibility. Even at its most productive, there is no simple process of inundation on the first order. On the general side of first-order responsibility, potential responsibility is not necessarily captured in the form of new rules or advice, and there is no guaranty that a participant's hypersensitivity in relation to second-order responsibility translates into greater willingness and capacity to take responsibility. The second order might easily come to exist as its own decoupled logic of hypothetical conversations, which never result in action. We might even argue that citizens' growing capacity for and understanding of their potential responsibility do not necessarily make it easier to take responsibility in specific everyday situations. In fact, the burden of responsibility might seem so overwhelming that citizens decide to reject their responsibility altogether. Indeed, to the extent that the various responsibility dialogues, citizens contracts and games work, the amount of responsibility that needs to be prioritised grows accordingly. It is an irruption of the element of irresponsibility within the discourse of responsibility.

This also means increased and accelerated risk of disappointment. If the administration or the professionals look for hyper-responsibility as expressed through engagement, ability to imagine new opportunities, and desire to speak in terms of potentiality, they may be disappointed if citizens insist on following existing rules and guidelines. But the administration and professionals may also experience disappointment if those citizens who have shown engagement and participated in responsibility games and open dialogue do not subsequently translate the lofty words into action and no one signs up to bake a cake for the next meeting or volunteers to join the parent dialogue group.

Reflection 8.1: Citizen management

Ask yourself:

1. How do you observe and meet citizens?
2. What do you expect of citizens?
3. Do you alternate between different sets of expectations? Are you aware of these shifts? Do you make citizens aware of these shifts?
4. Do you meet citizens with ambiguous expectations? Do you take responsibility for the power inherent in such ambiguity, eg when unilaterally demanding dialogue?
5. Do you ever view citizens as not having independent willpower?
6. What do you see as your responsibilities and those of citizens respectively? What concept of responsibility are you working from? Legal responsibility? Expert responsibility? Hyper-responsibility? Do you sometimes test citizens' willingness and capacity for personal responsibility? How do you justify such tests?
7. When do you invite citizens to contribute, engage and share responsibility? Is there a point when you feel that citizens get too involved? Too difficult, disrespectful, demanding?

NINE

The potentiality state

We began high above the clouds with a general perspective on the differentiation of society, and proceeded to zoom in more closely, first with a look at the general development in public administration, then observed from the perspective of individual organisations, and finally from the perspective of the boundary between organisation and individual. Now we zoom back out again, not all the way to the level of society's differentiation form, but to the political system and the question of the history of state forms.

In 1990, Bob Jessop, a leading writer on state theory for nearly three decades, asked the question 'What is the state?':

> Is the state itself best described by its legal form, its coercive capacities, its institutional composition and boundaries, its internal operations and modes of calculation, its declared aims, its functions for the broader society or its sovereign place in the international system? Is it a thing, a subject, a social relation, or simply a construct which help to orientate political action? (Jessop, 1990, p 44)

We address two questions. The first is: what are the governance possibilities from the perspective of the political system? This includes two sub-questions: How is it possible for the political system to govern other autopoietic social systems? And how have conditions for governance changed historically, for example, with changes to dominant legal and state forms? The second question is: what state form emerges from the historical trends we have described – in relation to developments in public administration, the historical development of individual welfare institutions, and the relation between state and individual? Are these developments merely 'organisational', or do they challenge the basic state form?

With regard to the first question, our premise is that the political system has no contact with the rest of society. It is an autopoietical function system operating by means of the code of power. The political system can only operate politically. It cannot operate in the other systems. It cannot even determinate non-political operations. The political system can observe society. It can communicate about it but it cannot decide over it. The political system can only govern in relation to excess meaning produced by the self-governance of other systems. From this perspective, structural couplings are essential to the political system's ability to govern. Thus, we will answer the first question based on the premise that politics basically can only govern itself.

With regard to the second question, our premise is that the state represents the political system's self-description. The state is not an actor, a capacity or an institutional construct. In historical terms, the state as a concept emerges at the moment when the political communication system is finding it increasingly more difficult to describe its unity. Traditionally, the political system has been symbolised by a person (for example, the king) or by means of specific institutions such as the police or the army (which is why we used to teach the history of the political system as the sequence of kings). Gradually the internal complexity of the political system becomes so great that its unity can no longer be summed up in a simple concept. Thus, the state as concept emerges as a more abstract description of the unity of the political system. When we inquire into the history of state forms, therefore, it becomes a question of the way in which the political system constructs concepts to describe its unity in response to the increase in internal complexity. And it is also about describing the way that the political system describes its practice, function, possibility and boundaries – and their effects.

One of the theses in this context is that the state as concept changes from an indication of a given frame and premise for the multifarious functions of public administration to a concept that no longer presuppose such given structures. Instead, we see a reversal of the relationship between frame and function so that the frame is no longer presupposed but is constructed and chosen relative to the function. It is, in other words, a reversal of context and text so that the text defines its own context. This is only possible because we now have a number of parallel state concepts that individual operations can choose between. This is what we refer to as the potentiality state, a state whose form changes depending on the space of action it creates for individual operations within the system.

The possibility of governing: how the political system harvests the excess of self-governance

Our first question was, what is the possibility in the political system for governing other systems in society when its basic premise is that it can only govern itself? The political system can only govern in relation to the self-governance of other systems. And this happens primarily by means of the structural coupling produced by the legal system over time. Therefore, in order to more precisely diagnose the

Concept 9.1: Structural coupling
Systems cannot communicate with each other but they can observe each other and build internal structures for how to respond to each other's operations. A system connects to another system by making itself structurally irritable to the communication of other systems. A coupling is not something that exists in the space between systems. A coupling exists in the individual system where it both connects and separates the systems. A structural coupling can be defined as an internally structured element in a system, which makes the systems irritable in relation to other systems in a particular way while also leaving it indifferent (Luhmann, 1992b, p 1433). Structural couplings provide systems with a continual flow of disorder in response to which the systems must shape and change themselves.

governance possibilities within the political system, we need to move by way of the legal system.

The law is basically a system designed to take precautions against conflicts in society. The law's construction of rules and decisions does not solve conflicts but allows conflicts in society to be transformed into legal conflicts about who is right and who is wrong. The court does not solve a conflict about the children in a divorce case, but a legal decision can establish what is right and wrong in the case, even if the parents do not perceive this decision to be just. Rules and laws are programmes within the law that help the law decide about right and wrong.

But the law is not only an event in the legal system. The law is also an event in the political system, albeit a different event. Thus, the law functions as a structural coupling between the legal system and the political system. In the political system, legislation is a political decision-making process, and the law represents a collective decision on behalf of society. From the perspective of the political system, the legal system is a judicial power, designed to ensure that decisions made in the political system, as legislation, are implemented.

However, from the perspective of the legal system, laws are not viewed with the simplicity that the political system desires. To the legal system, a law is an internally established legal programme that serves as the reference point for the law's judgement on right/wrong. Even if the political system has adopted a law, it remains the responsibility of the legal system to judge the legality of this law; not only whether or not it counts as law – that is, adopted by the political system within the bounds of the law – but also how it counts as law and the implications for existing law. The courts have developed their own way of mediating existing law, and the law is only one point of reference among others when the court makes a decision in a case. The state of law cannot simply be deduced from individual laws. The court weighs laws up against each other, prior decisions, international law, special circumstances, etc.

The political system sometimes suffers from the misconceptions that the adoption of a law automatically results in strict implementation of its policies. However, this is not how the law works in the legal system. The political system cannot independently enforce a law. Only the legal system can do this. Therefore, the political system depends heavily on the law as structural coupling.

Additionally, the law does not determine behaviour in society. What the law does is to prescribe norms. Norms function as expectations about expectations. Patient expectations about the expectations that apply when we visit the doctor constitute norms. Norms are expectations capable of surviving disappointment. We do not change our expectations because the expected did not happen. The law deals with the norms and formation of norms in society. The law does not define the norms. It observes the formation of norms in society's other systems and prescribes those. This is how the law functions. When the legal system judges in cases about patient rights, for instance, the law is not simply asserting its norm. The court listens to the evidence and looks at the norms involved in the case –

disappointed or not, conflicting or not – and makes a statement regarding which norm is right and which is wrong.

Table 9.1: The law as structural coupling

System	Construction of the law	Observations of each other's observations of law
Political	A collective decision on behalf of society	The court puts the law into practice
Legal	A programme for the decision of right and wrong	The law is only valid if it has been legally adopted by the political system

Because it needs to be able to harvest the excess of self-governance in the legal system, the political system remains highly dependent on the development of the law, its internal differentiation of different legal programmes and its capacity to prescribe norms (Teubner, 1991). We now take a closer look at the historical development of legal programmes before speaking further of the possibility for the political system to harvest the governance excess of the legal system's self-governance. We ask how the legal system prescribes norms in other systems. What does the legal system's programme for prescription look like? How does it become part of the legal system's prescription of norms to create structural couplings between function systems? And how does this allow for the political system to not simply govern in relation to the surplus in the self-governance of the law, but also in relation to the law's prescription of structural couplings between different function systems? We broadly identify four prominent legal programmes over the past century: formal law, substantial law, reflexive law and hybrid law (Teubner, 1983, 1986, 1988, 1992; Willke, 1986). These four legal programmes have not substituted but rather supplemented each other, and continue to affect each to this day. Below we try to describe these forms with reference to public administration (we described them in more rudimentary terms in Chapter Six in relation to the development of contract forms).

Formal law observes public administration as an organisation that makes administrative decisions, and the law decides which administrative decisions public administration is authorised to make and under which conditions. Formal law thus assigns to public administration the right to make specific types of decision, but at the same time, the law establishes criteria for what makes an administrative decision invalid. Formal law operates by means of conditional programmes. It is constructed around if/then sentences (Teubner, 1988). This means that it is directed at stipulating actions. We might use the social services department as an example. A rule would be formal if it established unambiguous conditions for when citizens are entitled to receive specific services. If a citizen shows up in the social services department needing glasses, the department would be able to refer to the law and ask, 'Is this something we are allowed to make decisions about?' If so, the law will also provide information about what kind of financial support the department can give and within which time frame. In social politics, this is referred to as rule-based services and was the dominant legal programme until the Social Security Act 1974 (Law no 333). Formal law leaves no room for other professional considerations within the social services department other than the law itself. This means that social policies can only come into effect when there is an explicit legal basis for services. In formal law, the question of providing assistance to a client is purely a question of legality. And the more detailed the legislation, the easier it is to subsequently make a decision in the case of a disagreement between a citizen and social services department, and to establish who is right and who is wrong according to existing law.

With *substantial law*, public administration is not only observed as responsible for making administrative decisions but also for delivering legally based services (Wiethölter, 1986). Substantial law assigns to public administration the right and independence to pursue specific legally established objectives, for example, educating children for such and such purposes or operating the railroad for such and such purposes. Substantial law programmes the law according to purpose. The law is organised around the effort to manage the purpose and result of social processes within public administration, but does not prescribe individual action. The law operates in accordance with the difference means/end, but only establishes what legally counts as an end. The means remain open-ended. In the case of social security legislation, the social services department is assigned responsibility for choosing among alternative means and conducting an objective review of the best methodical intervention in response to a client's acknowledged need for help. In this way, substantial law paves the way for self-management in public administration based on prescribed non-legal considerations. The social services department is given the right to weigh legal consideration against care and assistance-based considerations. This gives considerations such as care and assistance an independent platform within public administration next to the law but without the authority to define the purpose of assistance. In the context of the public school the same would apply to pedagogical considerations, at universities to research considerations, at hospitals to health considerations, etc. Thus, substantial law grants public administration a certain level of methodological freedom in terms of how to achieve given goals. This means that legislation no longer requires the same level of detail. The term used is 'framework law'. This means that it no longer anticipates the same forms of conflicts; it only anticipates conflicts regarding objectives and output. Thus, substantial law does not primarily regulate the actions of public administration but rather the structural coupling between organisation and function system. It is the definition of public administration objectives that marks the coupling between public administration and function system and makes it the object of a regulation, which produces freedom for the organisation and the specific function system at the same time as they become structurally coupled and come to serve as each other's external environments.

With *reflexive law*, the law observes the public sector as a set of independent organisations establishing their own objectives with reference to the law's specifications of considerations that the objectives must reflect (Teubner, 1986; Willke, 1986). In reflexive law, legal sentences are increasingly procedural and indicate the considerations that public administration must reflect in its objectives. Let us use again social legislation as an example: the law no longer prescribes individual actions. It also no longer prescribes the specific purpose of assistance. Procedures regulate the structural conditions for how to formulate goals and objectives, for example, who is responsible for formulating the goals and the general considerations that should be reflected in the goals. The Social Services Act 1997, which replaced the Social Security Act 1974, outlines detailed requirements about the formulation of an action plan for individual children in the case of administrative decisions to forcibly remove them from their homes. Thus, the law no longer defines the specific circumstances required for the authorisation of out-of-home placements. The law does not even prescribe the purpose of removing children. Instead, the social services department is required to work with the parents and child to formulate an action plan that outlines a specific goal, which then serves as the basis for decisions about specific interventions and sub-goals. This not only allows non-legal considerations to play a role in the definition of means; it also allows for an indefinite amount of non-legal considerations in the definition of goals (for example, parents' rights, the needs of the child, effects on education and health), to the extent that a goal is even established and the process follows existing procedures. Reflexive law now regulates multiple structural couplings between organisations and a specific number of function systems. These couplings come to include reflexive elements. It is prescribed that they be coupled but not how. The effect is the possibility for ultra-cyclical couplings where the systems are in a process of ongoing noise production that continually requires a response. In other words, systems react not only to specific operations in other systems but also to each other's reactions. Thus, we are dealing with much stronger structural couplings. Paradoxically, such couplings do not simply restrict the involved systems. Instead, the ultra-cyclical couplings continue to strengthen the systems' autopoiesis. Paradoxically, it becomes both a question of increased regulation and increased self-management.

Hybrid law puts in play the very line between law and non-law within the form of law. We have to admit to a certain level of uncertainty about our description of this final legal form. What we do know is that there are new developments taking place in the law's self-programming, which indicates that the law is adapting to its dependency on other systems (at the same time as it is becoming more specialised). However, we are still hesitant to make any firm conclusion about this development. Concurrently with the development of extremely specialised knowledge and technology in science and economics, the law has developed regulation that employs a similarly specialised terminology. The internet or biotechnology, for example, can only be regulated by a legal semantic that matches the complexity of technical innovations in these fields, and regulation takes the form of close co-dynamics between the semantics of the regulated systems and legislation in the fields. With hybrid law, therefore, it becomes difficult to decide whether the regulatory terminology is legal terminology or technical terminology from the regulated system (Sand, 2012). Hybrid law appears to cause the law to further retreat while also seeking to install the law in the objects of regulation. Thus, hybrid law can be said to operate as an intensification of reflexive law because it is driven by a further desire to support and exploit the reflexive capacities of other systems.

Moreover, hybrid law also entails that the law seeks to constitute the object of its regulation as a hybrid with many conflicting expectations. The effort to construct hybrids with built-in tension, paradoxical and ambiguous expectations and unresolved structural couplings seems to constitute a legal programme that considers the growing mutual interdependence of different systems and the necessity of having a flexible and changeable regulatory form. The use of internal contracts in public administration creates a governance hybrid that simultaneously communicates hierarchy and market. Administrative units represent a unilaterally constructed hierarchy. A contract represents a bilateral commitment to the market that exists between two or more independent parties. The internal contracts mark a form of governance in which the market is folded into the hierarchy. Formal governance law is translated into a far more ambiguous contract governance in which a superior party within the hierarchy communicates to subordinate parties as if they were independent legal subjects who can choose not to enter into a contractual agreement (see Ladeur, 2007). The communication says, 'Do as I say – be independent'. In terms of government, this is like eating one's cake and having it too, and its productive effect is that this double-bind inherent in the form of governance creates certain freedoms for both governing and governed parties. And because this form of governance rests on such paradoxical grounds, it remains in play and open for ongoing negotiation. It becomes a legally given framework and also absence of framework for governance. And the involved parties have to independently contribute to the creation and stabilisation of their legal framework conditions.

Networks, partnerships, citizens contracts and state-owned corporations are other examples of such governance forms. The Danish company DONG, for example, is legally constituted in the tension between operating as a private independent company in the marketplace, on the one hand, and a public hierarchically subordinate public sector institution working to implement national finance and energy policies, on the other. Or we might point to changes to divorce legislation. In the past, parents used the law to resolve mutual disagreements over how to organise their shared parenting responsibilities. The law could award sole custody to one parent and thus make a decision about who was right and who was wrong. Today, the law can return the conflict to families by requiring parents to collaborate. In this way, the law makes itself dependent on the family's ability to take on the job of self-regulation, but at the same time, the law's presence in the family is also intensified because the family is deprived of the possibility of leaving the decision up to the legal system. We might say that the legal system simultaneously makes a decision and refuses to make a decision. In one sense, the legal system withdraws from the family but only in the attempt to establish an even closer connection between the legal system and the family system. The law imposes self-regulation on the family, who has to independently determine right and wrong even though it would prefer not to.

Hybrid law regulates multiple structural couplings between organisation and an *in*definite number of function systems. Hybrid law designs second-order couplings. The law prescribes coupling but does not specify with whom or how. Inherent in the function of coupling is the need to continually seek out possibilities for coupling. Hybrid law enforces paradoxes for exploration on regulated entities. It remains an open question which systems to engage through coupling and how. Thus, couplings become open, dynamic and fragile at the same time. Structural coupling serves as a potentiality machine, and regulation becomes a question of creating maximum intensity in the couplings.

We have summed up the developments within the legal programmes in Table 9.2.

We have pointed to the fact that the political system's access to governance in society is tied to its structural coupling with other systems. Directly, the political system can only govern itself. The law represents the political system's most significant structural coupling to the legal system. To the extent that the legal system not only prescribes behaviour but also structural couplings between function systems, the political system not only harvests the governance surplus in the legal system but also indirectly the governance surplus in other systems. This means that the political system, despite its inability to govern beyond itself, achieves increased possibility for governance through developments within the internal programmes of the legal system. However, as a result, its governance becomes less specific. The political system can only achieve greater governance potential via the strengthened autopoiesis of organisations and function systems. The level of governance increases along with the level of ungovernability.

Table 9.2: Developments in the legal system

Form	Formal law	Substantial law	Reflexive law	Hybrid law
Programme	Conditional orientation	Goal orientation	Procedural and reflexive orientation	Hybrid orientation
Object of regulation	Prescribes behaviour directly. Result of behaviour is outside regulation	Prescribes direct results of social processes but only indirect behaviour and procedures	Prescribes procedures, which indirectly and on the second order prescribe and facilitate self-creation and self-management. Result remains outside of regulation or open	Prescribes paradoxes, contradictions and ambiguity for purposes of self-regulation and self-creation of legal order
Conflict anticipation	Conflicting behaviour	Conflicting goals and results	Conflicting interests and discourses	Conflicting constitutions
Openness to non-legal concerns	Very limited	Open to professional assessment of need for services as well as professional prioritisation of alternative means to achieve formally established ends	Open to indefinite number of considerations to the extent that they contribute to the formulation of a goal and a plan within the scope of formal procedures for these	Open to constant oscillation between law and non-law
Example	*If* unemployed *then* entitled to unemployment benefits	The purpose established by the Social Security Act 1974: 'The state is obligated by the rules of this Act to provide assistance to anyone who resides in the country and who, for the sake of him or herself or his or her family, is in need of counselling, financial or practical assistance, support for development or rehabilitation of ability to work or care, specialised treatment or educational support'	Paragraph 111 in the Social Services Act about the formulation of action plan as a basis for defining goals	The law about shared custody

Developments in the concept of state

What kind of state emerges from this enormous rise in the complexity of political systems as well as the structural couplings between society's diverse systems?

Corresponding to the legal forms we have described, we distinguish between four state formations that all produce unity within the political system in four different but supplementary forms. We distinguish between the constitutional state, the welfare state, the supervision state and the potentiality state.

Constitutional state

The gradual rise of the *constitutional state* meant that the creation of a type of constitutional order became the central problem. In the constitutional state the leading scientific mode is legal science. The state is described in legal terms. Using the constitutional state to describe its unity, the political system establishes the centrality of the boundaries of the state. The constitutional state is employed by the political system to create a clear distinction between state and society, which simultaneously restricts the political system's operations and governance of society. In other words, the political system defines a limit to its own power within society. In the constitutional state, governance is perceived solely in terms of the negative legal regulation of the sphere of action of individuals, organisations and companies. The basic function of the state is to grant legal freedom rights to individuals, organisations and companies, such as, for example, property rights, freedom of speech, political rights, etc. This creates private autonomous spaces of action in which individuals, organisations and private companies are viewed as free legal subjects. This allows these entities to mutually establish their own legal order by entering into legally binding relationships with one another, for example, by establishing associations, marriages or contracts. Thus, the creation of private autonomy is not simply a question of granting freedom rights to individuals, but also of defining a demarcated space for private regulation and legislations. The state can then subsequently regulate by restricting such spaces by means of specific and calculable rules and prohibitions. It is important in the constitutional state for legal subjects to know their legal space of action, which is why rules and prohibitions must be specific and calculable. This allows individuals, organisations and private companies to take on responsibility for the realisation of the freedoms they have been granted. The constitutional state does not regulate affirmatively, meaning that individuals, organisations and private companies are not required to obtain affirmative permission to engage in specific activities. Through rights, private subjects are granted a space of action in which everything that is not explicitly prohibited is permissible.

Welfare state

After the Second World War, and more specifically from around the 1960s, we see a new kind of state formation, which adds itself to the constitutional state. Whereas the constitutional state bases itself on the regulation of the individual's space of action, what will later be known as the *welfare state* subscribes to an idea about the redistribution of the goods distributed by the marketplace. The central problem in the constitutional state was to ensure a form of civic order, whereas the fundamental problem in the social welfare state is to address poverty. With the constitutional state, the political system sought to govern by harvesting the governance surplus in the legal system. In the welfare state, the political system seeks to govern the development of society by harvesting the governance surplus in the economic system, and redistributing the economically scarce resources by means of the budget, tax laws and municipal agreements. This period adds to the political system an economic self-description. The state no longer simply negatively regulates the space of action of legal subjects by means of legislation; it also seeks to regulate how these subjects use their freedom by redistributing resources in society.

> **Example 9.1: The constitutional state**
>
> The constitutional state gradually emerged around the end of the 1800s, but its development intensified from the 1920s on. However, not until the end of the First World War do we see a sustained elaboration of a semantic for the constitutional state reflective of the complexity that the previous four or five decades had created. In a Danish context, law professor Alf Ross played a central role in the formation of such a semantic. Having taken over the professorship in state constitutional law at the Law School at the University of Copenhagen, he wrote the book *Statsretlige studier* (*Studies in constitutional law*) in 1959 (Ross, 1959, p 9, emphasis in original). Here is a snippet:
>
>> When the legislative branch has issued a law, we do not assign this action to the physical persons who participated – the King and members of parliament – but view the legislative act as a constitutional act implemented through the legislative branch. Similarly, we say that the state, using the King as its tool or organ, negotiates treaties with foreign countries, or, using the judge, passes verdicts, or, using ministers, constructs railroads, builds hospitals and operates schools. What characterises this language is that certain *actions, which have actually been performed by specific people* – who else would perform an action? – *are referred to as performed not by said physical persons but by a subject termed "the state."* We might say that the action is attributed to "the state".
>
> Ross raises two questions here: (1) Under which circumstances is a specific action attributed to the 'state' rather than the acting subject? And (2) What does the term 'state' mean as a name for the subject to which action is attributed?
>
> Actions that can be attributed 'may be either legal actions or actual actions'. A legal action is defined as one that 'results in force of law' (for example, a promise, a will, a verdict or administrative measure), whereas actual actions are performed by a person endowed with the legal authority and competence to act on behalf of the state.

Only a person or authority that has been assigned legal qualifications may perform legal actions. Ross (1959, p 13) makes a distinction between two forms of qualifications: private autonomy and public authority. 'The social function of private autonomy is to enable individuals, within the boundaries of the constitutional order, to shape their own legal matters according to their self-interest.' The social function of public authority and the power it entails, 'is to serve the interests of the collective, what we also refer to as "the common good".' The concept of state 'indicates that individual authorities do not exist in isolation but are mutually coordinated into a systematic whole through rule of law. The unity of the "state" corresponds to the systematic unity of the constitutional order as expressed in the constitution.'

In response to the question, 'What does the term "state" mean as a name for the subject to which action is attributed?', Ross writes somewhat puzzlingly that there is no logical subject behind the grammatical subject in sentences such as, 'the state built...', 'the state decided...' or 'the state has informed...'. The grammatical subject does not refer to an actual subject. It does not refer to anything. It simply signifies the constitutional order in which it is possible to attribute certain actions to the state as either legal dispositions (as when a railroad is built at the expense of the state) or as legal action (for example, when a public authority discloses an administrative measure).

Example 9.2: The welfare state

The concept of the welfare state appears in a Danish context in the 1950s. At this time, it was not a positive term. Initially, the word primarily served as a counterconcept used in particular by the Danish Conservative People's Party (Det Konservative Folkeparti) as a way to critique the social policies of the Social Democrats (Bredsdorff, 2000, p 70). The following is an excerpt from a 1956 article written by Poul Møller, a leading conservative at the time:

> The social welfare state is a society in which the state is obligated to assist individual citizens through all of life's difficulties and in which the state must take on every economic, cultural or social responsibility in order to ensure the greatest possible welfare for the greatest number of citizens. The motivation behind the welfare state is that human beings are the product of either nature or environment, that they cannot independently decide their lives, and that it is the responsibility of society as a whole to assist individuals through the struggles of their lives. When nobody can be held directly responsible, it would be unjust – in education, crime control or in the struggles of life – to allow individuals to suffer the consequences for missteps or miscalculations, which they cannot be made responsible for. Many people would reject this fundamental principle of the welfare state; however, it remains a danger, precisely because it does not require of its supporters a principled approval but finds the concrete to be entirely satisfactory. And in a society where everyone has long since become accustomed to calling on the state to be responsible and contribute to the solution of almost any task,

> the welfare programme may indeed prove a windfall for its party. The phrase, "it is the fault of society" is so widespread in the discourse of all social circles as to serve as a precise description of the general understanding of responsibility and fault in the modern state. (Møller, 1956, quoted in Petersen et al, 2012, pp 135-6, own translation)

Supervision state

From around 1980, the most prominent political problem ceases to be redistribution and becomes instead the mutual ignorance among function systems caused by increased differentiation. This includes the political system's seizure of society's economic resources at the expense of the economic system's own dynamics. The fundamental problem becomes the management and control of this ignorance, and this effort leads to the formation of the *supervision state* (Willke, 1992). The task of the supervision state is to train the function systems to govern themselves, which means considering systems-external elements and reflecting on their own boundaries and limitations. Whereas the political system in the constitutional state harvests the governance surplus in the legal system by linking political intentions to the legislative processes, and whereas the political system in the welfare state harvests the governance surplus in the economic system through the authoritative redistribution of scarce resources, the political system in the supervision state seeks to harvest the governance surplus in a multiplicity of function systems by creating structural couplings among them through reflexive law. With the formation of the supervision state, the political system develops an eye for society as communication and for function systems as communication systems.

Potentiality state

Whereas the supervision state primarily focused on the dysfunctionality caused by increased social differentiation, the new *potentiality state*, taking shape in the first decade of the 21st century, appears to be the result of growing awareness of the potential for innovation in the systems' mutual interference with each other. It is no longer simply a question of harvesting the surplus of the self-governance of individual systems, but of harvesting the surplus of the systems' mutual interference with each other. Thus, the potentiality state develops an eye for 'the productive force' inherent in the mutual noise-making between systems, and rather than minimising the noise, it seeks to potentiate the noise. It strives for intensity in the structural coupling of systems. What we have termed the potentiality state also refers to awareness in the political system of the governance potential in the choice of different concepts of state. In the potentiality state, images of the state provide a reserve of contingent ideas, which can be exchanges and experimented with. Thus, the potentiality state asks: which concept of state may work as a suitable framework for this particular governance situation? Accordingly, we see in the first decade of the 21st century a proliferation of alternative descriptions of the unity of the political system, so that, in addition to constitutional state, welfare state and supervision state, we also encounter the network state, the competition state, meta-governance, the contract state and the security state. Many of these alternative descriptions share the fact that they completely dissolve the boundary between state and society by describing the political system in terms of society, for example, welfare society, smart society, network society, experience economy, risk society and knowledge society.

Concept 9.2: Harvesting the surplus of self-governance
Systems are not simply dependent on each other's services. The autopoiesis of one system does not restrict that of another. Conversely, the closed dynamics of one system may strengthen the dynamics of another system. In metaphorical terms, a system can only harvest the self-governance surplus off another system through a productive misunderstanding of the communication and meaning formation of the other system as a way to pursue its own values and goals. This is possible because individual communicative operations always produce a surplus of possible interpretations. Observing the trades and transactions of the economic system, the law sees patterns and repetitions, which it productively misunderstands as economic norms that the legal system has to respond to. Thus, the law harvests the governance surplus of the economic system when it creates a cause for new legislation based on fictions about norm formation in the economic system. Similarly, the political system can be said to harvest the pedagogical system's governance surplus when it productively misunderstands pedagogical discussion about the relation between society and the individual. Such productive misunderstanding causes the political systems to make decisions about examination methods, homework cafes, etc. On the other hand, political governance initiatives might lead to increased self-governance in the system that the political system seeks to govern. A municipality might decide that all municipal nursery schools need to develop a business plan. The only requirement is that individual institutions describe their strategies and plans for the coming year. Individual institutions may then harvest the governance surplus in the municipal decision by productively misunderstanding it as an occasion for a comprehensive strategy and dialogue process between managers, employees and parents. A nursery school invites speakers to talk about the latest pedagogical research initiatives and initiates a long-term value development process, a new staff policy, a new plan for parent collaboration, etc. The political system may subsequently respond to such extra activities and assign them political meaning and value.

Example 9.3: The state as a societal partnership
In 2012, the Danish Minister of Research, Innovation and Tertiary Education, Morten Østergaard, invited a broad circle of business and interest organisations, principals, educational institutions and public representatives to participate in the preparation of a new innovation strategy (INNO+) under the heading 'Societal challenges to drive innovation'. INNO+ was intended to 'form the basis for prioritising new partnerships between the business community, knowledge institutions and the public sector to increase innovation and produce new solutions to specific challenges in society' (Press release, own translation).

The concluding report from 2013 states that, 'solutions to major challenges in society often require collaboration between many actors across sectors and professional distinctions. Each focus area in the catalogue can serve as framework for social partnerships about innovation with participation from businesses, knowledge institutions and government' (Ministeriet for Forskning, Innovation og Videregående Uddannelser, 2013, p 45).

The goal is to encourage partnerships across different social systems, and a broad spectrum of institutions is invited to contribute proposals. It is a requirement that the proposals not only propose new forms of partnerships, but that they also propose a societal diagnosis for the partnerships to reference. Thus, the Ministry is not only awarded with individual projects but also with a semantic framework for the relationship between state and society designed to promote the formation of partnership and productive connections. The different images of future relations between state and society should focus on areas in which 'Denmark holds particular potential for the creation of innovative solutions' across distinct silos.

'Smart Society' is the name of Aarhus University's proposal for such a future image of the relationship between state and society, which may serve as framework for 'a societal partnership'. The following is an excerpt from the proposal:

> "Smart Society refers to a vision for a society with a coherent and transparent generation, accessibility and use of digital data. Today, we – in Denmark and everywhere else – are miles removed from this vision – public and private systems largely function as individual silos without any view to a larger whole [...] But the desired effect of open and public data can only be achieved in the setting of a Smart Society with a coherent public and private digital infrastructure. Technical solutions must be complemented by administrative and partnership models capable of meeting the challenges inherent in the creation of new publics with digital relations between citizens, the public and the business community [...] Moreover, Smart Society requires design and development of new forms of interaction including innovative challenges with respect to realtime visualisation and user interface [...] the development of new forms of interaction and coordination with the physical environment will allow Denmark to assume a leading position in the areas of design, architecture and information and communication technology. Citizens' movements across a Smart Society will require the need for a special effort with respect to digital identity – an identity which on one hand allows individuals to take advantage of the many new services while securing, on the other hand, citizens' right to digital privacy. Research and knowledge about surveillance, culture and art will play an important role for the exploration of personal identity. The solutions to the innovative challenges will require an authentically cross-disciplinary approach that involves the greater sections of technology, the Humanities, social sciences, (industrial) design and architecture. Moreover, it requires a comprehensive dedicated effort by relevant public and private companies as well as the incorporation of users in the form of citizens, companies, regions and municipalities [...] The development of Smart Society,

> therefore, calls for a broad societal partnership. The establishment of a Smart Society presupposes legitimacy, transparency and administration on a level that does not exist anywhere at this point in time. Denmark has a well-established tradition for interdisciplinary collaboration and a unique tradition for user-driven innovation, which can and should be taken advantage of in a Danish contribution to Smart Society" (Aarhus Universitet, 2013, own translation)

Table 9.3: The form of state in transition

State form	State problem	Political reform
Constitutional	Order	Reforming a law complex
Welfare	Poverty	Reforming the public organisation changing the capacity of reforming
Supervision	Intersystemic ignorance	Reforming the boundaries of the public sector creating a 'running' reform
Potentiality	Scarcity of noise and productive mutual interference	Reforming 'society' to reform itself

Example 9.4: Contemporary images of state and society

The competition state

> 'I believe in the competition state as the modern welfare state. The truth is that we are engaged in an incredibly positive agenda about strengthening and modernising the welfare state, and that the result of that change will prove to be a much better society than the one we have today,' states Bjarne Corydon, who rejects what he refers to as a 'decline mythology' about an 'unambitious bookkeeper government who submits to market forces' (quoted in *Politiken*, 8.23.2013, own translation).

The security state

> I believe that it is important that we take a critical look at surveillance. The tendency is increasingly in the direction of a security state, surveillance state and control state, not only with respect to terror but also other areas such as healthcare policies. (Hans Jørgen Bonnichsen, Kronikken, *Politiken*, 3.14.2011, own translation)

The knowledge and network society

> The virtual high school offers students a high school education that helps them develop into mature and complete human beings and contributes to preparing them for the knowledge and network society.... Society's growing complexity and rate of change makes it impossible to base one's actions on a predetermined foundation of professional knowledge and abilities. Knowledge is produced, actualised and becomes obsolete at a fast pace, and the individual has access to an enormous amount of information, which is potentially relevant for handling and making decisions in a given situation. (Danish Ministry of Education, 2001, own translation)

The knowledge society and late modern society

> The mixture of knowledge and culture at public libraries is a long-standing tradition. Concurrently with the developments of society and globalisation, this combination has taken on new significance because culture plays an important role in citizens' capacity to navigate an increasingly more complex, less transparent and more directionless society in which continual change is a basic condition. Competence development in the knowledge society, therefore, is also a matter of personal development. Society viewed from this perspective is referred to as the late modern society. In the late modern society everything is questioned. This allows for cultural freedom, which promotes innovation and change but it also makes it difficult for individuals to define a stable identity. Knowledge and identity development becomes an ongoing project that takes place in more transient and fluid communities and often through cultural experiences. Thus, culture becomes an important focal point for identity formation. (Committee on Public Libraries in the Knowledge Society, 2010, p 10, own translation)

> *The risk society*
>
> The risk society and interests: We live in a society in which risk is an unavoidable dimension of our consumption and lifestyle. Risk has become the unexpected and unforeseen effects of production, technology and science. In many cases, we have only limited knowledge of specific risk factors, and it is almost paradoxical so that the more knowledge one has and receives the more uncertain one feels. At the same time, science is not objective but marked by the context conditioning individual scientific studies.... Today, risk cannot be assessed on the basis of unambiguous objective parameters like cause and effect. Risks have become social constructions. Risk conflicts can be divided into three types: Factual – concerning evidence, probabilities and actual or lacking knowledge. Trust – in relation to institutions, science, experts and individual experiences. Value-based – social and cultural norms, ethical questions, ideology and life philosophy. (Danish Ministry of the Environment, 2004, own translation)

Reform in the different state forms

Changes in the state forms also change how reforms are conceived and practised. We have resumed the transformation of the form of state and form of reforming in Table 9.3 on page 228. The question we pursue in the following is what does it mean to make a political reform within the different forms of state?

In the constitutional state where the problem is legal order, political reforms target larger complexes of laws. We are talking here about 'doing a reform' when the political system does not simply change a single law, but a number of laws together, thereby redirecting a particular policy area. An example might be a social policy reform that targets all social law, and reformulates them so that they all follow the same basic principal, that is, universality. In the constitutional state, a reform is a coherent reformulation of a whole complex of laws.

In the welfare state, political reforms not only target legal laws; they also target the ways in which public organisations implement the laws. To reform, then, is also to reorganise a policy area. With the welfare state we begin to talk about 'administrative reforms'. These represent a kind of second-order reform: they build the internal capacity of public planning and problem-oriented decision-making. And we here have the tension between a reform theorist believing in

Example 9.5: Reform as revolution, the case of New Nordic Schooling
In the spring of 2012, the Danish Minister of Education launched a new initiative entitled New Nordic Schooling. The title evokes the combination of innovation and the reinventing of old regional values and ingredients known from the gastronomic movement of New Nordic Cuisine. What was to be reinvented in New Nordic Schooling was the way in which Danish schools had traditionally been successful in taking a point of departure in democratic values, community building, creativity and independent thinking. And what is presently not good enough and in need of innovation is the performance of Danish schoolchildren and the ability of the Danish education system to provide all children with equal possibilities of unfolding and realising their potential (Danish Ministry of Education, 2014, p 4).

New Nordic Schooling is based on co-ownership and democratic influence. The initiative is *not* constituted by predefined goals and guidelines. As stated: 'The initiative is an encouragement to the professional employees and managers – the experts of the everyday – to reconquer and reformulate the public agenda of development and education of our children and young people' (Danish Ministry of Education, 2014, p 6). This means that every participating organisation defines their own development goals and paths with a point of departure in the manifesto and the dogmas of New Nordic Schooling.

To become part of this reform, schools or daycare institutions have to apply. The minimum criteria for being accepted is that the management, local politicians and 85 per cent of employees commit themselves to change, improvement and collaboration (Danish Ministry of Education, 2014, p 12). Moreover, to become part of the reform requires, as it reads, 'that parents, teachers, pedagogues and pupils catch the ball – because they all desire to change' (Danish Ministry of Education, 2014, p 6). And finally, 'it is compulsory to transgress habitual thinking about known practice and one's own potential for development' (Danish Ministry of Education, 2014, p 12).

When a school or daycare institution has been accepted as part of New Nordic Schooling they are invited into networks with other organisations where they are to collaborate and work with a common challenge formulated by the network itself.

Just to give a few examples of the framework of New Nordic Schooling, the first dogma reads: 'We can do it ourselves, and we should do it: Actions before words' (Danish Ministry of Education, 2014, p 12). And the fourth reads: 'We will be systematically exploring and open to change: We will be curious, proactive, innovative and willing to take risks to realise the potential of individuals. To change the world we need to discover that something could be different and be willing to change the way we work' (Danish Ministry of Education, 2014, p 17).

New Nordic Schooling is an example of a reform where the hierarchy between reform and implementation is reversed. It does not provide the participating schools with concrete goals or expected results. Rather, the reform is an approach to life, schooling and professional

> work based on collaboration, professional development and dedication. It an offer from the Ministry to the local institutions, an offer that the object of the reform, the local institutions, have to apply to become part of; they even have to be able to document their sincere dedication and desire to become part of the reform. Thus, it is a form of reform where the Ministry provides an invitation, criteria for being accepted, network, a knowledge bank, competence development of individuals and groups and a number of tools to create professional reflection and knowledge, but where the goals are to emerge as part of the implementation of the reform.

more rational decision-making and planning with clear distinctions between problems and solutions and others who are more into muddling through and incremental politics (Lindblom, 1959, 1979). Thus, administrative reforms are reforms to reform the capacity of the state.

In the supervision state, not only the internal public organisation, but also the boundaries of public administration become the target of reforms (as we know it from the NPM discourse). These are boundaries such as public/private, administration/citizen, politics/administration and public institution/hierarchy. With an emphasis on constant change, we get a kind of 'ongoing reform' anchored in the independent change management of a multiplicity of institutions.

And finally, in the potentiality state, the political system begins to describe itself as a society: the society as such becomes the target of efforts to reform. But the political system cannot reform society as if the state was outside society and from that position be able to determine it. So what is more precisely happening is that the *interplay* between societal institutions (organisations as well as function systems) is in focus, as this interplay is marked by a particular description of the society as the frame of the interplay. To make this workable, the distinction between policy and implementation is deconstructed. The more substantial goals and policies are to emerge in the reform process.

Reforms that target communities rather than public organisations

In the potentiality state, what is to be reformed is no longer the public sector, which means that the object of government becomes rather elusive and more and more difficult to delimit. In the following we give a few examples.

In recent years, many Danish municipalities have experimented with new self-descriptions that make the object of governance the society as such. For instance, in 2013, the municipality of Aarhus launched a discussion paper, entitled, *The municipality of love. Future health care in Aarhus.* Its quite utopian vision is to renew public welfare by rethinking it as something that emerges in communities as a set of services. In the introduction it reads:

> We understand the municipality of love as the potential community which exists and emerges when human beings live, reside and work

together. It is the totality of the diverse community and potential for loving relations we have as neighbours and colleagues, in local associations, in the nursing and in the local society we call Aarhus. (Municipality of Aarhus, 2013, p 6)

Thus, the object of governance transgresses the individual welfare organisation and the public sector. Moreover, the object of governance is not only actual partnerships between public, private and volunteer organisations. Rather, what is installed as that which is to be governed are communities – the totality of human beings and organisations within a local area and the future, potential relations of love and care that might emerge within this geographic area.

In another municipality, Skanderborg, the self-description of the public sector is 'Municipality 3.0'. The municipality explains:

Here, the public service station is shut down and replaced by an active local society where the public sector interacts with citizens to create an everyday in which everybody actively participates: citizens, employees and politicians. (Local Government, Denmark, 2014, p 6)

Welfare managers are expected to think holistically and to dismantle boundaries between citizens and welfare organisations. As they put it in Skanderborg:

A part of this entails to think differently of the municipality. Not an organisation of employees, but a community of citizens. We are all in the basic situation that we should help each other. (Pleimert, 2015)

As this also indicates, the self-description 'Municipality 3.0' is used to suspend the boundary between who is formally employed in the municipality and who is not. The senior chief director of the municipality states:

It is an organisation without boundaries. If we dismantle the boundary between who is employed and who is a citizen, then we arrive at the "unboss" situation. And that is precisely what we want. We want to see everybody as equally engaged and active. (Pleimert, 2015)

The senior chief director emphasises that it is a matter of ending an outdated way of thinking where it is the public sector against the citizens, and where 'municipal employees forget that they are also citizens and citizens forget that they are part of a municipality' (Pleimert, 2015).

Although such descriptions of local government are also meant to bring matters to a head, serve to brand the municipality as highly innovative and maybe even provoke a bit, they capture the spirit of contemporary efforts to describe the object of public government as the totality of actual and potential relations between human beings and their ability to care for and help each other. The mayor of the municipality of Skanderborg is therefore not simply described as the political governor of the municipality understood as the public institutions; the mayor is observed as the leader of the total population in the community including private firms, families, single individual citizens, social movements, private sport organisations, and so on, and they are all expected to recognise this leadership. In the potentiality state, the object of government is expanded to such a degree that it almost becomes impossible to delimit it. Since the object of government is the totality of a community including everybody in it, and actual as well as potential capabilities to take responsibility for the wellbeing of the entire community, there is nothing outside the object of government. Simultaneously, it becomes highly difficult to delimit the responsibility of welfare managers. They can no longer assume that the boundary for their responsibility is confined by organisational boundaries, by who is employed, or by pre-defined service-delivering to particular citizens, namely, those who have been formally granted such a service. Welfare managers must learn to 'see beyond [a narrow understanding of their particular organisation] and see the broader context in which their enterprise is part of,' as another municipal senior chief executive puts it (quoted in Reiermann, 2011, p 17).

When the object of government becomes the entire community and all the actual and potential relations in it, the aim of government is not strictly to produce certain results, but also to foster buzzing life and activity out of which possible chances of forming new relations in which people may help each other and have a positive influence on each other's quality of life. The future partnership to build a new nursing home for elderly people described in Chapter Six is a lucid illustration of this. The planned nursing home is precisely not described as a nursing home, but as a small local community, where there are not only rooms and apartments for elderly people, but also for young couples with small children. In the project description it reads:

> Generally, it is buzzing with activity in Vonsild Garden, which is no longer called a 'nursing home'. Now it is just a modern community centre for the entire local society, as well as for the elderly residents at the centre. A large part of the ground floor is assembly halls and activity rooms, where many different associations come, hold meetings, do gymnastics, play cards and many other activities. Using the rooms is free of cost, but it is a precondition that the activities contribute to a lively atmosphere of the centre ie, by involving the residents in the activities. (Municipality of Kolding, 2012, p 8)

What is to be reformed is not the organisation, the nursery home or its employees and residents; rather, the object of government is the life, energy and level of activity at the centre. It seems that what is important is not precisely *what* comes out of the activity in terms of, for example, the health of the residents. The activities are not necessarily a means to something else. It is a goal in itself that the atmosphere of the centre is lively, that a lot is going on. Welfare governance is simply a matter of making local societies buzz with energy, activities and life.

As du Gay (2002) has noted, the fact that individuals, firms, 'communities', schools, parents and housing estates must themselves take on – as 'partners' – a greater proportion of the responsibility for renewing public welfare, involves a double movement of 'responsibilisation and autonomisation'. On the one hand, all actors, all communities and even potential relations between different people and collectives are to become more responsible for public welfare, that is, to consider how they are part of and naturally embedded in the public sector. And on the other hand, it is precisely by being different from what is often described as an impersonal, inefficient, path-dependent public sector that volunteers and local communities are seen as part of an innovative approach to welfare production. In the above-mentioned description of the new nursing home, it is explained how one of the tenants (not an elderly resident), named Yvonne, often solves small conflicts and helps the nurses and care personnel to talk to the residents. It is precisely because Yvonne is not formally employed that she sees and hears things that the professionals do not notice and are not told. Therefore, she can always provide insights into how to arrange everyday life more in accordance with the wishes of the older people. Moreover, she talks to the families of the residents, and suggest how they can assist and help make life at Vonsild Garden happier for everybody (Municipality of Kolding, 2012, p 9): 'It helps that it is Yvonne who speaks to the families of the residents because she knows how it feels to be a relative' (Municipality of Kolding, 2012, p 10). Thus, to be of service in producing public welfare, communities, associations and individuals need to be different from public servants. However, what happens to how we can assume and assign responsibility and accountability in the public sector and in processes of producing public welfare? Tasks and responsibilities that were once enmeshed in the bureaucratic lines of government of the state become distributed, not only to organised volunteer associations but also to potentially emerging relations of care in small communities. How can a public sector assign responsibility when so much political hope is invested in non-employed people and collectives' willingness and ability to take more responsibility?

The problem is not only how to divide tasks and responsibilities between public servants and volunteer citizens. If this were the case, transparency and accountability would not be unattainable. Instead, the difficulty lies in how the potentiality state is reluctant to divide tasks and responsibility beforehand. Indeed, not to decide in advance on division of roles and tasks is seen as a resource. To assign tasks and responsibilities to public, private and volunteer organisations on beforehand, before entering into partnerships is seen as a risk that may result in opportunities not being discovered and utilised. In an interview about how to create renewal in the public sector, an influential former municipal senior chief executive recognises that once in a while boundaries have to be made in relation to which tasks volunteers can be assigned and which tasks the professional have to be in charge of. 'However', he emphasises, 'it is increasingly difficult to draw that line on beforehand. We have to try things out and work out things collaboratively' (Reiermann, 2011, p 17). Roles, divisions of tasks and boundaries between who is formally employed and who is not should thus be kept open and undecided, and only temporarily, processually and experimentally be determined.

Combinations of state concepts

As a result of the four layers of different forms of states it becomes an open question that forms of governance and reforming should be used. In the potentiality state, if a municipality is faced with having to regulate independent self-governing institutions, it can ask itself: how does it change the relationship between municipality/self-governing institution to employ either the constitutional state, the welfare state or the network state as a given governance context? If the context is defined as the constitutional state, the municipality can only regulate rights and obligations. If the municipality defines the network state or the supervision state as its context, it might be able to see the governance potential inherent in having a multiplicity of different institutional constitutions, which may productively learn from each other. And instead of thinking according to the logic of rights and obligations with regard to the relation municipality/institution, the municipality could engage the notion of mutually developing partnerships. If the point of reference is the contract state, unity in the institutional practice is not achieved by means of a comprehensive holistic policy. Instead, as Andreas Abegg writes, the whole has been 'split into a multitude of small contracts' between the political system and society's institutions (Abegg, 2013, p 144). Thus, the potentiality state reverses the relationship between *context* and *operation*. As context, the state form is no longer given in advance as that which defines the governance operation and its conditions. The governance operation is given priority and is allowed to choose its own context through the choice of state form. In this way, the potentiality state becomes a form of *playful state*, which plays with state forms and their governance potential (Andersen, 2009, 2011a). Included in this playfulness is the eye for structural coupling of systems, and it becomes clear that different state forms increase while others weaken the political system's eye for the governance surplus in different function systems. The notion of 'knowledge society', for example, clearly strengthens the eye for the potential of the couplings between the sciences and other systems whereas the network state weakens the focus on the values of the legal system. Thus, it becomes a highly political act in the political system to choose and connect with specific models of state and society, whether the point of reference is state, region or municipality.

Management challenges

As we have said, the main challenge is this: how can the political system make collectively binding decisions on behalf of society when society cannot be represented in society? The political system pretends to be able to represent the whole or an approximate whole, but this remains a dangerous systems-internal fantasy, and one that is even sometimes shared by political science, which fancies itself a form of 'master science'. The state has definitively stepped down from its elevated position and can only govern by harvesting the surplus of other systems' self-governance (Willke, 1997).

The political system is forced to reflect on how it is perceived by other systems as a service. Or more specifically in the context of the welfare state: legislative measures in the social sector, educational sector and healthcare system have to consider how these measures might be perceived from within the systems as a service contributing to the continuation of the systems' internal operations. The challenge is to recreate the state in its role of governing a multiplicity of self-governance in other systems. This kind of state has to reflect on its own boundaries and prefers to provide guidance rather than intervene.

Supervision governance provides the political system with the opportunity to govern in accordance with the self-reflection of governed systems. This allows the state to indicate procedures instead of dictating goals, and hence to govern by taking advantage of the capacity in individual systems for formulating independent goals and strategies. This form of governance does not idolise its own specialised mode of operation, but governs in accordance with the capacity of governed systems to make use of their own specialised programmes in their development of goals. It invites the governed systems to consider which professional concerns should be reflected in the goals and action plan. The political system can govern by inviting other systems to reflect on their possibilities for taking responsibility for societal issues.

The governance limit is therefore drawn by the self-reflection capacity of the systems, which means that the political system has to increase its ability to produce reflection in other systems. Accordingly, effective governance can take the form of offering methods for sub-systems to increase their ability to observe themselves and their operations from a critical perspective. But at the same time, the political system encounters a number of paradoxes related to how to demand and sanction reflection.

With the law's developments toward a hybrid form we see the emergence of a form of governance increasingly more capable of matching the complex knowledge, technology and operations of the governed systems. This form of governance takes advantage of the ability in the governed systems to handle tension, conflicting goals and paradoxes. It is a flexible form of governance in the sense that it is able to oscillate between regulation, on the one hand, and contributing to the continued specialisation of systems, on the other. Precisely because the governed systems can be construed ambiguously (for example, as both public and private, as both part of a hierarchy and as independent entity, as both economic and political subjects, etc), hybrid governance is better equipped to handle uncertainty and unpredictability, including the fact that there is no way to predict the developments within the governed systems. Instead of delivering unambiguous prescriptions that risk not matching the complexity of the conflicts at hand and that might therefore become dysfunctional for the regulated systems, the political system can take advantage of the regulated system's conflict management capabilities. This allows a great level of freedom for the political system and for governed systems; however, it also results in a more intensive relationship between governing and governed systems because the very framework of the relation is up for continual negotiation, and because conflicts and paradoxes function as the very driving force behind the self-governance imposed on governed systems.

This means that the limit of governance is governed systems' ability to handle contradictions and paradoxes. The political system has to expand its ability to expand other systems' ability to tolerate and handle conflicting conditions and to use conflicts as the springboard for own development.

Ultimately, this means that the political system has to ask itself how to govern when the object of its governance is the specific and specialised self-governance of other communication systems, including the conditions for structural coupling between these systems. The big question is how to harvest the self-governance surplus off other systems to benefit one's own governance ambitions.

We have summarised some of the challenges and paradoxes here:

- How can the political system govern via the law with openness toward structural coupling of an unlimited number of function systems?
- How can the political system take advantage via the law of structural coupling among function systems for purposes of political governance? How can it govern through structural couplings that have been internally constructed in other systems?
- How to govern from the outside when it can only be determined from the inside whether and how one's governance initiatives can be translated in specific terms into meaningful reflection?
- How to govern in a way that supports rather than restricts self-regulating elements in other systems?
- How to implore the economic and pedagogical systems to recognise themselves as political and legal subjects with responsibilities for society and for their own legal constitution?
- How may political governance strategically seek recognition as offering support of the self-identification processes of other systems?

The political system's experimentation with its self-description creates a boundary problem. The potentiality state experiments with the potential effects of describing itself as a society rather than a clearly delimited state. This is the basis of the concept of Big Society and other contemporary models for the incorporation of civil society, voluntary groups, local associations, and so on in welfare solutions. But when the political system experiments with the description of itself as society, it becomes exceedingly difficult for it to place certain issues outside itself. Any system must draw a distinction between system and environment, and accordingly, the political system must distinguish between politics and non-politics. This boundary has been a difficult and contested site since the beginning of the welfare state, because once an issue becomes articulated as a political issue, it is difficult not to act on it when the primary concern of the state is considered the common welfare. And when the state additionally becomes identified as 'the whole' – when society comes to represent the unity of the political system – it becomes rather difficult to distinguish between politics and non-politics. There are very few issues today that can be described as outside the responsibilities of the political system. The state becomes limitless.

As mentioned in Chapter Eight, this shift has a number of implications for the state's relation to its citizens. And it also has a number of implications for the relationship between the state and private companies. On the one hand, the state accelerates its expectations of companies. They are invited to be socially, ethically and environmentally responsible and actively engage in political issues and offer solutions. On the other hand, however, this also accelerates the state's expectations of itself about watching out for the companies. Increasingly, it is seen as a political responsibility to make sure that private companies do well (Frankel, 2004).

The potentiality state thus accelerates the inherent tendency in the political system to respond to an issue once it has been defined as political (Luhmann, 1990). It is a political system that on the one hand disempowers itself through its perpetual awareness of and attention to obvious political solutions outside the political system (civil society, voluntary systems, public involvement). On the other hand, however, the state becomes limitless because it continues to elaborate the dissolution of boundaries as a source of political value. Increasingly, the political system operates by challenging the boundaries between the citizens' private and public sphere, between public and private, and between voluntary and public.

As in previous chapters, we have shown the increasing difficulty of establishing unambiguous factual premises for decisions in the public sector. And in this chapter we point to the fact that even the 'outermost' premise – the state – has assumed a more transient character through a process of constant experimentation with new images of the unity of the political system. Some of these images, such as 'the constitutional state', portray a precise and well-defined unity. Others refer to an almost limitless unity in which state and society merge, such as, for instance, the term 'the welfare society', where agents that were previously viewed by the constitutional as its 'outside' are now seen as partners. The question of which actions can be attributed to the state changes in accordance with the image of the state as either state or society. More significantly, however, is that the attribution of actions to either the first, second, or third state form also indicate the specific rules one chooses to take on or not take on. When the state is no longer viewed as a given frame but is viewed instead as different forms that one can locally subscribe to, the local operation has to assume responsibility for what it defines as state and hence the rules that apply. It would amount to flight from responsibility to both view the state as an open reservoir of forms and at the same time refuse to take responsibility for one's choice of attribution and reference.

With the potentiality state's new entrepreneurial approaches to welfare and with the political hope invested in non-state actors playing a greater role in the welfare service, a question of accountability becomes more and more pressing. Since the first the experiments of marketisation of public services in the 1980s, many scholars have warned that such experiments lack the constitutional fit of traditional bureaucratic forms of organising (Johnson, 1993; Chapman, 1996; Rohr, 1998; du Gay, 2009). They argue that an emphasis on efficiency, innovation, performance and responsiveness cannot stand alone, since something valuable is lost in the process, namely, public service as a unified constitutional bureaucracy (du Gay, 2009, p 360). The point of such a warning is not simply that the disadvantages of cautious, predictable, ordered bureaucratic administration may ultimately be more politically acceptable than the disadvantages of a more entrepreneurial, experimental, creative and risky style, but that the traditional bureaucratic ethos of office has a constitutional fit (Rohr, 2002, p 478). The bureaucracy is designed so as to make public officials act as custodians of the constitutional values that are easily forgotten or neglected in the search for efficient and innovative public management. Johnson argued as early as 1983 that although experimentations with entrepreneurial and innovative welfare production may be important in and of itself, perhaps the constitutional and political limits of such experiments need to be recognised (Johnson, 1983, p 194). As du Gay concurs, simply representing the public bureaucracy as an inefficient, unresponsive, outmoded or conservative form of organisation fails to take account of the crucial constitutional role bureaucracy plays (Rohr, 2002).

With the potentiality state and its reluctance to define beforehand whether it is the rules of the constitutional state, the welfare state, the supervision state or the potentiality state that count, unambiguous assigning of responsibility becomes difficult. The potentiality state aims to produce more possibilities precisely by making it an open question who holds responsibility for welfare production and service. When the state is no longer viewed as a given frame but as different forms that can locally be subscribed to, the local operation has to assume responsibility for what it defines as a state, and hence the rules that apply for how responsibility can be assigned.

Conclusion: toward a premiseless management philosophy

We began this book with the question: 'If management is the case, what then lies behind it?' We can now answer that question: the dissolution of premises for management.

Management appears all across the welfare state as the answer to almost any problem. Anything from stress, poor PISA results, limited public involvement, lacking innovation to poor quality eldercare is described in terms of management problems. Accordingly, better management education is often perceived as the obvious path to improved welfare. With this book, we wanted to show how the demand for management is directly connected to the dissolution of premises for management caused by the welfare society's attempts to handle increasingly complex issues.

In Chapter One, we focused on the machine that drives the acceleration of management expectations, and traced it back to the emergence of a new understanding of time in the public sector. With descriptions of the future as something we cannot possibly imagine from the perspective of the present, the future that we navigate according to becomes a horizon beyond the horizon that we are able to imagine in the present. We referred to this temporality as *the future of the future*.

This temporality shift undermines the factual premises for welfare management because the question of how facts are defined is simply displaced onto the temporal dimension as always a question of exploring what a welfare service or welfare organisation could be in the future. The displacement of factuality onto the temporal dimension creates enormous management expectations because there is no limit to the unknown future potential of an organisation and its services. Managers are precisely expected to confront the organisation and its elements with the question, 'Could it be different?'

The rank between decision premises and decision-making is turned upside down. In the attempts to expect the unexpected, it becomes almost impossible to fix decision-premises before taking the decision. Factual grounds, goal orientations and procedures all become elements that have to be suspended until the decision is taken. Not until the decision is taken can it become possible to add the goal, the factual arguments etc. And even at this point it is difficult because you want to keep the decision open. This is far from the Weberian ideal of a calculable bureaucracy, and the prize is a huge loss of accountability or at least accountability becomes something very different as a kind of hyper-responsibility (as we narrowly discussed earlier regarding the concept of citizenship). Accountability is then not simply an attribution of responsibility for events in the past, but attribution of responsibility for anticipating potential future events.

The potentiality machine identified in Chapter One is not unambiguously or directly accessible 'somewhere' in the welfare society. There is no simple way to predict how the ideal about the future's future manifests itself and its effects in such different areas as public administration, welfare organisation, relationships between state and citizen, ideals about the good employee, etc. In this book we have gradually mapped the effects of the potentiality machine throughout the welfare society.

However, we began our analyses way above the ground in Chapter Two, not with the organisation, but with society as systems reference. We described today's society as functionally differentiated and constantly undergoing further differentiation. Function systems remain open on the social dimension (regardless of status, everyone is in principle relevant to communication), but closed on the factual dimension (their communication of factuality). In that sense, function systems are providers of factual perspectives. The greater society's functional differentiation, the higher the potential number of mutually exclusive factual perspectives. The result is a society that cannot represent itself within itself. There is no comprehensive unity of the many functionally differentiated perspectives. Instead, each system creates its own comprehensive image. And despite the fact that individual social systems develop self-reflexive semantics about their dependence on other perspectives, there are no 'bridges' or overlaps connecting the function systems since the reflexivity of each system remains tied to its own coding. Hyper-reflexivity does not open up closed systems. On the contrary, the self-reflection of the function systems only extends their closedness.

Chapter Three focused on public administration and explored changes to the internal organisation of the public sector through the 1900s until today. We described the way that increased complexity has historically compelled new modes of differentiation and management in the public sector so that today we have at least four co-existing organisational forms within public administration: formal bureaucracy, sector administration, supervision administration and potentiality administration. This undermines governance premises for management as a result of the shift from hierarchical organisation, premised on unilateral statements from the top, to a form of organisation in which contingent and multiple leader–subordinate relationships are included as elements of governance. Throughout public administration, the question of which form of governance applies remains open. The reason that management expectations can be so radically expanded in public administration is that much greater demands can be made on governed systems than in traditional case management based on prior cases and the implementation of planned change. Supervision and potentiality administration include the expectation that governed systems continue to surprise with new forms and models of independence. Governed systems can be made responsible for independently deciding when to follow instructions and when to create management space and innovation possibilities by rejecting existing structures and rigid rules.

Conclusion

In Chapter Four we zoomed in on the individual welfare organisation. How might a welfare organisation act when it is governed at one and the same time as an innocent, professional, strategic and potential organisation? Expectations directed at the potential organisation create a rather peculiar form of governance according to which welfare organisations are recognised as independent by refraining from seeing their identity as given. Organisations are expected to continually confront themselves and reflect on how a given action, service or procedure could be carried out differently, could be rethought. This undermines the factual premises of management. The question of what quality means, how to describe the welfare organisation and how to mark the limits of its responsibility cannot be taken for granted but remain an open question. This paves the way for rather extreme expectations about the effect of organisational independence. Welfare managers are basically expected to translate the impossibilities, logical contradictions and paradoxes of management into internal strategy formation and innovation.

Chapter Five showed how the differentiation of society affects welfare organisations and turns them into heterophonic and communication-seeking organisations. This means not only that the codes for shaping communication can never be taken for granted and that heterogeneous interests have to be continually weighed against each other, but also that welfare organisations become responsible for seeing conflicts between codes and professional competences or between differentiated units as productive and translating them into value as improved welfare. We described the way in which any given factuality is deferred to make room for potential and alternative factualities. Factual premises are not permitted to obstruct the communication-seeking operation. This accelerates expectations placed on welfare management because there are no demarcated limits for the achievable potential as long as welfare organisations continue to seek out the potential of the different function systems for the development of questions, facts, organisational descriptions, strategy formulation, etc.

In Chapter Six, we explored the implication for public sector collaboration of changing forms of governance and their impact on welfare organisation. How can the increasingly complex dependencies between welfare institutions be managed? We showed how today partnerships are viewed as an appropriate mode of collaboration in response to public organisations' framing of the future as unknown, since partnerships can defer elaborations and agreements into the future. The efforts to create flexible and dynamic forms of collaboration also serve to dissolve a number of premises: the object of exchange is no longer a given, the content of what is being promised is in a state of perpetual change, and the question of what defines a relevant partner becomes multiple and fluid. On the one hand this allows for very high expectations of the partnership since the premise is that the partnership will automatically generate more possibilities than what anyone can imagine. However, on the other hand, management conditions become rather fragile because, despite its support for speed dating, its delegation of competences, coaching, mediation, and so on, management cannot establish and maintain, not to mention control, partnerships.

Chapter Seven zoomed in even closer on the relation between organisation and employee. We showed how the supplementation of formal membership by new models of self-enrolment fundamentally change the conditions of employment so that employees are given responsibility for their self-development, for their passionate engagement in the organisation and for potentialising themselves. From a model where membership was defined by formal appointment with a set of appertaining expectations about specific assignments and responsibilities, we arrive at fluid and transient conditions and continual self-enrolment. Employees no longer perform only by actualising competences and results, but also by demonstrating an ability to potentialise their self-relation, that is, by remaining flexible and transgressive in the way they reflect themselves as a way to provide the organisation with a surplus of possible future identities. The relation between employee and organisation has to be continually reinvented, and there is no way to know the premises that apply in particular situations.

In Chapter Eight we took a look at growing expectations directed at citizens as the co-creators of welfare. We described how ambitions about citizen management have increased so that not only citizens' self-motivation but also their ability to explore possibilities for thinking differently about themselves, their abilities and potential become relevant objects of management. This undermines the basic understanding of the private sphere as the limit of the public sector's regulation of the citizen. This premise does not vanish entirely – the citizen perceived as legal subject still exists – but it becomes contingent so that an aspect of citizen management becomes to experiment with the boundary between citizen and state. This also means that the professional premises for what it means to be a professional in relation to citizens are similarly undermined. It cannot be established in advance what counts as quality for individual citizens, or which kind of invitation to co-creation individual citizens will react positively to. Expectations directed at professionals are accelerated because they become responsible for ensuring the availability of a surplus of opportunities for citizens to take responsibility and explore and discover their potential – albeit on the condition that the definition of responsibility remains diffuse and potentially limitless.

Finally, in Chapter Nine we described the historical development from constitutional state to potentiality state, a shift that reverses perceptions about the relation between *context* and *operation*. As context, the state form is no longer given as a premise, which defines the governance operation and its conditions. The governance operation becomes the primary focus and chooses its own context, its own state form. In this way, the potentiality state becomes *a playful state*, playing with different state forms and their governance potential. This form of play centres on this question: which notion of state as framework is appropriate for this particular governance situation? Moreover, this perspective serves as an experimental productive power-centred eye for the potential inherent in individual state forms for the creation of intensive and potent couplings between different systems.

A shift from a given whole to contingent multiple wholes

The peculiar ways in which governance and self-governance today become folded into each other cannot simply be described as self-governance within a politically established framework. What we are seeing is much more complex than what concepts such as goal and framework management can capture. Not only is the management space of welfare managers created through constant negotiations of how to understand the boundary between general goal and local agency. Today, experimentation with multiple descriptions of how to understand such frameworks is part of the way governance operates.

Table C.1: Developing forms

Administrative form	Institutional form	Relation between institution and function system	Form of contact	Form of membership	Form of citizen	State form
Formal bureaucracy	Innocent institution	Formal institution	Formal contract	Formal membership	Citizen as legal subject	Constitutional state
Sector administration	Professional responsible institution	Homophonic institution	Material contract	Double membership	Citizen as recipient	Welfare state
Supervision administration	Strategic organisation	Heterophonic organisation	Reflexive contract	Pedagogical and intimate self-enrolment	Citizen as active fellow citizen	Supervision state
Potentiality administration	Potential organisation	Communication-seeking organisation	Partnerships	Playful self-enrolment	Citizen as potentiality	Potentiality state

Self-perpetuating management?

Irrespective of the specific point of observation and specific forms, the historical movement seems to be one of a gradual undermining of the possibility for decision premises to serve as unambiguous premises. Whereas premises in the past were produced as clear and relatively unambiguous, expectations increasingly lose the unambiguous role of premise formation. Given premises are replaced by the intensity of operations. And this undermining of premises allows for new and extremely inflated expectations of management. Managers are no longer simply the people who implement political reforms in local contexts, and also not simply the producers of frameworks and conditions for welfare production. Today's managers are perceived as value-creating in themselves.

Have we painted a picture of a welfare society that is becoming increasingly desperate to create possibilities out of infinite challenges and scarce resources? A public sector so overwhelmed by its own historical excess left behind by different governance models that its only mode of innovation is to diffuse existing premises? A welfare society whose only strategy for creating possibilities out of impossibilities is to define as contingent such figures as welfare, organisation, employees and citizens?

In any case, there is a tragic element to the way the demand for increased management results in a kind of self-perpetuating logic. Premises are undermined at still higher rates, in part as the result of attempts by the welfare society to manage complexity by pushing it outward into local welfare organisations. In an effort to incorporate independence as a way to create better conditions for management and greater efficiency in governance, given frameworks and an organisational identity are undermined, which leads to an even greater need for management in order to translate open contingency into possibilities. Thus, we look for managers who can make the organisations ask themselves, 'Is this the right premise?' or 'Could it be different?' This preserves and perpetuates the demand for management. Management forms lead to new ungovernability, which then require new initiatives, which again increase ungovernability. Ultimately, therefore, management continues to ensure its own necessity.

Possibilities for management

These developments, however, do not add up to an unambiguous narrative of decline. It is not only a story of the loss of rights, job security and clear responsibilities and their replacement by a breach of rights, insecurity and infinite responsibility for self-development. Instead, as we have argued in several chapters, the movement in the direction of transience and turbulence is about the public sector's ability to handle complexity. Thus, it would be naïve to imagine that it would be possible to return to unambiguous governance forms, homophonic welfare organisations or the clear separation of the employee as either role or person, or the clear separation of public and private spheres.

The potentiality machine means that welfare managers on every level – to the extent that they master the game 'Do as we say: be inventive and independent' – are invited into the processes through which the welfare society develops. This results in a welfare society that remains theoretically open to management capacity from below or without. Previously, the management premise was that the higher up in the public hierarchy one found oneself, the closer one would be to the political, and the more important and significant would be the decision one made. This meant that political science was mandatory training for anyone seeking influence and power. It was regarded as better to work for the state than for the municipalities and better to work in the Ministry of Finance than in more peripheral ministries. There was a strong idea about power as centralised and the political as happening close to the centre of power.

The developments we have traced turn management on all levels of the welfare society into an exciting challenge. Or, if nothing else, it means that management becomes a political job at all levels. It is not possible to speak of management separate from the political battles over what welfare is or should be. Being a manager in municipalities or institutions no longer means simply implementing decisions that have been made elsewhere. Today's managers have to take much greater and more complex responsibility. It is much more involved than making sure things operate and function within a given framework.

Welfare politicians

All this does not make being a manager any easier. However, being a politician has also not become easier. Politicians might not always be aware of how much politics take place across public administration departments, but it would be naïve to think that, in a society as complex as today's, politics would not be involved in the production and delivery of welfare. Politicians are required to develop methods for formulating policies, which do not make themselves blind to the extent to which all aspects and all relations within the welfare society have become political. At the same time, politicians are not in a position to even approximately be able to survey and comprehend all welfare processes. As history has shown, there is a constant risk that efforts to create more transparency simply contribute to the lack of transparency. Even initiatives such as d-bureaucratisation reforms seem to strengthen bureaucracy rather than soften it.

Perhaps it is necessary to imagine a new role for politicians, which finally lays to rest the notion that politicians reside somewhere above the world in a place from which they may survey, comprehend and plan society. This produces disempowered politicians. Accordingly, what is required of today's politicians is courage. At the same time, the risk of scandals is great, because what is perceived from one perspective as innovation can be viewed from a different perspective as a failure to live up to legal requirements.

Welfare professions

Moreover, this book shows how conditions for professions being recognised as such have changed radically. One thing is clear: the professions no longer stand in a given and natural relationship with the welfare organisations that they historically helped establish and whose professional knowledge they monopolised for years. A daycare institution is no longer just a professional care institution in relation to which the administrative bureaucracy serves as framework and professional methodologies and assessments as content. Therefore, the welfare professions have to base their activities on an understanding of the complexity of the organisations they bring together.

When welfare organisations become heterophonic, the professions find themselves in a competitive situation where they risk being excluded at the benefit of other areas of professional knowledge. And with the emergence of the communication-seeking and potential organisations, welfare professions come to represent potential horizons of possibilities for the practices of welfare organisations. This is very different from being their given and natural horizon. The professions have to continue to find new ways to make themselves attractive to welfare politics and decision-making. And in the context of a potentiality regime, this means constantly reinventing oneself through new relations and modes of collaboration. This places the professions in a somewhat complex strategic position. On the one hand, individual professions are perceived as a contribution because of their specialised knowledge and specific competences, but, on the other hand, expectations with respect to the potential of interdisciplinary efforts and collaboration across professions run extremely high. Thus, despite the fact that professions may perceive themselves as contributing the appropriate professional knowledge in a given situation, their inclusion relies both on their core qualities of who they are and also on their reinvention of who they are for this particular situation, in this particular partnership with another profession.

The profession of social educators and its role in a current public school reform in Denmark may serve as an example. It is precisely by being who they are, meaning something different than teaching professionals and teacher-related professional knowledge, that social educators come to play the role of significant resources in the efforts to create a more diverse school day. However, at the same time, the reform calls for a reimagining of the relation between the professional knowledge of social educators and the concept of learning since their activities are now described as education support. Thus, as the example demonstrates, professions have to continually reinvent themselves in order to serve as a beneficial contribution qua themselves. This presents itself as a rather complex strategic situation – also for labour unions. Social educators, doctors, social workers, nurses and teachers all have to formulate a more flexible and connective role and function within the welfare organisations.

Labour unions often respond to these shifts by criticising the tendencies toward a generalist approach and the loss of professional knowledge in public administration, and call for a return to core professional values. There is ample reason for frustration in welfare organisations where it remains an open question how professional knowledge and competences may become relevant in particular cases and situations. But it is not simply a question of control versus trust. It is not possible to simply 'take back professional competences' or return to the professions' core responsibilities. Instead, labour unions have to engage in the process of developing a new language for how to be a profession in a hyper-complex welfare society. It is not possible to simply reconstitute unambiguous professional premises since it has become an integrated element of governance to continually experiment with professional premises. Today, too much political hope is invested in the possible outcomes and effectiveness of interdisciplinary efforts and the dissolution of boundaries to imagine a return to professional autonomy.

Three welfare management challenges

It is precisely because the object of management becomes increasingly diffuse that the expectations directed at management intensify. But what kind of management is required? How do managers establish any form of structure when any attempt to establish a stable 'outside' proves illusory and can only be stabilised through 'violence'? Much management philosophy points to values, but one might ask why values would serve as a credible 'outside'? Would it be imaginable instead to establish what we might refer to as a 'premiseless management philosophy'? Such an approach would have to define contingency and operation as its basic foundation.

Despite the fact that we no longer have just one ideal for how to design public administration or how to conduct welfare management, we still believe that the complexity of today's society makes some specific demands for attitudes toward welfare management. All welfare management must base itself on a polycontextual worldview. All welfare management must contend with a basic level of unmanageability. And all welfare management must acknowledge management as also political.

Polycontextualism

The first premise for a premiseless management philosophy is that all welfare management would have to base itself on a polycontextual worldview. As previously, we distinguish between a monocontextual and a polycontextual worldview. From the perspective of a monocontextual worldview, an observer sees what they see. The world is expected to be what it appears to be. From the perspective of a polycontextual worldview, by contrast, the observer still sees what they see but also knows that what they see is seen differently by other observers. This does not mean that observers are able to observe their own blind spot or see what other observers see. However, it is an insight into the fact that the world is observer-dependent and that a person's own observations derive from a specific perspective that they can never gain full insight into.

Polycontextualism, thus, is a worldview that takes into consideration the idea that what a person sees is probably seen differently by another observer. Every observation has a blind spot. Observers see what they see but cannot see what they cannot see. Any observation of the world is always framed by a particular perspective or way of seeing, which allows observers to see but also equips them with systematic blindness. When a person sees, they do not see the perspective they see from. This is a condition of all observation, all analysis, all thought and all communication. Nothing exists that is not observer-dependent. Everything is something for an observer.

In a hyper-complex context in which many different systems remain highly dependent on each other, we believe that it is critical to assume a polycontextual worldview. Any management situation has become complex in the sense that it is observed from a multitude of different perspectives involving a multitude of different systems. A manager's object of management appears differently from the perspective of different positions or places in the organisation and from the perspective of other systems in the organisation's environment. And when there seizes ceases to be a pre-defined definition of the function system that professionally grounds a specific welfare organisation, it becomes a critical management insight to be sensitive to different perspectives and to the way that each perspective frames factuality and professional knowledge differently. A monocontextual manager is unable to consider perspectives other than the one they have adopted. Monocontextual management asserts its worldview as if it were the only way to observe the world, and thus risks reducing the possibility for other systems to operate. In a complex society, monocontextualism easily becomes a form of violence.

Thus, today's welfare management must account for the complexity that surrounds it as countless worldviews, perspectives and systems. A central element of a modern welfare management perspective is to be hyper-sensitive to the systems ecology within which it operates. Otherwise, management runs the risk of causing more damage than value.

We believe that managers have to relinquish all notions of a single place from which society can be governed and planned. Decisions in the political system do not determine the activities of other systems. In the functionally differentiated society, one system cannot serve as the model for others. Politics does not serve as a model for economy. The free market cannot serve as a model for politics and care. This would destroy the capacity for self-governance in those systems and reduce the possibilities for handling complexity.

Polycontextualism does not mean that all perspectives are equal or that all perspectives must be considered or included. It simply refers to the acknowledgment that any perspective works by excluding other perspectives, an exclusion that the system must claim responsibility for. Many welfare professionals working in welfare organisations feel that they are prevented from doing what they consider to be their jobs. Polycontextualism also provides an insight into whether or not specific governance technologies risk suppressing what many people consider to be core professional responsibilities and values. This includes awareness of what we might refer to as 'structural corruption.' Structural corruption happens when one system serves as a parasite on another system so that it can no longer fulfil its internal function and is reduced to external service. Structural corruption would apply, for example, in cases when the sole function of unemployment training programmes is control and regulation and the programmes barely make sense as actual training. Structural corruption happens whenever service is valued above function. Accordingly, polycontextualism in this context means to have an eye for the independent values of independent systems.

Ungovernability

The second premise for a premiseless management philosophy is that all welfare management has to contend with a level of basic ungovernability.

As we have made clear, we write within the context of a systems theoretical tradition. Systems theory was basically founded as governance theory. In the 1950s, we saw a radical rupture within system theory. This rupture shifted systems theory from what was called first-order cybernetics to second-order cybernetics. First-order cybernetics is about optimising the governance of a system by building models of it. The governing agent is viewed as positioned outside the system it seeks to govern. The governed system is fundamentally seen as an opaque black box that operates like a machine by continually repeating particular patterns of cause and effect. Thus, by accumulating knowledge about the functioning of this machine and building a model of it, it becomes possible to calculate the system's response to governance. The governing agent intervenes in the system (input). This leads to an effect (output), which then serves as feedback for the governing agent. The output can be compared to the defined governance goal, and the governing agent may then subsequently correct itself in order to more precisely target the desired governance goal. Over time, the governing agent learns to master its governance. This first-order cybernetic idea of governance exists today in many areas of society. A vast number of national economists, for example, think in terms of first-order cybernetics. They construct models of the world perceived as an economic system. They provide modes of intervention into such systems and modes of calculation of various interventions, and the effects of specific interventions serve as material for the further elaboration of the models to become even more precise in their predictions. They assume that objects of governance are simple predictable machines.

Second-order cybernetics fundamentally rejects this idea of governance. Second-order cybernetics sees systems not as trivial machines but as self-creating (autopoietical) systems, which create order out of chaos (Hansen and Clarke, 2009). The systems that serve as objects of governance are also perceived as self-governing. They create themselves and continually change themselves. Therefore, autopoietical systems have to be considered fundamentally unpredictable. Autopoietical systems do not respond to the world in a simple way. They are not simple machines operating through the repetition of certain causal mechanisms. They establish their own relations with their external environment and always produce a surplus of possibilities for their own continuation. They continually produce disorder. Their operations are always contingent, which means that the systems always have alternative models for operating. The system's choice of possibilities is fundamentally open, and its choice further produces possibilities for operation. To an outside perspective, therefore, these systems are not predictable but rather chaotic. From this perspective, the condition of all governance is a fundamental sense of ungovernability. It is fundamentally impossible to calculate another system since it is not constructed around simple and endlessly repeatable cause and effect relations. The systems continually change as do their modes of operation, and they establish their own perspective on the governing agent's attempt at governance.

We believe that welfare management needs to account for the limits of governance. We are not governance optimists. We believe that governance has a better chance of being effective if it is based in an understanding of the fundamental ungovernability and unpredictability of systems. To acknowledge ungovernability as a point of departure is to acknowledge an always radically limited insight into the way the world appears to the system one seeks to govern. This leads to a form of 'humble governance' that knows that a person's worldview cannot be made the model for the worldviews of others, and that management needs instead to contend with complexity.

Management as political

Finally, the third premise for a premiseless management philosophy is that all welfare management should acknowledge the political aspects of management.

If each moment contains a surplus of possibilities for ways in which new actions and operations within a system can connect to previous operations, and if the operative choice of connectivity simultaneously establishes and changes the system in question, we can no longer separate operation and constitution. And, moreover, if we adopt a discourse-analytical perspective on politics, which defines politics as 'the constitutive moment of the social', any operative choice is potentially always political. Politics are choices that affect the constitution of social conditions and the way in which systems create, operate and develop premises.

As decision premises increasingly lose their character of given premises, we see how local, practical and operative decisions increasingly become potentially political decisions. In that sense, politics becomes ubiquitous and no longer only takes place in institutions designed to be political. And in light of this, welfare management increasingly also becomes political management. Welfare management is political when welfare management decisions also change the premises for how welfare systems are constituted. And this applies on all levels of the hierarchy – to permanent secretaries, city managers, heads of department, heads of institutions, team leaders or self-managing employees.

When the coding of particular decisions is no longer given, and a decision therefore becomes both a decision and a decision about its factual coding, we are in the realm of the political. When the hierarchical leader–subordinate relation is not given but is defined in part by the subordinated institution, we are in the realm of the political. And when, in a partnership contract, the premises for the collaboration are not given and the goals of the collaboration have to be continually defined and redefined, we are clearly in the realm of the political.

And it is not unusual for decentralised decisions to directly address and re-elaborate fundamental values and boundaries as when a social services director decides to introduce contracts with at-risk single mothers about the conditions of motherhood, or when a public school decides to introduce individual pattern breaker contracts with students, which incorporate and intertwine schoolwork, family obligations and afterschool activities in relation to individual goals.

In effect, the formally political is forced to assume special responsibility for the practical implementation of the efforts of many welfare managers. Formal political structures (parliament, municipal councils, parent organisations, church councils, etc) need to acknowledge that politics take place in every corner of society. They should cultivate awareness of the ubiquity of the political within the administrative and the professional within public administration and in welfare institutions – public, private, voluntary or self-governing. Otherwise they become politically blind and run the risk of rendering formal political structures a matter of mere ritual in relation to the 'real' politics that happen invisibly everywhere else.

References

Aarhus University (2013) 'Smart society – Big Data udfordringen', Copenhagen: Ministry of Higher Education and Science, (http://fivu.dk/aktuelt/temaer/inno/modtagede-indspil/afsender/aarhus-universitet/smart-society-2013-big-data-udfordringen).

Abegg, A. (2013) 'The legitimacy of the contracting state', *Law and Contemporary Problems*, vol 76, pp 139-50.

Administrationsdepartementet [Administration Department] (1987) *Årsberetning 1987*, København.

Albertsen, K., Jeppesen, D. and Hvenegaard, H. (2012) 'Samarbejde om kerneopgaven', in *Sund Ledelse*, Danske regioner og Dansk selvskab for ledelse i sundhedsvæsenet.

Andersen, N.Å. (2000) 'Public market – political firms', *Acta Sociologica*, no 1.

Andersen, N.Å. (2003a) 'The undecidability of decision', in T. Bakken and T. Hernes (eds) *Autopoietic organization theory, Abstrakt, Liber*, Oslo: Copenhagen Business School Press, pp 235-58.

Andersen, N.Å. (2003b) 'Polyphonic organisations', in T. Hernes and T. Bakken (eds) *Autopoietic organization theory, Abstrakt, Liber*, Oslo: Copenhagen Business School Press, pp 151-82.

Andersen, N.Å. (2003c) *Discursive analytical strategies – Understanding Foucault, Koselleck, Laclau, Luhmann*, Bristol: Policy Press.

Andersen, N.Å. (2004) 'The contractualisation of the citizen – on the transformation of obligation into freedom', *Social Systems*, vol 10, no 2, pp 273-91.

Andersen, N.Å. (2005) 'Political administration', in D. Howard and J. Torfing (eds) *Discourse theory in European Politics: Identity, policy and governance*, New York: Palgrave Macmillan, pp 139-69.

Andersen, N.Å. (2007a) 'The self-infantilised adult and the management of personality', *Critical Discourse Studies*, vol 4, no 3, pp 331-52.

Andersen, N.Å. (2007b) 'Creating the client who can create himself and his own fate – the tragedy of the citizens' contract', *Qualitative Sociology Review*, vol III, issue 2, pp 119-43.

Andersen, N.Å. (2008a) 'The world as will and adaptation: the inter-discursive coupling of citizens' contracts', *Critical Discourse Studies*, vol 5, no 1, pp 75-89.

Andersen, N.Å. (2008b) *Partnerships: Machines of possibility*, Bristol: Policy Press.

Andersen, N.Å. (2009) *Power at play – The relationships between play, work and governance*, London: Palgrave Macmillan.

Andersen, N.Å. (2011a) 'Who is Yum-Yum? A cartoon state in the making', *Ephemera: Theory & Politics in Organization*, vol 11, no 4, pp 406-32.

Andersen, N.Å. (2011b) 'Conceptual history and the diagnostics of the present', *Management & Organizational History*, vol 6, no 3, pp 248-67.

Andersen, N.Å. (2012a) 'To promise a promise – When contractors desire a life-long partnership', in N.Å. Andersen and I.-J. Sand (eds) *Hybrid forms of governance – Self-suspension of power*, Basingstoke: Palgrave Macmillan, pp 205-31.

Andersen, N.Å. (2012b) 'Citizen's contract as a tricky steering medium', in N.T. Thygesen (ed) *The illusion of management control – A systems theoretical approach to managerial technologies*, London: Palgrave Macmillan, pp 108-32.

Andersen, N.Å. (2013a) 'Contract as a form of intersystemic communication', in A. Febbrajo and G. Harste (eds) *Law and intersystemic communication*, Studies in Sociology of Law, Aldershot: Ashgate, pp 129-54.

Andersen, N.Å. (2013b) *Managing intensity and play at work: Transient relationships*, Cheltenham: Edward Elgar.

Andersen, N.Å. and Born, A.W. (2000) 'Complexity and change: two "semantic tricks" in the triumphant oscillating organization', *System Practice and Action Research*, vol 13, no 3, pp 297-328.

Andersen, N.Å. and Born, A.W. (2001) *Kærlighed og omstilling*, Frederiksberg: Nyt fra Samfundsvidenskaberne.

Andersen, N.Å. and Born, A.W. (2007a) 'Heterophony and the postponed organisation – Organising autopoietic systems', *Tamara Journal for Critical Organizational Inquiry*, vol 6, issue 2, pp 176-86.

Andersen, N.Å. and Born, A.W. (2007b) 'Emotional identity feelings as communicative artefacts in organisations', *International Journal of Work Organisation and Emotion*, vol 2, no 1, pp 35-48.

Andersen, N.Å. and Born, A.W. (2008) 'The employee in the sign of love', *Culture and Organization*, vol 14, no 4, pp 225-343.

Andersen, N.Å. and Knudsen, H. (2014) 'Heterophoni and hyper responsibility', in M. Knudsen and W. Vogt (eds) *Systems theory and the sociology of health and illness: Observing healthcare*, Abingdon: Routledge, pp 81-100.

Andersen, N.Å. and Pors, J.G. (2012) 'Spielende Organisationen – Unbestimmtheit als Ressource', in J. Müller and V. von Groddeck (eds) *(Un)bestimmtheit. Praktische Problemkonstellationen*, München: Wilhelm Fink, pp 117-31.

Andersen, N.Å. and Pors, J.G. (2014) 'Playful membership. Embracing an unknown future', *Management and Organisational History*, pp 1-17.

Andersen, N.Å. and Sand, I.-J. (eds) (2012) *Hybrid forms of governance – Self-suspension of power*, Basingstoke: Palgrave Macmillan.

Andersen, P. (1924) *Om ugyldige Forvaltningsakter med særligt Henblik paa Ugyldighedsgrunde*, København: Arnold Buscks Forlag.

Andersen, P. (1926) 'Kontrakt eller forvaltningsakt?', *Nordisk Administrativt Tidsskrift*, pp 78-84.

Armbrüster, T. (2005) 'Bureaucracy and the controversy between liberal interventionism and non-interventionism', in P. du Gay (ed) *The values of bureaucracy*, Oxford: Oxford University Press, pp 63-88.

Baecker, D. (1999) 'The form game', in D. Baecker (ed) *Problems of form*, Stanford, CA: Stanford University Press, pp 99-106.

Bækgaard, J. (2009) 'Den autentiske fagperson', *Socialrådgiveren*, no 10, pp 22-3.

References

Bateson, G. (1955) 'The message "This is play"', in B. Schaffner (ed) *Group processes*, Transactions of the Second Conference, 9, 10, 12 October, Princeton, NJ: Josiaf Macy J.R. Foundation, pp 145-242.

Bateson, G. (2000) *Steps to an ecology of mind – Collected essays in anthropology, psychiatry, evolution, and epistemology*, Chicago, IL: University of Chicago Press.

Bauman, Z. (2008) *The art of life*, Cambridge: Polity Press.

Bjerg, H. and Knudsen, H. (2012) 'Når personkendskab bliver professionskundskab: Aktuelle udviklinger i lærerrollen', in M. Järvinen and N. Mik-Meyer, *At skabe en professionel*, København: Hans Reitzels Forlag, pp 76-97.

Bogdanor, V. (2001) 'Civil Service reform: A critique', *The Political Quarterly*, vol 72, no 3, pp 291-9.

Bourdieu, P. (1994) 'Rethinking the state: Genesis and structure of the bureaucratic field', *Sociological Theory*, vol 12, no 1, pp 1-18.

Bramming, P. and Johnsen, R. (2011) 'Love will tear us apart: Transformational leadership and love in a call centre', *European Journal of International Management*, vol 5, no 1, pp 80-95.

Bredsdorff, N. (2000) 'Fremtidens Danmark, socialdemokraterne og Keynesianismen', *Skriftserie fra Roskilde Universitetsbibliotek*, no 35, Roskilde.

Cabinet Office (1999a) *Vision and values*, London: Cabinet Office.

Cabinet Office (1999b) *Civil Service reform*, London: Cabinet Office.

Campbell, D. (2007) 'Relational contract and the nature of private ordering: A comment on Vincent-Jones', *Indiana Journal of Global Studies*, vol 14, no 2, pp 279-300.

Caroselli, M. (1996) *Quality games for trainers*, New York: The McGraw-Hill Companies.

Chapman, R.A. (1996) 'The end of the British Civil Service', in P. Barberis (ed) *The Whitehall reader*, Buckingham: Open University Press, pp 189-91.

Chapman, R.A. (2006) 'The ethics of enthusiasm', *Public Money and Management*, January, pp 5-7.

Christensen, S. (1987) 'Fremtidens personalepolitik i staten', *Samfundsøkonomen*, no 3, pp 19-21.

Clarke, J. and Newman, J. (1997) *The managerial state*, London: Sage.

Committee on Public Libraries in the Knowledge Society (2010) *Folkebibliotekerne i videnssamfundet*, Rapport, Styrelsen for Bibliotek og Medier.

Condren, C. (2006) *Argument and authority in Early Modern England: The presupposition of oaths and offices*, Oxford: Oxford University Press.

Corby, S. (1993) 'How big a step is Next Steps? Industrial relations developments in the Civil Service executive agencies', *Human Resource Management Journal*, vol 4, no 2, pp 4-19.

Costea, B., Crump, N. and Amiridis, K. (2007) 'Managerialism and "infinite human resources": a commentary on the "therapeutic habitus", "derecognition of finitude" and the modern sense of self', *Journal for Cultural Research*, vol 11, no 3, pp 245-64.

Costea, B., Crump, N. and Amiridis, K. (2012) 'Graduate employability and the principle of potentiality: an aspect of the ethics of HRM', *Journal of Business Ethics*, vol 111, no 1, pp 25-36.

Costea, B., Crump, N. and Holm, J. (2005) 'Dionysus at work? The ethos of play and the ethos of management', *Culture and Organization*, vol 11, no 2, pp 139-51.

Costea, B., Crump, N. and Holm, J. (2006) 'Conceptual history and the interpretation of managerial ideologies', *Management and Organizational History*, vol 1, no 2, pp 159-75.

Crozier, M. (2007) 'Recursive governance: Contemporary political communication and public policy', *Political Communication*, vol 24, pp 1-18.

Cruikshank, B. (2004) 'Viljen til at mægtiggøre: Medborgerskabsteknologier og "Krigen mod Fattigdom"', *Grus*, no 70, pp 30-48.

Dall, A.S. (2011) 'Du skal lede personer, ikke funktioner' (www.lederweb.dk/Strategi/Mangfoldighedsledelse/Artikel/85220/Slip-forskelskraften-los).

D'Amour, D. and Oandasan, I. (2005) 'Interprofessionality as the field of interprofessional practice and interprofessional education: An emerging concept', *Journal of Interprofessional Care*, May, Supplement 1, pp 8-20.

Danish Ministry of Education (2001) 'Det Virtuelle Gymnasium – Det almene gymnasium i viden- og netværkssamfundet', *Uddannelsesstyrelsens temahæfteserie*, no 37.

Danish Ministry of Education (2014) *Bliv en del af Ny Nordisk Skole*, Copenhagen.

Danish Ministry of Finance (1993) *Nyt syn på den offentlige sektor* [A new perspective on the public sector], Copenhagen.

Danish Ministry of Finance (1994) *Medarbejder i Staten –Ansvar og udvikling*, Copenhagen.

Danish Ministry of Finance (1995) *Værktøj til velfærd. Effektive institutioner* [Welfare tools], Copenhagen.

Danish Ministry of Finance (1998) *Personalepolitik i staten. Fra ord til handling, Sammenfatning*, Copenhagen.

Danish Ministry of the Environment (2004) *Risikohåndtering og risikokommunikation*, Miljøprojekt no 893.

Dean, M. (1995) 'Governing the unemployed self in an active society', *Economy and Society*, vol 24, no 4, pp 559-83.

Dean, M. (1999) *Governmentality: Power and rule in modern society*, London: Sage.

Dean, M. (2007) *Governing societies: Political perspectives on domestic and international rule*, Maidenhead: Open University Press.

Derrida, J. (1988) *The ear of the other*, London: University of Nebraska Press.

Derrida, J. (1992a) 'Force of law: The "mystical foundation of authority"', in D. Cornell, M. Rosenfeld and D. Gray Carlson (eds) *Deconstruction and the possibility of justice*, New York: Routledge, pp 4-67.

Derrida, J. (1992b) *The gift of death*, London: University of Chicago Press.

du Gay, P. (2008) '"Without affection or enthusiasm": Problems of involvement and attachment in "responsive" public management', *Organization*, vol 15, no 3, pp 335-53.

du Gay, P. (2009) 'In defense of Mandarins: Recovering the "core business" of public management', *Management & Organizational History*, vol 4, no 4, pp 359-84.

du Gay, P. and Vikkelsø, S. (2012) '"Reflections": on the lost specification of "change"', *Journal of Change Management*, vol 12, no 2, pp 121-43.

du Gay, P. and Vikkelsø, S. (2013) 'Exploitation, exploration and exaltation: notes on a metaphysical (re)turn to "one best way of organizing"', in M. Holmqvist and A. Spicer (eds) *Managing 'human resources' by exploiting and exploring people's potentials*, Bingley: Emerald Group Publishing Limited, pp 249-79.

Dunn, K. and Dunn, R. (1993) 'Teaching secondary students through their individual learning styles', *Practical Approaches for Grades*, pp 7-12.

Dunn, R. and Dunn, K. (1999) *The complete guide to the learning styles in service system*, London: Allyn & Bacon.

Dunn, R., Dunn, K. and Treffinger, D. (1992) *Bringing out the giftedness in your child: Nurturing every child's unique strengths, talents, and potential*, London: John Wiley & Sons.

Durkheim, É. (2013) *The division of labor in society*, New York: Palgrave Macmillan.

Ekman, S. (2012) *Authority and autonomy. Paradoxes in modern knowledge work*, Basingstoke: Palgrave Macmillan.

Esposito, E. (2011) *The future of futures. The time of money in financing and society*, Cheltenham: Edward Elgar.

Esposito, E. (2012a) 'The structures of uncertainty: performativity and unpredictability in economic operations', *Economy and Society*, vol 41, pp 1-28.

Esposito, E. (2012b) 'The time of money', in N.T. Thygesen (ed) *The illusion of management control: A systems theoretical approach to managerial technologies*, Basingstoke: Palgrave Macmillan, pp 223-36.

Finansministeriet, Undervisningsministeriet, KL (Kommunernes Landsforening [Danish Local Municipalities]) et al (2009) *Inspirationskatalog til renovering og byggeri af daginstitutioner og folkeskoler – udmøntning af kvalitetsfonden*, København.

Forvaltningsnævnet (Public Administration Comitee) (1960) 'Efteruddannelse af akademiske tjenestemænd', *Betænkning nr. 265*, Copenhagen.

Foucault, M. (1989) *The birth of the clinic*, London: Routledge.

Frankel, C. (ed) (2004) *Virksomhedens politisering*, Frederiksberg: Forlaget Samfundslitteratur.

Frankel, C. and Thygesen, N.T. (2012) 'Management as a temporal hybrid', in N.Å. Andersen and I.-J. Sand (eds) *Hybrid forms of governance – Self-suspension of power*, Basingstoke: Palgrave Macmillan, pp 102-24.

Freedland, M. (1994) 'Government by contract and public law', *Public Law*, Spring, pp 86-104.

Gittell, J.H. (2011a) 'New direction for relational coordination theory', in K.S. Cameron and G. Spreitzer (eds) *Oxford handbook of positive organizational scholarship*, Oxford: Oxford University Press, pp 74-94.

Gittell, J.H. (2011b) 'High performance healthcare: Using the power of relationships to achieve quality, efficiency and resilience', Presentation at Glostrup Hospital, 27 January.

Gjesing, B.S. (2010) 'Pas på etikken', *Socialrådgiveren*, no 7, p 20.

Greer, S.L. and Lillvis, D.F. (2014) 'Beyond leadership: Political strategies for coordination in health policies', *Health Policy*, vol 16, no 1, pp 12-17.

Hansen, M. and Clarke, B. (2009) *Emergence and embodiment: New essays on second-order systems theory*, Durham, NC: Duke University Press.

Hills, R.J. (1976) 'The public school as a type of organization', in J.J. Loubner, R.C. Baum, A. Effrat and V.M. Lidz (eds) *Explorations in general theory in social science*, New York: The Free Press, pp 829-56.

Højlund, H. (2012) 'Hybrid inclusion: multiple inclusion mechanisms in the modernized organization of Danish welfare services', in N.T. Thygesen (ed) *The illusion of management control: A systems theoretical approach to managerial technologies*, Abingdon: Palgrave Macmillan, pp 87-108.

Højlund, H. and La Cour, A. (2015) 'Polycontextuality and the body', in M. Knudsen and W. Vogd (eds) *Systems theory and the sociology of health and illness. Observing health care*, London: Routledge, pp 43-60.

Højlund, H. and Larsen, L.T. (2001) 'Det sunde fællesskab', *Distinktion*, no 3, pp 73-90.

Holbæk Kommune (2014) *Holbæk Kommune Kerneopgaver*, Holbæk.

Hørsholm Sygehus [Hospital] (2001a) *Udbudsbetingelser og vejledning til tilbudsgivere*, Hørsholm.

Hørsholm Sygehus [Hospital] (2001b) *Udkast til partnerskabskontrakt om varetagelse af serviceopgaver på Hørsholm Sygehus*, Hørsholm.

Hørsholm Sygehus [Hospital] (2002) 'Partnerskab mellem Hørsholm Sygehus og ISS', *Internt notat*, Torben Knudsen, 27/09/02.

Ibarra, H. and Petriglieri, J.L. (2010) 'Identity work and play', *Journal of Organizational Change Management*, vol 23, no 1, pp 10-25.

Järvinen, M. and Mik-Meyer, N. (2012) *At skabe en professionel [Creating a professional]*, København: Hans Reitzels Forlag.

Jenkins, K., Caines, K. and Jackson, A. (1988) *Improving management in government: The next steps*, London: The Stationery Office.

Jensen, L. (2003) *Den store koordinator. Finansministeriet som moderne styringsaktør*, København: Jurist- og Økonomforbundets Forlag.

Jensen, L. (2008) *Væk fra afgrunden. Finansministeriet som økonomisk styringsaktør*, Odense: Syddansk Universitetsforlag.

Jensen, L. (2012) 'The self-suspension of government: hybrid reform technologies as a response to the government's welfare state conundrum', in N.Å. Andersen and I.-J. Sand (eds) *Hybrid forms of governance – Self-suspension of power*, Basingstoke: Palgrave Macmillan, pp 124-47.

Jessop, B. (1990) 'Putting states in their place: State systems and state theory', in A. Leftwich (ed) *New developments in political science*, Aldershot: Edward Elgar, pp 141-72.

References

Jessop, B. (2003) 'Governance and meta-governance: on reflexivity, requisite variety and requisite irony', *Governance as Social and Political Communication*, pp 101-16.

Johnson, N. (1983) *Management in government: Perspectives on Management*, Oxford: Oxford University Press.

Jones, A. (1998) *104 activities that build*, Red Room Publishing.

Juelskjær, M. (2011) 'Når skolen bygger om. Hvordan ny arkitektur skaber nye betingelser for ledelse', in M. Juelskjær, H. Knudsen, J.G. Pors and D. Staunæs (eds) *Ledelse af Uddannelse. At lede det potentielle*, Frederiksberg: Samfundslitteratur, pp 53-80.

Juelskjær, M., Knudsen, H., Pors, J.G. and Staunæs, D. (2011) '"Vi holder af hverdagen": Ledelse som et tværfagligt, flygtigt og magtfuldt fænomen', in M. Juelskjær, H. Knudsen, J.G. Pors and D. Staunæs (ed) *Ledelse af uddannelse: At lede det potentielle*, København: Samfundslitteratur, pp 13-26.

Kane, P. (2004) *The play ethic: A manifesto for a different way of living*, London: Macmillan.

Keller, A. (2013) 'Art and architecture: Swiss Re's corporate culture and identity', in Swiss Re (http://next.swissre.com/en/index.cfm/stories/arts-and-architecture/art-and-architecture-swiss-res-corporate-culture-and-identity/).

Knudsen, H. (2010) *Har vi en aftale? – Magt og ansvar i mødet mellem folkeskole og familie*, Frederiksberg: Nyt fra Samfundsvidenskaberne.

Knudsen, H. (2011) 'The game of hospitality', *Ephemera: Theory & Politics in Organization*, vol 11, no 4, pp 433-49.

Knudsen, H. and Andersen, N.Å. (2014) 'Playful hyper responsibility: toward a dislocation of parents' responsibility', *Journal of Education Policy*, vol 29, no 1, pp 105-29.

Knudsen, M. (2006) 'Autolysis within organizations: A case study', *Soziale Systeme*, vol 12, no 1, p 79.

Knudsen, M. (2012a) 'Displacing the paradox of decision making: The management of contingency in a Danish county', in D. Seidl and K.H. Becker (eds) *Niklas Luhmann and organization studies*, Frederiksberg: Copenhagen Business School Press, pp 107-26.

Knudsen, M. (2012b) 'Structural couplings between organizations and function systems: looking at standards in health care', in N.T. Thygesen (ed) *The illusion of management control: A systems theoretical approach to managerial technologies*, Abingdon: Palgrave Macmillan, pp 133-58.

Knudsen, M. and Højlund, H. (2012) 'Organisational suspension: A desire for interaction', in N.Å. Andersen and I.-J. Sand (eds) *Hybrid forms of governance – Self-suspension of power*, Basingstoke: Palgrave Macmillan, pp 85-101.

Knudsen, M. and Vogd, W. (eds) (2015) *Systems theory and the sociology of health and illness. Observing health care*, London: Routledge.

Koch, A. (1982) *Socialt arbejde – helhedsprincip og behovsvurdering på fagligt grundlag*, København: AKF.

Kofoed, K.H. (1928) 'Bør Tjenestemandstillingen være en egentlig livsstilling eller et tidsbegrænset kontraktsforhold?', *Nordisk Administrativt Tidsskrift*, pp 1-17.

Kommunernes Landsforening [Local Government Denmark] and KTO (1995) *SKUP i leder- og medarbejdersamarbejdet*, København.

Kooiman, J. (2003) *Governing as governance*, London: Sage.

Kooiman, J. (2008) 'Exploring the concept of governability', *Journal of Comparative Policy Analysis: Research and Practice*, vol 10, no 2, pp 171-90.

Kooiman, J. and Jentoft, S. (2009) 'Meta-governance: Values, norms and principles, and the making of hard choices', *Public Administration*, vol 87, no 4, pp 818-36.

Kooiman, J. and van Vliet, M. (2000) 'Self-governance as a mode of societal governance', *Public Management*, vol 2, issue 3, pp 359-77.

Koselleck, R. (1985) *Futures past: On the semantics of historical time*, New York: Colombia University Press.

La Cour, A. and Højlund, H. (2008) 'Velfærd gennem det superviserende samarbejde', in C. Sløk and K. Villadsen (eds) *Velfærdsledelse*, København: Hans Reitzels Forlag, pp 197-226.

La Cour, A. and Højlund, H. (2012) 'The emergence of a third-order system in the Danish welfare sector', in R. Hull (ed) *Dialogues in critical management studies, vol 1, Critical Perspectives on the 3rd sector*, London: Palgrave Macmillan, pp 87-111.

Ladeur, K.-H. (2007) 'The role of contracts and networks in public governance: The importance of the "social epistemology" of decision making', *Indiana Journal of Global Legal Studies*, vol 14, no 2, pp 329-51.

Lauridsen, O. (2012) *Fokus på læring 3.0. Om læringsstile i hverdagen* [*Focus on learning 3.0. Everyday learning styles*], København: Akademisk Forlag.

Lewis, J. (2002) 'Individualisation, assumptions about the existence of an adult worker model and the shift towards contractualism', in A. Carling (ed) *Analysing families*, Florence, KY: Routledge, pp 71-6.

Lindblom, C.E. (1959) 'The science of "muddling through"', *Public Administration Review*, vol 19, no 2, pp 79-88.

Lindblom, C.E. (1979) 'Still muddling. Not yet through', *Public Administration Review*, vol 39, no 6, pp 517-26.

Linder, M.-O., Roos, J. and Bart, V. (2001) *Play in organizations*, Working Paper 2, Lausanne, Switzerland: Imagination Lab.

Lister, R. (2001) 'Towards a citizens' welfare state', *Theory, Culture & Society*, vol 18, no 2-3, pp 91-111.

Local Government, Denmark (2014) *Fremfærd. Et magasin om fremtidens velfærd i kommunerne* (Moving forward with welfare. A magazine about future welfare in municipalities), http://fremfaerd.dk/sites/default/files/fremfaerd-magasin-enkeltsider-020614d_0_0.pdf

Lüdecke, D. (2015) 'Sustainability in integrated-care partnerships: a systems and network theoretical approach for the analysis of corporation networks', in M. Knudsen and W. Vogd (eds) *Systems theory and the sociology of health and illness. Observing health care*, London: Routledge, pp 149-70.

References

Luhmann, N. (1971) *Politische Planung, Aufsätze zur Soziologie von Politik und Vervaltung*, Bielefeld: Westdeutscher Verlag Opladen.

Luhmann, N. (1977) 'Differentiation of society', *The Canadian Journal of Sociology*, vol 2, no 1, pp 29-53.

Luhmann, N. (1981) 'Communication about law in interaction systems', in K. Knorr-Cetina and A.V. Cicourel (eds) *Advances in social theory and methodology. Toward an integration of micro- and macro-sociologies*, London: Routledge and Kegan Paul, pp 234-56.

Luhmann, N. (1982a) 'World-time and system history. Interrelations between temporal horizon and social structures', in N. Luhmann (ed) *The differentiation of society*, New York: Columbia University Press, pp 289-323.

Luhmann, N. (1982b) 'The world society as social system', *International Journal of General Systems*, vol 8, pp 131-8.

Luhmann, N. (1986) *Love as passion*, Cambridge: Polity Press.

Luhmann, N. (1989) *Ecological communication*, Chicago, IL: University of Chicago Press.

Luhmann, N. (1990) *Political theory in the welfare state*, Berlin: Walter de Gruyter.

Luhmann, N. (1992a) 'The coding of the legal system', in G. Teubner and A. Febbrajo (eds) *State, law, and economy as autopoietic systems*, Milan: Dott. A. Giuffré Editore, pp 145-86.

Luhmann, N. (1992b) 'Operational closure and structural coupling', *Cardozo Law Review*, vol 13, no 5, pp 1419-41.

Luhmann, N. (1993a) 'Die Paradoxie des Entscheidens', *Verwaltungs-Archiv. Zeitschrift für Verwaltungslehre, Verwaltungsrecht und Verwaltungspolitik*, vol 84, no 3, pp 287-99.

Luhmann, N. (1993b) 'Observing re-entries', *Graduate Faculty Philosophy Journal*, vol 16, no 2, pp 485-98.

Luhmann, N. (1993c) 'Barnet som medium for opdragelse', in J. Cederstrøm, L. Qvortrup and J. Rasmussen (eds) *Læring, samtale, organisation – Luhmann og skolen*, København: Unge pædagoger, pp 163-90.

Luhmann, N. (1995) *Social systems*, Stanford, CA: Stanford University Press.

Luhmann, N. (2000a) *The reality of the mass media*, Oxford: Polity Press.

Luhmann, N. (2000b) *Organisation und Entscheidung*, Wiesbaden: Westdeutscher Verlag.

Luhmann, N. (2006) *Samfundets uddannelsessystem*, København: Hans Reitzels Forlag.

Luhmann, N. (2012) *Theory of society*, Volume 1, Stanford, CA: Stanford University Press.

Luhmann, N. (2013) *Theory of society*, Volume 2, Stanford, CA: Stanford University Press.

Maas, A. and Bakker, D.-J. (2000) 'Managing differences in a multi-paradigmatic partnership', in T. Taillieu (ed) *Collaborative strategies and multi-organizational partnership*, Leuven-Apeldoorn: Garant Publisher, pp 189-98.

Macaulay, S. (1963a) 'The use and non-use of contracts in the manufacturing industry', *The Practical Lawyer*, vol 9, no 7, pp 13-40.

Macaulay, S. (1963b) 'Non-contractual relations in business: a preliminary study', *American Sociological Review*, vol 28, no 1, pp 55-67.

Macaulay, S. (1985) 'An empirical view of contract', *Wisconsin Law Review*, p 467.

Macauley, S. (2003) 'The real and the paper deal: empirical pictures of relationships, complexity, and the urge for transparent simple rules', *The Modern Law Review*, vol 66, no 1, January, pp 46-7.

Mainemelis, C. and Ronson, S. (2006) 'Ideas are born in fields of play: Towards a theory of play and creativity in organizational settings', *Research in Organisational Behaviour: An Annual Series of Analytical Essays and Critical Reviews Research in Organizational Behaviour*, vol 27, pp 81-131.

Majgaard, K. (2008/09) 'Slip paradokserne løs!', *Økonomistyring & Informatik*, vol 24, no 3, pp 261-83.

Majgaard, K. (2013) *Offentlig styring, Simpel, reflekteret og transformativ*, København: Hans Reitzels Forlag.

Miller, P. and Rose, N. (1992) 'Political power beyond the state: problematics in government', *British Journal of Sociology*, vol 43, no 2, pp 173-205.

Ministeriet for Børn, Legestilling, Integration og Sociale forhold (2012) *Relations- og mentorarbejde*, Håndbogsserien 'Forebyggelse af ekstremisme', Copenhagen, Ministeriet for Børn.

Ministeriet for Forskning, Innovation og Videregående Uddannelser (2013) 'Sammenfatning af INNO+. Det innovative Danmark' (http://fivu.dk/publikationer/2013/filer-2013/pixi_web_interaktiv_enkeltsider.pdf).

Moe, S. (1998) *Den moderne hjelpens sosiologi. Velferd i systemteoretisk perspektiv*, Stavanger: Apeiros Forlag.

Møller, P. (1956) 'Svaret til velfærdsstaten', in *Til alle mænds tarv*, København, pp 83-103.

Mommsen, W.J. (1974) *The age of bureaucracy*, Oxford: Basil Blackwell.

Müller, J. and von Groddeck, V. (eds) (2013) *(Un)bestimmtheit. Praktische Problemkonstellationen*, München: Wilhelm Fink Verlag.

Municipality of Aarhus (2013) *Kærlig Kommune. Fremtidens sundhed og omsorg i Aarhus* [*The municipality of love. Future health care in Aarhus*, Mandag Morgen with Aarhus kommune.

Municipality of Kolding (2012) *Et godt liv på plejecenter. 12 hverdagsfortællinger*, Kolding, Seniorforvaltningen.

Nelken, D. (1987) 'The use of "contracts" as a social work technique', *Current Legal Problems*, vol 40, pp 207-32.

Newman, J. (2004) 'Constructing accountability: Network governance and managerial agency', *Public Policy and Administration*, vol 19, no 4, pp 17-33.

Newman, J. (2005a) 'Bending bureaucracy: leadership and multi-level governance', in P. du Gay (ed) *The values of bureaucracy*, Oxford: Oxford University Press, pp 191-210.

References

Newman, J. (2005b) 'Enter the transformational leader: Network governance and the micro-politics of modernization', *Sociology*, vol 39, no 4, pp 717-34.

Obling, A.R. (2013) 'Ascribing emotion to reasonable use in accelerated cancer services', *Journal of Health, Organization and Management*, vol 27, no 4, pp 432-48.

OECD (2004) *OECD-rapport om grundskolen i Danmark – 2004*, Uddannelsesstyrelsens temahæfteserie nr. 5, Copenhagen: Undervisningsministeriet

Parsons, T. (1939) 'The professions and social structure', *Social Forces*, vol 17, no 4, pp 457-67.

Parsons, T. (1956) 'Suggestions for a sociological approach to the theory of organizations – II', *Administrative Science Quarterly*, vol 1, no 2, pp 225-39.

Parsons, T. (1971) 'The strange case of academic organization', *The Journal of Higher Education*, vol 42, no 6, pp 486-95.

Pedersen, D. and Hartley, J. (2008) 'The changing context of public leadership and management: Implications for roles and dynamics', *International Journal of Public Sector Management*, vol 21, no 4, pp 327-39.

Pedersen, M. (2011) 'A career is nothing without a personal life: On the social machine in the call for authentic employees', *Ephemera: Theory & Politics in Organization*, vol 11, no 1, pp 63-77.

Pedersen, O.K. (1993) 'The institutional history of the Danish polity: From a market and mixed economy to a negotiated economy', in S.-E. Sjöstrand (ed) *Institutional change*, New York: M.E. Sharp, pp 277-300.

Peters, B.G. (1998) 'Managing horizontal government: the politics of co-ordination', *Public Administration*, vol 76, no 2, pp 295-311.

Petersen, J.H., Christiansen, N.F. and Petersen, K. (2012) 'Det socialpolitiske idelandskab', in J.H. Petersen, K. Petersen and N.F. Christiansen (eds) *Dansk velfærdshistorie. Velfærdsstaten i støbeskeen*, bind III, Odense: Syddansk Universitetsforlag, pp 87-152.

Pfeifer, S. (2013) 'Europe's utility groups forced to find new business models', *Financial Times*, 5 August (www.ft.com/cms/s/0/93e28206-f37e-11e2-942f-00144feabdc0.html#axzz3mZkwPNQu).

Philippopoulos-Mihalopoulos, A. (2009) *Niklas Luhmann: Law, justice, society*, London: Routledge.

Pierre, J. and Peters, G. (2000) *Governance, politics and the state*, Basingstoke: Macmillan.

Pleimert, T. (2015) 'Kommune 3.0. Interview with Lisbeth Binderup', Foreningung for UdviklingsKonsulenter (http://ffuk.dk/kommune-3-0-interview-med-lisbeth-binderup/).

Pors, J.G. (2009) 'Servile power. When something is rotten in the state of Denmark', *Power and Education*, vol 1, no 2, pp 201-13.

Pors, J.G. (2011a) *Noisy management: A history of Danish school governing from 1970-2010*, Frederiksberg: Copenhagen Business School (PhD Series, 24.2011).

Pors, J.G. (2011b) 'Evalueringssamtaler mellem skole og kommune: Selvledelse og gæstfrihed', in M. Juelskjær, H. Knudsen, J.G. Pors and D. Staunæs (eds) *Ledelse af uddannelse: At lede det potentielle*, Frederiksberg: Samfundslitteratur, pp 81-102.

Pors, J.G. (2012a) 'Avoiding unambiguity: tensions in school governing', in N.Å. Andersen and I.-J. Sand (eds) *Hybrid forms of governance – Self-suspension of power*, Basingstoke: Palgrave Macmillan, pp 30-45.

Pors, J.G. (2012b) 'Experiencing with identity: paradoxical government in times of resistance', *Tamara Journal for Critical Organization Inquiry*, vol 10, no 3, pp 33-42.

Pors, J.G. (2014) *Støjende styring. Folkeskolen mellem evaluering og innovation*, Frederiksberg: Nyt fra Samfundsvidenskaberne.

Pors, J.G. and Andersen, N.Å. (2014) 'Playful organisations: Undecidability as a scarce resource', *Culture and Organization*, pp 1-17.

Pors, J.G. and Ratner, H. (2013) 'Process theory in public management: Liberating value from structure or strange bedfellows?', Paper presented at the European Group for Organization Studies Annual Conference, Montreal, Canada, July.

Randers Kommune (2009) *Frihed gennem samarbejde og handling*, Randers kommunes personalepolitik.

Ratner, H. (2013) *Inklusion – Dilemmaer i organisation, profession og praksis*, København: Akademisk Forlag.

Ratner, H. and Pors, J.G. (2013) 'Making invisible forces visible: managing employees' values and attitudes through transient emotions', *International Journal of Management Concepts and Philosophy*, vol 7, no 3/4, pp 208-23.

Reece, H. (2000) 'Divorcing responsibility', *Feminist legal Studies*, vol 8, pp 65-91.

Reierman, J. (2011) 'Den mentale frikommune' [The free thinking municipality], *Mandag Morgen* [Monday morning], 9 May, pp 15-22.

Rennison, B.W. (2007a) 'Cash, codes and complexity – New adventures in the public management of pay scales', *Scandinavian Journal of Management*, vol 23, no 2, pp 146-67.

Rennison, B.W. (2007b) 'Historical discourses of public management in Denmark', *Management and Organizational History*, vol 2, no 1, pp 5-26.

Rennison, B.W. (2007c) 'Intimacy of management – codified constructions of personal selves', *Philosophy of Management*, vol 6, no 2, pp 47-60.

Rhodes, R. (1997) *Understanding governance. Policy networks, governance, reflexivity and accountability*, Buckingham: Open University Press.

Rodger, J.J. (2013) '"New capitalism", colonisation and the neo-philanthropic turn in social policy', *International Journal of Sociology and Social Policy*, vol 33, no 11/12, pp 725-41.

Rohr, J.A. (1998) *Public service, ethics and constitutional practice*, Lawrence, KS: University Press of Kansas.

Rohr, J.A. (2002) 'How responsible is "responsive" government?', *Economy and Society*, vol 31, no 3, pp 461-82.

Rose, N. (1999) *Powers of freedom*, Cambridge: Cambridge University Press.

Ross, A. (1959) *Statsretlige studier* [Studies in constitutional law], København: Nyt Nordisk Forlag Arnold Busck.

Roth, S. (2012) 'The multimedia organization', *Tamara Journal for Critical Organization Inquiry*, vol 10, issue 3, September, pp 5-6.

References

Sand, I.-J. (2012) 'Hybridization, change and the expansion on law', in N.Å. Andersen and I.J. Sand (eds) *Hybrid forms of governance – Self-suspension of power*, Basingstoke: Palgrave Macmillan, pp 186–204.

Sandelands, L. (2010) 'The play of change', *Journal of Organizational Change*, vol 23, no 1, pp 71-86.

Schirmer, W. and Michailakis, D. (2015) 'Two ways of dealing with polycontexturality in priority-setting in Swedish health-care politics', in M. Knudsen and W. Vogd (eds) *Systems theory and the sociology of health and illness. Observing health care*, London: Routledge, pp 63-80.

Stäheli, U. (2003) 'The popular in the political system', *Cultural Studies*, vol 17, no 2, pp 271-96.

Stahl, T, Wismar, M., Ollila, M., Lahtinen, E. and Leppo, K. (eds) (2006) *Health in All policies: Prospects and potentials*, Helsinki/Brussels: Ministry of Social Affairs and Health/European Observatory on Health Systems and Policies.

Statler, M. and Roos, J. (2002) 'Preparing for the unexpected', *New Practice from Imagination Lab*, vol 1, no 3, pp 1-2.

Staunæs, D. (2011) 'Governing the potentials of life? Interrogating the promises in affective educational leadership', *Journal of Educational Administration and History*, vol 43, no 3, pp 227-47.

Staunæs, D. and Raffnsøe, S. (2014) 'Learning to stay ahead of time. Moving leadership experiences experimentally', *Management and Organizational History*, vol 9, no 2, pp 184-201.

Stelling, C. (2014) *Public–private partnerships and the need, development and management of trusting: A processual and embedded exploration*, Frederiksberg: Doctoral School of Organisation and Management Studies, Copenhagen Business School.

Stevenson, N. (2003) 'Cultural citizenship in the cultural society: a cosmopolitan approach', *Citizenship Studies*, vol 7, no 3, pp 331-48.

Stichweh, R. (1997) 'Professions in modern society', *International Review of Sociology*, vol 7, no 1, pp 95-102.

Storm, R.K. (2010) 'From homophonic to polyphonic objectives: European team sports clubs in transformation', *Sport Science Review*, vol XIX, no 5-6, pp 93-120.

Sullivan, B. (1997) 'Mapping contract', in G. Davis, B. Sullivan and A. Yeatman (eds) *The new contractualism?*, Melbourne: Macmillan Education Australia Pty Ltd, pp 1-13.

Sundhedsministeriet [Ministry of Health] (1999) *Regeringens Folkesundhedsprogram 1999-2008*, København.

Swiss Re (2013) SONAR, June (http://news.naturalscience.org/wp-content/uploads/Swiss-Re.pdf).

Teamarbejdsliv og Center for industriel produktion (2014) 'Kerneopgaven for og med borgerne' ['Core tasks for and with citizens'], AAU KBH for fremfærd.

Teubner, G. (1983) 'Substantive and reflexive elements in modern law', *Law and Society Review*, vol 17, no 2, pp 239-85.

Teubner, G. (1986) 'After legal instrumentalism?', in G. Teubner (ed) *Dilemmas of law in the welfare state*, New York: de Gruyter, pp 299-326.

Teubner, G. (1988) 'Refleksiv ret', in A. Born (ed) *Refleksiv ret*, København: Nyt fra Samfundsvidenskaberne.

Teubner, G. (1991) 'Autopoiesis and steering: how politics profit from the normative surplus of capital', in R. Veld, L. Schaap, C. Termeer and M. van Twist (eds) *Autopoiesis and configuration theory: New approaches to social steering*, London: Kluwer Academic Publisher, pp 127-41.

Teubner, G. (1992) 'Social order from legislative noise? Autopoietic closure as a problem for legal regulation', in G. Teubner and A. Febbrajo (eds) *State, law, and economy as autopoietic systems*, Milan: Dott. A. Giuffré Editore, pp 609-49.

Teubner, G. (1996) 'Double bind: Hybrid arrangements as de-paradoxifiers', *Journal of Institutional and Theoretical Economics*, vol 152, pp 59-64.

Teubner, G. (1998) 'After privatization? The many autonomies of private law', *Current Legal Problems*, vol 51, pp 393-424.

Teubner, G. (2000) 'Contracting worlds: the many autonomies of private law', *Social and Legal Studies*, vol 9, no 3, pp 399-417.

Teubner, G. (2002) 'Hybrid laws: Constitutionalizing private governance networks', in R.A. Kagan, M. Krygier and K. Winston (eds) *Legality and community*, Lanham, MD: Rowman & Littlefield Publishers, pp 311-35.

Thygesen, N.T. and Andersen, N.Å. (2012) 'The polyphonic effects of technological changes in public sector organizations: A systems theoretical approach', in N.T. Thygesen (ed) *The illusion of management control: A systems theoretical approach to managerial technologies*, Abingdon: Palgrave Macmillan, pp 159-81.

Villadsen, K. (2008) '"Polyphonic" welfare: Luhmann's systems theory applied to modern social work', *International Journal of Social Welfare*, vol 17, no 1, pp 65-73.

Vincent-Jones, P. (2000) 'Contractual governance: Institutional and organizational analysis', *Oxford Journal of Legal Studies*, vol 20, no 3, pp 317-51.

Vincent-Jones, P. (2006) *The new public contracting*, Oxford: Oxford University Press.

Vincent-Jones, P. (2007) 'The new public contracting: Public versus private ordering?', *Indiana Journal of Global Legal Studies*, vol 14, no 2, pp 259-78.

Vincent-Jones, P., Hughes, D. and Mullen, C. (2009) 'New Labour's PPI reforms: Patient and public involvement in healthcare governance?', *The Modern Law Review*, vol 72, no 2, pp 247-71.

Vingesuset (2015) Virksomhedsplanen (www.vingesuset.dk/virksomhedsplanen.spp).

von Foerster, H. (1981) *Observing systems*, Salinas, CA: Intersystems Publications.

von Foerster, H. (1989) 'Wahrnehmung', in J. Baudrillard, H. Börhringer, V. Flusser, H. von Foerster, F. Kittler and P. Weibel, *Philosophien der neuen Technologie*, Berlin: Merve Verlag, pp 27-41.

von Foerster, H. (1992) 'Ethics and second-order cybernetics', *Cybernetics and Human Knowing*, vol 1, no 1, pp 9-19.

von Foerster, H. (2003) 'On self-organizing systems and their environments', *Understanding Understanding*, New York, NY: Springer, 1-19.

Weber, M. (1946) 'Science as a vocation', in H.H. Gerth and C. Wright Mills (translated and edited), *From Max Weber: Essays in sociology*, New York: Oxford University Press, pp 129-56.

Weber, M. (1978) *Economy and society*, Volume 2, London: University of California Press.

Weber, M. (1994) 'The profession and vocation of politics', in M. Weber, *Weber: Political writings*, Peter Lassman (editor), Cambridge Texts in the History of Political Thought, Cambridge: Cambridge University Press.

White, M. and Hunt, A. (2000) 'Citizenship: care of the self, character and personality', *Citizenship Studies*, vol 4, no 2, pp 93-116.

Wiethölter, R. (1986) 'Materialization and proceduralization in modern law', in G. Teubner (ed) *Dilemmas of law in the welfare state*, New York: de Gruyter.

Willke, H. (1986) 'Three types of legal structure: The conditional, the purposive and the relational program', in G. Teubner (ed) *Dilemmas of law in the welfare state*, New York: de Gruyter, pp 280-98.

Willke, H. (1992) *Ironie des Staates*, Frankfurt am Main: Suhrkamp.

Willke, H. (1997) *Supervision des Staates*, Frankfurt am Main: Suhrkamp.

Yeatman, A. (1997) 'Contract, status and personhood', in G. Davis, B. Sullivan and A. Yeatman (eds) *The new contractualism?*, Melbourne: Macmillan Education Australia Pty Ltd, pp 39-56.

Yeatman, A. (1998) 'Interpreting contemporary contractualism', in M. Dean and B. Hindess (eds) *Governing Australia*, Cambridge: Cambridge University Press, pp 227-42.

Index

Note: page numbers in *italic* type refer to tables and figures.

A

absolute responsibility 206, 207
accountability 129, 240, 241
active fellow citizens 183, 185–8, 191, 193–4, 202–3, 205
adaptability
  and radical innovation 74
  and self-development 156
  temporality and adapting to 11, 16–19
  under supervision administration 66, 69
administration *see* central administration; public administration
administrative decisions
  under formal bureaucracy 61
  under sector administration 63
administrative law 61
administrative reforms 230–2
  see also political reform
aesthetic centrism 53
Amiridis, Kostas 189
amoeba organisations 94–6
Andersen, Poul 151
annual plans 13
arbitrary judgement 113
architecture 26, 79
art system 48, 53
audience, professional roles in relation to 196–9
audience fictions 193, 194, 195
audience roles 192–6
authenticity 177, 199
authority 199

B

Baecker, Dirk 169
Bækgaard, Jane 199
Bakker, D.-J. 145
Bateson, Gregory 24, 169
Bauman, Zygmunt 165
Bertz, Jannie 197–8
Big Society 238
bilateral decisions 100
bilateral form of contracts 61, 134–6
bilateral statements 61
binary codes 36, 37, 38–40, 41, 46
Bjerg, Helle 198
Bonnichsen, Hans Jørgen 229
boundaries
  between function systems 43–6, 51
  organisational 96–7, 98, 101
  of public administration 232, 234–5
  of state and society 238–9
Bourdieu, Pierre 35
budget policy 70
bureaucracy 73–4, 240
  see also formal bureaucracy
business policies 12

C

care programmes, collaboration in 98
care system 39, 48
  heterophonic organisations in 114, 115–16
  homophonic organisations in 109, 110
  partnerships in 143–4
  see also eldercare
case management, under formal bureaucracy 15, 60, 75
catering services 98, 115–16
central administration
  and administration types 63, 70–1, 80
  and organisational partnerships 146–8
central planning 16, 62–5
change
  and adaptability 16–17
  role of play in 169–72
child, as medium 38, 155
citizenry (forms of) 183, 191
  active fellow citizens 183, 185–8, *191*, 193–4, 202–3, *205*
  legal subjects *183*, 184, *191*, 202, *205*
  as potentiality *183*, 188–92, 194–6, 203–5
  recipients *183*, 184–5, *191*, 202, *205*
citizens 244
  as audience of function systems 192–6
  challenges for management of 209–10
  personal responsibility 199–205

271

first-order responsibility 205–7, 209–10
second-order responsibility 207–10
professional roles in relation to 196–9
relations between administration and 74
citizens contracts 132, 186–8, 203
civil government, concept of 33–4, 35
climate issues 44–5, 71
cocreation 78
codes
  binary codes 36, 37, 38–40, *41*, 46
  function systems, organisations and 104, 108, 111, 115–16, 118, 119, 126
  legal in formal organisations 108–9
  love coding of self-enrolment 159–65, 166, 172–3, 179
  pedagogical coding of self-enrolment 154–9, 166, 172–3
  play coding of potentialised membership 167–75, 176
  in polycontextual partnerships 147–8
  self-development and doubling of 157
coercion 59
collaboration 78–9
  between organisations 96–7, 98, 101
  between schools and parents 103–4
  and communication-seeking organisations 122–4
  see also partnerships
communication 49
  and function systems 36, 37–9
  and roles 192
  see also codes
communication systems, relations between 135, 137, 138, 145, 146–7
communication-seeking organisations 105, 106, 107–8, 120–30
  potentialised playful membership *150*, 167–75, 176
communities, reforms targeting 232–6
community, and contracts 145
competence 157, 172
competence reviews 155, 156
competition state 229
complexity reduction management 28–30
conditional programmes 136
conflicts, and legal system 37–8
constitutional state 222, 223–4, 230
contingency
  open and fixed 14
  tension between decisions and 29
  see also adaptability
contractual relations
  between organisations 131–4
    bilateral form 61, 134–6
    challenges and paradoxes 145–6
    formal contracts 136–7
    material contracts *136*, 137–9
    partnerships *136*, 139–48
    reflexive contracts *136*, 139

citizens contracts 132, 186–8, 203
  and hierarchy 133, *134*
  internal contracts 68–9, 70, 219
  typology of 132–3
controrgs 133
coordination 5, 6, 64, 73
  relational coordination 122–3
  see also collaboration; interdependence; partnerships
core tasks/responsibilities 123–5, 128–30
Corydon, Bjarne 229
Costea, Bogdan 189
coupling see structural coupling
Crump, Norman 189
cybernetics 24, 251

D

D'Amour, Danielle 122
Danida 107–8
decentralisation 70–1
decision-making 241
  noise of alternative decisions 97–9
  self- and external reference in 89–97
decisions
  as containment of future uncertainty 13–15, 75
  in formal bureaucracy 15, 61
  levels of 75–6
  potentialisation and paradox of 26–8
  in sector administration 63
  tension between contingency and 29
  unilateral and bilateral 100
defense system 43–6, 111
  see also security system
Denmark, welfare management in v
Derrida, Jacques 134–5, 206
dialogue, as governance technology 186
differentiation see functional differentiation of society
discourse management 71
dismissal of employees 178
divorce law 219–20
divorcing responsibility 208
double membership 150, 152–4
drug use 125–7
drug users 197–8
du Gay, P. 73, 240
Dunn, R. 196
Durkheim, Émile 134

E

economic centrism 52–3
economic system 48
  as basis of governance 52–3
  contractual coupling with law 136–7
  heterophonic organisations and 116
  and political governance 223
education

and citizen as potentiality 188
core responsibilities 129
and flexibility 25–6
learning styles 195–6
planning for future 12, 19
political reform of 231–2
potentiality administration in 79–80
teachers' self-development 158–9
see also pedagogical system; schools
Ekman, Susanne 173
eldercare 98, 110, 143–4, 188–9, 234
employees
  challenges of self-enrolment for 178–80
  clients as 187
  contracts with 132
  employee–organisation relationship 3, 149, 244
  double membership *150*, 152–4
  formal membership 150–2, 154, *176*
  management challenges 175–80
  potentialised playful membership *150*, 167–75, *176*
  self-enrolment *see* self-enrolment
empowerment 186
engagement
  of employee with organisation 160–1
  and play 174
Enneagram Test 196
environmental issues 44–5, 71
Esposito, Elena 21
evaluation culture, in education 158–9
evaluation reviews 72, 87
expectation machine 2–3, 4, 7
expectations, in contractual communication 138
experience managers 74, 162
external reference (in decision-making) 89–90
  and innocent institutions 90–1
  and potential organisations 94–7
  and professionally responsible institutions 91
  and strategic organisations 91–3
extremism, prevention of 200–1

F

factual dimension 25
factuality, and contractual obligation 142
family services 187–8
firing of employees 178
first-order contracts 139–40, 141–3, 144–5
first-order cybernetics 251
first-order responsibility 205–7, 209–10
fixed contingency 14
flexibility
  in employee–organisation relations 164
  in potential organisations 94–5
  and potentiality administration 73, 78

value of 25–6
foreign aid 45–6, 107–8
formal bureaucracy 60–2, 82
  institutions' external reference under 90–1
  institutions and function systems under *106*
  and temporality 15–16
formal contracts 136–7
formal institutions 105, 106, 108–9
formal law 106, 108, 216–17, 221
formal membership 150–2, 151, 154, 176
formal responsibility 202
Foucault, Michel 46
framework law 217
freedom
  in constitutional state 222
  and obligation 134–5, 145
  and power 59
  and responsibility of citizens 185
  see also independence
freedom charter 77–8
function systems 242
  citizens as audience of 192–6
  concept of 35–7, 41
  contractual coupling 135, 136–7, 139, 144–5
  examples of 37–41
  harvesting self-governance surplus from 226
  hyper-reflection of 43–9, 50–1, 120
  interdependence of 42–3, 48–9
  professional roles in 196–9
  reflection on boundaries 43–6, 51
  relationship with political system 213, 214–21, 222, 223, 225, 236–40
  relationship with welfare organisations 103–8, 243
    communication-seeking organisations 105, *106*, 107–8, 120–30
    formal institutions 105, *106*, 108–9
    heterophonic organisations 105, *106*, 107–8, 113–20
    homophonic organisations 105, *106*, 107, 109–13
    return to core responsibility 128–30
    role of law in coupling 214–15, *216*, 217, 218, 220
  and roles 192–6
  simultaneity of 47–8, 49–50
  see also care system; legal system; mass media system; pedagogical system
functional differentiation of society 5, 34–42, 242
  hyper-reflection of systems 43–9, 50–1, 120
  implications for governance 51–4, 225
  interdependence of systems 42–3, 48–9
  simultaneity of systems 47–8, 49–50

future
  Possible Predictions game 171
  predicting 12
  supervision administration focus on 18, 69, 73
  win/wip model 81
  see also temporality and time

G

general responsibility 206, 207
generalists 152–3
Gittell, Jody 122–3
governance
  and community targeted reforms 232–6
  concept of civil government 33–4, 35
  concepts and frameworks of iv, 245, 251
  forms of citizen governance *191*
  and forms of public administration 242
    challenges 82–7
    formal bureaucracy 60–2
    potentiality administration 74–5, 84–6
    sector administration 62–5
    supervision administration 66–72, 83–4
  of functionally differentiated society 51–4, 225
  management challenges 236–40
  and political system 52, 213, 214–15, 236–40
  and power 58–60
  of self-governance 89
  and ungovernability 251–2
  see also external reference
governance technologies 183, 185–6, 191

H

hash conversation 125–7
Health in Play game 204–5
healthcare programmes, and function systems 121–2
healthcare system 48
  boundaries of 46
  communication-seeking organisations and 121–2
  heterophonic organisations and 114
  homophonic organisations in 109, 110
  and horizontal governance 71
  partnerships in 140–1
heterophonic organisations 105, 106, 107–8, 113–20
hierarchical contracts 133
hierarchies
  and contractualisation 133, *134*
  in formal bureaucracies 60, 61–2, 90
  potentiality administration and 78
  societal 34, 35
Højlund, Holger 146–7
homophonic organisations 105, 106, 107, 109–13

hospitals 114, 140–1
hybrid governance 237–8
hybrid law 106, 218–20, 221
hyper-reflection 43–9, 50–1, 120
hyper-responsibility 201, 207–10, 241

I

Ibarra, Herminia 170
identity play 170
imagination 168–9, 172
indefinite responsibility 203
independence and self-management 4
independence of welfare organisations 90
  challenges for management 100–2
  function of noise 97–9
  governance and 83–4
  self- and external reference 90–7
individual responsibility 122
individualisation 192, 194
individuals
  relationship with society 33
  see also citizens; employees
individual–external contractualisation 132
individual–internal contractualisation 132
information, in mass media system 39–41
initiative 161, 166, 173
INNO+ strategy 226–8
innocent institutions 90–1, 97, 99, 100, 150–2
innovation 74–5, 77–8
institutions
  definition 90, 92
  see also organisations
instruction 111–12
  see also pedagogical system
integration 5–6, 43
interdependence 5, 42–3, 48–9
internal contracts 68–9, 70, 219
interprofessionality 122
ISS catering 115–16

J

Järvinen, Margaretha 198
Jessop, Bob 213
Johnson, N. 240
judgement 113

K

Kane, Pat 170, 173, 174
knowledge, and function systems 42
knowledge and network society 229
knowledge society 229
Knudsen, Hanne 198, 203
Kofoed, Kristian Hansen 150–1

L

La Cour, Anders 146–7
labour unions 248
language, and contracts 134–5, 145
late modern society 229
latent motivation 188
law
  basis of formal bureaucracies 60–1
  formal law *106*, 108, 216–17, *221*
  hybrid law *106*, 218–20, *221*
  as medium of employee membership 152, 153, 154
  and organisation–function system relationship 104–5, *106*, 107–8, 110
  reflexive law *106*, 218, *221*
  substantial law *106*, 110, 217, *221*
law reform 63
learning styles 195–6
legal subjects, citizens as 183, 184, 191, 202, 205
legal system 37–8
  contractual coupling with economy 136–7
  development of 216–21
  and political system governance 214–21, 222
  and structural coupling 104–5, 136–7, 214–15, 217, 218, 220
legally based judgement 113
love coding of self-enrolment 159–65, 166, 172–3, 179
Luhmann, Niklas 24, 34, 36, 38, 40, 45, 99

M

Maas, A. 145
Macaulay, Stewart 138
management
  and political power 246–7
  of self-management 4–5, 69–70, 72
  see also welfare management
managers, use of term 69–70
manifest motivation 188
mass media system 39–41, 48, 115, 116
material contracts 136, 137–9
meaning dimensions 25
media
  of function systems 36, 37, 38, 39, *41*, 117–18
  see also mass media system
mentoring work 200–1
methodological autonomy 112
Mik-Meyer, Nanna 198
military organisations 111
Ministry for the Environment (Denmark) 71
Ministry of Finance (Denmark) 67–8
Ministry of Health (Denmark) 71

Møller, Poul 224–5
Mommsen, Wolfgang 60
monocontextualism 54, 249, 250
motivation, of citizens 184–5, 187–8, 191

N

national security 46, 48
  see also defense system
network society 229
New Nordic Schooling 231–2
new public management (NPM) 66
noise 24–6, 43, 97–9, 225
norms 215–16
nursing homes 143–4, 234
nutrition policy 202

O

Oandasan, Ivy 122
obligation, and freedom 134–5, 145
open contingency 14
operational time 6
order
  of contracts 135, *136*
  potentialisation, noise and 24–6
organisational boundaries 96–7, 98, 101
organisational needs, anticipation of 159–65, 172
organisations
  definition 92
  and function systems 105
  and potentialisation 20–8
  and time 12–13
    changing figures of temporality 15–22
    decisions 13–15
  see also contractual relations; employee–organisation relationship; welfare organisations
organisation–external contractualisation 133
organisation–internal contractualisation 132
outsourcing 114, 115–16
over-inclusion 177–8

P

Parsons, Talcott 110–11
partnerships 78–9, 133–4, 243–4
  challenges and paradoxes of 145–6
  as second order contracts *136*, 139–45
  state and societal 226–8
  supervision and potentialisation of 146–8
past *see* temporality and time
pedagogical coding of self-enrolment 154–9, 166, 172–3
pedagogical system 38–9, 48, 50–1
  communication-seeking organisations and 120

harvesting self-governance surplus from 226
heterophonic organisations and 114
homophonic organisations in 109, 110, 111–12
see also education; schools
perceptual time 6
performance contracts 132
performance roles 192–3, 194–5, 198–9
  professional roles 196–9
personal responsibility 199–205
  first-order 205–7, 209–10
  general and absolute 206, 207
  playful hyper-responsibility 201, 207–10, 241
  second-order 207–10
personality, as organisational resource 162
personality typologies 196
Petriglieri, Jennifer 170
planning
  concept of 45
  and temporality 13, 16
  under sector administration 62–5, 75
play, concept of 169
playful hyper-responsibility 207–10
playful membership 167–75, 176
playful state 236
political power, and management 246–7
political reform 228, 230–6
political system 48, 49–50
  as basis of governance 52, 213, 214–15, 236–40
  and formal institutions 108
  and heterophonic organisations 115, 116
  and homophonic organisations 111
  relationship with other systems 213, 214–21, 222, 223, 225, 236–40
  self-descriptions of 213–14, 222–30, 238
politicians 66, 86–7, 247
politics
  relationship with management 252–3
  role in public administration 66, 67–8, 86–7, 247
polycontextual partnerships 147–8
polycontextualism 54, 249–50
polyphonic supervision of partnerships 146–7
Possible Predictions game 171
potential organisations 94–8, 99, 101
potential responsibility 207–10
potentialisation 242
  concept of iv, 22–3
  order and noise 24–6
  and paradox of decision 26–8
  and temporality 20–3
potentialised playful membership 150, 167–75, 176
potentiality, citizens as 183, 188–92, 194–6, 203–5

potentiality administration 73–81, 82, 84–6, 94–7, 106
potentiality decisions 75–6
potentiality principle 189
potentiality programmes 141
potentiality state 225–30, 232, 233–5, 238–9, 240
power 59, 186
preschools 93, 103–4, 110
present *see* temporality and time
private companies, function of 111
private sector 66, 133, 143–4
private sphere, in employee–organisation relationship 163–5
procedural programmes 139
professional autonomy 112
professional competencies 128–9
professional knowledge 3, 153
professional roles 196–9
professionally responsible institutions 91, 97, 99, 100, 104–5, 150, 152–4
professionals
  and communication-seeking organisations 122–4
  and employee–organisation relationship 153
  relationship with citizens 191–2
  shared perspective with citizens 185–6
professions 112–13, 247–9
programmes, and contracts 135, 136, 137, 139, 141
public administration
  and challenges for governance 82–7
  employee membership
    double employee membership *150*, 152–4
    formal employee membership 150–2, 154, *176*
    potentialised playful membership *150*, 167–75, 176
    self-enrolment *see* self-enrolment
  and forms of citizenry 183–92
  forms and development of 58, *82*, 242
  formal bureaucracy 60–2, *82*
  potentiality administration 73–81, *82*
  sector administration 62–5, *82*
  supervision administration 66–72, 73, *82*
  and legal system 216–21
  and organisational partnerships 146–8
  role of politics in 66, 67–8, 86–7, 247
public buildings 26
public (market), relationship with society 33
public sector
  changing figures of temporality in 15–22
  and reform targeting communities 232–6
  relationship with private sector 66, 133, 143–4

see also welfare organisations; welfare state
public sector management 1–3
  see also welfare management
public servant, semantic of 150–2
purposive programmes 137

Q

quality 68–9, 98
quality management tools 78

R

radical change, role of play 169–72
radical innovation 74–5, 77–8
Ratner, Helene 195–6
reality, play and 174–5
recipients, citizens as 183, 184–5, 191, 202, 205
Reece, Helen 208–9
reflexive contracts 136, 139
reflexive law 106, 218, 221
reflexivity and reflection
  of function systems 43–9, 50–1, 120, 237
  hyper-reflection 43–9, 50–1, 120
  of professionally responsible institutions 91
  teachers' 158–9
reform (political) 228, 230–6
regulation, and contracts 135, 136
relational coordination 122–3
religious centrism 53–4
religious system 53
responsibility
  of active fellow citizens 185
  and employee–organisation relations 175
  first-order 205–7, 209–10
  formal 202
  general and absolute 206, 207
  for own learning 195–6
  personal 199–205
  playful hyper-responsibility 201, 207–10, 241
  second-order 207–10
responsibility technologies 205
responsibility-seeking employees 159
reviews see evaluation reviews
rights 184, 222
risk society 230
roles
  changing professional roles 196–9
  and function systems 192–6
Roos, Johan 168, 170
Ross, Alf 223, 224
rule-based services 217

S

sanctions 59
Sandelands, L. 172–3

schools
  architecture 26
  flexibility in 25–6
  and function systems 103–4, 109, 110, 111–12, 113–14, 120
  New Nordic Schooling 231–2
  as potential organisations 94–6
  potentiality administration in 79–80
  preschools 93, 103–4, 110
  as strategic organisations 93
  teachers' self-development in 158–9
  see also pedagogical system
scientific system 42, 112
second-order audience fictions 194
second-order contracts 139–45
second-order cybernetics 251
second-order responsibility 207–10
sector administration 62–5, 82, 91, 106
security state 229
security system 46, 48
  see also defense system
segmentary differentiation 34, 35
self-descriptions
  of organisations 106, 108, 111, 118–19
  of political system 213–14, 222–30, 238
self-development 155–9
self-enrolment 150, 154
  challenges of 175, 176–80
  love coding of 159–65, 166, 172–3, 179
  pedagogical coding of 154–9, 166, 172–3
  and play code 172–3, 174
  as postponed membership 165–7
self-governance
  governance of 89
  harvesting surplus 213, 214–15, 226
  and power 59
  threats to 52–3
  under formal bureaucracy 61
  see also self-reference
self-image 197–8
self-management
  and active fellow citizens 185–8
  management of 4–5, 69–70, 72
  under supervision administration 69–70, 72
self-reference (in decision-making) 89–90
  and potential organisations 94–7
  and professionally responsible institutions 91
  and strategic organisations 91–3
self-reflection see reflexivity and reflection
self-relation
  and active fellow citizens 185, 186, 194
  and citizen as potentiality 188, 189–91
self-worth 190
shared perspective 185–6
simultaneity 5–6, 47–8, 49–50
Smart Society 227–8
social dimension 25

social educators 248
Social Security Act (1974) 221
Social Services Act (1997) 218
social services departments 114–15, 216–17, 218
social systems see function systems
sociality, and contractual obligation 142
society
  boundaries of state and 238–9
  civil government concept of 33–4
  contemporary images of state and 229–30
  functional differentiation of 5, 34–42, 242
    governance of differentiated systems 51–4, 225
    hyper-reflection of function systems 43–9, 50–1, 120
    interdependent function systems 42–3, 48–9
    simultaneity of function systems 47–8, 49–50
  potentiality state as 238
  segmentary differentiation of 34, *35*
  stratifactory differentiation of 34, *35*
specialists 152–3
speed 48
spending cuts 101–2
stability 16, 24
state
  boundaries of 238–9
  combining forms of 236
  contemporary images of 229–30
  defining 213
  forms of 222–30, 236, 244–5
  management challenges of potentiality state 238–9
  and political reform *228*, 230–6
  relationship with political system 213–14, 222–30
  relationship with society 33, 35
  as societal partnership 226–8
  see also welfare state
state centrism 52
Statler, Matt 168, 170
strategic organisations 91–3, 97, 99, 100
  employee self-enrolment *see* self-enrolment
strategy
  and temporality 18–19
  under supervision administration 69, 73, 75
stratifactory differentiation 34, 35
stress 178–80
structural corruption 250
structural coupling
  concept of 214
  coupling function of contracts 135, 136–7, 139, 144–5

role of law 104–5, 214–15, *216*, 217, 218, 220
structures, and potentiality administration 76
substantial law 106, 110, 217, 221
supervision, of partnerships 146–7
supervision administration 66–72, 73, 82, 83–4, 91–3, 106
supervision governance 237
supervision state 225, 232
Swiss Re 20
symbols, in function systems 36, 37, 38
systems
  and concepts of time 6
  see also function systems
systems theory 251–2

T

teachers 25, 129, 158–9, 198
technology 79
temporal dimension 25
temporal integration 5–6
temporality and time 241
  changing figures in public sector of 15–22
  concept of 17
  and contractual obligation 142
  and decisions 13–15
  forms of 6
  and organisations 12–13, 15–22
  and potentialisation 20–3
  problems of planning for future 12
  simultaneity and function systems 47–8
  see also future
terminology, of hybrid law 218–19
Teubner, Gunther 133

U

uncertainty
  decisions as containment of 13–15, 75
  as risk and resource 20–1
undecidability 99
ungovernability 251–2
unilateral decisions 100
unions 248
unity 5
  central planning to restore 16, 63, 64
  and political self-description 214, 222, 226, 239
  and temporal integration 6
  see also coordination; integration
universities 111, 112

V

voluntariness, and play 174
von Foerster, H. 99

W

war system
  boundaries of 43–6
  see also defense system; security system
Weber, Max 60
welfare institutions *see* innocent institutions; professionally responsible institutions; welfare organisations
welfare management
  Danish example v
  diagnosis and critique 3–4
  expectations of 2–3, 245–6
  as political 252–3
  possibilities for 246–7
  as self-perpetuating 245–6
  tensions and challenges iv, 2–3, 4–6, 249–53
    citizen management 209–10
    complexity reduction management 28–30
    contracts and partnerships 145–6
    employee–organisation relationship 175–80
    independence of organisations 100–2
    organisation–function system relationship 113, 120, 127–8
    political governance 236–40
welfare organisations
  employee relationship with *see* employee–organisation relationship
  governance and self-governance of 89
  independence of *90*
    challenges for management 100–2
    function of noise 97–9
    governance and 83–4
    self- and external reference 89–97
  relations between 131, 243–4
  see also contractual relations
  relationship with function systems 103–8, 243
    communication-seeking organisations 105, *106*, 107–8, 120–30
    formal institutions 105, *106*, 108–9
    heterophonic organisations 105, *106*, 107–8, 113–20
    homophonic organisations 105, *106*, 107, 109–13
    return to core responsibility 128–30
  responsibility for personal responsibility 201–2
  and welfare professions 247–9
welfare state
  citizen as active fellow citizen in 185
  citizen as potentiality in 188–9, 192
  citizen as recipient in 184–5
  political reform in 230–2
  as self-description of political system 222–3, 224–5
'whole employee', organisational interest in 163–5
win/wip model 81
work-life balance 177–8

www.ingramcontent.com/pod-product-compliance
Lightning Source LLC
Chambersburg PA
CBHW080356030426
42334CB00024B/2894